TRAVELING SOUL

THE LIFE OF
Curtis Mayfield

Todd Mayfield WITH TRAVIS ATRIA

CHICAGO
REVIEW
PRESS

An A Cappella Book

This biography has not been authorized by the estate of Curtis Mayfield.

The Library of Congress has cataloged the hardcover edition as follows:
Names: Mayfield, Todd, author. | Atria, Travis, author.
Title: Traveling soul : the life of Curtis Mayfield / Todd Mayfield with
    Travis Atria.
Description: Chicago, IL : Chicago Review Press, 2016. | Includes
    bibliographical references and index.
Identifiers: LCCN 2016027301 (print) | LCCN 2016028753 (ebook) | ISBN
    9781613736791 (hardback) | ISBN 9781613736807 (PDF edition) | ISBN
    9781613736821 (EPUB edition) | ISBN 9781613736814 (Kindle edition)
Subjects: LCSH: Mayfield, Curtis. | Singers—United States—Biography. | Soul
    musicians—United States—Biography.
Classification: LCC ML420.M3369 M39 2016 (print) | LCC ML420.M3369 (ebook) |
    DDC 782.421644092 [B] —dc23
LC record available at https://lccn.loc.gov/2016027301

A list of credits and copyright notices for the Curtis Mayfield songs quoted in this book can be found on page 318.

Cover design: Marc Whitaker, MTWdesign.net
Cover photo: Michael Putland
Interior design: Jonathan Hahn

Printed in the United States of America

To my parents, Curtis and Diane, and to my daughter
and greatest inspiration, Corinne Lee Mayfield

Contents

FIRST IMPRESSIONS . . . . *vii*

1 THE REVEREND A. B. MAYFIELD *1*

2 MY MAMA BORNED ME IN A GHETTO *11*

3 TRAVELING SOULS 23

4 THE ORIGINAL IMPRESSIONS *43*

5 KEEP ON PUSHING 77

6 PEOPLE GET READY *109*

7 CURTOM *135*

8 NOW YOU'RE GONE *157*

9 MOVE ON UP *175*

10 SUPER FLY 207

11 BACK TO THE WORLD 235

12 WHEN SEASONS CHANGE 271

13 NEVER SAY YOU CAN'T SURVIVE 295

LASTING IMPRESSIONS *315*

ACKNOWLEDGMENTS *317*

SONG CREDITS *318*

NOTES 323

BIBLIOGRAPHY *341*

INDEX *347*

First Impressions

"Try and understand I'm an unusual man."
—"Love Me (Right in the Pocket)"

Atlantic City, 1969—My father stalks around his dressing room. The Impressions are ready to hit the stage for their second set, but first he wants his money. He's hip to this game; he takes no mess. He turned sixteen onstage at the Apollo Theater in Harlem, and since then he's seen every type of crook run every type of con. He knows getting paid after the show often means not getting paid. These days, he demands a percentage up front and the rest between sets, sliding the money into his vest pocket, where you'd have to go through him to get it.

The promoter in Atlantic City is a wiseguy, though. He slithers into the dressing room clutching cash in one hand, steel in the other. He levels the gun at my father's head. "How bad do you want this money?" he demands.

Everyone freezes.

"I want it bad enough to let you pull that trigger."

He says it coolly, his voice barely rising above the soft, measured sigh that has graced countless hit records.

The promoter lowers the gun. My father gets his money.

He strides on stage, the music kicks in, the crowd shouts in ecstasy, the Impressions finish with a flourish and walk straight out the front door of the auditorium to their cars, leaving the band playing inside. They gun their engines into the night toward the next show and the next promoter foolish enough to pull another stunt like that.

————

Curtis Mayfield has seen scarier things than a gun in his face. His father deserted him when he was five years old. He witnessed his mother abused and abandoned, powerless to help her. He spent long, hunger-wracked nights battling starvation in a squalid single-room apartment. He knows as much about pimps and prostitutes as he does about the Bible and Jesus. The first he learned from the rotten slums where he grew up a nothing child, destined to become another boyish, shiftless jigger. The second he learned from his grandmother's church, where she practiced a cultish mixture of Christianity and the black arts called Spiritualism.

These experiences gave him the courage to stare down the barrel of a gun in Atlantic City without flinching. They made him who he is—a contradictory, unpredictable, brilliant man who dropped out of high school and built a musical empire. A man who spends much of his public life on stage and much of his private one locked in his bedroom. A man capable of legendary cool and flashes of temperamental violence. A man revered around the world but tormented by insecurity. A man gifted with tremendous powers of imagination but little ability to master the mundane day-to-day mechanics of life. A man who somehow manages to be both present and absent as a father. A man who sings of endless love but can't remain faithful to any woman. A man hell-bent on control who sometimes relinquishes that control to the wrong people.

In becoming that man, he's plucked the sweet fruits of the American Dream—money, fame, women—and choked down the despair of the American nightmare—degradation, deprivation, and humiliation because his skin was the wrong color. And the hardest part of his journey hasn't even begun. Like everyone, he can't see the future. As he speeds away from Atlantic City, he doesn't know the greatest tragedy awaits him in the place he least expects it. He can't foresee this tragedy will lead to his greatest triumph of spirit and a slow, agonizing death. He can scarcely imagine life will soon teach him the ultimate impossibility of control.

———————

A few would-be biographers have tried to tell my father's story; none have done it well. They failed because they had no access to his inner life, to what drove him. They had no knowledge of his deep insecurity over his dark skin, big teeth, and small stature; of the humiliation he suffered at the hands of schoolmates because of his family's desperate poverty; of his profound need for control over music, money, and relationships; of his deeply divided nature as a Gemini. Even astrology agnostics would have to agree, if such a thing as a true Gemini exists, my father was one. Everyone who knew him affirms that he changed his mind so often and with such ease, they never knew exactly what he felt, what he wanted, or what he'd do. Only with music was he constant.

These writers also failed because they didn't know where he came from. They didn't spend time with the people who raised him, but those people are integral to his story. You most likely didn't pick up this book to read about Curtis's grandmother, but without her, he might never have become a musician, and he couldn't have written songs such as "Keep On Pushing" and "People Get Ready." In interviews throughout his life, he always mentioned her as a main influence and inspiration. To understand him, then, you must understand her.

You most likely didn't pick up this book to get a history lesson, either. But my father's music was integral to the civil rights movement, which he lived through and helped mold even as it molded him. To understand him, you must understand his times. We'll follow the movement as it flowers and flutters. Part of that movement concerns racial terminology and what it signified, so we'll use the correct nomenclature of the times—from "Negro" in his childhood, to "black" by the late '60s, to "African American" in the last two decades of his life.

Another issue of terminology arose while writing this book. Growing up with a famous father, I saw many sides of him. I called him different names depending on the situation—he was "Dad" at home; he was "my father" in public, around people who might have wanted something from us; he was "Curtis" later in life when I helped him run the Curtom label. Since I knew him as all three during his life, I will use all three throughout the book.

During his life, my father guarded his privacy jealously. After his death, we have done the same with his legacy. But the world deserves to know the real Curtis Mayfield. A wise man once said, "To the living we owe respect, but to the dead we owe only the truth." Perhaps we don't have to choose. Maybe it's possible to show my father his due respect by the very act of telling the truth, just like he did in his songs. He told more truth than any musician of his era, capturing the hope, fury, despair, strength, and love of his people in a way no one else could. As *Rolling Stone* said of him, "More than Marvin Gaye, more than Stevie Wonder, maybe even more than James Brown, Curtis Mayfield captured the total black experience in America during the '60s." Of course, his music wasn't just for black people—scores of fans from every race and ethnicity can attest to that—but it was from our perspective. As he said in his legendary concert at the Bitter End, he was always "believing very strongly in equality for all, but basically telling it like it is."

In presenting his story through my eyes, I have tried to tell it like it is and like it was, even when a crafted piece of public relations would have made him look better. After all, as the man himself once sang:

> *Pardon me, brother, while you stand in your glory,*
> *I know you won't mind if I tell the whole story.*

1

The Reverend A. B. Mayfield

"People get ready, there's a train a-coming
You don't need no baggage, you just get on board."
—"People Get Ready"

Mansfield, Louisiana, circa 1910—Slavery was dead, but its terror still hung in the hot air over the cotton fields near my great-grandmother's house. The crack of the master's whip echoed through the generations of her family up to her own grandparents, who as slaves were worth almost $800 on the trading block in their prime. After suffering in bondage so long, they couldn't help but feel their current freedom was negotiable.

Like much about my great-grandmother's birth, a cloud surrounds her real name. She sometimes introduced herself as Gertrude, while others knew her as Annabelle, but most likely she went by Annie Bell. Such confusion about names occurred often in the land of slavery. Negroes could never know their true last names, and even first names could carry the indelible imprint of the plantation. For almost two centuries, they traded in nicknames and pseudonyms, perhaps as a way to assume control of their identity in a world that gave them none.

Annie Bell's father, Elmore Scott, toiled at a sawmill—a comparative luxury. He earned enough money to let his wife, Lula, stay home—

another luxury, although she had to pick up jobs on the side with her old Singer sewing machine. Their hometown of Mansfield was a tiny, stifling place occupying less than four square miles of land. Cotton took to the black, fecund topsoil there, and its downy tufts had formed the backbone of the economy since slavery times. By Annie Bell's birth, most Mansfield Negroes had become sharecroppers—a kind of virtual slavery that kept them in perpetual debt, eking out an existence on the knife-edge of starvation. Still, Elmore and Lula hoped their daughter might have a better chance at life than they did, just as they once had a better chance than their parents. They also knew how nominal the definition of "better" could be.

Lula kept her little house spotless, decorating the inside with a three-foot-tall porcelain collie. Out back, she tilled a garden, showering special adoration on her elephant leaves and four-o'clocks. Annie Bell loved exploring the enchanting garden in the afternoon when the four-o'clocks would open as if by some magic, right on time. The house had running water but no bathroom, so Annie Bell, born severely nearsighted, trudged cautiously through the chicken yard rain or shine to reach the dilapidated outhouse. Sundays Lula took the family to a country church where the preacher sweated and moaned, conjuring the Spirit from thin air. The church provided the only true sanctuary for her family, as it did for Negroes across the South. Within its sacred walls, they had the freedom to drop their defenses and spill out their troubles like vessels filled to the brim. As Annie Bell grew, these gospel-drenched sounds became part of her flesh and blood and bone.

While Elmore and Lula struggled to raise her the best they knew how, Jim Crow drew lines around them they couldn't control. They couldn't always see those lines, so Annie Bell had to learn to sense where they stood. If not, she could meet her demise at the hands of the lynch mob, the South's most gruesome death sentence. During Annie Bell's childhood, Louisiana citizens lynched a Negro once every four months, by a conservative estimate. It served as a grim warning of what happened when you didn't know your place.

Jim Crow laws in Louisiana reinforced that message at every turn. Under those laws, Annie Bell couldn't ride the same streetcars as whites, drink or buy alcohol from the same taverns as whites, or build a house in a white neighborhood. It was illegal for her to marry a white man, buy tickets for public events at the same window, occupy the same jails, attend the same schools, or rent in the same buildings as white people.

As awful as segregation was, better days beckoned like unfulfilled promises. In 1909, the scholar W. E. B. DuBois helped form the National Association for the Advancement of Colored People, which would soon set in motion the legal death of segregation. The NAACP took most of its membership from the Negro middle class, so Annie Bell and her family in Louisiana didn't know much about it at the time. Soon, though, it would cause significant improvements to Negro life throughout the country, hers included.

By confronting the power structure, the NAACP created niches for more radical groups like Marcus Garvey's Universal Negro Improvement Association and planted the seeds for the great civil rights movement that would begin three decades later. Unlike the NAACP, Garvey recruited poor, working class, and rural Negroes. As Annie Bell neared her teenage years, she might very well have heard of Garvey and his exhortation "Up, you mighty race! You can accomplish what you will."

The event that affected her most personally, though, was the first Great War. At the end of the Civil War in 1865, Negroes began slipping out of the South to the promised land north of the Mason-Dixon Line, but when America entered World War I in 1917, the trickle burst into a flood historians call the Great Migration. Over the course of six decades, six million Negroes, my great-grandmother among them, left the South and spread across the country in search of anything better.

Annie Bell's father might have considered fleeing as the exodus began around him, but the South was all he knew. He stayed in Mansfield with his family while many of his friends harked to the siren song of northern factories, sometimes only taking the clothes on their backs for fear their white bosses might find out what they were up to and stop them—or worse.

Weaker ties bound Annie Bell to Louisiana, and while the war thundered on, major changes in her life pushed her closer to leaving. First, she found Spiritualism, a belief system that didn't square with her mother's

Christianity. Spiritualists believe they can communicate with the dead through a medium. The movement started in the late 1840s, when a woman in a New York farmhouse claimed she communicated with the spirit of a man who was murdered there years before. After that, it mushroomed but faded almost as quickly once most of the Spiritualist seers proved to be simple hucksters. It gained steam again during World War I, when Annie Bell found it.

Though Lula wanted no part of the strange quasi-religion, Spiritualism fit naturally in Louisiana, especially around New Orleans, where African voodoo still suffused the culture like incense. Slaves had carried voodoo within their bones across the horrors of the Middle Passage and never exactly let it go, even though their masters on a new continent tried to beat it out of them. Once in America, it mixed with a dab of Christianity and became something different. Annie Bell drank deeply from this mixture of African religion and American experience, and soon she claimed to have a spirit guide, a dead person she could talk to and see.

At the same time, she found romance. In the early 1920s, she met Willie Cooper, and soon they married. In 1923, just barely a teenager herself, Annie Bell gave birth to a girl she named Mercedes. The next year, she had a boy named Curtis Lee, whom everyone called Mannish because he exhibited some of the less flattering aspects of manhood from an early age. Soon after Mannish's birth, Annie Bell and Willie split.

As she raised her children under the Louisiana sun, the exodus continued around her. With her hometown becoming ever more stifling, my great-grandmother contemplated her options. She had grown into a storm of a woman with a thunderous temper, which could only mean trouble in Louisiana. Even if she managed to survive Jim Crow, she knew it would put a permanent lid on her children's dreams. As great hordes of people fled north, sometimes returning to visit with the trappings of modest wealth, it seemed her best hope rested on a train chugging away from home. Sometime in 1928 she made up her mind. Annie Bell said good-bye to her family and the only world she'd ever known, bundled Mannish and Mercedes up tight, and plunged into the Great Migration.

When the young family left the South, they most likely boarded a train on the Texas & Pacific Railway in Mansfield, which connected to the Illinois Central Railroad in Shreveport, thirty-seven miles north. From there they would have traveled to New Orleans and caught the Illinois Central's most famous train, the Panama Limited—a hulking hunk of steel spewing smoke high into the sky. Annie Bell used the same train, renamed the City of New Orleans, to visit Louisiana with her grand-children later in life. The Panama Limited was state-of-the-art—an all-Pullman consist featuring luxurious cars, though Annie Bell's skin likely barred her from being allowed to enjoy most of the luxuries.

The Panama Limited crawled from the muddy mouth of the Missis-sippi Delta up through the waving cotton fields, all the way to Chicago near the cool, blue shores of Lake Michigan. Along the way it deposited untold thousands of Negroes in new, exciting places. The trip took a full day and night and part of the next day, which left Annie Bell ample time to think about the world ahead and the one just left behind. She never talked much about her feelings, but it isn't hard to imagine what she must have felt sitting on that train with two fidgety little ones at her side. Perhaps she dreamed of how life would change for her, and her children, and their children as she dozed off in the train car, one sleep from Chicago.

———

After twenty-five jostling hours, the train steamed into Chicago's Central Station, at Roosevelt Road and Michigan Avenue. Annie Bell collected her luggage and her children and stepped onto northern ground. The city she saw around her might as well have been a different planet. The station itself was jaw dropping compared to Mansfield's ramshackle huts. Its brooding brick building towered nine stories above the tracks and con-nected to a thirteen-story clock tower topped with a Romanesque spire.

The streets stretched on as far as the eye could see, dotted here and there with Model T Fords. People—millions of them, it seemed—rushed from place to place, always in a hurry. Women, in thrall to the flapper craze, wore straight-line chemises with cloche hats covering their bobbed

hair. Men wore sporty suits, Oxford shoes, and fedoras, homburgs, tril-
bys, or straw boaters. The city buzzed with kinetic energy. It was a thrill-
ing spectacle for a country girl used to outhouses and cotton fields.

Chicago in the late '20s was embroiled in an era of heavy tensions
and epic capers. Prohibition had brought the scarred face of organized
crime, as Al Capone's notorious Chicago Outfit put the city in a choke-
hold through a toxic mixture of bribery and murder. Frank Lloyd Wright
had brought architecture with Prairie School designs, all horizontal lines
and overhanging eaves, including his legendary light court in the Rook-
ery building, commissioned in 1905. Steel had brought industry to construct those designs, providing work for thousands of men.

When Annie Bell arrived, steelworkers plodded to work each morning in a city still reeling from the race riots that had exploded near the
stockyards less than a decade before. In the summer of 1919, Eugene
Williams, a Negro teenager swimming in Lake Michigan, crossed an
informal line of segregation between the Twenty-Ninth Street Negro
beach and the Twenty-Fifth Street white beach. As a mob of white beach-
goers pelted him with stones, he became disoriented and drowned. Their
bloodlust awakened, whites and Irish immigrants unleashed a flood of
aggression upon Negroes in Chicago. Violence ruled for thirteen agonizing days, as roving white gangs scoured the streets around the Black Belt
looking for buildings to burn, possessions to loot, and Negroes to kill.

It was the worst race riot in Chicago's history, and it formed part
of the infamous Red Summer. During that summer, some twenty-five
riots busted through Washington, DC, Omaha, Knoxville, and several
other cities. Most of the violence was white on black, although that
would change in coming decades. One thing wouldn't change, though,
and it would exact a massive toll during my father's life: summer always
remained a good time for riots.

———

Dazzling as it was, Annie Bell learned her new city imposed limitations
almost as severe as the ones she had left in Louisiana. Upon her arrival,
almost all Chicago Negroes were crammed into the South Side, with

some overflowing into parts of the West Side. In a sliver of land measuring seven miles long and one-and-a-half miles wide, a quarter-million people lived, breathed, worked, slept, ate, made love, fought, showered, shaved, bought groceries, cooked, cleaned, got drunk. People called it the Black Belt, also known as Bronzeville, also known as "North Mississippi." As Great Migration historian Isabel Wilkerson wrote:

> Up and down Indiana and Wabash and Prairie and South Parkway, across Twenty-second Street and down to Thirty-first and Thirty-ninth and into the low Forties, a colored world, a city within a city, rolled out from the sidewalk, the streets aflutter with grocers and undertakers, dressmakers and barbershops, tailors and pressers, dealers of coals and sellers of firewood, insurance agents and real estate men, pharmacists and newspapers, a YMCA and the Urban League, high-steepled churches—Baptist, Holiness, African Methodist Episcopal churches practically transported from Mississippi and Arkansas—and stacked-heeled harlots stumbling out of call houses and buffet flats. The living conditions [were] not much better than those back home and, in some cases, worse . . . Front doors hung on single hinges. The sun peeked through cracks in the outer walls. Many rooms sat airless and windowless, packed with so many people that some roomers had to sleep in shifts.

This was Annie Bell's new home, and it came with a dizzying array of new experiences. She got her first chilling taste of the Hawk, the not-so-loving nickname given to Chicago's bitter winter wind. Years later, Chicago native Lou Rawls painted a gripping picture of life as a poor Negro trying to survive the Hawk: "There was nothing to block or buffer the wind, the elements / Keep them from knocking my pad down," he raps on the song "Dead End Street." "The boiler would bust and the heat was gone / I would have to get fully dressed before I could go to bed."

At some point during that first year, Annie Bell met a man named Walter Mayfield, or "Wal" to friends. She and Wal didn't get married, but they moved into a small apartment together and lived with Mannish and Mercedes in a situation that would be known today as common law. Marriage certificate or not, Annie Bell changed her last name to Mayfield, and her children became Mayfields too.

Grim job prospects confronted the Mayfields. In Chicago, three out of four Negro men toiled at unskilled, semiskilled, or servant jobs. These jobs locked them in constant poverty. To earn a full month's salary as a Pullman porter, for instance, a Negro had to work four hundred hours or log eleven thousand miles—either way required more than ten hours of work, seven days a week. Annie Bell saw those porters as she left Louisiana on the Panama Limited, giving her a glimpse of what Negroes had to do to survive in the North.

For many Negro women, the best they could hope for was to land a servant's job with a wealthy white family. Worse still, the stock market shattered like sugar glass a year after Annie Bell's arrival, making jobs a scarce commodity even for white people. But she brought something from Louisiana that set her apart, something that kept her in money for most of her life—Spiritualism.

A thousand miles from home, she had a captive audience of fellow migrants who trusted the word of a Spiritualist seer in a place where such attuned people were hard to find. She began attending a church on Division Street on the near West Side, where she'd soon find a nice little house. There, she made friends with the congregants, people who missed the close touch of a down-home church and might not have received the kind of spiritual guidance they needed from stuffy northern preachers.

Annie Bell knew these people. She knew how they talked, where they came from, what they believed. She also had her spirit guide. She told her new friends she was clairaudient, which meant she could hear things in other dimensions, as well as clairvoyant, which meant she could see them. Then she went to Madame Mary Overa, who ordained her as a reverend, and she set up shop in the tiny apartment she shared with Wal, Mannish, and Mercedes. She filled the parlor with plaster statues, pungent incense, mysterious potions, and special roots, all lit by the flitting flames of yellow, black, and red candles. It cast an eerie vibe, but soon people packed in every day to get a reading, a healing, or advice from the spirit guide through their medium—the Reverend A. B. Mayfield.

Even as the 1930s slogged on and the Great War gave way to the Great Depression, the Great Migration continued, which meant Annie Bell could count on a steady income from Louisiana migrants searching for a piece of home in the big city. While lines of languid men with hollow, frightened eyes stood downtown for hours waiting on a few pieces of bread, Annie Bell worked. Outside her cramped apartment, the city and nation grew desolate. Inside, with the incense snaking, candles flickering, and spirits reaching across the void, bread stayed on the table.

As the 1930s limped to their end, Mercedes began dating a tall older man with dark brown skin named Charles Hawkins Jr. Their marriage started the way many do, with a pregnancy followed by a ceremony. They didn't have enough money to set out on their own, so Charles moved in with Mercedes and her family. With the addition of another man to the apartment, Annie Bell—the only one with money—began looking for a bigger place.

Meanwhile, Mannish met Marion Washington, a scholarly, bookish girl, at school. Marion stayed mostly to herself, nose buried in a volume of Paul Laurence Dunbar, one of the most famous Negro poets, and she was a self-proclaimed ugly duckling. Mannish showed her some attention, and soon the two became involved.

Six months younger than Mannish, Marion was a Chicago native. Her father, Kenneth "Joe" Washington journeyed to the city from Oklahoma roughly a decade before Annie Bell. He worked hard painting and wallpapering houses. After arriving in Chicago, he met and married another transplant, Sadie Ann Gillard, in 1922. Sadie came from Knoxville, Tennessee, in the first wave of migrants. She did everything from domestic work, to factory jobs, to homemaking, and she was a superb cook.

When high school ended, Marion earned a scholarship to college, but she never got the chance to use it. Sometime near the end of 1941 her life took an unexpected turn, and six months before her eighteenth birthday she went with Mannish to see Reverend Horace Hayden at his church on 1250 Wabash Avenue. On February 7, 1942—two months to the day after the Japanese bombed Pearl Harbor—Marion and Mannish married, her belly already full with his boy child.

2

My Mama Borned Me in a Ghetto

"My mama borned me in a ghetto!
There was no mattress for my head.
But, No! She couldn't call me 'Jesus.'
'I wasn't white enough,' she said."

—"KUNG FU"

Chicago, June 3, 1942—The baby came. Marion named my father Curtis Lee, after his father. His life would put Annie Bell's gamble to the test. He'd never suffer the indignity of "colored" signs barring him from bathrooms, or watch his dreams wither under the foul cloud of Jim Crow, or fear the hangman's noose.

Yet, even in Chicago the invisible lines of race still bound my father. While most white children of his generation dreamed of soaring through the sky like Superman or swinging vine to vine like Tarzan, Curtis knew from an early age he'd never be quite like them. No hero looked like he looked or lived where he lived—he was black and poor in a world that wouldn't let him forget it. If those prospects seemed glum, just across the ocean a maniac goose-stepped through Europe, hell-bent on conquering the Earth to assert the primacy of the white race.

While Marion adjusted to the rhythms of her newborn boy, she became pregnant again, this time with a girl. A mere nine months and eight days after Curtis's birth, Judith arrived prematurely. Now my grandmother had two lives to protect with the same money that often couldn't cover one. Even though Annie Bell's finances allowed her to take special care of her only son, her largesse didn't extend to Marion and Mannish's family, so Marion had to go on relief—known today as welfare. She lived hand to mouth, never sure she'd have enough to feed her babies or that her husband would provide support.

When Mannish came home, which wasn't often, his belligerence ruled. He had a temper like his mother and fought Marion constantly. He wasn't even twenty years old and couldn't provide for his family, which often brings the worst out of a man. Still, he'd soon desert his wife and children, leaving Marion to do the hard work the best she could.

The second Great War opened opportunities for Negroes the same way the first one had, so Mannish joined the service and was stationed in California, giving him a steady salary. The money helped, but Marion now had to negotiate the internal anguish of watching her husband leave without knowing when, or if, he'd come back. He shipped out for duty as millions of Negroes shipped in from the South, the Great Migration still flooding forth.

As the new arrivals sought jobs, food, and shelter, racial passions ran high. In June, roughly three months after my aunt Judy's birth, race riots rocked Detroit. Unlike the Chicago riots of 1919, Detroit in 1943 represented a turning point. As Wilkerson wrote:

Until the 1943 uprising in Detroit, most riots in the United States . . . had been white attacks on colored people often resulting in the burning of entire colored sections or towns. This was the first major riot in which blacks fought back as earnestly as the whites and in which black residents, having become established in the city but still relegated to rundown ghettos, began attacking and looting perceived symbols of exploitation, the stores and laundries run by whites and other outsiders that blacks felt were cheating them. It was only after Detroit that riots became known as primarily urban phenomena, ultimately centered on inner-city blacks venting their frustrations on the ghettos that confined them.

This subtle shift in the nature of riots would have massive and destructive repercussions in the coming years, but at the time it only caused Marion to worry for her children.

Two thousand miles away from the riots, Mannish had plenty of room to live wild and free, leaving his marriage behind on the cold banks of Lake Michigan. At some point, Marion decided to visit him. She dropped Curtis at her mother's house—he loved Grandma Sadie's sweet potato pies—and left Judy with Annie Bell, perhaps because Judy had also been born severely nearsighted. Whatever her reasoning, when Marion returned to pick up Judy, Annie Bell refused to give her back.

Marion found a way to get along with just about everybody, but losing her daughter strained her gentle soul until it almost burst. Worse still, Annie Bell had money, which meant no government agency was likely to force little Judy to return to live with her mother in abject poverty. So, in a bizarre way, Judy was stolen. No one talked much about it. Judy grew up calling Annie Bell "Mom," and although she had some inkling her real mother was the woman who visited on weekends, it would take many years and a bit of snooping to figure out what had happened.

My father didn't have to wait long for new siblings, though. After Mannish went AWOL from his military duty, changing his name to Kenneth Washington to avoid trouble, he returned home and fathered three more children with Marion—Carolyn Mercedes in '45, Gary Kirby in '46, and Kenneth in '47. Time apart had done nothing to help the couple, and their fighting grew worse as responsibilities piled up. Soon after Kenny's birth, Mannish left for good. His children didn't miss him; he had no presence in their lives, and as Muddy Waters once sang, "You can't lose what you ain't never had." But for Marion, life only got harder. Deserted, dejected, emotionally battered by her husband and his family, powerless to reclaim her first daughter, she began battling a new foe—depression.

Fortune hadn't finished dealing her fresh blows, either. Soon after his birth, Gary—whom everyone called Kirby—contracted measles, which led to acute encephalitis. He slept straight through a week or two as though in a coma, Marion sitting by his bedside in anxious agony the whole time. When he awoke, she noticed his movements had changed. The sickness had left Kirby mentally challenged. My grandmother would have to watch him like a baby his entire life, which meant she couldn't take a job until one of the other kids got old enough to handle the responsibility. From an early age, Curtis helped with the small things—Marion remembered that by three years old, he could diaper Carolyn as well as she could. Still, she was the only adult and had to handle the big things. With government aid now her only possible source of income, she stared desperation dead in the eye.

Hunger hounded the family, but my grandmother kept them alive any way she could, stretching every dollar until the eagle grinned. Most times they ate rice, or beans, or anything that cheaply filled a grumbling belly. Meat was a delicacy enjoyed maybe one weekend of every month, and it consisted of chicken necks, or backs, or any other part of the animal that people with money wouldn't eat. "Mom had this great big pot and she would cook beans and neck bones," Aunt Carolyn recalls. "She'd cook it on Monday, and we'd eat all the meat out on Monday, but it was always on the table until we ate up all the beans. I just now learned how to eat beans again, because I swore when I got grown, I would never eat beans."

The family lived on the run, chased by creditors and landlords from one seedy flophouse to the next. Being a poor Negro in Chicago meant you rarely got a sense of belonging anywhere. After Mannish deserted the family, they lived in a dingy apartment on South Washtenaw Avenue, where Marion began dating a man named Eddie who abused her. One of Aunt Carolyn's earliest memories is scrambling up the fire escape to Grandma Sadie's apartment, which was just above theirs, and begging her to come down and stop Eddie from hitting Marion. "Mama was kind of on the timid side, and Grandma was just very boisterous," Aunt Carolyn says. "Mama wasn't a fighter, but Grandma was. And [Eddie] didn't mess with Grandma. Grandma ended up putting him out."

Sadie was often the family's only refuge. "She was always around," Aunt Carolyn recalls. "She was Mom's backbone." Not affectionate by nature, Sadie possessed the kind of steel will necessary to survive the Chicago slums. She worked all day cooking in rich white people's kitchens, and at night she often brought home food her employers didn't eat to feed her daughter and grandchildren. Many times she saved them from starvation.

At home, young Curtis watched his mother get beaten; at school, he took the beatings. With a cruelty special to children, his classmates roughed him up and zeroed in on his every imperfection. They mocked his poverty, although they were most likely poor too. They picked on him because of his short stature and big teeth. Perhaps most hurtful, they made fun of him because of his dark skin. He'd never forget the derogatory nickname they slung at him like a stone—Smut. They used the word in its original sense, meaning a dark stain or blot. This bred in him insecurities that would take decades to shake.

———

Soon, Marion left Eddie and moved the family to the White Eagle, a decaying hotel on Eighteenth Street between Indiana and Michigan Avenues. Of all the cheap digs, the White Eagle haunted my father's memory most. He recalled it as a dark, dreary joint where hookers stalked the sidewalk day and night, and many more lived in the neighborhood nearby. He never saw a pimp at the time, though. "I guess pimps are a luxury of wealthier neighborhoods," he said later.

Outside, trash choked the sidewalk and broken windows made the building's face leer like a jack-o-lantern's smile. Inside, prostitutes, dope pushers, and drug fiends lived on one side, while poor families huddled on the other—mostly single mothers struggling to raise their children in the jaws of nighttime's vices. At the White Eagle, the whole family lived in a single room the size of a postage stamp. Marion slept on a let-out sofa bed, and the children shared a bunk bed, Curtis on top, Carolyn, Kenny, and Kirby down below.

Their floor had eight units but only one communal bathroom, so young Curtis had to trudge out to the hall to use it, not unlike Annie Bell's beaten path to the outhouse in Louisiana. The bathroom was a nightmare—putrid, cramped, filthy, full of exposed pipes and crumbling walls. Residents stuffed newspapers into crevices to stanch water leaks, while exposed light bulbs dangled from dangerous wires overhead.

Life in the White Eagle reflected the building's shabby state. Most nights, Curtis and family went to bed hungry and woke up itching from bedbug bites. As Aunt Carolyn remembers, "Many Christmases, we didn't have anything. Mama would fix corn bread and a bowl of sugar to make syrup. We thought it was a treat, but that's all she had." Grandma Sadie moved into the building, as did Marion's siblings, Uncle Son and Aunt Edith. Having family close by did nothing to make the White Eagle a homier place, though. At age seven, Aunt Carolyn narrowly escaped a pervert trying to lure her into the bathroom.

Under such duress, my dad had to grow up fast. He lived in a world that snuffed out innocence, a world that forbade the luxury of childhood. At age five, he became the man of the house through no choice of his own. The word "man" is instructive here—there's no such thing as child of the house. When Marion wasn't around, Curtis exerted control like an adult, and he got used to having others look to him for that control. As Aunt Carolyn says, "If anything went on, we looked to him if Mama wasn't there because he was the oldest one around at that time." It fit his natural tendencies as a Gemini, and for much of his life, if he couldn't control something completely, he wouldn't do it.

Marion's situation taught him the dangers of living without control. At the same time, she also taught him about the strength of the spirit to survive, and the importance of art as a way to manage despair. She couldn't provide creature comforts, but she kept the family respectable through sheer force of will and artistic talent. Whatever clothes she couldn't afford, she could knit, sew, or crochet just as well. She also loved working at puzzles—jigsaw and crossword—and she always had a book in hand, which provided endless entertainment for her children. She'd tell them stories from the books she read, and often she'd recite her favorite Dunbar poems, like "How Lucy Backslid":

> De times is mighty stirrin' 'mong de people up ouah way,
> Dey 'sputin' an' dey argyin' an' fussin' night an' day;

An' all dis monst'ous trouble dat hit meks me tiahed to tell
Is 'bout dat Lucy Jackson dat was sich a mighty belle.

She was de preachah's favoured, an' he tol' de chu'ch one night
Dat she travelled thoo de cloud o' sin a—bearin' of a light;
But, now, I 'low he t'inkin' dat she mus' 'a' los' huh lamp,
Case Lucy done backslided an' dey trouble in de camp.

The stanzas churned around young Curtis's mind, powerfully influencing his sense of rhythm and rhyme. While Dunbar's poetry left a mark on my dad, it also eased his transition into a world that would force him to have two identities. Dunbar's work is mixed, with some poems written in formal English verse and others, like "Lucy," written in Negro dialect. This dual identity as a poet struck at the heart of Negro existence in America. It represented an artistic expression of a phenomenon that DuBois, at roughly the same time as Dunbar's writing, called "double-consciousness." DuBois wrote:

> It is a peculiar sensation, this double-consciousness. . . . One ever
> feels his two-ness,—an American, a Negro; two souls, two thoughts,
> two unreconciled strivings; two warring ideals in one dark body,
> whose dogged strength alone keeps it from being torn asunder.
> The history of the American Negro is the history of this strife,—
> this longing to attain self-conscious manhood, to merge his double
> self into a better and truer self. In this merging he wishes neither of
> the older selves to be lost . . . He simply wishes to make it possible
> for a man to be both a Negro and an American, without being
> cursed and spit upon by his fellows, without having the doors of
> opportunity closed roughly in his face.

Double-consciousness held true for every station of Negro life. From the common laborer to the most successful celebrity, all had to be proficient in two languages, two ways of acting, two modes of dress, two sets of rules—one for the white world, one for the Negro. As Curtis grew, he encountered these two worlds. Often the encounter was silent and subconscious, like listening to his mother recite Dunbar's poems in two voices. Within a few years, however, the encounters would grow deafening as the worlds crashed together.

For now, my father kept to himself, like his mother and Annie Bell. Quiet and solitary, he preferred doing most things alone—he'd remain that way even as a world-famous musician. Marion recalled, "When other children came by to play, Curtis would tell them he was on punishment and couldn't have any company." When the other kids left, he'd break open a box of crayons and lose himself in drawing.

Still, he had a deep curiosity about the world. He plied his mother with questions, wanting to know how everything worked, and where, and when. His favorite question, though, was, "Why?" Even if he knew the answer, he still asked why. It seemed a magical question, always producing new perspectives.

He also had a keen interest in music. During his youth, the smooth sounds of Nat King Cole, Lena Horne, and Dinah Washington poured from the radio like honey, salving the wounds of a war-weary nation. At the same time, a new movement of jazz musicians flouted the unwritten code that a Negro performer mustn't ever threaten the status quo. Miles Davis led the pack, and whatever anyone thought of him, he "took no shit off of nobody," as he often said, white or Negro. Living in blues central, Curtis also heard the plaintive moans of Muddy Waters, Howlin' Wolf, John Lee Hooker, and others who electrified nightclub stages down the street from his home.

Curtis meanwhile took his own first steps on a different kind of stage. As Marion remembered it, "He used to stand on the tree stump in front of my grandmother's house in Du Quoin, Illinois, and sing 'Pistol-packing Mama' to the engineers driving the trains by." He was a born performer, and no poverty or hardship could take away my grandmother's joy at watching her eldest son strut across a tree trunk with the confidence only a child can feel.

Marion also had a voracious appetite for music, listening to opera, classical, country, gospel, and rhythm and blues at home. She had a collection of gospel records she played from her dusty old Victrola while Curtis peeked his little head over the turntable's edge, watching the black-and-white Specialty Records labels turn in hypnotic circles.

Specialty singers like Claude Jeter and the Swan Silvertones ingrained Almighty God in the grooves of their records. Jeter's lilting falsetto—the precursor to my father's vocal style, and inspiration for legions of doo-wop singers—gave sound to the human soul. When that soul-sound bounced off the White Eagle's grimy walls, the unfathomable took fleeting shape in Curtis's mind. Only music had this divine, ecstatic power, and my father was enthralled. He'd found a love as intimate as his own skin.

My grandmother raised her family gently and respectfully. "She was a reasonable mother," my father recalled, "a woman of mentality, of mind, that could talk, express herself." Despite her expressive mind, however, her financial situation remained dire. On Kenny's fourth birthday, she gave him a quarter and asked him not to tell Curtis or Carolyn because that was all the money she had. Annie Bell offered little help, and Mannish had remarried a few times. He fathered more children (who were given the surname Washington, after the new name he took when he went AWOL), leaving him with fewer reasons to think about his first family. "I never will forget this one Christmas," Aunt Carolyn says. "[Mannish] came over and brought a basket of food and it had a doll in it. This basket of food, that's how we happened to have a Christmas meal, and I finally got a doll for Christmas. That's when he was with his third wife, Gracie . . . and he and Gracie were having an argument. They were arguing because the basket of food was not supposed to come to us. It was supposed to go over to [my half sisters] Tanya and Ann's house, but they weren't home. So he brought it to us. I was so upset, when I got home, I took the doll and broke the head off. I remember throwing it because it wasn't meant for us."

While Mannish continued to ignore the family, depression gnawed at Marion like an open sore. Sometimes the children heard her crying alone in her room at night because she had nothing to feed them. Curtis and his siblings made a game of it the way children do, filling their little bellies with water and jiggling it around just to hear the noise of something inside other than hunger pangs. Otherwise, they'd squeak by with canned food, and powdered milk, and salad-dressing sandwiches until Marion's relief check came again.

When it came, she had twenty-five dollars to feed her family for the next month. She had to stock up on staples, but every once in a while she'd buy some popcorn, pop it up, and gather the family around the table, telling the children stories from her books as they munched away. Or, she'd splurge by taking Carolyn down to Woolworth's and buying a banana split. No matter how much she needed every red cent, she knew sometimes it was a mother's duty to pamper her children.

———

Marion's struggle shaped my father. As he watched her battle to do something as simple as survive, depression became part of his mind. But he had another role model in Annie Bell. She lived in relative opulence because of her work as a reverend. From her, he learned that one way to have what his mother didn't—success, money, power—was to possess something special, something mystical even, something that set him apart the way Spiritualism set Annie Bell apart.

His family hoped he'd become a preacher, but he knew from a young age that was something he'd never be. Other ways of being special existed though, and he didn't have to look far to find them. They juked all night in the clubs down the street and shook the walls at the church meetings he attended. Their voices came tinny from the radio speakers like magic every night and crept through the phonograph needle into his wondering ears each day. Muddy Waters was special. Louis Armstrong was special. John Lee Hooker was special. Sam Cooke was special. They held a magical power that seemed as strong as religion itself—music. Like many great preachers, musicians attracted all the things that seemed impossible to attain for a ghetto child insecure of his looks and his poverty—money, fame, power, even sex.

———

As America eased toward the innocuous 1950s, flush with returning soldiers and financially solvent again, the country celebrated and convalesced. The celebration for Negroes, however, was muted. They still chafed under an oppressive homeland for which they had just fought and died by the thousands. They also fought, as always, for their rights.

In 1944, a woman named Irene Morgan refused to give up her seat on an interstate bus in Virginia, violating Jim Crow laws. She was arrested, and by '46 her case rose to the US Supreme Court with the help of Thurgood Marshall, legal counsel of the NAACP. Right around Kirby's birth, the Court struck down the Virginia law as unconstitutional. The ruling prompted a new civil rights organization, the Congress of Racial Equality (CORE), to launch a series of nonviolent protests challenging segregation laws on interstate public transport, setting the stage for the great bus boycott that would begin the civil rights movement a decade later. Of course, my father didn't know about CORE or Thurgood Marshall yet, and he felt no personal gain from the ruling. After all, no one complied with it, and the federal government either would not or could not enforce it. Even so, the violent changes that would shape his life stirred once again, with two more key players stepping into the spotlight.

Demonstrations didn't matter to him yet—Dad had fallen in love with the radio. Later in life, he'd say, "Aside from the gospel music in the church all I'd hear was the R&B stations . . . I got nothing but Muddy Waters, Jimmy Reed, Howlin' Wolf, John Lee Hooker, and all these guys." He couldn't avoid it. In the 1940s and '50s, Chicago had DJs like Holmes "Daddy-O" Daylie, whose *Jazz from Dad's Pad* aired on WAIT, and Al Benson, "a whiskey-drinking Democratic precinct captain" who slogged out ten hours on the air every day. Several stations interspersed Negro DJs playing R&B with Greek, German, Lithuanian, Polish, Czech, and other ethnic shows, filling my father's head with strange, exotic combinations of sound. No one wielded more influence, however, than Herb Kent "the Cool Gent." Kent began as a country and western jockey, but his doo-wop and R&B playlists would come to form the backbone of many a Chicago musician's sense of rhythm, taste, and style, my father's included.

The radio stations were extensions of Chicago's jumpin' and jivin' club scene, and though Dad was too young for these clubs, they imprinted the fabric of his world. By the end of the 1940s, Chicago had become arguably the best city in America for live jazz, with at least seventy-five clubs on the South Side alone. At places like the Club DeLisa, one could see Fletcher Henderson's band, featuring a young Sun Ra (when he was still known as Sonny Blount), as well as blues singers like Big Joe Turner, Gatemouth Moore, and Dr. Jo Jo Adams, a flamboyantly dressed man who performed X-rated blues numbers in top hat and tails and did a knock-kneed dance Chuck Berry would make famous a decade later.

During my father's youth, Chicago also flowered with a cultural and artistic explosion much like the Harlem Renaissance of the 1920s. The Chicago Black Renaissance, which began in the '30s, reshaped American literature with authors like Richard Wright, Gwendolyn Brooks, and Margaret Walker. The accompanying musical explosion inspired a young generation including Curtis, Ramsey Lewis, Herbie Hancock, and Maurice White.

In addition to so much enticing secular music, Dad saw firsthand the power of gospel music. At Union Hall near Forty-Eighth and State, he watched bands like the Pilgrim Travelers, the Bells of Joy, and the Staple Singers, as well as Sam Cooke, who would profoundly influence his direction in life. He'd also never forget watching Archie Brownlee, singer of the Five Blind Boys of Mississippi, dart up and down the aisles like a man possessed, pouring sweat and howling until it seemed the sky would split and Christ Himself would appear.

These singers inspired my father to try his own voice at gospel music, and he'd soon have the chance. Around this time, Annie Bell had saved enough money to rent a small basement at 2310 West Maypole Avenue, where she set up her first church. And there again was the lesson—because of her mystical power, Annie Bell could afford not only food, clothing, and a house, but also her own place of business. If young Curtis had any question about what he wanted to do with his life and how it could help him achieve the control he desired, he wouldn't have to wait long for the answer.

3

Traveling Souls

"I know I believe in the spirit,
Traveling Soul was alone, a part of me,
Out in this world, it don't take your eyes too long to see."
—"Sweet Exorcist"

Chicago, 1950—Down in a dank basement on Maypole Avenue, forty or fifty people crammed into neatly lined rows of chairs facing a small pulpit. They met every Sunday to chase spiritual ecstasy, arriving impeccably dressed, the men in double-breasted suits, the women in felt hats with grosgrain ribbons. Service commenced with an early morning Bible study followed by Reverend A. B. Mayfield's sermon from nine until noon, during which she'd recount the stories of Jacob, whose brothers sold him into slavery, and Abraham, who nearly slaughtered his own son, and Job, whom Almighty God persecuted the way a cat toys with a bug. She wove these parables into the flow of her congregants' lives—few audiences could identify with Job more than a room full of Negroes—and as she spoke, she cast a spell over the room. The old folks swayed and murmured; the children, of course, dropped like little flies, bored straight to sleep.

Annie Bell didn't celebrate Christian mass, so at some point she called on her spirit guide with rhythmic incantations that snaked around the basement like frankincense. As she channeled the unutterable essence of the divine, her congregation erupted with testifying shouts and moans. They stomped and sang, the spirit alighting where it would—now here, now there.

On street level, pedestrians swaddled in their Sunday best strolled by the sky-blue building. The only clues to what went on below their feet were the words painted in big white letters on the front window: Traveling Souls Spiritualist Church.

It wasn't big, but it was hers. In the twenty-odd years since she had fled Jim Crow's clutches, Annie Bell had clawed her way to self-sufficiency, a miraculous feat for a Negro woman at the time. She was slight of frame and just over five feet tall, but Jesus said it only takes faith the size of a mustard seed to move mountains. If anyone could move a mountain, Annie Bell could. She even earned enough money to buy a little house in a racially mixed neighborhood at 2214 W. Division, where she continued her work as a seer. Most of Traveling Souls' congregation visited her during the week, and her house was usually lousy with people. Apart from Mercedes, Charles, and their children, at any given moment one might see clients, relatives, latchkey kids, and the occasional moocher hoping to snag a free meal.

Despite so many people surrounding her, my great-grandmother had few friends. She cultivated an aloofness, preferring her own company to that of others. She did most things in her bedroom, and to deal with her usually required doing it in her room, on her terms. Sometimes she'd come out and mingle with the constant stream of visitors, but as soon as she grew tired of socializing, she'd disappear without ceremony into the sanctuary of her room. She passed these traits unchanged to my father.

Her detachment gave her a kind of power. It kept her accessible yet distant, in the mold of all great religious healers. She projected that air, self-stylized as it was, and the multitude packed in every day to breathe it in, bodies weaving around each other, hemmed in by piles of junk. Annie Bell was a hoarder, and she crammed the house full of trinkets from Riverview. Pink and yellow policy slips sat in messy stacks on her dinner table, and Aunt Carolyn earned many a rebuke for playing with the pretty slips. "Don't touch that! Put that down," Annie Bell would hiss, with good reason. Policy formed an important part of her income.

In those days, policy was a little like the modern lottery and a lot like a gambling racket. Number runners prowled the neighborhood, marking down wagers in little books kept in their pockets. At the end of the day, whoever picked the right number won a piece of the pie. Annie Bell had a knack for picking the right number. She claimed they came to her in dreams, which was easier to believe after she won again, and again, and again. She'd stash the cash in wads under her mattress, using it to fund Traveling Souls, make house payments, and splurge on a new car just about every year. Annie Bell loved Buicks.

For Aunt Judy, the constant commotion and clutter created a chaotic living space, made worse by the volatile personalities housed within. Annie Bell passed on her raging temper to her children, as Marion had learned with Mannish. Mercedes exceeded them both in cruelty. She and Annie Bell often shook the house with screaming spats, each on opposite sides of a room shouting in no uncertain terms what would happen if the other put so much as a toe over *this line*.

Meanwhile, every new weekend brought a trip from Marion with my father, Carolyn, Kirby, and Kenny in tow, adding more bodies to the stew. Annie Bell usually hid Judy when my grandmother arrived, so Marion rarely got a chance to see her daughter. Worse, Marion still struggled mightily to keep food on the table, while Judy always had new clothes and plenty of food. Perhaps inevitably, Curtis, Carolyn, and Kenny looked at her as the *have*, while they were the *have-nots*. The constant shuffling between the *have-nots* of Marion's hovel and the *haves* of Annie Bell's house further ingrained the message in Dad's mind—possessing a special talent earned control, and control brought security.

Curtis and the rest of the kids sometimes stayed the weekend at Annie Bell's. It was the only time they got a decent meal. Sundays, they'd slink out of bed rubbing sleepy eyes and pad toward the kitchen where Mercedes's husband, Charles, prepared breakfast. He worked over the food poetically, pots and pans clanging, smoke curling through the house carrying the savory smells of scrambled eggs, steamed rice, hot biscuits, crispy bacon, fried sausage, and steak smothered in tangy gravy. He sang spirituals while he cooked as if they added seasoning, and when he set the food out for a feast just like you'd see on television, it seemed God Himself had been listening to his songs.

After breakfast, a sinister Sunday ritual followed. As Aunt Carolyn remembers, "It wasn't a pleasant home, because every Sunday morning, you had the big alley fight, cuss-out fight before we went to church. Cuss all the way to the church, and then after church, you'd come home and cuss all the rest of the day." Only in church would the cussing cease, as no one wanted to cuss in front of the Bible. My father watched these fights, and even though he possessed a much cooler temperament, at times he'd repeat them in his romantic relationships later in life. If Annie Bell's congregants knew about their reverend's unholy temper, however, they didn't seem to mind. They showed up dutifully to Sunday services, and Traveling Souls thrived.

––––––––––

The word "traveling" did not earn top billing in my great-grandmother's church by accident. Soon after starting the church, she joined the National Colored Spiritualist Association of Churches, a long title made longer by the fact that whites and Negroes in America were separated even before God. The NCSAC held meetings in big cities around the country, and little Spiritualist churches from all over attended, home-grown gospel groups in tow, competing to see who had the best one. Annie Bell wanted Traveling Souls to attend these national meetings, so she had Charles form a quartet featuring his two sons, his stepson Eddie "Paddyfoot" Patterson, and Jerry Butler, a young man with a voice so rich it would change my father's life.

Jerry's family transplanted to Chicago from Sunflower, Mississippi, when he was three years old. Like many Southern migrants, they fled home under duress. "My father had a doctor," Jerry recalls, "and the doctor was the father of another doctor. They had the same name. My father went in and asked the lady for the doctor, and she said, 'He won't be in until such and such a time.' And [my father] said, 'Well, I want to speak to the old man.' She got offended, because this black had the audacity to call her boss an old man, and she called the sheriff. The sheriff came and chastised my father for being disrespectful. My mother got so angry, she said, 'We've got to leave this city because somebody's going to die here.' She made him pack up and bring us to Chicago." Such was the situation in Mississippi that two poorly chosen words changed the Butlers' lives forever.

Even at such a young age, Jerry's voice made him the clear choice for the quartet's lead singer. They went by the Northern Jubilee Singers, and as Jerry remembers, "We sang traditional gospel songs. At the time that we started, Sam Cooke was a major star in gospel music. And so anything that Sam sang, we wanted to sing. But we never limited it to that. We did 'I'll Fly Away,' 'Pilgrim and a Stranger Traveling Through This Wearisome Land.' Most of these songs were made famous by some other spiritual or gospel group."

My father begged to get in, but no one wanted him. He was only eight years old, and they stood on the cusp of their teenage years—it was simple politics. He didn't give up, though. He might have been a loner, but he craved the acceptance of these older boys who did what he dreamed of doing. He'd soon find the key to unlock the door to those dreams.

By this point, Dad's musical ability had begun to blossom. On a trip to visit Sadie's relatives in Du Quoin, he discovered the piano, sitting before it like an archaeologist trying to make sense of a hieroglyph. As his fingers fumbled around the keys, he noticed the black ones sounded like the boogie-woogie music he heard on the radio. Soon, he could pick out little melodies on the sharps and flats. He seemed naturally drawn to the instrument, although as he would remember later in life, he didn't need much prodding. "I never really had to acquire an interest in music," he said. "I just grew up around people who were a constant inspiration."

Regardless of his burgeoning piano skills, the older boys didn't want him hanging around—Annie Bell didn't have a piano in the church, anyway. But then came one of those moments in life where fate, that dreamy concept, seems to become a living, breathing thing. As my father remembered it:

> [Eddie Patterson] brought a guitar with him to my grandmother's house. And this guitar would just sit in a corner and sit there and sit there, and no one would touch it. Of course, with my curiosity about music, it just kept pulling me and pulling me until I had to pick up that ax . . . I picked up this guitar, and when I strummed across it, it was in the standard Spanish tuning, which means when you strum across, you don't get a chord . . . Well, I didn't know what to do. So I tuned the guitar to the black keys on the keyboard . . . That's how I taught myself to play guitar.

Without knowing it, he had tuned his guitar to open F-sharp, which meant that when he strummed across the strings without putting his left hand on the fret board, the guitar played an F-sharp chord. No one told him to tune the guitar that way; it happened by that mixture of chance and God-given talent often called genius.

Genius is a much-abused word, of course, but it must apply to a child inventing his own system of playing a six-stringed instrument. No guidebook exists to learn guitar in open F-sharp tuning, no reference manual with chord shapes, scales, or fingerings. It is hard, if not impossible, to think of any other guitarist in the history of the instrument who played it that way. My father had no teachers but his ear and intuition.

Playing the guitar came with secondary benefits. The instrument fascinated the older boys, but only Curtis took the time to learn it. Now he had something they wanted. Within the year, he joined the Northern Jubilee Singers.

The group grew stronger with my father in the lineup. It turned out he had a sweet tenor voice and, even better, he could write songs. At first he wrote gospel music, songs heavily indebted to traveling church acts like the Soul Stirrers and the Staple Singers. As my father recalled, "The church had plenty of little affairs with other churches and we'd go visit other churches and they'd visit us and every church would have a group, a young kid singer vocalist or someone who was singing music. So we got a lot of that. A lot of a cappella and group singing . . . I was a quartet man, the four and five man groups . . . I just loved harmony. So that's where the foundation was laid down for me."

A whole circuit existed for these gospel acts, and Uncle Charles wanted to get the boys on it. Annie Bell held a service in early 1953 to send the Northern Jubilee Singers off. Winter still hovered, the Hawk slicing its talons into every crack and crevice as congregants shuffled downstairs to the church. The service took place in the evening, which made it feel special. A potbellied stove burned in the back of the basement, providing some semblance of heat. Uncle Charles gathered the children around and explained they would begin attending Spiritualist conventions in other cities. Annie Bell even splurged on new transportation, peeling off a few bills from the wad under her bed and purchasing a bus.

In no time, Uncle Charles had the group running. They hit Detroit and Cleveland, dipping down into Louisiana where Annie Bell visited the family she left behind, then back to Chicago. As leader of the Northern Jubilee Singers, Charles became a hero to the children and a father figure for Curtis. Charles was the guy he could talk to when he had problems, the one who disciplined him when he got out of line. He was the only adult male who offered Curtis tenderness, affection, and guidance.

He also gave Curtis his first taste of life on the road. In the summer of 1953, the group traveled down to Tampa, Florida, to perform at a convention. Few southern states at the time treated Negroes worse than Florida, and as Annie Bell's bus grumbled into Tampa early in the morning, Curtis and the other boys discovered what they had missed by being born up north. As Jerry remembered, "A group of white boys looking for trouble threw things at the bus, made faces, and called us 'sanctified niggers.'" Jerry found to his amazement Negroes in Tampa didn't treat them much better. They didn't like that these northern cats swooped down and stole the spotlight and, perhaps more important, the girls. He recalled, "They seemed to know only one phrase: 'You ain't shit, man.'"

The convention took place at the Pallbearers Union Hall, where the Northern Jubilee Singers sang every night. My father learned from these gigs. Watching how Uncle Charles arranged the quintet, he learned how to voice harmonies, how to structure call and response, and how to write for multiple singers. Soon, he got his own guitar, or something like one. "It was a twelve-string, and it looked more like a lute," he said. "My grandmother bought it for me. I always wanted a guitar, you know, but I guess she had no idea what one was. She found something that was quite ancient . . . and it had a very strange shape."

Later, Marion bought him a Roy Rogers guitar, and he progressed quickly. Though gospel music was still my father's main interest, secular music lured him like a siren. The blues, after all, weren't that different from gospel—one was about a woman, the other about God, but the intent was the same. Plus, he heard the blues everywhere he went. He even lived them. It came as no surprise when he formed a loose little blues group with a friend on harmonica and another on snare drum. "When I first started playing guitar I remember that's what I used to play—strictly down blues," he later said. "I guess that gave me my basics of being able to understand just the simplicity of those one, two, three changes and the funkiness of blues itself. And the church gave me the inspiration and the harmony overall to be able to take a lyric and build it into other things that might help to inspire or motivate people."

He still used his unique F-sharp tuning, which gave the licks he copied from Muddy Waters and Little Walter a twist. On Saturdays while Uncle Charles shot pool, Dad's group played in the back of Charles's car. Every now and then someone walking by would toss a quarter or two their way. By the end of the day, Dad usually had a few coins to rub together.

Music, both holy and secular, now dominated his life. Sixth grade couldn't compete with the high of hurtling from gig to gig while the country blurred by before his eyes. When he stood on stage, he felt safe from the schoolyard taunts of "Smut," safe from jabs at his looks, height, or poverty, and safe most of all from the insecurity that otherwise never left him alone. People treated him differently after seeing him on stage. *Girls* treated him differently, although in a way, his guitar was the closest girlfriend he'd ever have. He kept it at hand constantly, even in bed. He fell asleep cradling it. He woke up strumming it. He played it gently, lovingly, using his fingers to caress the strings. "It was my other self," he said. "It dictated to me as much as I dictated to it. The guitar was my twin."

Out on the road, Dad felt his calling, but he still lived under his mother's thumb, so his dreams of ditching school for the life of a professional musician would have to wait. He found little encouragement in school, though, and shuffled through at least nine grammar schools before high school. He summed up his scholastic experience saying, "My education didn't give me any background, not even any back*bone*, as a black. It just didn't mean anything. My whole education for whatever I do know was brought to me right here on the road."

Meanwhile, the social rumblings that framed Curtis's birth now threatened an all-out tempest. In 1951, a Negro family had moved into Cicero, Al Capone's former stronghold and Chicago's most virulently segregated suburb. Cicero's white residents greeted them with a riot, burning their building and destroying their possessions. The National Guard had to be called to restore order. Curtis and the kids were old enough to know what had happened and why. Marion worried especially for Kenny, who had a tendency to speak his young mind. Whenever racial trouble stirred, she'd usually send him to Annie Bell's until the threat diffused.

Trouble seemed to be stirring all the time, though. By the early '50s, the Nation of Islam—a group ideologically influenced by Marcus Garvey—began gaining strength and buying real estate all over the South Side of Chicago. The Nation promoted a mixture of Islamic theology and a theory known as Yakub's History, which held that an evil black scientist named Yakub genetically engineered the white race. The theory said all American Negroes were actually Asiatic, a term uniting Arabs, Egyptians, Chinese, Japanese, Negroes, and many other ethnicities into one group.

The Nation was founded in Detroit in 1930 and moved to Chicago under the leadership of Elijah Muhammad in 1935. As the Nation grew in Chicago, many of Annie Bell's clients joined its ranks, and her house swirled with political debates, social theories, and heated discussions. Soon, Annie Bell got caught in the tide. As Aunt Carolyn recalls, "When we were little she told us we weren't black; we were Asiatic. I came home, and I told mama, 'We're Asiatic.' Mama said, 'That's a flu.'"

Marion might not have been swayed, but the Nation continued growing, spurred on by a prodigiously talented speaker and lightning rod of a man, Malcolm X. Malcolm had the laser-like focus and unyielding ethics often found in a reformed sinner. He discovered the Nation in prison and became its staunchest defender and strongest promoter upon release, heading Harlem's Temple Number 7, one of the Nation's most important sites.

While the Nation baited white racists, referring to whites as "devils" and spouting fiery rhetoric about black supremacy, the NAACP stirred the pot in another direction, one that hit closer to home for my father. Led again by Thurgood Marshall, the group now leveled its sights on segregated education. Soon, several NAACP cases came before the US Supreme Court as *Brown v. Board of Education of Topeka*. In mid-May 1954, the Court delivered one of its most revolutionary rulings, declaring the doctrine of separate-but-equal unconstitutional. For the better part of a century, separate-but-equal formed the legal underpinning for Jim Crow segregation. The Court's ruling effectively lopped off one of Jim Crow's legs, leaving it hopping on one foot, violently trying to regain its balance across the South.

With *Brown*, the movement directly interested my father for the first time. He was nearing high school, and although Chicago had no laws requiring segregated schools, common practice kept Negroes out of white schools just the same. The Court's ruling wouldn't change that, but if Negroes could integrate schools across the South, anything seemed possible.

Of course, neither Curtis nor his friends understood the legal complexities of the case. "*Brown v. Board* was what the grown-ups talked about," Jerry recalls. "Black kids going to school was what we talked about. We didn't know about the Supreme Court and no other stuff attached to that but we knew that there were these black kids trying to get into schools who were our age." My father was just old enough for such a huge moment to imprint his mind with visions of how the world could change. He was also young enough not to fully grasp how much struggle, toil, and death it had taken for Negroes to achieve that change. The old folks viewed it warily, knowing all too well the brutal force of American racism. Dad didn't have the same baggage, although he heard about it from his elders. *Brown* brought him pure excitement.

Soon enough, however, he learned why the old folks reacted with such ambivalence. In 1955, three Negro boys in the South were murdered as a reaction to *Brown's* forced integration, including fourteen-year-old Chicago native, Emmett Till. My father and Till shared much in common. They were roughly the same age, and both came from southern migrants who fled to Chicago. In August of '55, Till returned south to visit family that hadn't made the migration, just as Dad often did with Annie Bell. The similarities ended there.

No one knows exactly what happened next—the official story goes that Till walked into a store and flirted with Carolyn Bryant, a married white woman, perhaps whistling at her, perhaps even saying something suggestive. He most likely just wanted to show off to his southern relatives, filled with the natural cockiness of a teenager and unaware of the South's unwritten rules. Unfortunately, his first lesson in southern living was also his last.

On Sunday, August 28, between 2:00 and 3:00 AM, Bryant's husband Roy and his half brother J. W. Milam kidnapped Till, flung the boy into the back of a pickup truck, and drove him to a barn where they tortured and killed him. They then drove to the Tallahatchie River, tied a seventy-pound cotton-gin fan around Till's neck with barbed wire, and heaved his corpse into the water. Three days later, two fishermen found his remains.

The murder made national headlines and affected my father deeply. Till's mother insisted on an open-casket funeral, wanting the world to see what Mississippi racists had done to her boy. Both the *Chicago Defender* and *Jet* magazine—two huge Negro publications—ran pictures of Till's hideously disfigured face. My dad saw the pictures, and he'd never forget them or the story of Till's death. For the first time in his life the sadistic extent of racist violence confronted him. It could have just as easily been him in that coffin.

————

As my father mourned Till's murder, changes rushed over him with breathtaking speed. Around 1955, Marion moved the family into the Cabrini-Green housing projects. Constructed the year Curtis was born in an attempt to house the migrant flood washing into Chicago, the project was built on the site of an old Sicilian neighborhood nicknamed "Little Hell." It eventually offered two choices of residence—tiny row houses that squatted along Cambridge and Chicago Avenue, and a cluster of high-rises known as the Cabrini Extension. Due to their redbrick construction, everyone called the first Cabrini high-rises "the Reds." Several years after Marion moved the family into a row house at 966 Hudson Street, the city completed another high-rise on the north side of Division called the William Green Homes, or "the Whites."

For Marion and the family, the row house on Hudson was a dream come true. Looking at it later in life, my father must have wondered how his family ever fit inside the narrow building, but compared to the White Eagle, it seemed a mansion. "We felt we were up in Pill Hill," Aunt Carolyn remembers, referring to one of Chicago's most exclusive black neighborhoods at the time. "We were finally in a two-bedroom place, and it had a back yard and front yard." My father remembered it the same way: "It was really high-class living. We had our own toilet and two full bedrooms in our own apartment. Such luxury seemed too good to be true."

The front door of the row house led into the kitchen, which joined a small living room. The house had a bathroom, closet, pantry, and back and front yards carpeted in lush green grass. The backyard had enough space to hang clothes to dry; the front yard was big enough for a garden. Finally free from the endless treachery of the slums, the darkness that consumed my grandmother lifted just a bit. She was still so poor she could only outfit her new house with what mismatched furniture she happened to find, but she had a safe place to raise her children, and now that Carolyn was finally old enough to take care of Kirby, she could look for a job. She began working at Marshall Field's in Evanston, and soon moved to a job at the post office, where she'd work for decades.

Before leaving the White Eagle, Marion had also met and married a man named Albert Jackson. Albert courted her and treated her better than any man ever had. On his payday, he'd even bring food to the family. But though he treated Marion well, he abused Kirby, and the children didn't like him. It seemed my grandmother couldn't find a man who treated both her and her children with respect. Regardless, Albert moved into the house on Hudson and stayed until their relationship ended a few years later.

Cabrini thrust my father into a brave new world. The homes were racially mixed, with Jewish, Italian, and Latino families living in relative harmony alongside Negroes. The Italians threw a block party every year, with floats, a carnival, and, of course, food. Residents took great pride in their homes and kept the project clean. Littering earned a three-dollar fine, and the Chicago Housing Authority inspected the apartments, stairwells, and hallways for cleanliness. People roller-skated, danced in the streets, and slept with their doors unlocked. They shopped at the local stores on Larrabee Street like Pioneer Meat Market, Big Frank's, Del Farms grocery, Greenman's department store, and a Negro-owned store called Jets. At night, juke houses along Larrabee jumped with the latest music, and two of Chicago's biggest Catholic churches brooded nearby, in case one did a little too much juking and needed to confess the next morning.

Soon after moving into the house on Hudson, Dad entered high school, walking to Wells High and taking with him all the awkwardness of a teenager. For someone already insecure about his looks, he now had to negotiate puberty. His brief attempt at straightening his hair only made matters worse. High school held one major difference from grade school, however—his musical skills now made him one of the most popular students in class, when he attended. He even made friends with a white boy named Jimmy, who had a little money and never minded helping fund creative endeavors.

Those endeavors now ranged beyond the Northern Jubilee Singers and Chicago blues. Following the example of his hero Sam Cooke, who had just crossed over with the pop hit "You Send Me," Curtis put together a secular group called the Alphatones with Al Boyce, James Weems, and Dallas Dixon. "We used to harmonize and sing Frankie Lymon tunes and the Spaniels and the Dells," my father recalled. "We had two or three entrances to apartments where we had plenty of echo, and we was happenin' with all the doo-wop."

Curtis and the Alphatones weren't unique; Cabrini-Green crawled with doo-wop groups, the air around the project hanging thick and sweet with multipart harmonies. The groups practiced in rehearsal rooms at Seward Park. "We were all trying to sing," Billy Butler, Jerry's brother, said. "That was the only thing to do really. The area didn't have street gangs at the time. Everyone would form a group and go into Seward Park."

Seward Park stood just a short walk from the row houses. It contained a big gymnasium and several small rooms where people could play Ping-Pong, take arts and crafts classes, or hold rehearsals. When word got around Cabrini that all the doo-wop groups practiced at the park, crowds of eager young kids lined up outside the doors to get a peek at the likes of the Capris, the Players, the Medallionaires, and the Van Gayles. The Alphatones became one of those popular groups, with people lined up for their practices. Soon there was always someone coming by the house looking for Curtis. He liked the attention, but sometimes he'd get tired of it, and, showing his mercurial nature, he'd tell Carolyn, "Get rid of those people," or he'd disappear into his bedroom, just like his grandmother.

As he rehearsed with the Alphatones, he developed a unique style on guitar, almost tickling the strings rather than strumming them, and strengthened his naturally high tenor voice. He continued writing songs, mostly knockoffs of whatever doo-wop was popular. He also discovered a new influence in the music of Ray Charles, who had just set the R&B

charts on fire with hits like "I Got a Woman" and "What'd I Say." Charles did something altogether different from most acts of the time—he began his career making secular music rather than gospel, though his songs clearly came from the church. He mixed the holy with the profane, gospel with pop, R&B with jazz. The resulting music was all of those things and none of them at the same time. Dad paid close attention to Charles's music as he worked on his own songs and honed the Alphatones into a tight unit.

He also noticed something else that had been happening, not knowing it would change the course of his life. On December 1, 1955—eleven years after Irene Morgan's similar stand—Rosa Parks stepped onto a bus in Montgomery, Alabama, took a seat near the front, and refused to give it up to a white person when ordered to by the bus driver. Her refusal set in motion a chain of events that would revolutionize American race relations. Cops arrested and booked her, but her arrest seemed a blessing in disguise. Local activists had been waiting for a case like this for years, one they could take to the US Supreme Court and likely win.

As Montgomery civil rights leaders plotted a Supreme Court challenge, others planned a boycott of the city's buses. Negroes had attempted bus boycotts across the South many times before, but gains had been minimal or nonexistent. Of course, no one involved with the Montgomery bus boycotts expected them to make great progress in race relations—they just wanted minor changes to laws that would allow Negroes greater freedom in bus seating. Boycott leader Ralph Abernathy said, "We thought that this would all be over in three or four days."

They underestimated white recalcitrance. Instead of ceding to their modest demands, the white community dug in, forcing the boycott to continue for months. Soon, news stories across the country began covering one of the most brazen affronts to segregation ever mounted. Even though the boycott mostly concerned southerners, northern Negroes paid close attention, my father among them.

As the boycott slogged on, Martin Luther King Jr. reluctantly emerged on the world stage after a delegation of Montgomery's civil rights leaders, including Abernathy, voted him to lead the protests. King initially did not want the role. He viewed himself as a simple preacher better suited to studying and teaching religion than leading a movement. But the times often pick the man. Even though King was young and baby-faced, he was a respected pastor, which the civil rights establishment believed would attract conservative Negroes to the movement. At the same time, he railed against segregation and racism, which Abernathy and company hoped would attract the more militant faction of Negroes.

Like millions around the country, my father felt great hope as King grew in stature. He supported the bus boycott and then rooted for King's Southern Christian Leadership Conference. Finally, something stirred him as deeply as music.

———

As the '50s progressed, a new breed of singers elbowed onto street corners beside Chicago's electric bluesmen and hip beboppers. These young kids with processed hair and smooth-as-silk voices wove intricate harmonies into a new style. They sang anywhere and everywhere—on the corners, in stairwells, or in years to come, at one of Herb Kent's sock hops.

Paralleling the competitions between gospel groups, which Dad had experienced, and anticipating hip-hop freestyling competitions two decades later, doo-wop groups battled each other for street-corner control. Reggie Smith, a member of the Five Chances, remembered my father hanging around the Five Chances' turf at Forty-Fourth and Prairie, saying, "We'd tell him to get away from us with all that noise, 'cause we're trying to sing, [but] he went on to beat us to death."

Doo-wop was bigger than Chicago, though. Every city seemed to have its own collection of aspiring teenagers honing their harmonies, and in 1953, five young friends in Chattanooga, Tennessee, formed such a group. Sam Gooden, Fred Cash, Emanuel Thomas, and the brothers Richard and Arthur Brooks called themselves the Roosters. After Thomas quit the group, his sister Catherine joined, and they became Four Roosters and a Chick.

Catherine soon married and left, but the Roosters continued even though Fred's religious parents never approved of the group. He was

barely a teenager, and they didn't want him out all night singing that
secular music. Like most teenagers, Fred found a way around their disapproval. "Once they'd gone to bed, I'd slip out of the window and join the
other guys on the corner, and then we'd go do to this little club on East
9th Street called Memos, where we'd sing," he said. "And then, once we'd
finished, I'd come home, slip back in through the window, go back to
bed. And neither my mom nor my dad would ever know I'd been out."

Chattanooga had no record labels to speak of, and after the Roosters
tried to cut a record in Nashville to no avail, they faced a dilemma. Any
serious singer knew that to make it in the music business, you had to
go to Chicago, Detroit, Los Angeles, or New York. Those places were
far away and full of unknown dangers, though. With no other options,
they took a chance. The Brooks brothers had a sister in Chicago, so the
band loaded up on bologna sandwiches, packed into a car, and drove six
hundred miles north to the Windy City.

Fred's parents wouldn't let him go, which meant Sam, Arthur, and
Richard had to find a replacement in Chicago. After a little searching,
they met Jerry, who was working a dead-end job as a short-order cook.
With his strong voice, he got the gig. As Jerry remembered the group on
first meeting them:

> Arthur was stockily built with a light complexion. Sam, who was
> about my height and complexion but thinner, had narrow facial
> features that enhanced a big, broad smile. Richard, Arthur's brother,
> was about my age. Much skinnier than Arthur, Richard had dis-
> tinctive sandy, curly hair that he combed constantly.
>
> Arthur and Richard were dead serious, but I always got the feel-
> ing that Sam really didn't give a damn. I remember him saying once
> that if he didn't make it singing, he could always play baseball. After
> watching him play one day, I could see why. He could really play.

Soon, they worked out a practice schedule—Jerry went straight to
meet the guys after work around midnight. He'd sing all night, work all
day, and do it again the next night. It didn't take long for them to get

tight. Even though they had grown up in different cities, they shared a common link in the church. Sam's father was a minister and his mother an organist. His parents forced him to sing solos in church, which he hated doing. Jerry had grown up in Annie Bell's church with Curtis, listening to and singing the same gospel tunes. Unlike Sam, he loved the spotlight.

They all knew the basic rules of singing gospel and shared a love of doo-wop, but Jerry knew the group lacked a key element—a musician who could tie it all together. He thought first of my father and asked him to join the group. Always bent on control, Dad saw no reason to leave his own group, where he was the leader, for one where he'd be just another member. Jerry pleaded with him, "If you join us, man, with the way you play the guitar and the way they sing, we'll come up with a different sound." Dad didn't bite. Jerry cooked up a scheme. "Dig, Curt," he said. "Let's do it like this—you rehearse three nights a week with us and three with your group. Whoever improves first, or seems to have the most potential, will be the group you go with." Even at such a young age, my father knew a good business deal when he heard one.

Jerry's persistence paid off—Curtis soon dropped the Alphatones and joined the Roosters. Wasting no time, they began working on original material, dreaming of writing the next big hit. "We wood-shedded for a good year," Dad said, "and finally we came along with a few songs." One of the songs, an emotional, spoken-word ballad called "For Your Precious Love," would become the group's calling card. It owed a good deal to Ray Charles's genre-bending style—it wasn't quite gospel, R&B, or pop, but contained all those elements. It also shared quite a bit in common with the Gospel Clefs' "Open Our Eyes," which Herb Kent used to close his radio show. Structured around Curtis's plucked guitar chords and set in a slow 6/8 meter, "For Your Precious Love" played almost like a hymn. My father's high falsetto rode atop the heavenly backing vocals, providing a lush bed for Butler's chocolate-rich voice.

As they perfected the song, they also looked for a break. The Roosters entered a talent show at Washburne High School in 1957 and challenged some of the best groups in Cabrini, including the Medallionaires, who held the distinction of releasing a single called "Magic Moonlight" on Mercury Records. The Medallionaires were so professional they even had a manager, Eddie Thomas, who drove a canary-yellow Cadillac with glinting white trim. As Eddie recalls, "The Medallionaires thought they were hot stuff. Girls were screaming and hollering, going crazy, and they had a song they had just written and recorded on Mercury Records. I have a feeling they bought all the copies that were sold themselves. It didn't do that well."

Eddie came to the talent show to watch his group perform, but he'd also heard of the Roosters and made sure he caught their set. That night, the Roosters harmonized on Sam Cooke's "You Send Me," and despite struggling with a single microphone that kept cutting out, they took the house by storm. "Their harmony was mind blowing," Eddie says. "The lead singer had a great smooth, sexy baritone voice. They had a young guitar player who had a very unusual style of playing his guitar. When they learned that I was working with this group called the Medallion-aires, they asked me could I work with them too."

Eddie, a born hustler, agreed—on one condition. He demanded the group axe the name Roosters. "Too country," he said. My father heartily agreed. "We couldn't get through a song after we told the audience the name," he said. "They'd be crowing and making all kinds of barnyard sounds." There was only one problem: no one had a better name. For a while everyone threw around suggestions, but they couldn't make any-thing stick. It didn't help that Arthur, Richard, and Sam didn't want to change the name. "We're gonna lose a lot of sales in Chattanooga," they protested. "The Roosters are very popular there." Eddie explained he had his eye on a much bigger picture. "I can't see it on a marquee," he told them. "I can't see it at the Regal Theatre." Besides, a publicist could alert fans of the name change once the group had something to promote.

"What's the new name then?" they demanded.

They kicked around a few clunkers, but still nothing seemed to stick. After several failures, they wrote down ideas and threw them in a hat. Sam reached in and pulled out a scrap. He nervously unfolded it.

Scrawled on it was one of Eddie's ideas, conceived after recalling how impressed he had been the first time he saw the Roosters perform.

"How about the Impressions?" Sam said, reading the paper. It stuck.

4

The Original Impressions

"Taking all that he can take,
Gambling with the odds of fate,
Trying to get over."

—"SUPERFLY"

April 5, 1958—The Hawk screeched through Chicago overnight, blanketing Hudson Street in sparkling snow. Dad woke to find drifts piled five feet high, glinting in the cold sunlight. Of all the times for a freak snowstorm, this one threatened to ruin the Impressions' audition with Vee-Jay Records. Early that morning, they humped their gear through the not-quite-winter wonderland to Record Row, breath jetting out in steamy spurts, looking for a record deal or bust.

They had endured this before, minus the snow. In previous months, the guys had taken "For Your Precious Love" to Savoy Records, where owner Herman Lubinsky suggested Jerry sing the lyrics rather than speak them. Jerry took his advice, but Lubinsky passed on the group. They had also solicited King Records, where Ralph Bass, head of Artists & Repertoire, passed as well. Bass had enough work breaking a young singer named James Brown. After that, Eddie set up an audition with an A&R man at Mercury Records who took the Impressions into a small studio, listened to their material, and said he dug the sound but couldn't sign the group because his roster was already too heavy.

He offered the Impressions an opportunity to do some background singing with a singer named Eddie Howard, which they happily took. "I had never heard of [Eddie Howard] myself," Jerry said, "but for $25 an hour per side, I was willing to do some serious chirping." Still, the gig didn't represent the success they sought.

Options dwindling, Eddie Thomas went to a tiny label called Bandera, where he met founder Vi Muszynski—a large woman in her forties with platinum blonde hair. "She talked very fast, squirmed in her seat, and smacked her lips when she talked," Jerry recalled. "She always seemed too heavily made up to me. She was such a nice woman, though, that you tended to overlook everything else." Around town, everyone knew Muszynski as "the record lady." She wanted to the sign the Impressions, but Bandera lacked the funds to publish a record. The label's pittance of publishing went through a much more successful label, Vee-Jay, and Muszynski couldn't cut a deal without Vee-Jay's approval.

At that time Vee-Jay reigned over Negro music in Chicago. Its office was a sort of headquarters where everyone in the business went after hours, no matter where they worked during the day. As renowned Chicago producer Carl Davis recalled:

Vee-Jay had an employee lounge that turned into a nightspot after working hours. Industry personalities would be up there trading stories and shooting the breeze, while others would be playing cards. The people who didn't want to gamble would sit around the makeshift bar, which was really a lunchroom counter, and have a few drinks . . . Vee-Jay had the luxury of having everybody promoting Vee-Jay. Vee-Jay set the standard. Vee-Jay kept you in the know. We all took some pride in the fact that it was *the* black record company, and to even be indirectly affiliated with them gave us all welcomed credibility.

Muszynski scheduled an audition for the Impressions with Vee-Jay's A&R man, Calvin Carter, on April 5. With better intentions than taste, she selected several songs that were "an inch away from being country," according to Jerry, and had the Impressions learn them. "We thought they were ridiculous, but we went along because we didn't want to hurt her feelings," Jerry said. "We . . . tried to make them as soulful as possible."

In one version of the audition story, when the Impressions arrived that snowy day, they knocked on the door at Chess Records first. They made eye contact with a security guard sitting inside but he didn't let them in, so they crossed the street and went to Vee-Jay. While romantic, this version doesn't square with the other facts known about that day. First, Eddie recalled unsuccessfully offering "For Your Precious Love" to Chess Records before meeting Muszynski, which makes a return to Chess unlikely. Second, Muszynski scheduled an audition at Vee-Jay, which makes a spur-of-the-moment drop-in at Chess equally unlikely.

Regardless, when the Impressions reached Vee-Jay's offices they met label president Ewart Abner, a thin, dapper Negro with kind eyes and an immaculately trimmed moustache. He sat with his ever-present Great Dane slobbering by his side. Abner was a slick man, a charmer, and one of the most powerful men in the business. Trembling, the Impressions climbed the stairs to the rehearsal room and played a few of Muszynski's numbers for Carter, who sat unimpressed. "Do you have any original material?" he asked. They played a few originals, which Carter liked better, but still not enough to sign the Impressions.

The audition had just about reached its end, and it looked like another failure. My father put down his guitar and everyone stood in awkward, nervous silence. Carter said, "Gee, I really want to record you guys, but I don't really hear that hit song." Then, an idea struck him. "Sing something you're ashamed to sing. Sing something you don't usually feel like singing in public."

They only knew one other song, so Dad picked up his guitar, plucked a few chords, and Jerry let out a velvety blast, "Your precious love means more to me . . ." The group fell in behind him in perfect harmony, and by the time the song ended, Carter's eyes beamed with the electricity of a man who suddenly *believed*. He shouted, "That's it! That's it! That's the one! Abner, get me some contracts. Vi, you, Eddie, and Abner better talk."

My father stood in stunned silence trying to play off the bottle rockets of emotions shooting through him. Then, as if his mind wasn't blown enough, Pookie Hudson and the Spaniels—one of his favorite doo-wop groups—walked into the room. "Hey, y'all, sing that 'Precious Love' song again," Carter said to the Impressions. "I want them to hear it."

Just then, paranoia set in. Dad and the group had heard horror stories of crooked producers hiding tape recorders in their desks, stealing songs from unknown youngsters desperate for a break. "Here comes the rip off," Jerry thought. "He likes our song and he wants [the Spaniels] to record it. That's why they called them and told them to come over right away. This ain't no accident. I'll bet that bastard's got a tape recorder in his desk."

They nervously played the song again. As soon as they finished, the Spaniels started slapping hands and telling stories about what the Impressions would go through when the record hit. The paranoia subsided. "We were very happy and very grateful," Jerry said. "Mostly, though, we were very surprised that a group like the Spaniels, with all their success, would be that decent and down to Earth."

Muszynski and Abner drew up a contract signing the Impressions to Bandera for one year, with an option to renew within five days of its expiration. Vee-Jay would distribute the records. The Impressions got two points, which in the music industry's arcane lingo meant they'd earn 2 percent in royalties out of every 90 percent of records sold. Bandera didn't have a standard contract form, so they borrowed one from Vee-Jay, crossing out the Vee-Jay masthead and typing Bandera's below it. Everyone signed, and since my father, Richard, and Jerry were minors, their mothers also had to sign the contract.

Saturday morning, the Impressions had their first professional recording date. They arrived early and stood outside Universal Studios on Walton Street, trying to stop their nerves from jangling. Finally, Arthur broke the macho facade, saying, "I ain't gonna lie, I'm scared as hell." Everyone burst out laughing and calmed down.

They entered Studio A, "a huge room with the control room way up in the air, like an airport," according to the recording engineer that day. The Impressions began with one of my father's earliest compositions, "Sweet Was the Wine," a song straddling the line between doo-wop and rock 'n' roll, a genre just beginning to take the white world by storm in the form of a swivel-hipped dynamo named Elvis Presley. It took a few passes to warm up, but as Jerry remembered it, "Four or five takes later, we got into a good groove. My voice cracked on one note. [Carter] played 'Sweet Was the Wine' back a couple of times to convince himself it wasn't too bad. Then he asked us to do 'Precious Love.'"

From the days rehearsing in Seward Park, the Impressions were used to singing a song again and again until they had it just right. But after half a dozen takes of "Precious Love," it still sounded wrong. Due to union rules, my father couldn't play guitar on the record, so two other players named Lefty and Guitar Red filled in. They might have been great session men, but with their standard tuning, they weren't getting the *sound*. Carter, to his credit, recognized the problem.

He told Curtis to grab his guitar. Taking Lefty and Guitar Red aside, he asked them to sit out without telling the union—such a breach could get Vee-Jay into an expensive legal battle. Carter returned to the recording console and told the Impressions to hit the song again. Two takes later, it was perfect. Carter wanted to send it to the pressing plant right away. In fact, he liked it so much he had several acetates, or test pressings, cut that day so he could take one home.

Carter gave one of the acetates to his sister Vivian (as cofounder of the label, she was the "Vee" in "Vee-Jay"), who hosted a radio show in Gary, Indiana. She told the Impressions she'd play it that night. When the time came, the group huddled around a radio in the Brooks house aching with anticipation. Finally, Vivian introduced the song and Curtis's opening guitar notes seeped from the radio's speakers. Jerry recalled, "When we heard that song coming across that little box that was sitting there over in the corner, we started out jumping up and down on the bed, grabbing, hugging each other, and then we started to cry because it was overwhelming. And we didn't really know how good it sounded

until we heard it on the radio. Then people started calling, 'Play it again.'
She must have played it five or six times."

The young Impressions had little time to bask in the glow of their
radio debut. The next day, they returned to the studio to record two
more songs, including another of Curtis's compositions, "At the County
Fair," on which he sang lead for the first time.

A few days later, official copies of "For Your Precious Love" arrived
from the pressing plant, and Eddie drove the group to the Vee-Jay office
in his Cadillac. This was the most important moment. Signing a contract, recording in a professional studio, and getting on the radio marked
huge milestones, but nothing said success like seeing your name on the
label of a record. That was something tangible, something permanent
and undeniable.

They tore open the boxes, passed around the records, and gazed at
them the way a father looks upon his firstborn child. As they read the
label, the room fell silent. Under the song title, it read "Jerry Butler" in
huge letters. Beneath that, in tiny typeface, it read, "and the Impressions." Without consulting the group, Vee-Jay had decided to put Jerry
out front as the star that would outshine the nameless, faceless "and the
Impressions." The sting set in immediately. Jerry said:

> I knew that Curtis, Sam, Arthur and Richard didn't like it one bit.
> Each of their faces was twisted into a half smile that did nothing
> to hide their hurt and envy. I finally spoke. "You'll have to reprint
> the label so it reads 'The Impressions.' If you don't, we're going to
> have dissension in the group before we ever get started." Sam and
> Arthur mumbled in agreement. Curtis and Richard just kept staring
> at the record and shaking their heads. Eddie was nervous. He hadn't
> known about it either. Still, he remained silent. He later told us that,
> at the time, he thought it unwise for us to be raising questions at that
> meeting, when we were so close to getting things off the ground.

Eddie had good reason to worry. Abner wasn't about to take directions from a no-name kid whose career rested in his industry-savvy hands.

When he replied to Jerry's request, he spoke matter-of-factly, a hint of anger coloring his words. He explained how much it would cost to reprint fifty thousand labels and why the company chose to feature Jerry on the label. It would help them get more airplay, Abner said. Besides, Vee-Jay knew more about promotion than they did, and the company only had their best interests in mind. He promised Vee-Jay would not do anything to break them up. They simply couldn't reprint the labels, and even if they could, it would take two or three weeks before they could get the record out. "By the time he got through talking, we were feeling sorry for feeling sorry," Jerry said. "Abner was like that. He was one of those guys who could sell you the Brooklyn Bridge and then buy it back five minutes later for half the price." Abner's speech worked for the moment, but tensions remained just below the surface. "The rift over the phrase 'Jerry Butler and the Impressions,' and later 'The Original Impressions,' was irreparable, and would remain even after forty years," Jerry said.

For Vee-Jay, the decision was pure business. Every label worth its salt had long realized that once a group had a hit, the company could multiply its money by separating the lead singer and creating two acts. It happened to Dee Clark and the Kool Gents, Clyde McPhatter and the Drifters, James Brown and the Famous Flames, and Frankie Lymon and the Teenagers. After separating the front man from the group, the story usually ended the same—the lead singer soared to fame if he was good (and lucky) while his former band put out a few tepid records and faded into obscurity.

The Impressions didn't know that then. None of them expected such a thing to happen. They had made it this far together, and they intended to succeed or fail together. "You can understand all these fellows having worked and sacrificed evenly in trying to become somebody, for anyone's name to be put out front was a sort of a blow," my father said. "When disc jockeys played the record, it was 'Now here's Jerry Butler and "For Your Precious Love."'" And of course the fan mail would come, which we got gobs of, to Jerry Butler."

Despite the hard feelings, success had a way of ironing out differences, at least temporarily. Within two weeks, "For Your Precious Love" sold 150,000 copies and charted in every city where it played. When rumors began swirling that the debonair R&B star Roy Hamilton planned to cover the song, Abner decided to set up a promotional tour for the Impressions. Hamilton had a string of smash hits like "You'll Never Walk Alone" and "Unchained Melody." Abner could just see him driving women wild with "For Your Precious Love," making it his song before the unknown Impressions could even begin making a name for themselves.

To get the scoop on Hamilton and build the Impressions' name, Vee-Jay and Eddie booked dates in Detroit, followed by an appearance on Jim Lounsbury's *Bandstand Matinee*—Chicago's version of *American Bandstand*—as well as stops in Philadelphia, Miami, and the prize of them all, Harlem's Apollo Theater.

———

Before leaving for Detroit, the Impressions went to Maxwell Street Market to buy uniforms. Known to many in the Negro community as Jew Town, the market featured "cigar-chomping hawkers in ramshackle kiosks, barking 'Hot dogs! Polish sausages! Thirty-five cents!'" Jerry recalled, "The musky smell of grilled onions, mustard and sausages always hung in the air. Then there were the merchants who would literally force you into their dark dingy shops, insisting that you buy something."

The market also boasted Goldstein's music store, Leavett's—a popular bar where musicians hung out—and Smokey Joe's. The latter was the primary purveyor of hip clothing in the city, its racks full of continental suits with narrow lapels and Dior dresses with the so-called New Look. The space surrounding the kiosks served as an unofficial stage where musicians could set up and plunk out their tunes for a few coins tossed into their open guitar cases or upturned hats. Once upon a time, a shopper could browse the market while the likes of Jimmy Reed, Muddy Waters, or Howlin' Wolf provided the soundtrack. It had a festival atmosphere—between Maxwell and Fourteenth Street on Newberry, crowds gathered in an empty lot to listen to the music under a cottonwood tree, or dance in the streets to songs like Waters's "Mannish Boy" and Wolf's "Moanin' at Midnight."

The Impressions left the market that day with matching suits—gray silk jackets, black pants, white shirts, black ties, and pocket scarves. Suits were the standard uniform for vocal groups at the time. The Spaniels wore them. So did the Dells, the Flamingoes, and just about everyone else trying to make it in show business. These suits were especially important for Negro entertainers wanting to project an air of debonair worldliness. Suits opened the door to the white supper-club scene, which meant serious money. They didn't hurt with the ladies, either. Coming years would witness a generational divide regarding Negro performers dressing up for the white world, but for the time at hand, if my father and the Impressions wanted to work, they'd have to do it in suits. For a bunch of kids accustomed to hand-me-downs and whatever ragtag clothing their parents could afford, being forced into a sharp-looking suit wasn't the hardest sacrifice to endure.

With their threads in place, they hit the road for their first professional engagement. The Brooks brothers had another brother who lived just outside of Detroit, and the Impressions spent the night in his house playing cards—Dad loved bid whist—and preparing for the work ahead. The next day, they made rounds to the Negro radio stations in the area, and they also appeared on Soupy Sales's television show. Sales had three shows at the time, including *Soup's On*, which he used to promote his love of jazz. Artists like Louis Armstrong, Duke Ellington, Miles Davis, and Coleman Hawkins had graced the stage the Impressions stood on that night.

It was heady stuff, but the Impressions got a much different reception than expected from Detroit's white show business professionals. "We were treated like a bunch of kids, young kids at that," Jerry said. "In the black community [in Chicago], despite our youth, we were treated with respect, like heroes. To black people, young and old alike, we had grasped that elusive thing called success, and, if only for a moment, we symbolized their dreams and aspirations. Black males, for example, saw us as symbols of hope. Black females saw us as suave, worldly guys who had gone places, done things. We were special." In Detroit, they were just another act.

The trip took them down another peg before it ended. Famous Detroit DJ Larry Dixon sweet-talked the Impressions, telling them how good their record sounded and how Abner would get them on Ed Sullivan's show. Then, he sprung the trap. He promoted a concert every Saturday, he said, and if the Impressions would perform there—just a song or two—it would help their sales in Detroit. They explained that they had scheduled an appearance on *Bandstand Matinee* back in Chicago. "Don't worry," Dixon said. "I'll call Abner on Friday and straighten it out. It's ridiculous to spend the money to come here and not get all the publicity you can out of this town." All day Friday, WCHB played "For Your Precious Love" once or twice every hour. Late Friday night, Dixon called to say he had spoken with Abner and worked everything out.

Around seven o'clock Saturday evening, the Impressions arrived at the club, where people already stood in line waiting to get inside. The full force of the house band hit the crowd as it cascaded in. The band showed up too late to rehearse the Impressions' material—the first sign something was about to go wrong.

Close to nine o'clock, Dixon appeared "dressed like some fairytale prince." He walked to the bandstand and shouted, "It's show time!" After the house band played a few more songs, Dixon introduced Eddie Holland, who sang Jackie Wilson's "Reet Petite" with mesmerizing accuracy, down to every nuance of Wilson's routine. Holland would soon cowrite some of the biggest hits in popular music history at Motown, the label run by "Reet Petite" cowriter Berry Gordy.

After Holland finished, Larry started his rap: "Ladies and gentlemen . . . all the way from Chicago, Illinois . . . five young men who have the hottest record in WCHB land! The creators of the monster hit 'For Your Precious Love' . . . Here they are . . . our special guest attraction tonight . . . Jerry Butler and the Impressions!" The crowd erupted in cheers.

As the Impressions performed, electric energy pounded through their veins. The audience carried them on a wave of ecstasy that felt downright holy. "I got the same feeling that night that I had experienced with the Northern Jubilee Singers when the church was with us," Jerry said. "It's a feeling of pushing up to your limit and then over, and your spirit lifts your body. It all becomes so real that it's unreal. We finished, and the audience applauded and screamed. 'More! More! More!' We had two encores, singing the same song. After the third time, Larry got us off. Afterwards, there were young, pretty women with pieces of paper wanting autographs, fat ladies with big bosoms and whiskey on their breath wanting to hug and kiss us, and the boyfriends and husbands of these women wanting to kick our asses."

It is no secret that many insecure people find themselves drawn to the stage. The attention, spotlight, and applause help ease the pain of their insecurity and replace it with an often-fleeting sense of self-worth. My father was one such person. He knew a few things about how women treated performers, but the crowd's reaction in Detroit was something else. Standing on that stage, he felt powerful and confident, maybe for the first time in his life.

The stage offered him more than just sex and self-worth, though. As the crowd went wild in Detroit, he saw a way out of the constant hardship that had plagued him and his family throughout his life. The stage legitimized him. It raised his social status. It gave him the power to do what his father couldn't or wouldn't do—take care of his mother and siblings.

It did another thing as well. As a loner, he had few close friends. The stage provided him support, adulation, and maybe even love. At the same time, it let him control those things. He could protect his insecurities by choosing how close he let others get. This didn't always work in his favor when it came to personal relationships, especially romantic ones. But in that moment, it all seemed too good to be true. Until the end of the night.

Coming down from the performance high, the Impressions realized that Dixon had disappeared with the $3,000 made at the door without offering them a cent—he "didn't even buy us a hamburger," Jerry said. Worse yet, when they slunk back to Chicago, a furious Abner chewed them out for missing *Bandstand Matinee*. They tried to explain, but Abner didn't want to hear it. Of course he never authorized their extended stay in Detroit. They'd been duped, exploited, and taught a hard lesson about show business. My father catalogued these disappointments. He hated someone taking advantage of him, and he studied ways to make sure it didn't happen again.

———

Back in Chicago before the next tour began, the Impressions played several of Herb Kent's sock hops. "Curtis was so broke in those days, his guitar didn't even have a back," Kent said. "Whenever you saw him, he was always facing you, because he didn't want people to see the back of that guitar."

Curtis might have been broke, but it didn't break him down. He spent most nights on the run, crashing either with friends or at Annie Bell's. Staying with Annie Bell, however, meant submerging deeper into Spiritualist traditions. Before the Impressions left for Philadelphia, Annie Bell asked them to see a healer named Mrs. Washington and receive her blessing. "Mrs. Washington was a very hip old lady and we did it more out of respect for her than from the belief that it would do any good," Jerry said.

The little old lady prayed with the group, blessed some water in the name of God, and sprinkled it on Sam, Arthur, and Richard. Something changed when she got to my father and Jerry. She flung the rest of the water in their faces, ending the spectacle by throwing the cup at Jerry's face. On the way out, my father muttered, "She sure did bless the hell out of us, didn't she, man?" For all his soft-spoken seriousness, Dad always had a cutting, wry sense of humor.

With Mrs. Washington's odd blessing, and three St. Christopher medals hung around their necks to ward off evil spirits, the Impressions prepared for their longest promotional tour yet. They piled into their green Mercury station wagon—a gift from Vee-Jay—and set off to perform for the famous Philadelphia DJ Georgie Woods.

Woods had a special power to break records. He served as Dick Clark's inside man, alerting Clark to Negro music worth featuring on *American Bandstand*. In such a way, Woods formed a link between race records and the mainstream pop market. Impressing him was crucial.

Unfortunately, the Impressions' first show at Philly's Uptown Theater suffered immediate trouble. That night, they replaced Ed Townsend, who had just had a huge hit with a doo-wop ballad called "For Your Love." Townsend, who would later write for the Impressions, had become an overnight sensation. When Woods announced that Townsend wouldn't perform, the crowd responded with thundering boos. The Impressions stood backstage trembling with fear. They hadn't rehearsed with the orchestra because the show was in progress when they arrived. They had no arranger, which meant they had no lead sheets for the band. On top of that, the crowd was now furious.

As boos rained down, Woods yelled into the microphone, "Wait a minute! Wait a minute! When I tell you who's replacing Ed, you'll know you're in for a treat. These guys have a new record called 'For Your Precious Love.'" Just like that, the crowd turned. Girls started screaming. It seemed there was no problem a hit song couldn't fix.

While in Philadelphia, the group stayed in a rooming house on North Broad Street called Mom's, along with other acts on the show like Mickey and Sylvia, Lee Andrews and the Hearts, Huey Smith and the Clowns, Robert and Johnny, and Patti LaBelle. Mom's served as a second home for most of the acts playing the Uptown Theater—even in the North, they had to lodge on the outskirts of town with other Negroes who made a living housing traveling performers. Within a few years, Woods would use his shows at the Uptown Theater to promote civil rights. He'd even receive an award from the NAACP in 1963. His voice was so strong in the Negro community, he helped disperse the Philadelphia race riots that occurred near the theater in 1964. But, for now, the unwritten rules that forced people like my father to stay in dingy boarding houses and people like Woods to limit their career aspirations to "race" music still stuck firmly in place.

Not even oppression dampened the Impressions' spirits, however. They were young, relatively famous, and making more money than they ever imagined. Plus, the camaraderie among the artists turned even the harshest situation into a chance for fun. "We used to play tricks on one another," LaBelle said. "Like the time we were performing with the Impressions at the Uptown Theater in Philadelphia. We stuffed their shirts with paper and filled their shoes with water. But they paid us back. At the end of the engagement, Jerry, Curtis, and Sam came to our dressing room and sang 'Goodnight Sweetheart' in wonderful harmony. We were touched. When they finished, as we hugged them goodbye, they stuck us with pins!"

Practical jokes aside, the Impressions finished the week at the Uptown Theater, picked up their money, and prepared for the biggest engagement of their lives. Next stop, Harlem.

———————

This was *it*. The world-famous Apollo Theater. Mecca and Nirvana wrapped in one for the Negro performer. Mount Rushmore, even—an eternal badge of success. It made everything else look rural. And yet, upon arriving, the mood soured when they saw the billing on the marquee. The Apollo marquee was, after all, a hallowed place. Night and day, it sparkled like a diamond alerting all of Harlem, which meant the world, that the names in bold black were worth something. It once held the consecrated names of John Coltrane, Sarah Vaughan, Miles Davis, Josephine Baker, Billie Holliday, and Joe Louis. Like every Negro performer, my father dreamed of seeing his name in those lights, and his chance had finally come.

Only, he didn't see it. Right there on that sacred marquee, the name "Jerry Butler" loomed in giant letters over the much smaller "and the Impressions." Once again, the rest of the group had been cast as also-rans, bruising their barely healed egos. They threatened to walk out, and they might have done it had Abner not flown in and repeated the speech he made in Chicago. Still, passions ran high. Jerry said, "I felt like a stranger among guys who were my friends."

Strangers or not, the Impressions had a weeklong gig to get through, and they had reached the pinnacle of Negro entertainment, no matter how the billing read. Before the first show, Dad waited nervously backstage as the promoter, Harlem DJ Jocko Henderson, warmed up the crowd. "Jocko was number one in Harlem," Jerry said. "He had his own television show and everything. He was famous for his so-called 'Rocket Ship Show' on the radio and a rap that goes like this: 'Eeeh tiddy yock. This is the jock. Back on the scene with my record machine saying, ooh pooh pah dooo. And a how do you do? We got good music just for you. Mommio and Daddio, this is Jocko with the rocket ship show, get up you big bad motor scooter'n lets go!'"

As Jocko performed his rap at the Apollo, a picture of a rocket ship was projected onto the theater's huge movie screen. When he finished, the screen lifted to reveal him on stage in his space suit and helmet. Then, the Kodaks did their set, followed by the Story Sisters, Lee Andrews and the Hearts, Huey Smith and the Clowns, and Robert and Johnny. Finally, it was time for the Impressions. Curtis and the guys rubbed the Apollo's famous tree of hope for good luck as they strode onto the stage. What they saw almost stopped them dead.

Faces—a sea of them—faces stacked on faces, stacked on faces, towering as high as the eye could see, which wasn't too high because the stage lights mercifully expunged the upper rows, which were themselves full of faces, upon faces, upon faces. A crowd that size has a way of making its presence felt, though, and the young Impressions heard it stirring with a thousand little noises, breaths, grunts, and groans. My father, guitar in hand, led the group into some crowd-friendly fare. They opened with a cover of "Wear My Ring Around Your Neck," a rollicking song Elvis had just taken to the top of the R&B chart. As Jerry explains, "Since we were going to New York, we knew we had to be super sophisticated, and what was more sophisticated than to do an Elvis Presley tune?"

The only problem with crowd-friendly fare was, this was no friendly crowd. The Apollo crowd has never suffered fools, and if a performer didn't know that going in, he learned quickly. My father's first lesson came after the Impressions finished their Elvis cover. As the final notes died out, someone shouted, "Y'all take that white shit someplace else and sing what I came here to hear!" The restive audience burst into pockets of laughter and applause.

It was a shaky start, but it contained an important message. The Negro performer existed between two worlds. The white world had money but rarely accepted Negro artists. The Negro world offered a support base that could last an entire career but couldn't bring the same riches. This left Negro performers like my father on a tightrope. Sure, it was possible to cross over to the white market and massive fame and fortune—Ray Charles and Sam Cooke had done it a few years before. But it was just as possible to stray too far from your core audience trying to appease the white market and end up unceremoniously dropped by both.

The person who shouted at the Apollo subconsciously warned the Impressions they were wobbling on that tightrope, in danger of falling. My father would never forget this lesson—he couldn't. It restated the unspoken rule he learned listening to Dunbar's two-voiced poetry, and it was a part of the music business that would plague him for decades. Like everything else about American life, whites and Negroes remained separate in the music business, too.

As the laughter settled down at the Apollo, Dad hit the opening notes of "For Your Precious Love." The effect was devastating, like lighting a fuse that made the theater burst. When the song finished, the crowd demanded three encores. After their set, the Impressions floated backstage, jubilant, sweaty, bubbling with excitement. Bobby Schiffman, manager of the Apollo, greeted them. "I'll tell you what to do," he said. "I want you all to sing 'For Your Precious Love,' and if you get an encore, I want you to sing it again, and if they call you back a third time, I want you to sing it again." For the rest of their engagement, they did just that.

———

At the end of the night, the Impressions returned to their rooms at the Grampion hotel in Harlem. The Grampion wasn't so different from the White Eagle, the seedy hotel where Curtis grew up. "Plenty of junkies and rats," Jerry recalled. To make matters worse, Carter had warned that junkies would creep up the fire escape at night to steal anything that wasn't nailed down. He suggested the Impressions leave their money on the dresser—that way the junkies wouldn't have to wake them up with a pistol to take it.

They couldn't help but feel nervous, although they didn't own much for a junkie to steal. The group pulled in $1,250 for their week's work at the Apollo, which seemed an astronomical sum on paper, but after paying commissions and expenses, it didn't amount to much once split between five band members.

During their stay at the hotel, they lived in adjoining rooms. Sam, Richard, and Curtis shared the front room; Arthur and Jerry took the back room near the window and fire escape. As they settled down that first night, shining their shoes and preparing for the upcoming shows, they told jokes and ghost stories until Jerry dozed off. With Carter's warning and the unease they all felt, Dad couldn't miss an opportunity for a great practical joke.

As Jerry slept, a loud crash near the window jolted him awake. He opened his eyes, saw a hand in front of his face, and screamed in terror. This sent Curtis, Arthur, Sam, and Richard into paroxysms of laughter. The crash came from a shoe Curtis threw against the wall, and the hand was Jerry's own dangled before his eyes. That was life on the road with my dad. He was the type of guy who would throw a bucket of cold water on you in the shower and lose himself in laughter.

———————

The second day of their engagement, Sunday, a line stretched from the Apollo box office halfway down Seventh Avenue while they rehearsed inside. During one rehearsal, the Apollo house musicians couldn't figure out how my father was getting *that sound* out of his guitar. They couldn't follow his chord fingerings either. That's how he found out he tuned his guitar to open F sharp, from a bunch of grizzled old pros that had never seen or heard anything like it. In no time, all the great guitarists around—session guys mostly—came to the Apollo to watch this kid create something new and magical with his instrument.

Monday, the performers could get a little money in advance of the full payment to pay off debts they incurred from food-and-clothes expenses, or the constant gambling backstage. After the second show, the Impressions asked for $300 to pay their food tab and have some spending change. As soon as they got their money, the underworld rose to meet them. "Every junkie and booster in Harlem had been standing around the corner waiting for the eagle to fly," Jerry said. "When it did, they swooped down on the theater with hot suits, hot watches, televisions, radios, rings, socks, underwear, shirts—everything, in your size, shape, and color. You name it, they had it. If they didn't, they promised to have it by the last show, which was payday." It was a cutthroat world for a bunch of kids. The next day, Tuesday, my father turned sixteen onstage at the Apollo.

Sometime during the whirring blur of that week, the Impressions also appeared on a local TV show hosted by Alan Freed. Freed was famous for coining the term "rock and roll," and his show gave Negroes a great chance to cross over to the white market without teetering off the tightrope. In fact, although he was white, Freed had recently tripped on that same rope, in the opposite direction. In 1957, he hosted *The Big Beat* on ABC, a weekly music show that was canceled after Negro singer Frankie Lymon danced with a white girl in the studio audience after his performance. Such was the state of racial progress in America.

Still, the Impressions needed the show. "We had sold only so many records with Jocko and the other black deejays playing our song," Jerry said. "With Freed playing it, we potentially could sell 200,000 copies in New York alone."

The TV appearance flashed by like lightning. The Impressions rode in a limousine to the television studio, met Freed, and strode on his stage dressed in pink after-six jackets, crisp white shirts, jet-black pants, black bow ties, pocket scarves, and patent-leather shoes shined to shimmer. Curtis slung his guitar around his neck, although like most television shows at the time, the musicians didn't perform live. Canned music started from the control room, the floor man swiveled his finger at the Impressions signifying they were *on*, and they mimed along as "For Your Precious Love" played. Two minutes and forty-seven seconds later, the crowd screamed, clapped, and whistled, and the Impressions left the stage and stepped into another limousine that sped through Central Park and deposited them back at the Apollo. It almost didn't seem real.

Freed and Georgie Woods did the trick. A few days later, Abner got a call from Red Schwartz, one of Vee-Jay's top promotion men. "Turn on *American Bandstand*," Schwartz shouted into the phone. "Why?" said Abner. "They're gonna play 'For Your Precious Love,' that's why," Schwartz huffed. "Somebody go across the street and get a TV!" Abner yelled, almost dropping the phone. "Dick Clark is playing our record!"

Dick Clark was *the* channel to the white market, bar none. His acceptance plugged a Negro artist into white American youth culture, and that brought money. In essence, Clark's approval was a badge—*these Negroes are safe*. It was a stupid, racist game but it was the only one going.

———

Racism in the country remained strong while the movement briefly floundered. Whites across the South violently battled desegregation using the old tricks—racist judges, economic intimidation, and terrorism in the form of homemade bombs chucked through windows in the dead of night, or rocks flung at protestors' heads, or guns cocked and pointed at a line of marchers. As local governments in the South met the movement with open hostility, the federal government dragged its feet, offering the same old platitudes. King met with President Eisenhower seeking federal action, but Ike wasn't about to mar the last years of his antiseptic reign with the stain of Negro rights.

Vice President Richard Nixon seemed more willing to help, but nothing came of it. King said, "Nixon has a genius for convincing one that he is sincere . . . he almost disarms you with his apparent sincerity. If Richard Nixon is not sincere, he is the most dangerous man in America." King wouldn't live to witness the irony of his words.

King rallied supporters with high oratory. "This is the creative moment for a full scale assault on the system of segregation," he said. "We must practice open civil disobedience. We must be willing to go to jail *en masse*. That way we may be able to arouse the dozing conscience of the South."

Dad listened to these words. He felt an increasing sympathy with the movement as the situation for Negroes in Chicago became more desperate. The State Street Corridor between Cermak and Fifty-First Street, where Negroes had crammed since before Annie Bell arrived, could hold no more. The only other option was the growing West Side ghetto, where conditions were even worse. Racist whites made easy targets for blame, but these conditions existed and thrived with the approval, unspoken or otherwise, of the Negro power structure, which depended on de facto segregation to retain its power. It was a thorny, impossible mess of a problem. Curtis wouldn't live in Cabrini much longer, and he could escape these problems on the road, but his mind would never stray far from them.

For the moment, my father's life had become too exciting to focus on any hardship for long. By the time the week in Harlem ended, the Impressions had smashed the Apollo's box-office records. It was estimated that upward of five thousand people lined the streets each night to see them—the Apollo could only seat fifteen hundred, leaving many fans disappointed. At the same time, "For Your Precious Love" rode near the top of the charts, hitting number eleven pop and three R&B. The rest of the tour went well except for occasional flare-ups about the billing, but as Jerry said, "We were making more money than any of us had ever made in our lives, and going places that we had only read about or seen pictures of. A place that had once seemed alluring suddenly became just another town that never quite compared to what the pictures and postcards and books had led us to believe."

The Impressions returned to Chicago at the end of July 1959, and my father and Jerry went back to Cabrini-Green as heroes. Royalty checks started coming in, the first containing $332.69 for each member. For a kid who was once thrilled at getting a couple of quarters playing in the back of Uncle Charles's car, Curtis could hardly comprehend making so much money off of one song.

The first thing he did was buy matching furniture for the house on Hudson. "We never had decent-looking furniture," Aunt Carolyn says.

"We had different odd pieces here and there. When Curtis bought Mom some furniture, Mom was at work, and he and I were playing, running all over the new furniture. We were sword fighting and just having a good time because he had been gone all this time." Picturing my father jumping across the furniture, playing make-believe with his sister, it is impossible to forget he was little more than a child at the time. If not for the money and success, he would have been a sophomore in high school.

For Jerry, the homecoming didn't feel quite as sweet. "All of a sudden, the smells we used to ignore—the pee in the elevators and on the stairs, wine bottles and junkies suddenly become too much to bear," he said. Worse, the Chicago Housing Authority informed Jerry's mother she could no longer stay in Cabrini-Green. According to the city, because of Jerry's success, she now had too much money. Little did the city know, while one hit single could raise a person's social status, the long-term financial picture didn't change. What the Impressions needed was another hit.

Dad was about to learn another important lesson on the rough road to stardom, though—one hit does not guarantee another. The Impressions followed "For Your Precious Love" with "Come Back My Love," a retread of the former that went to number twenty-nine on the R&B chart and missed the pop chart. At that session, they recorded two more similar ballads—"The Gift of Love" and "Love Me." Neither had much impact. "Love Me" marked the last time my father, Jerry, Sam, and the Brooks brothers recorded as the Impressions.

While home between tours, Curtis met Helen, a pretty, brown-skinned girl with a round, open face. "Helen used to come over the house and see me, but actually I think she was coming to see him," Aunt Carolyn says. "When Curtis started going on the road, he'd just started courting her. He'd take her for walks." Soon, he began dating Helen seriously, or at least as seriously as he could date anyone. The road offered temptations he couldn't resist, and soon after recording "Come Back My Love," Vee-Jay sent the Impressions on the road for thirty-one days with

the Coasters and Clyde McPhatter—thirty-one days where every show
ended with eager young girls wanting to touch success and my father
only too happy to oblige.

The groupies complicated his relationship with Helen, as they would
with every serious relationship throughout his life. But they also eased
the relentless physical, mental, and spiritual grind of one-nighters—endless car rides, a new city every day, a new venue every night, ramshackle
boarding houses, and then back on the road where there was no place for
a Negro to stop and eat or even go to the bathroom.

Sometimes the Impressions engaged in a bit of trickery to secure a
few warm beds in white-only southern hotels. Richard Brooks, who was
"as close to white as we ever got to in our group" according to Eddie,
would rent a room and let the rest of the group in the back door. The
ruse fell apart one night, though, reminding them of the severe danger
they faced. "We let Richard go ahead and check us into the hotel, and we
came through the back way once he got situated," Eddie says. "We were
doing fine until Sam, with his dumb self, decided to go out and get ice
cubes or something, and a white man saw him and said, 'What is that
nigger doing in here?' The man called the desk, the desk called the police,
the police came and told us to get packed and get out right away. I said,
'We got to get out. These people will lynch you down here. They don't
play. The police will back them up and they'll never find you.'"

Of all the southern cities they toured in, Atlanta treated them best.
The show's promoter arranged for a crowd to greet the Impressions at
the airport. Then he set up a motorcade to carry them all over Atlanta's
Negro community. The guys rode in sleek cars that had banners taped to
the sides with JERRY BUTLER AND THE IMPRESSIONS emblazoned in bold
red set on dazzling white paper. "Young girls, seeing the spectacle and
recognizing the name, pointed at the car, screamed, and covered their
faces in embarrassment," Jerry said. "Prostitutes boldly yelled to us, 'Y'all
wanna have a good time?' and patted their behinds."

The motorcade headed down Auburn Avenue, to WERD, America's
first Negro-owned radio station. Then they made the rounds to WAOK
and met DJs Piano Red, Alley Pat, and Zena Sears. "They all interviewed

us and made us feel at home," Jerry said. "For the first time, I understood what people meant by Southern hospitality. Everyone wanted to feed us, take us wherever we wanted to go, and help in any way they could." Thus began my father's long love affair with Atlanta, where he'd spend the last years of his life.

———————

Tensions within the group continued to mount as the month-long tour slogged on. The fights usually centered on the billing—"Jerry Butler and the Impressions"—as well as the natural stresses and strains of five young guys forced to live together close as husband and wife for a month straight. In San Antonio toward the end of the tour, the Impressions could no longer hold their wounded egos in check.

They had an appearance scheduled in Philadelphia the next day, but upon reaching the venue in Texas, they realized the money from the show wouldn't cover their plane tickets. Butler called Abner and said the road manager refused to give them more money without Abner's assent. "Okay, baby," Abner said. "I'll call and straighten it out. You'll have the money tomorrow. You guys do well, and I'll see you when you get back home." The receiver went dead. Just then, Arthur asked to talk to Abner. Jerry explained Abner had just hung up. Arthur didn't believe him.

What happened next sealed the original Impressions' fate. As Jerry described it:

Arthur pitched a bitch, starting in again with that stuff about me wanting to be the boss and always wanting to do all of the talking for the group. "Well, we ain't going on," [Arthur] finally said, "and you can do all the singing!"

"Who the fuck are 'we'?" I asked, trying to stay calm. But I could feel my anger rising. "Me and my brother," said Arthur. Richard said nothing, but Sam was quick to respond. "I ain't going on, either," he said. All eyes then turned to Curtis. . . .

"I'm goin' on, man," said Curtis, "because I want to get paid."

. . . Sam had second thoughts. "Well, if that's the way it's gonna be," he said, "I guess I'll go on too." Arthur and Richard were obstinate. "Fuck you, man," they said, mumbling to themselves and walking off from us. . . .

As I sang our first couple of songs, with Curtis playing guitar and him and Sam adding background voices wherever they could, I kept wondering if Arthur and Richard would cut out all of the bullshit and join us on stage. I didn't realize how stubborn they could be.

It occurred to me, as we went along that night that Arthur and Richard weren't missed at all. Sil Austin's horn section was playing their part. No one in San Antonio even knew they existed. It was then that I made my decision to leave the group.

My father, true to form, had his eye on the bottom line. He wanted money more than he wanted to get tangled in some silly fight. During the tour he'd been sending part of his earnings to his mother and family in Chicago. With that money, Aunt Carolyn recalls, "[Mom] bought this great big freezer and filled it up. I think she bought a half of beef, and a half a pig, and filled it up, and boy did we have food then. I sent [Curtis] a letter thanking him for the food." Dad needed the money for himself and his family—it was a desperate need. He refused to go back to poverty as intensely as he cared about music.

For his part, Jerry cared about the music too, but Carter and Abner pressured him to go solo. "I found out later they offered him a brand new Mercury, a couple thousand dollars cash," Eddie says. "Can you imagine, a kid from Cabrini-Green?" Jerry had little choice but to take the offer, especially since Abner planned to split the group anyway.

———

After Jerry quit, the Brooks brothers returned, and the Impressions no longer had to worry about billing. Unfortunately, the tension they'd had with Jerry transferred to my father, who at sixteen years old stepped into the lead spot. No one else could handle the role. He was the only one who could write a song and the only one who had sung lead on any

Impressions record other than Jerry. Before Jerry left, Dad didn't mind taking a backseat—Jerry had been the lead singer since the Northern Jubilees, and it felt natural. With Jerry gone, Dad's controlling nature came to the fore. He now led the group, and after assuming that role, he wouldn't relinquish it for nearly twenty years. As a result, when the Impressions looked for someone to fill out the quintet, it had to be someone who sang backup.

On a swing through Chattanooga, Richard, Arthur, and Sam stopped by Fred Cash's house, the kid they knew from their days in the original Roosters. Fred had followed the Impressions' success from Chattanooga. The first time he heard "For Your Precious Love" on the radio, he thought, "Hey, this a great record, but this can't be the same fellas I used to sing with, because we couldn't sing!" Still, the last thing he expected was to see them drive up the hill to his house in their green station wagon. "Hey, that looks like the fellas in there," he thought as the green machine crested the hill and parked in front of his house. Then, out spilled his old buddies, everybody smiling, laughing, and slapping hands. Someone whipped out a big roll of money and held it up for Fred's inspection. "Oh boy! What have I missed here?" Fred thought. He'd soon find out.

Toward the end of 1959, Vee-Jay gave the Impressions—now featuring Fred Cash—a couple of records, playing out the usual script for vocal groups. True to that script, the Impressions couldn't buy a hit. They recorded one of Curtis's compositions, "At the County Fair," and even though Herb Kent put his considerable powers into breaking the song, it never got out of Chicago. "We scuffled some," my father said. "For a time we would do gigs as the Impressions, but nobody was really aware of the Impressions. So it was quite hard for us to get gigs."

For a few months, they scraped by with small gigs in what my father called "the lowlands, like down in Mississippi, just in little night spots," often billing themselves as Jerry Butler and the Impressions and letting Sam sing "For Your Precious Love," since no one knew the difference anyway.

As 1959 ended, Vee-Jay dropped the group. Chief among their reasons was that my father couldn't come up with another hit. Also, Carter never felt excited about Curtis's falsetto voice, and he felt less excited about butting heads with a teenager over royalties and song ownership. Even at such a young age, Dad understood the importance of owning himself. Once he took over the group, he often argued with Abner and Carter about his rights. "There were so many fights," he remembered. "They couldn't understand it. 'He wants his publishing!' they would say to each other. Like it wasn't mine to have." He might not have finished high school, but he was no fool. Nobody could dupe or bully him into giving away a single cent. Unfortunately, that attitude left him out of a job.

After the Vee-Jay deal fell through, Eddie couldn't get the Impressions another contract. Defeated and deflated, they took whatever menial jobs they could find. Around this time, my father began a working relationship with a guy he knew from high school, Major Lance. Major had become a featured dancer on Jim Lounsbury's show, *Time for Teens*, and wheedled his way into a one-off single on Mercury Records. He couldn't write songs, so he turned to the one man he knew who could. "He was always coming round and looking through my bag for songs that I'd written but didn't want to do with the Impressions," Dad said. "He was pretty good at picking them, too." Unfortunately, the first one he picked—a middling doo-wop number called "I've Got a Girl"—got no traction.

My father now dealt with the possibility that his life as a musician, which had been his main passion, might suffer an early death. After all, the music business was littered with the carcasses of has-beens and one-hit wonders. Curtis had no guarantee of getting even one shot to hit it big, and he'd just seen that shot come and go in a flash. Sure, he was only seventeen years old, but he already had the baggage of failure hanging around his neck.

He spent the beginning of 1960 living in Cabrini-Green, working a dead-end job selling cigars with Alfred Dunhill Co. In later years, he'd often boast it was the only job he ever had outside of music. He spent his days going to fancy office buildings in the Loop, Chicago's central business district, trying to sell cigars to white businessmen. Often, they'd either harass him or throw him out. A Negro—even one selling cigars—had no place in the white business world. As for the Impressions, they lessened the blow by calling their breakup a hiatus. Of course, the word hiatus implies things will resume, and none of them knew when or if that would happen.

Real progress, however, was being made in race relations, which gave Dad something to focus on. In 1960, John F. Kennedy became the youngest president in American history. He seemed sympathetic toward Negro rights, giving those in the movement reason for hope. Less than a month after his inauguration, the movement received another positive jolt when four young Negro men sat down at the counter of a Woolworth's in Greensboro, North Carolina, and refused to leave when denied service. Within a week, similar protests occurred across the state and into South Carolina. The era of sit-ins had begun, and the movement entered its most successful phase—one in which my father would play a major role. Then, as if the roller coaster of 1960 hadn't given him enough to think about, he proposed to Helen.

Curtis married Helen in a double ceremony alongside Fred and his first wife, Judy. After the marriage Curtis and Helen moved into an apartment outside of Cabrini, where Uncle Kenny visited them often. "We were still living in Cabrini-Green," Kenny says, "and I went over to his house one time, and it was the first time I ever had a shower in my life. I think I was about fourteen years old then. That kind of stays in my mind. A lot of things I could say that I done in life was because of my brother."

In fact, even though he had married and lived apart from his family, Curtis still played the role of the protective brother. Aunt Carolyn recalls him coming to her rescue after she got into a fight with a schoolmate. "I beat her up, and the next thing I heard was that her brother was looking for me," she says. "I remember Mama talking about it, and Curtis was in the house doing whatever he did—he always acted like he wasn't paying attention, but he was. And he said, 'Who is that?' They told him who it was. He said, 'Oh, OK.' The next thing I know, he left, and I didn't have no more problems with the brother. Whatever he said, that took care of it. He used to say, 'If anybody asks you for something, tell them to ask me.'" Now seventeen years old, my father still embraced his role as man of the house, the part he'd played for more than half his life. It made him older than his years. Perhaps that's why he decided to get married at such a young age.

Unfortunately, he wasn't ready. His relationship with Helen faced trouble from the start. "I don't think that relationship ever came together properly," Eddie says. "Curtis was a very unusual person because he was a genius, and geniuses have idiosyncrasies going and coming. Sometimes a woman can't deal with them, or the man can't deal with it. Basically, they couldn't get it to fit. That's just the way it went."

Whatever problems Curtis and Helen had going into the marriage were heightened by an unexpected turn of events that sent him back on the road. In mid-1960, the IRS came after him for $400 in taxes. Even though royalty checks still trickled in, he didn't have that kind of money. He did own a Webcor tape recorder, on which he recorded snatches of potential songs that came to him while he noodled around on his guitar between shifts at the cigar store. The IRS wanted him to sell the tape recorder to pay off his debt, but he needed it too much. His creativity came in torrents, and the tape recorder was the only way to hold onto the hundreds of chord progressions, melodies, lyrics, and song structures he discovered before they disappeared back into the ethereal cloud where ideas are born. Curtis needed an escape. Just then, fate stepped in.

Jerry spent most of 1960 touring the chitlin' circuit trying to break as a solo artist. One day in New York, his guitar player—Phil Upchurch, who would soon play on much of my father's work—announced he was leaving the band. Stuck in a bind, Jerry called and asked my father to meet him in New York. "Man, I don't know anybody's songs but yours," Curtis said into the phone. "Well, just play those—that's all I'm singing," Jerry replied. "Well, I don't have no amplifier," Curtis said. "Get here," Jerry said. "I'll have your amplifier when you get here." So, my father jumped right back into life on the road. "When Jerry called, I had nothing to do," he said later. "I got away from [the IRS] by playing for Jerry. I did nothing but play for Jerry and sleep with my guitar and write songs."

Curtis didn't just sleep with his guitar, though; he also shared a bed with Eddie to save money. When Jerry had started his solo tour, he had hired Eddie as a valet, a position Eddie saw as demeaning but necessary. "I was his chauffer—or flunky, that's what I called it, carry his shoes, go to the bathroom with him, wipe his behind, whatever it takes," Eddie says. "Swallow your pride, that's what you call it."

When Dad joined, he and Eddie became closer than ever. "We were living together like man and wife almost," Eddie says. "You don't get any closer than that. We were always planning and scheming, maneuvering, what we were going to do. He was always writing something, asking what did I think of it."

Eddie also learned that despite the humiliations he suffered as Jerry's valet, the job came with hidden benefits. As he explains that period:

> I was making history with radio stations and disc jockeys. I had their names, their home phone numbers, their kids' numbers. I had a book of DJs. You name a place, I'll tell you something about it. I would live with the jocks. I had a strong bond. I was like a powerhouse. I could come to town with no money, other guys come to town with a couple thousand dollars in their pocket to go on the radio station, but the [DJs] always gave me a pass because they knew I was broke and poor, and I could take them to get a cup of coffee and a hamburger or something, but they accepted me because they felt me from the heart. I was at radio stations promoting Jerry but at the same time promoting Eddie Thomas.

As winter approached, Curtis had been on the road for almost two years, making it easy to forget Helen back home. Despite the fact Jerry occasionally traveled with his wife and that Curtis slept with Eddie most nights, they were three young men who had women falling at their feet. Curtis had already experienced a taste of what fame could bring in terms of female attention, and he liked it. Being on the road with Jerry, he got another heaping plateful.

In regard to their marriages, Jerry says,

> I can assure you that we did it very poorly. It was not an easy thing to do. But why wasn't it easy? Because we had nothing to compare it to. We were treading in new territory. You know, you're young. Never had enough of anything. And all of a sudden, everything is coming at you in great abundance. How do you deal with it? There was no [Uncle] Charles around to say, "Don't do that." And you always felt that everybody around you was trying to hustle you. Nobody was around you because they really liked you. They were there because they liked what you represented. Or they liked what you had. And they became vicariously stars in their own way. And pretty soon, you got to the point where you couldn't trust anyone.

Call it the famous man's curse—thousands of acquaintances but few real friends. It plagued my father and Jerry throughout their careers, and as Jerry said, they had no mentor to help them deal with it. While Curtis was away, both Uncle Charles and Wal Mayfield left Annie Bell's house on the same day, never to return.

———————

One night, watching the miles flash by between Philadelphia and Atlantic City, Jerry started humming a melody. My father sat splayed in the back seat with his guitar, as he usually did on tour, and he began putting chords behind Jerry's voice. "He always had an instrument close to him if he could," Jerry says. "I mean sometimes we might not have space, but that was rare. Because usually he'd be in the backseat with my wife and the guitar, and Eddie and I would be in the front seat driving to wherever we had to go." As they worked on Jerry's melody, they went through the normal conversation of whether it should be fast or slow, what the lyrics should say, and so on. Soon, they had polished off an up-tempo number called "He Will Break Your Heart." It would become Jerry's first number-one R&B hit as a solo artist and a national top twenty record, featuring my father on guitar and backing vocals. It shared a similar rhythmic backbone with "Lonely Teardrops," a song made famous by Jackie Wilson two years earlier, cowritten by Berry Gordy.

At that time, Gordy had cowritten another single that began making its way up the charts—"Shop Around." Released on Gordy's new label, Tamla, it introduced to the world a group called the Miracles with Bill "Smokey" Robinson. "Shop Around" sold one million copies on its first release. Soon, Tamla would become Motown, Smokey Robinson would be a household name, and Gordy would run the most successful Negro-owned business in the country. My father surely heard "Shop Around" on the radio as he flashed from city to city, and he felt the fire to make a hit for himself.

He saved up nearly $1,000 on tour with Jerry, and he had a song he wanted to cut with the Impressions. He'd begun writing it when he was twelve years old after watching a Western movie. Even at such a young age, his imagination could carry him far from the ghetto's claws. He introduced it to Eddie one night in his usual way—"Hey, Tom. What do you think of this?" Then, he played a few licks and began singing about a mysterious gypsy woman dancing around a campfire. "Yeah, that's a hit, I hope," Eddie said. "But I think we might be starting a new trend because right now it's all doo-wops. We're coming up with something different, and something different might be acceptable. Let's go for it."

On a stop in Chicago, Eddie called the Impressions to his apartment. That night, Curtis, Fred, Sam, Arthur, and Richard sat around catching up on old times, and then Curtis played them the song—"Gypsy Woman." They wanted to hear it again and again. Each time he played it, another voice found a harmony to sing. Soon, the air grew full with five voices intertwined. By the end of the evening, the Impressions were a group again.

Before beginning his last leg with Jerry, Dad booked a session at Universal Studios in Chicago to cut "Gypsy Woman." The recording they made that day creeps from the speakers and settles over the listener like fog on a dark night. Castanets and finger cymbals accent a nasty snare-drum pattern that splits the difference between funk and a marching beat. The Impressions provide the perfect backing, blending doo-wop and gospel, laying a plush bed for Curtis's trilling falsetto to lie upon. Curtis's guitar is a quintessential lesson in understatement, especially the lick he rips off after the line "She danced around and 'round to a guitar melody"—two notes so perfectly placed and executed they hit like a punch to the gut.

Everyone knew the song had legs; they just needed a break. As luck would have it, Jerry's tour stopped next in Philadelphia, playing for Georgie Woods at the Uptown Theater again. Eddie knew the radio stations in Philly could break "Gypsy Woman," so he spent ample time at WDAS and at Philly's other major station, WHAT. "I was there with my tin cup begging that guy to play the record," Eddie says. "I had to see the program director. I sold him a bill of goods, you know, I had my hand crossed behind my back. He said, 'OK, we'll give you a shot. We'll put it on the extra list, but you're going to have to talk to the jockey personally to get him to play it, because on the extra list, they're not required to play it.' So now I got to go to the jocks one on one, take my time, come back a different time, ask them to plug my record."

Eddie had one other asset in his favor in Philadelphia: a good promotion man named Manny Singer. "I used to take him out to dinner a couple of times," Eddie says. "I'd say, 'Manny, I need your help on this.' So, he would talk to the jocks, too."

Still, it was Georgie Woods who ultimately held the key to Philadelphia. Eddie told Woods, "This is me, man; this is for me." Woods put the record in heavy rotation, and it took off in Philly, became bigger than bubble gum. The fire spread to Maxie Waxie in Baltimore and DC, followed by Bill Summers in Louisville and Porky Chedwick in Pittsburgh. Through sheer gumption, Eddie was slowly creating a radio smash.

"Eddie was such a hustler, man," my father said. "Everywhere we went, anything even looked like an antenna, maybe five or ten miles away, we'd come on and Eddie would hustle 'Gypsy Woman' to whoever was there. . . . Country and western, gospel, any kind of station, didn't matter what the format was. Eddie would pull over and take us into the station. People just appreciated you coming in and making the stop, so they'd give you a play. So that's how we began to build up 'Gypsy Woman.'"

Even Jerry helped promote the song. As "Gypsy Woman" picked up steam on local radio, the Impressions received an invitation to perform on television. The rest of the group couldn't make it in time, so as Curtis pantomimed the song for the cameras, Jerry and Eddie stood in the background, just close enough to the lights so the crowd could tell they were there, but far enough in the shadows so no one could see who they were.

With television and radio promotion going strong, "Gypsy Woman" continued gaining traction. Meanwhile, Jerry returned to the Apollo as Eddie scoured New York for a new record deal. It seemed just days ago he was begging around Record Row in Chicago trying to sell the original Impressions, but even after so much hard work, he had to begin from the bottom again.

Eddie went to Laurie Records first, which had Dion and the Belmonts and the Chiffons. They passed. Next, he went to Scepter Records, home of the Shirelles and Tammy Montgomery, who would later score massive hits as Tammi Terrell, singing with Marvin Gaye for Motown. Scepter passed. Then, Eddie went to RCA Records on Fifth Avenue and played the demo for A&R man Ray Harris, who thought my father looked like a rabbit with his front teeth sticking out. Harris said, "No, I can't see this group singing about a gypsy woman and the kids getting into it."

Undaunted, Eddie kept on his dogged way to ABC/Paramount Records on Broadway. ABC existed in another stratum from the labels that had already rejected "Gypsy Woman." When Eddie plucked up his nerve and walked into the building, he stood in the house of B. B. King, Fats Domino, Lloyd Price, and perhaps biggest of all, Ray Charles. Charles had signed with ABC the year before and negotiated a contract virtually unheard of for a Negro at the time, with a $50,000 annual advance, high royalties, and eventual ownership of his masters. That last part did not go unnoticed by my father.

At ABC, Eddie met A&R man Clarence Avant, and played him "Gypsy Woman." It didn't knock Avant out, but for some reason he decided to help. "He was black, and I'm black, and I guess we had to stick together," Eddie says. "And he knew it wouldn't cost them anything to put it out because they were known for being cheapskates, which meant that they would only give you enough advance money to put in your pocket." Eddie showed how much hustle he had, telling Avant, "Being with Jerry Butler, I know a lot of DJs across the country. I got their home phone numbers and everything. I think I can support this record. If you guys will distribute it, I can get the airplay to get it started."

Avant played "Gypsy Woman" for ABC president Samuel Clark and told him it was a great record, although he didn't quite believe it himself. True to form, Clark signed the Impressions with no advance money offered. ABC would only release the song regionally in Philadelphia, Baltimore, DC, and New York, and the label passed off most, if not all, promotional responsibilities to Eddie and the group. If the song hit—and the odds were stacked against it—ABC would release "Gypsy Woman" nationally. If the song missed, which was much more likely, the Impressions were out of the business. Eddie said, "Man, we're going to have to roll our sleeves up and hustle the best we can," but my father already knew that.

After the last Apollo show, Dad told Jerry he wouldn't be playing guitar for him anymore. Jerry said later, "I could see it coming, but I didn't know it would come that soon. Curt was anxious to try new ideas and explore different sounds. And so we parted again, this time more amicably."

My father explained it like this: "Everybody who was part of the Impressions could see that it was God's calling." He wasn't a religious man, but he'd endured enough of Annie Bell's droning sermons to recognize the sound of that heavenly phone ringing.

All he had to do now was answer.

5

Keep On Pushing

"Maybe someday I'll reach that higher goal,
I know I can make it with just a little bit of soul."
—"KEEP ON PUSHING"

New York City, late 1960—The sidewalk outside the Brill Building bustled with hungry young songwriters seeking a break. Inside, the major music publishers in New York sat ready to prey on these desperate youngsters. The publishers had everything set up in the boxy building on Broadway—songwriters toiling in tiny offices, arrangers who could write a quick lead sheet for a sawbuck, an in-house demo studio, and radio promoters who pushed songs into nationwide rotation. "Brill was a building where songwriters would go up to the eleventh floor and would come down on the elevator and stop at each floor, trying to sell their songs at every office," said Mike Stoller, who cowrote many of Elvis's hits.

Only the best writers earned offices in the building—Carole King, Phil Spector, Burt Bacharach, Paul Simon, and other soon-to-be famous names. Roving musicians and lesser writers lingered in phone booths at the Turf, a restaurant on street level, hoping for a crack at the big time. "If a songwriter was doing a demo session and someone hadn't shown up, they'd run into the restaurant and shout, 'I need a bass player,' and he'd get one," Stoller said.

My father spent a lot of time hanging out near the Turf while in the city, and he heard the songwriters gripe about their travails. Race didn't seem to matter there; black or white, they all got the same lousy deal—twenty-five dollars a song. For writers on a hot streak, like Ellie Greenwich, who cowrote early '60s blockbusters like "Chapel of Love" and "Leader of the Pack," the Brill Building publishers might raise the price to fifty or one hundred dollars—a pittance compared to the millions they raked in.

From his experiences near the Brill Building, my father learned that having a hit record meant little without owning the publishing rights. With publishing, Dad saw another way to gain the control over his life and finances his mother never had. "I believed very early in life that it was important to own as much of yourself as possible," he said. "I think that came from my insecurities as a child, coming up as a poor young student from a family that was poor." He'd repeat that phrase like a refrain throughout his life—own yourself, own yourself, own yourself. It was perhaps the most important lesson his childhood and his experience in the music business had taught him. If you owned yourself, you could control your fate. If not, all the hits in the world couldn't stop some record company from taking your money and leaving you in the lurch when your career dried up.

After fighting with Carter and Abner at Vee-Jay and learning how the music business scammed naive artists, my father knew he'd rather have fifty percent of something than one hundred percent of nothing. He said, "Publishers were hitting the lottery off of people's material. Of course, what was considered black money was a Cadillac and $2,500 in fives, tens, and twenties. Nigger rich. When I started recording, I saw very few people who owned themselves." In fact, when my father started recording in 1958, no Negro artist did. Sam Cooke became among the first to change that, starting his own label, SAR, in 1961. Though he used SAR exclusively to record other artists, he also founded a publishing company to control royalties from his work on RCA Victor.

Already one of Dad's heroes in music, Cooke became his hero in business, too. At eighteen years old, Dad followed in Cooke's footsteps and founded his own publishing company. He called it Curtom, under-scoring how close he and Eddie had become. He always called Eddie "Tom," a shortening of Eddie's last name, and Eddie called him "Curt." Curtom seemed a natural fit.

At the same time, my father diversified his interests, buying into Queen Booking with Jerry. Queen booked some of the biggest acts around—they'd eventually work with Gladys Knight, the O'Jays, and Aretha Franklin, among many others—and they made gobs of money. Gobs of money meant Mob involvement in Chicago. Soon, a mobster named Gaetano "Big Guy" Vastola snatched control of the agency and ran it on Mafia principles. Jerry said, "My friends were being intimidated into signing contracts with personal managers and agencies that openly cheated them, and black newcomers were being channeled onto the same chitlin' circuit treadmill that the older artists had fought so hard to either expand or upgrade." Once they saw the way things were going down at Queen, my father and Jerry got out almost as fast as they had bought in.

Queen wasn't the only factor forcing Negro performers onto the chitlin' circuit, though. Even with the past decade's advances, the circuit was still the only consistent gig open to them. They needed it to sustain their careers. My father knew that. He sought to get back to it with "Gypsy Woman." As Eddie promoted the single on local radio, Curtis called the Impressions to New York to cut a gorgeous ballad called "As Long as You Love Me" for the flip side. The two songs together showed his growing prowess as a writer, singer, and guitarist.

"As Long as You Love Me" opens with a devastating guitar lick, the kind of lyrical hammer-on and pull-off lick that became my father's sig-nature sound. That sound accomplishes in a few notes what most guitar-ists couldn't with an entire album. Then, the Impressions chime in with soaring five-part harmony, and the song becomes almost as enchanting as "Gypsy Woman." The chorus repeats the phrase "for your precious love," perhaps to remind people who the Impressions were in the first place.

By the time the Impressions finished "As Long as You Love Me," Eddie had already helped make "Gypsy Woman" a regional smash. ABC had to press thousands of copies to meet the demand, and, as Eddie says,

"Once they saw that, they released it on a national level, and 'Gypsy Woman' was just solid as a rock." The single rose to number two on the R&B charts and number twenty pop, roughly equaling the relative positions of "For Your Precious Love." The Impressions were back.

Then, Fred got hit with a scare courtesy of the US Army. Since the mid-'50s, the army had been quietly amassing troops in Vietnam to stanch the tide of communism flowing through the Far East. As President Kennedy escalated troop deployment, a few attentive citizens guessed how serious the affair had become. Fred, like many others, did not. In 1961, he received papers to report for an army physical, but he couldn't have predicted the bloody war brewing or how it would brutalize his generation within a few short years. For the time being, he only worried what the call to duty would mean for his career. "I was scared to death," he said. "I was like, 'Oh my God, I'm going to miss out on [the Impressions] again.'" Luckily, the recruiters only chose every other man for active duty, and Fred wound up the odd one out.

With that scare over, the Impressions watched from Chicago as "Gypsy Woman" sold half a million copies. ABC president Sam Clark offered Eddie a job as a national promotional manager. Now, in addition to the Impressions, Eddie promoted everything from Ray Charles's *Modern Sounds in Country and Western Music*, to the Tams' "What Kind of Fool (Do You Think I Am)," to releases by B. B. King, Tommy Roe, and others. ABC also offered the Impressions a five-year contract, which they gladly signed. After years of hustling, grinding out one-nighters, and swallowing their pride, they had a solid footing in the music business for the first time.

Curtis had little time to spend at home with Helen before leaving on another hectic sprawl across the country. The tour for "Gypsy Woman" played out like any other: more one-nighters, more miles piled in the green wagon, more girls after each show making it easy to forget the wife back home. "Girls were there by the fortress," Eddie said. "I mean, dozens, and dozens, and dozens, specifically on Curtis." My father found it impossible to say no, as he would for most of his life.

On tour they hit the usual places—the Apollo in New York, the Regal in Chicago, the Uptown in Philly, the Howard in DC, the Royal in Baltimore—and Dick Clark featured them twice on *American Bandstand*. At the Apollo, they performed alongside B. B. King as he made his debut at the hallowed venue. King was so nervous before going on stage, he turned to Fred and said, "Man, you think the people are gonna like me?" Fred replied, "B.B., people are gonna love you here." The Impressions had seen enough to know the real thing. They were old pros.

Touring took a lot out of my father. "The country was our neighborhood," he said. "We were putting on 150,000 miles a year. It was a grind." Making matters worse, traveling through the South was still dangerous for Negroes, even famous ones. After a show in Jackson, Mississippi, the Impressions steered the green wagon toward a Negro boarding house. Though the speed limit on the road was thirty-five miles per hour, they went a bit slower just to be safe. Soon, lights flashed in their rearview mirror, and a cop pulled them over. "You're driving too slow. Where are you going, where are you from, and what are doing here?" he demanded. He gave the Impressions a ticket, and the next day, as Eddie recalled, "We went downtown to pay the ticket. Guess how much the ticket was? A dollar! I can't forget that. All these little petty things they'd do, just things to interrupt you."

The Impressions did everything possible to avoid trouble. They registered the green wagon under the company name to forestall white cops from wondering how a bunch of Negroes got such a nice ride. They also learned to fill up on gas early in the day to avoid stopping in dangerous towns after sundown. Nighttime was long in the South. The Klan burned crosses at night; King's house was firebombed at night; Emmett Till was murdered at night. It seemed racists found violent courage when the moon was the only witness.

Even with those precautions, the Impressions crawled cautiously as sheep in a wolf's den through places like Mississippi, Georgia, and Alabama. "Oh Lord, it was rough," Fred said. "We were just scared to death a lot of times."

If they managed to avoid trouble with cops, they often ran into it at gigs. "A lot of auditoriums that we played, the people that were running the sound would just be so nasty," Fred said. "They'd say you got to be out by a certain time. You couldn't go a minute over that time, because they'd turn the mics off, they'd turn the lights off. I don't care if you're in the middle of your song or what."

They couldn't stay in white hotels, so Negro rooming houses became their only oases. Negro artists worked out an impressive network for finding these houses. Backstage on the chitlin' circuit became gossip central, and groups hung around exhausted from the work but exhilarated from the cheering crowds, talking about money, and girls, and life on the road. When the Impressions heard from their peers of a rooming house with good Southern cooking—greens, black-eyed peas, smothered steak, and all the fixings—they'd check it out and pass the word to the next group they met. In such a way, an entire economy grew in the Negro community based upon housing traveling musicians.

The rooming houses were often nothing more than spacious private homes. "You had your room, but everybody shared a bathroom," Fred said. "And it was like your mom cooking in the kitchen, everybody go in there and eat, sit down at the table." Dinnertime at those houses was quite a scene. Since most artists toured together in package shows and crossed paths with others doing the same thing, it is possible to imagine the Impressions huddled around a table breaking bread and dishing gossip with the Four Tops, Jackie Wilson, Marvin Gaye, Smokey Robinson, Patti LaBelle, Martha Reeves, James Brown, and others.

In these boarding houses, Curtis usually stayed to himself in his room—a habit he inherited from his mother and grandmother. "When the fellows would go out to have fun and maybe there'd be parties after the set, they would leave all their wallets with me," he said, "and I'd sit in my room and live through my own fantasies and write." He liked to write late at night, sitting on the edge of his bed. Sometimes he'd come up with something special, pad down to Fred or Sam's room, knock gently on the door and say, "Hey, come listen to this." Fred would soon hear one of the most important songs the Impressions ever recorded that way.

Even at home, my father spent a good deal of time alone with his music, either in his den playing guitar or holed up in the studio trying to score another hit. "During those times of my life I was sleeping with my guitar and writing every feeling," he said.

> Anger, love, everything in my life would come out on paper. . . .
> It was even an escape if I was hurt too bad or if something wasn't
> going right. I could always retire to writing my sentiments and my
> personal feelings. A lot of times those songs were mostly for me. I
> was the one trying to learn the first lesson because I didn't have the
> answers. My fights and arguments, even with God, went down on
> paper. Why, when, what—well, this is how I feel about it.

As a child, he used to ask those questions of his mother. Now, he asked his guitar.

———

Unfortunately, the next songs Curtis wrote for the Impressions failed to even sniff success. The first attempt, a doo-wop-flavored number called "Grow Closer Together," had a similar rhythmic feel to "Gypsy Woman." While it featured some choice guitar licks and a warm blanket of backing vocals, it wasn't perceived to have the brilliance of its predecessor melodically or rhythmically.

The next effort, 1962's "Little Young Lover," failed to impress the pop charts, despite opening with a swinging, driving beat and ending with one of my father's most breathtaking guitar licks. It peaked at number ninety-nine. Curtis did write two songs that achieved minor success—"Find Another Girl" and "I'm A Telling You"—but he wrote them for Jerry, not the Impressions.

During this dry streak, the Brooks brothers grew antsy. "Our style was so different than what was really going on," my father said. "My music and my own personal creations were so dominant. They being from the South, Chattanooga, the people they loved were the Five Royales, the Midnighters, James Brown. [The Impressions] just wasn't their music." For the Brooks brothers, the Impressions seemed stuck in the doo-wop age while Brown inched toward funk with songs like "Night

Train." At the same time, Motown blazed a new path of rhythmic pop, releasing smashes like Marvin Gaye's "Hitch Hike," the Miracles' "You Really Got a Hold on Me," the Marvelettes' "Beechwood 4-5789," and dozens of other songs by artists like Little Stevie Wonder, the Supremes, and Eddie Holland (the same Eddie Holland who performed Jackie Wilson's routine with the Impressions three years before). To Arthur and Richard, it seemed Curtis didn't have his finger on the pulse of hit music.

As 1962 wore down, the Impressions cut "I'm the One Who Loves You," an up-tempo, doo-wop-tinged song. When it disappeared without notice, the Brooks brothers snapped. "They were wanting to do stuff like Little Richard was doing," Fred said, "whereas we kept telling them that we needed to have our own identity and that we couldn't just be doing what everyone else was doing. So they got really mad, took the record, threw it in the garbage, and said 'We're quitting! We're gonna sign to End Records instead!'—because at the time Little Anthony & The Imperials were really hot on End Records." The Brooks brothers left the group in Chicago and went to New York to create their own short-lived version of the Impressions.

My father, Fred, and Sam had felt the split coming for a while. They'd even begun rehearsing as a threesome whenever Richard and Arthur went out to eat between shows. "Sam, Curtis, and I had become really tight," Fred said. "When the time came and they threw the record in the garbage can, we didn't make no big fuss about it. We just kept on going and rehearsing. It was a lot of work perfecting that sound that we had with just the three of us."

———

Before they could perfect their sound, my father was called away on other business. Just after the Brooks brothers left, Carl Davis hired him as a staff writer for OKeh Records—a great break for him but tough for Fred and Sam, since they now took a backseat to his new job. He had to take the offer, though. Davis was one of the hottest record producers on the planet, having scored an enormous hit with Gene Chandler's "Duke of Earl," released on Vee-Jay in January 1962. "Duke of Earl" hit number one on both the R&B and pop charts and held the number-one slot on the *Billboard* Hot 100 for three weeks. Chandler became a household name, and Davis soon joined Columbia Records as producer and head A&R man for the subsidiary OKeh label.

Davis, another son of Louisiana migrants who settled in Chicago, felt a strong connection to my father. "I wanted Curtis more for his guitar playing than his singing," he said. "He was a true innovator like T-Bone Walker and B. B. King. He was a songwriting genius, and his guitar style has done more for rhythm and blues than anyone's."

For nine months, Fred and Sam were relegated to singing backup on other people's records while Curtis helped create what became known as the Chicago Sound. Three basic elements form the Chicago Sound—my father's guitar, Davis's production, and the arrangements of jazz-bassist-turned-arranger Johnny Pate.

Unlike the bass-heavy gutbucket soul coming out of Stax and Muscle Shoals, the backbone of the Chicago Sound is Curtis's guitar. "Because I play with my fingers and play a chord along with the melody, my style suggests two guitars," Dad said of his playing. "I [felt like I should try standard tuning] when I was around fifteen or sixteen, but by then, I was writing hit records and it was working. I felt proud because I had finally developed something that was totally mine."

Of course, he couldn't help but invent something unique. Tuning a guitar the way he did changes the tension of the strings, which changes the way they relate to the body of the guitar. In essence, it changes the dialect of the guitar. Curtis could play the same notes as another player and have them sound completely different because his guitar had an accent, *his* accent.

He went further in depth about his guitar style, saying:

My voicings are different compared to the standard. And even my favorite keys are unorthodox. For instance, F# or A, or B instead of B flat. When I first started, I played flat, like a steel guitar. And I was fretting with my thumb. You can play a lot of grooves that way. Eventually, I turned the guitar upright. Still, I thought, "My left thumb is closer to the bass string, why not use it?" So I carry the bass line with my thumb, where the average guitarist doesn't. That's not in the book. In the beginning, I used a clamp [capo]; that's how I changed keys. But after a while, I outgrew that. I've never taught myself to use a pick. That's why there are many things I can't do. When you can't do something, you find a way not to need it anyway. I pluck the strings very gentle. Almost the way I sing. I don't do nothin' hard. Rather than do a single-note lead part, I use chord movement . . . If it wasn't guitar, it would be piano. If it wasn't piano, it would be harp. It would have to be something that would give me a full chord movement. To sing a melody, I need a chord to ride upon.

If Curtis's guitar provides the backbone of the Chicago Sound, Johnny Pate's arrangements form the musculature. Davis said, "I chose to use Johnny in particular with the OKeh records because I wanted to develop what I thought was indicative of the Chicago kind of things. I always felt we were a bit of the South and a bit of the North combined. So I liked the syncopated rhythm and I liked the fact that he did the things with horns." Johnny's string and horn lines are particularly interesting when considering Chicago's history of big band and swing. In a way, he provided a link between Nat King Cole and soul.

––––––––

My father became a true producer through his experience at OKeh. He wrote the music, melodies, and lyrics, coached the artists on how to deliver them, and often presided over the sessions as they cut his songs—dozens of them, including Walter Jackson's "That's What Mama Say" and "It's All Over," and Major Lance's "You'll Want Me Back" and "Think Nothing About It." He'd always wanted control over all things in his life. Now, he had more of it than ever. He still felt insecure about his looks, his teeth, his stature, but with each new success, the sting of "Smut" momentarily faded.

He had no shortage of songs to keep success coming, either. Gerald Sims, one of Davis's partners at OKeh, said, "I used to go out to Curtis' house a lot of times, and Curtis would have a shopping bag full of tapes, and a lot of them were songs that he would only have six or eight bars to. Because when Curtis used to get an idea he would go to a tape recorder and put the idea down. Then he would go off into something else, and he would come back to it later on. A lot of times you'd pick up a tape and play it, and you'd get off into it, and then it would stop! You'd have to go back and ask him to finish this tune or finish that tune. So he would do it; he was very obliging about it and would go write you a complete tune."

Near the end of 1962, Major went through Dad's bag of songs again and cut one called "Delilah" for OKeh. It didn't chart, but it made enough noise for people to start paying attention. At the same time, Gene Chandler recorded a slow burner of my father's called "Rainbow." The song came out as the B-side to "You Threw a Lucky Punch," which Davis wrote as a response to Mary Wells's Motown smash "You Beat Me to the Punch." "Rainbow" ended up a surprise hit that rose fourteen places higher on the R&B chart than the A-side.

In rapid succession, Chandler hit again with another sultry Curtis tune called "Man's Temptation," which features revealing lyrics such as "This woman won't leave me alone / She's going to ruin my happy home with a man's temptation." The song reads as a deeply personal one, considering what my father was going through with Helen. The lyrics show a man in the painful position of having to choose between two women, and while Dad often wrote songs like this from his imagination, he had indeed begun courting another woman.

Earlier that year, a beautiful young girl named Diane had taken three of her girlfriends to see the Impressions at the Apollo. Even though she preferred the Miracles—after all, the Impressions just *stood* there on stage—Diane loved "Gypsy Woman." In fact, she knew most of the Impressions' music, though she didn't know Curtis by name. He wasn't quite famous enough yet, and although he sang lead, he didn't seem an obvious choice for the group's leader. He didn't have Sam's handsome facial features, and standing a squat five-foot-seven, he seemed diminutive next to Fred's heft and height. Anyone close to the group knew he held the power, though. Diane would soon find that out for herself.

Leaving the Apollo, the Impressions slipped into a limo and their road manager Eddie Suitor gunned the engine toward the hotel. At the same time, Diane and her friends crossed the street to get to the subway. As the limo bore down on them, Suitor slammed on the brakes, just missing the girls. Fred and Sam got out, apologized, and offered them tickets to the show the next night in Brooklyn. Curtis, ever the loner, sulked in his plush seat without saying a word.

After the show in Brooklyn, Diane and her friends went backstage where a gaggle of hangers-on milled about, everyone dressed to the nines. The Impressions still wore suits or tuxedos, while many other men sported the Mod look—bright, colorful suits with frills and cravats, wide ties, trouser straps, leather boots, and collarless jackets popularized by the Beatles. Diana Ross led the way for Negro women, with classic wigs, knee-length flared dresses, and fake eyelashes. For the adventurous, the miniskirt had just been invented; for those wanting to project chic airs, Jackie Kennedy's pillbox hat became iconic.

Curtis, Fred, and Sam mingled with the stylishly garbed crowd, but they were men set apart. Youth culture was exploding, and they stood at its vanguard. Beautiful women cast flirting looks at them. Men gave them soul-brother handshakes. The whole place crackled with post-performance energy and the manic hum of a bunch of young guys trying to get laid. My father wasn't the only one cheating—Fred and Sam already had New York girlfriends.

Eventually, Curtis found Diane. He didn't say much that night, but as the evening wore on, people disappeared until it was just the two of them. At that point, he warmed up a bit. They exchanged numbers and arranged middlemen and middle-women, since Diane was married and had a young son named Tracy, and the two parted company.

Diane found Curtis to be attractive in his sincerity; he seemed to deeply believe whatever he said. She also didn't mind that he had a little bit of money, since she came from the same low-income background he did. The Impressions pulled in about $100,000 a year, and my father's work with OKeh also poured in royalties—quite a sum for 1962.

No matter how much money he made, Dad always lived a modest life. He appreciated fancy things, like a sleek new Jaguar bought with the proceeds from "Gypsy Woman," but that's not why he wanted money. He wanted it because it gave him the power and control no one in his family had growing up, except Annie Bell. Money made him *the man*, which meant he could buy his family new furniture and food. It meant he could afford a nice home. It also meant he could attract women.

In the furtive early days of their relationship, he'd call Diane and say, "What did you do today?" to which she might answer, "Well I was just window shopping," and he'd reply, "Was there something you saw? Because I'll send you the money for it." In such a way, the relationship deepened. It reinforced the message Curtis had learned from Annie Bell—music made him special. It brought him everything he wanted, including beautiful women who might not have looked at him twice if not for his money and fame. He and Diane rarely saw each other—he was either on tour or in Chicago, and she lived in New York—but she'd make a point to see him whenever the Impressions swung through her region. The rest of the time, they'd write letters or talk on the phone.

———

As 1963 dawned, Davis offered my father a job as associate producer, and the two presided over OKeh's renaissance as a soul label. My father faced incredible pressure, like a juggler with too many balls in the air, but somehow he managed it all without losing his cool aloofness. He continued adding to his fame, fortune, reputation, and, most important, control.

He'd spend all week producing and recording in the studio. On weekends, he'd shoot around the country on tours with the Impressions, only to come back for more writing, rehearsing, and recording. Somehow he also kept up relationships with Helen, who was now pregnant, and Diane, who left her husband (and would become pregnant with me two years later).

Curtis received the news he'd be a father at roughly the same age as his father, and his first son would be born into a house just as fraught with marital tensions. If nothing else, his son wouldn't face the same financial hardship. Dad knew the more he wrote, the more he'd earn, and after he penned a minor hit called "We Girls" for Jan Bradley, Chess Records wanted to hire him as a writer. He would have taken the job, but Chess wanted a piece of the publishing, and he wouldn't give it up. That was his business sense—owning himself meant more than anything, more even than working for one of the nation's biggest labels.

He didn't need the gig anyway. While Fred and Sam grumbled about doing background work, ABC grew restless watching them score hits for OKeh. After almost a year of silence, the Impressions cut a slow ballad called "Sad, Sad Girl and Boy." It didn't fare well on the charts, but it did hint at the Impressions' new direction.

During their hiatus, my father, Fred, and Sam pushed themselves to create a new sound as a trio. Fred and Sam lived next to each other in Chicago, and Curtis would drive out to them from his house in Markham, a small suburb south of the city. They'd sit in Fred or Sam's basement, working all night. Curtis would pick out their vocal notes on guitar, and they'd sing them over and over until they figured out how to make three voices do the same work five used to do. Their bond became unbreakable in that basement—just three kids camped around a guitar with everything to prove and one goal in mind.

Other than Eddie, Dad would never have closer friends than Fred and Sam. For a decade, they spent more time with each other than they did with their families. Dad grew to trust and love them. He looked at them as brothers. But brothers or not, they'd eventually learn my father could easily separate friendship from business. It was one of many areas where his dual nature as a Gemini came into play. He could cherish a filial bond; he could be kindhearted and generous—but, as Miles Davis often said, geniuses are selfish. My father was a genius, and when it came to money, power, and control, he wanted all of it. If he had to harm or end a close relationship in the process, he would.

That wouldn't happen to Fred and Sam for a few years, though. Practicing in the basement, they became three parts of the same voice. The trio left no room for ego—Dad had to learn to fall into backing harmony as he traded leads with Fred and Sam. Sam also had to adjust, as the new arrangements forced him to sing uncomfortable notes. "They were taking me out of my range," he said. "When the whole group was together, I was doing a lot of bass singing. After the Brooks brothers left, they started raising me up."

Sam stretched himself to hit those notes because he understood the power of singing in a range where few other male singers could compete: "We were trying to establish something that nobody else had, so we said we'll sing higher than anybody else."

With their new format, the Impressions found something unique in R&B music, although that sort of interplay among voices—trading parts of the lead back and forth, singing in unison and then breaking off into harmony—was nothing new. As Curtis said, "In gospel, you knew how to sing lead and also how to incorporate yourself into the group, how to blend in. Sometimes everyone would come out and sing harmony with a portion of the lead. It made us [as] a three-man group stronger than we were as a five-man group. It locks everybody in; you really know where the voices are. When you have four or five men, if one moves up, the other doesn't know where to go." Many artists had drawn from gospel's deep, holy well to make great secular music, but none had done it in the harmonic way of the Impressions.

"Sad, Sad Girl and Boy" represented an important step leading the Impressions forward as a trio. It also marked five consecutive failed singles. Even worse, despite all his success for other artists, Curtis still had not written a real blockbuster. He knew to reach that level, he needed to come up with something truly inspired.

————

Back on the chitlin' circuit at the Top Hat in Nashville, Tennessee, the Impressions hired Bob Fisher and the Bonnevilles (sometimes referred to as the Barnevilles) to open for them. The Bonnevilles featured a young guitarist named Jimmy Hendrix, who had kicked around the circuit playing for the likes of the Isley Brothers, Little Richard, and even Jerry Butler. Hendrix looked like he could use a good meal, but he could play the hell out of his guitar, and he revered my father, copying his lyrical style of play-ing. Four years later, Jimmy would become Jimi and change the course of music history. For the time being, he was just a kid playing alongside one of his idols (according to one story of that tour, Hendrix borrowed Dad's amplifier without asking and turned it up so loud, it broke).

During that stop, my father wrote two of the most important songs of his life. One was a catchy tune called "The Monkey Time," written to go along with a new dance craze called the monkey. The Impressions didn't do dance numbers, so Dad put it in the bag to await another artist, as he always did when he wrote a song Fred and Sam didn't want.

The other song came to him after the first set at the Top Hat. Sit-ting in the green wagon with Fred and Sam waiting for the next show to begin, Dad "got to talking and running off at the mouth and just dreaming about ideas and things that might happen to us in the future," Sam recalled. "Fred kept answering back . . . 'Well, all right, well, that's all right,' you know. Before I knew it, it rang in my head. We had a real hook line, 'It's All Right,' so I said, 'Say it's all right.' Before we knew it, we had actually written two-thirds of that tune right there in the car! We could have gone on stage for the next show and sung it."

They often worked that way, constantly rehearsing and tightening their sound anywhere and everywhere. Between sets, while other artists might take a break or chase girls, the Impressions worked on their har-monies. Even jostling from town to town in the cramped wagon, my father always had his guitar slung across his body. "I drove most of the time," Fred said, "and Curtis would be in the back, playing the guitar, Sam sitting on the passenger's side. And he'd be writing and playing songs for us to kind of bounce them off of us."

When they returned to Chicago, Major Lance had nothing to work on, and Davis couldn't wait to get him back in the studio for several reasons. Chief among them, Major was hard to deal with when not busy. Davis said, "He knew that I liked coffee, so he'd run out and get me cups of coffee. Every five minutes, he would run out and get me another cup. It got to the point where either I had to keep him busy in the studio, or have a stroke from a caffeine overdose."

To find Major a song, Davis paid a visit to Curtis's house in Markham. He couldn't believe the number of songs my father had in the works. After playing the potential songs, my father said, "Which one do you like?" Davis replied, "I like all of 'em! What ones are you not going to do on the group?"

"Well, I know we're not gonna do 'The Monkey Time,'" Curtis said, "because that's a dance tune, and Fred and Sam don't want to do dance tunes." Of course, that was the song Davis wanted in the first place. "You had to learn to work around Curtis," Davis said wryly. He took the song to Johnny Pate, who wrote the arrangement, and Major cut it.

The song charted at number eight pop and number two R&B, making Major a bona fide star. It also propelled the fad dance to the height of pop culture, along with Smokey Robinson and the Miracles' "Mickey's Monkey." After the song's success, Major even bought a monkey, causing my father to have a little fun at his expense.

One day, Major made one of his regular visits to Grandma Sadie's house—as Uncle Kenny says, "A lot of [Curtis's] entertainment friends would hang out at Grandma's house, because Grandma loved to cook rolls, and when Grandma cooked rolls, the whole neighborhood lined up." When Major arrived with the monkey on a leash, Uncle Kenny recalls, "We were peeking in the car and [Curtis] was saying, 'Which one is Major?'"

"The Monkey Time" also featured Fred and Sam on backing vocals, making it the first session where all three Impressions worked with Johnny Pate. "That was my first introduction to arranging," Dad said. "Everything prior to that, we'd just try to nail the rhythm and get it through. But Johnny gave me my first encounter with real arranging. . . . He was the love of my life as far as real arrangers go." After the session with Major, my father approached Johnny and said, "My group's the Impressions, and we're with ABC/Paramount. We got a session coming up, and we'd like to have you do the arrangement on it." Johnny agreed.

Working with Johnny changed their lives. Sam said, "He started putting brass, and he put funky rhythm in our track, and he would enhance the vocal. Man, it just made you sing." For his part, Johnny approached the gig philosophically, saying, "I never tried to cover what Curtis was doing, because Curtis was the artist. He was the star, and the Impressions were the star. I was merely background."

From the first session, something special happened when Johnny and the Impressions came together. Usually the group ripped through three or four songs in one day—a pace Dad kept up most of his career. But when they recorded "It's All Right" in August 1963, the song stopped them dead. "We didn't record anything else that day," Fred recalled. "We just kept on playing that song over and over again, and we were just wondering if this was a hit. Then Gene Chandler said, 'Let me tell you something—if y'all don't want that song, give it to me. This is a hit.'"

My father left that day with the only acetate, but Fred and Sam were so intoxicated by the song, they drove all the way out to Markham from Chicago just to hear it. They knew Chandler was right. "When we recorded that song, I discovered what it meant to make the magic," my father said.

———

"It's All Right" was Curtis's first great party song. Shedding the mystical, lovelorn overtones that colored much of his previous work, his lyrics simply invite the listener to have a good time. A finger-snapping shuffle drives the song, punctuated by Johnny's horn blasts. It cruises on that groove as Curtis trades the call-and-response chorus with Fred and Sam. It is deceptively simple, though. A close listen shows how tight and intricate the Impressions' vocal arrangements had become, trading between lead and background, harmony and unison with expertly timed precision.

"It's All Right" shot to the top spot on the R&B chart. My father finally had a single digit beside one of his songs. In fact, the Impressions would never record a more successful song. As Fred recalled, "That song bought Sam's home, Curtis' home, and my home; we all bought homes off that song. By twenty-one, twenty-two years old, we all had our own homes and Cadillacs in the doggone garage."

It came just in time. While Motown continued pushing R&B music onto the pop charts with Marvin Gaye's "Pride and Joy" and the gospel-drenched "Can I Get a Witness," as well as Little Stevie Wonder's "Fingertips (Part 1)," and Martha and the Vandellas' "(Love Is Like a) Heat Wave," Stax began flowering with Booker T. and the M.G.'s, Rufus Thomas, and Otis Redding. On top of that, in February, Vee-Jay released "Please Please Me" by the Beatles, a group of guys about my father's age from Liverpool, England. Even though the song wouldn't hit in America for a year or so, it was a portent of things to come.

Still, party music was not my father's forte, and somewhere deep down he knew it. Serious changes were afoot in America, treacherous ones. The movement had entered a new phase the year before when James Meredith desegregated the University of Mississippi in Oxford. It took five hundred armed guards to allow Meredith to register, and even then, sneering students assailed the marshals with stones, bottles, bricks, clubs, iron bars, gasoline bombs, and guns.

Then, in early May 1963, the movement had its most public, iconic, and brutal moment yet when the Birmingham police turned skin-searing fire hoses and snarling dogs on a group of peaceful demonstrators. Water cannons ripped the clothes off the demonstrators' backs, and images of the travesty rocketed around the world.

My father paid rapt attention to the news. More than that, he watched the country seethe in turmoil as he traveled the South. The Impressions performed in Birmingham around this time and Eddie remembers, "The hatred was strong, strong in Birmingham. We did our show and we left. We didn't stay around." The indignities my father suffered traveling through the South, and those he watched others endure, stirred the soul deep within him.

In August, Martin Luther King Jr. and his allies pulled off the biggest public demonstration the movement would ever stage—the March on Washington. They hoped to pressure the government into passing the Civil Rights Act, which Kennedy had quietly introduced months before.

On a sunny Wednesday morning, more than two hundred thousand people marched to the Lincoln Memorial, and the movement elbowed its way to center stage in American life. "The Negro is shedding himself of his fear," King said, "and my real worry is how we will keep this fearlessness from rising to violent proportions."

Fortunately, the march remained nonviolent, and when King rose to give his speech, the spirit of the crowd overtook him. "I started out reading the speech," he said, "and all of a sudden this thing came to me that I have used many times before, that thing about 'I had a dream,' and I just felt that I wanted to use it here. I don't know why, I hadn't thought about it before the speech."

King's "I Have a Dream" speech might have been off-the-cuff, but it was recognized immediately as one of the great pieces of oration in American history. A poet himself, my father recognized the speech's beauty and latched onto its spirit, even as another faction of the movement mocked King's hope. This other faction, less patient and peaceful, was summed up by Malcolm X's reaction to the speech: "You know, this dream of King's is going to be a nightmare before it's over." Two weeks later, dynamite blasted apart Birmingham's Sixteenth Street Baptist Church and killed four young Negro girls attending Sunday school.

A few months later, a bullet ended President Kennedy's life in Dallas, Texas, throwing the country and movement into panic. Kennedy was the most sympathetic president to Negro rights since a bullet ended Abraham Lincoln's life a hundred years before. An eerie similarity between the two assassinations existed—in 1963, as in 1865, a southerner named Johnson ascended to the presidency. Lincoln's successor, Andrew Johnson, ended the Reconstruction and plunged Negroes back into quasi-slavery for the next hundred years. No one knew how Kennedy's successor, a tough, drawling Texan named Lyndon Johnson, would react to the fight against Jim Crow.

During this time of great uncertainty, many movement activists adopted "It's All Right" as a message song. They took strength and solace from lyrics like "When you wake up early in the morning / Feeling sad like so many of us do / Hum a little soul, make life your goal / And surely something's got to come to you." My father didn't mean it that way—he wasn't quite mature enough as an artist. Regardless, the song spoke to the activists, giving them the assurance they needed to continue their difficult, dangerous work. Noticing the way people interpreted his song inspired Dad and opened his mind to new possibilities.

———

As 1963 drew to a close, it seemed everyone was talking, arguing, and worrying about the country's state. James Farmer, director of CORE, eloquently outlined the movement's goals on a PBS panel discussion featuring Malcolm X, Wyatt Tee Walker, and *Ebony* magazine editor Alan Morrison, saying:

> We aren't going to stop until black skin is no longer considered a badge of deformity by the American people, we are not going to stop until the dogs stop biting little children in Alabama, until the rats in tenement slums in Harlem and the hundred Harlems throughout the country stop biting our people. We are not going to stop until the bigots of the South and the North no longer challenge a man's right to live simply because he is asking for the rights which the Constitution says are his . . . We are not going to stop, in a word, until we have the same rights that all Americans have. We are not going to stop until we have jobs and are not walking the street unemployed in a proportion which is more than two times as great as among whites. We are not going to stop until we have the right to a house, a decent home, an apartment, any place we choose to live. We are not going to stop until we have the right to enter any place which serves the public all over the country. We are not going to stop, in a word, until America becomes America for all people.

At the same time, Malcolm X continued sniping at the stated purpose and so-called gains of the movement: "If the NAACP can tell me that they won a desegregation decision for me ten years ago, but yet the schools haven't been desegregated, this is a victory with no victory. It's a

victory that you can talk about, but it's a victory that you can't show me
. . . We don't want to be equal with the white man. He's not the criteria
or yard stick by which equality is measured. He's not in a position to tell
us we are equal. It's not his right. It's not his to do."

As these factions battled within the movement, pop music joined
its ranks. The recent events of the era inspired Bob Dylan to write a
powerful message song called "Blowin' in the Wind." When Dad's idol,
Sam Cooke, heard the song he couldn't believe a white man had written
it. Cooke decided to make his own statement, producing a three-minute
opus called "A Change Is Gonna Come."

Dad heard these songs, and he also heard the people around him
talking about their struggles, fears, hardships, and hopes. With the birth
of his first son—Curtis III, nicknamed "Curt Curt"—in 1963, he contemplated the invisible box that constricted American Negroes through
the eyes of his child. He yearned to throw his own work into the growing
fray of socially conscious songs. He knew he could add something valuable to the fight. Even at such a young age, he was a big-picture thinker.
He wasn't the type to pick up a sign and start marching or get involved in
the day-to-day machinations of the movement. Rather, he could observe
it from a wide angle and use his poetic mind to craft something that
spoke to people's souls, same as the gospel tunes he sang in Annie Bell's
church.

He didn't have much time to write such a song, though. On top of
the demands of a new baby, which Helen bore the brunt of, he also had
to capitalize on the success of "It's All Right" and write new material
for Major and other OKeh artists. To cover the gap, ABC released the
Impressions' first album—a compilation of their singles to date. It featured ten of my father's compositions, as well as a song credited to Richard Brooks, and the Impressions' cover of Johnny Ace's doo-wop classic
"Never Let Me Go." The latter is particularly interesting—it proves the
Impressions could have been a hell of a doo-wop group had they wanted,
but Curtis's mind had long since wandered to other places.

In January 1964, the Impressions released "Talking About My Baby,"
which rose to number twelve on the pop chart. Like "It's All Right" before
it, "Talking About My Baby" was made for the party crowd. The song

shows the Impressions continuing to perfect the gospel-tinged interplay among the three voices and also contains another example of my father's brilliance on the guitar. Listen to how he phrases the first three chords of the song, how he flicks those first two hard and then lays back and lets the third just *happen*, dead in the pocket with the sock cymbal. That's his genius.

The next month, the Beatles debuted on *The Ed Sullivan Show*, marking the beginning of the British Invasion, which would crowd the pop charts for the rest of the decade. Even so, Curtis found space for several hits cut by Billy Butler, whom he taught to play guitar. Billy played with the Enchanters, and they toured with the Impressions, Gene Chandler, the Vibrations, and the Drifters throughout '63 and '64. They didn't have a hit until Curtis wrote "Gotta Get Away," which spent three consecutive weeks on the R&B chart, followed by "Nevertheless," "You're Gonna Be Sorry," "Does It Matter," and "I'm Just a Man." Gene Chandler also recorded a dozen of Curtis's songs, most hitting the R&B charts.

Major needed new material too, so Curtis gave him songs like "It Ain't No Use," "Girls," and "Rhythm." At the end of 1963, Major had released another of my father's songs, "Um, Um, Um, Um, Um, Um (Curious Mind)," and by early '64 it had become bigger than "The Monkey Time." It seemed impossible that one man could write so many hits in such a short time, but Dad's prolific pen never ran dry.

"Um, Um, Um, Um, Um, Um (Curious Mind)" gave Carl Davis his first taste of my father's uncompromising business sense. The original lyrics told the story of mystical sirens who sang a song so beautiful, dumbstruck sailors couldn't help but steer toward the island and shipwreck. Davis didn't think this Homeric tale had legs in the pop market, so he asked Curtis to rewrite the lyrics and include a love story.

With any other artist, Davis's suggestion would earn him songwriting credit. But as he recalled, "[Curtis] would never share any of the writing credits with me or anyone else. Because of that, he never shared any of the revenues with me either. That's something that Curtis just wouldn't do . . . He wouldn't give up any of his publishing or writing credits. If you worked with Curtis, you had to do things his way." Or, as Herb Kent put it: "If you made a dollar, then Curtis made five."

My father remained this way throughout his career, causing irreparable rifts with some of his closest friends. But, for as many royalties as Davis lost, Dad lost something perhaps more valuable by allowing so many other artists to score huge hits with his songs. It kept him obscure. If these hits had all come out on the Impressions, which they could have, the true extent of his genius would have been impossible to miss. Diffused as the songs were, my father remained just under the radar. No one could complain too much, though, as "Um, Um, Um, Um, Um, Um" hit number five on the pop chart and went to the top of the R&B chart—my father's second number one.

He was on a serious roll. Unlike at Motown, where a factory of writers created the hits, at OKeh, Curtis *was* the factory. He didn't spend too much time worrying about where the credit went, as long as the money came to the right place, and the next Impressions single kept the money rolling in. "I'm So Proud" was a gorgeous ballad that hit high on the charts, although the group never wanted it released as a single. As Fred recalled:

> The record company called and said, "We're gonna release 'I'm So Proud.'" We had a fit. We were still writing it, and we wanted to release an up-tempo tune called "I'm the One Who Loves You." They bet us any amount of money that this song, "I'm So Proud," was going to be a big hit for the Impressions . . . Man, that killed our groove for the whole day . . . We were young, not knowing that the record company had the money; they could make it a hit record if they wanted to. And they did. That was one of our biggest records. After they got through with it, they said, "All right, what do y'all think now?" We had to eat our words.

The label's decision turned out fortuitous for more than just the Impressions. At that time, three kids in Jamaica formed a loose little group called the Wailers, and they based their sound and style on the Impressions. The trio of Bob Marley, Peter Tosh, and Bunny Wailer even dressed like the Impressions. As Bunny recalled, "We were fascinated by the way they did this song, 'I'm So Proud.' Out of that song came [the

Wailers'] 'It Hurts to Be Alone.'" When the Impressions toured Jamaica that year, the young Wailers sat in the first row of the Carib Theatre.

At the time of the Impressions' visit, Jamaica suffered under a racist system similar to America's, and the island's own civil rights movement had just begun burgeoning. As my father watched his Caribbean brothers struggle, it reignited his passion to write songs that spoke to the times. He dipped back to his days listening to Annie Bell's sermons, pondering the power of the church while watching his country change around him.

Across the South, movement activists continued to die grisly deaths. Closer to Curtis's home, comedian and activist Dick Gregory led protest marches through Mayor Daley's segregated neighborhood in Chicago. Martin Luther King Jr. was nominated for a Nobel Peace Prize—he'd already been *Time* magazine's Man of the Year for 1963—and Congress seemed tantalizingly close to passing the Civil Rights Act. Meanwhile, great antagonism electrified the gap between militants like Malcolm X and moderates like King. My father revered King and believed Negroes couldn't let these divisions stop their momentum.

With all that in mind, he started scribbling lyrics and fitting them to a melody. He finished the song in a hotel room on tour. Around two in the morning, Fred heard a gentle knock on his door. He cracked it open and squinted into the hallway light. He could just make out my father standing there in his pajamas. "Hey man, come and listen to this and see what you think of it," my father said. "I wrote something that maybe can help motivate the people."

Cradling his guitar at the edge of his bed, he played "Keep On Pushing" for the first time. When he finished, Fred stood dumbstruck. "Where did you come up with all these words?" he finally asked. My father replied, "I'm living."

Dad had been training to write a song like "Keep On Pushing" his entire life. It used the same rhythms he learned in Annie Bell's church, only now the terms had changed. He said, "All I needed to do was change 'God gave me strength, and it don't make sense not to keep on pushing,' to '*I've* got my strength, and it don't make sense.'. . . Nothing else needed to be changed."

"Keep On Pushing" explodes from the speaker with a crash cymbal, while Dad's guitar flutters around the beat like a hummingbird. He sings the whole song in falsetto and hits an extra gear in the chorus, pushing himself near the limit of his range. Up there, he unleashes a gorgeous warble from a place few men can reach. During the verses, Johnny's hypnotic horn line echoes the vocal melody, flirting with the waltz rhythm, and providing a contrapuntal call-and-response as my father, Fred, and Sam sing:

> *Look a yonder, what's that I see?*
> *A great big stone wall stands there ahead of me*
> *But I've got my pride, and I move the wall aside*
> *And keep on pushing. Hallelujah! Keep on pushing.*

The song was a call to arms, a salve to the fractures within the movement, and a message of hope. "Move up a little higher, some way, somehow," my father urged. He never wanted to be a preacher, but he'd just written his first sermon. Like the best sermons—King's "I Have a Dream" speech, for example, which still rung in Dad's head—it had a strong hook and made the impossible seem within reach.

Unlike a religious preacher, though, Dad paired his sermons with melody and rhythm. DJs put them in heavy rotation on radio stations across the country. In such a way, he could preach to people who never set foot in a church, and do it without them knowing it. "Painless preaching," he'd later call it. The single came out in July and rose to the top slot of the R&B chart—my father's third number one.

Curtis the messenger had arrived.

————

After "Keep On Pushing," Dad became an icon. People began recognizing him when he went out to dinner or walked down the street. They'd approach him breathlessly, sometimes wanting an autograph, sometimes just wanting to shake his hand. He'd smile from ear to ear and charm them with his soft voice. He always reacted graciously, and he noticed the effect he had. His fans seemed to glow as they walked away from meeting him. "It wasn't like they were starstruck," my brother Tracy recalls. "It was more admiration, humble admiration for him."

Now he had more than just money. His face became a form of currency—dark skin, big teeth, and all. It set him apart in a good way. The name Curtis Mayfield was currency too. It meant something. Uncle Kenny recalls going to a convenience store with Curtis and Marion, and when Curtis walked up to the counter to buy something, the cashier said, "Man, you look like Curtis Mayfield." Dad said, "I am Curtis Mayfield." "Aw, you lyin'," the man said. In later years, after the novelty of fame had worn off, my father might have let it drop at that, happy to get away unmolested. For now, he said, "There's my mother, there's my brother— you ask them." The cashier glowed, too. That was the power of fame.

The added attention cut both ways, though—it helped relieve my father's insecurities, but it also added new ones. He could never know who his real friends were. People came at him from all directions. If someone went out of their way to treat him well, he had to gauge their motives. A host of hard questions faced him at every turn—who do you trust, who do you let close, how do you know if they want to hurt you? Sometimes—as Fred, Sam, Eddie, and Johnny would soon learn—he'd put his trust in the wrong people, treating friends like enemies and vice versa.

As "Keep On Pushing" rode high on the charts, the eponymous album followed in suit. *Keep On Pushing* was the Impressions' first proper album, as opposed to a collection of singles, and it reflected the growing trend in pop music. The album as a statement existed long before 1964, but it was fast becoming the dominant art form in a world once ruled by singles. The Impressions released *Keep On Pushing* into a musical landscape still quaking from the Beatles' *A Hard Day's Night*, Dylan's *The Times They Are A-Changin'*, Otis Redding's *Pain in My Heart*, and the Supremes' *Where Did Our Love Go*. These came out alongside landmark albums by the Rolling Stones, the Kinks, Sam Cooke, Muddy Waters, the Beach Boys, the Miracles, and a plethora of other soon-to-be icons. With *Keep On Pushing*, the Impressions put themselves at the forefront of this exploding musical landscape and exited the doo-wop age forever.

The album contained five top forty pop and R&B singles, including a version of a spiritual called "Amen," which my father reimagined with Johnny Pate as a triumphant march. He'd decided to cover the song after he heard Sidney Poitier sing it in the 1963 film *Lilies of the Field*. Johnny came up with the idea to open with an allusion to the old Negro spiritual "Swing Low, Sweet Chariot," and he also suggested the marching beat groove. The song hit number seven on the pop chart and provided Dad with his fourth number-one R&B hit within one year.

His seemingly endless string of hits continued with a catchy song called "You Must Believe Me" and two B-sides that also charted. The first of the B-sides, an epic, haunting ballad called "I've Been Trying," showcased my father's increasing finesse as a songwriter and highlighted the inherent rhythm in his guitar playing. It was also a perfection of the falsetto vocal style the Impressions had begun working on after the Brooks brothers left. As Johnny said, "On the end of 'I've Been Trying,' the group went into some high falsetto harmonic things that was really unheard of. Nobody had really done that. After Curtis and the guys did that, we just kind of flipped over it, the way it came out. A few sessions down the line, Curtis came up with a tune called 'I Need You,' and they did it again. This began to be a signature thing for the Impressions."

The second charting B-side, "Long Long Winter," made a further argument for Curtis as one of the great guitar players and songwriters of his era. Bob Marley and the Wailers would soon cover it as well as the album's closing track, "I Made a Mistake."

———

"Keep On Pushing" helped take the movement further into the mainstream just as Congress passed the Civil Rights Act in July 1964. The act outlawed discrimination against "racial, ethnic, national, and religious minorities, and women," and ended "unequal application of voter registration requirements and racial segregation in schools, at the workplace, and by facilities that serve the general public." When President Johnson signed it into law, Negroes breathed a sigh of relief. It seemed Kennedy's successor would be a friend—or at least not an outright enemy. With the act in place, hope within the movement reached its pinnacle.

At the same time, my father experienced two great losses. On June 28, Kirby died of an enlarged heart. Only eighteen years old, he lived his entire life with severe mental disabilities. Even Mannish showed up at the funeral, where Uncle Kenny recalls seeing his father for the first time since he left.

As my father mourned Kirby and toured *Keep On Pushing*, he decided to leave Helen. His relationship with Diane had only deepened, and he yearned to pursue the woman in his heart. After his mother wrote him a letter that no longer survives, he wrote back from New York on November 14, 1964. His writing seems at times stilted and too formal, perhaps trying to make up for his lack of schooling, but his reply shows a tenderness and maturity uncommon for someone so young:

Dear Mother,

Here's hoping that you are doing well. I did receive your letter and have read it several times as you have asked. Of course your letter is nothing new to me for all you have said has been in my mind for a great length of time before my love son was born, in which I think has been time enough to consider carefully your letter. Despite of my success in the business world, I must submit to being young, therefore I am considered under rank as you might say. But how old must I be to know my own mind? Or realize what is best for myself, my wife, and my beloved son? I am sure there is no doubt in your mind of my loving our Curt Curt. Might I live with him or away from him, I know I would be a better father to him than some with their sons, and yet I know this is not enough, for it does take two in most cases to give a child the teaching and guidance he needs. We both agree.

I have now been married over three years. I am sorry to say that I've been unhappy a large portion of this time. My wife is a good woman, I need not tell you this despite of her ways. And yet things have happened within our home that has caused my love for her to die. For over a year because of our child to come I have tried and failed in arousing my love for her. Mother, I am not one to pretend I do not love my wife, which I have told her, and my respect for her will not let me lead her on as I have in the past. A woman with a child needs more than a husband. She also needs love and affection, in which now only my son receives because of the lost feeling for my mate. Maybe you say Curt Curt's a child and don't know the difference, so resolve in some more constructive way, as thousands do . . . But Curt Curt is not enough. I do not believe an unhappy marriage helps a child or children in any way. Children are people with their own minds. Sooner or later, anything concealed from him will come out. Living with him or away shall amount to the same problems he'll have to face. I am not so worried about Curt Curt, for if he's anything like his daddy, he'll have a mind of his own.

I can still respect my father as a man, and so can you. Would you rather live with him and he not love you? You did this with Al [Jackson] and what came of it? It only brought bitterness and unhappiness of yourself and your children toward a man who didn't love you. You asked the question, "Would I deliberately condemn my baby son of the same misfortune?" Our only misfortune was being poor. I imagine it was harder on you of not having a husband than our not having a father. I love my son and respect his mother, and there's nothing I wouldn't do for the both of them. It is not my intention to say, "The Hell with it, shucking my responsibilities for some corner of the Earth." I think I have proved myself to you and my family. But I must be happy too if it means giving up everything I have. Call it selfish interest if you must. But I don't think it will deprive the little one of anything. I could not pretend to him that all is well when it is not.

Always your son,

Curt

Despite the losses, my father's life had taken several dramatic turns for the better during 1964. *Keep on Pushing* and his work at OKeh made him successful and rich beyond his hopes, and his new relationship with Diane lessened the sting of his failed marriage. He couldn't marry Diane since he hadn't divorced Helen—she wanted money as part of a settlement, and my father never liked parting with money. Regardless, like Annie Bell did with Wal, my mother changed her name to Mayfield, making Tracy a Mayfield too.

No one told Tracy that Curtis wasn't his biological father, echoing the situation between Judy and Annie Bell. He had to figure it out later in life. But, as Tracy recalls, Dad welcomed him as his own flesh and blood. "On his part, I didn't feel any iota of a difference," Tracy says. "He never once made me feel less than or different at all. When I looked at his face, I saw my father's face. When I heard his voice, I heard my father's voice."

After leaving Helen, Dad moved into a posh apartment in the Marina Towers, one of Chicago's most recognizable landmarks. The building looks like a multitiered spaceship, and he lived near the top of that spaceship, on the highest floor but one. From the windows, he could look down over the well-heeled theater district like a king observing his domain. The building stands less than two miles southeast of Cabrini, but it was a long way from the ghetto. The control he'd chased all his life seemed within his grasp, at least for the moment.

Dad enjoyed earning enough to carve out a place for himself and his family in a stuffy, upper-class white area. His elevation in social status was still new to him, though. He had the money, but not the manners. "He had poor table manners," my mother recalls. "We were somewhere and he was eating some ribs, and he was licking his fingers. Oh, that just turned me off. I was like, 'Curtis, can you just use your napkin?'"

Though he lived in a wealthy circle, his friends, family, and acquaintances still struggled with the same old poverty and hardships. He made sure to include them in his new wealth whenever possible, but the fact remained that he now straddled two worlds—the old world of the White Eagle, Cabrini-Green, and never having enough of anything, and the new one of fame, fortune, and excess.

My mother never felt comfortable in that new world. She says of Marina Towers, "The building basically was white people who had money, and you got a doorman. Nobody ever said anything, but maybe that was my insecurity, being a little girl from Harlem in this building with all these people who probably had a lot of money."

Aunt Ann felt uncomfortable there too. One day she came by but arrived while my parents were out. When they finally came back, Ann sat by their door waiting. She told them the doorman recognized her and let her up, and their white next-door neighbor saw her and invited her inside to wait, but she preferred to wait outside. The white residents of the building weren't hostile, but it was simply too hard coming from the slums to feel safe and comfortable in upper-class white America. The danger was real, as my mother learned on a trip to Cicero, the neighborhood that destroyed an entire building in 1951 when a Negro family moved there. "They called us names, and it scared me, and I turned around and went home," she says. "I didn't ever go back."

Though she didn't feel comfortable in the plush apartment, my mother felt more at home with Dad's family. On a visit to Grandma Sadie's house in Cabrini, she picked up some tips on how to make her greens better. She also cultivated close relationships with Marion and Annie Bell.

As the year wound down, everything seemed to be moving in the right direction for Dad. He had just experienced the most successful year of his life. He could even relax slightly when touring the South. Driving through Mississippi earlier in the year, the Impressions pulled to the side of the road, exhausted. They knew they couldn't stay there, but they couldn't drive on without risking falling asleep at the wheel. Stuck in a bind, Dad decided to go to a nearby Holiday Inn and see if they'd give him a room. Fred and Sam waited nervously outside as he entered the building and approached the clerk. A few minutes later he appeared again, a grin pasted on his face. He waved them inside. They'd stay at Holiday Inns exclusively for the next several years.

Life had never been so good. Then, two weeks before Christmas, Sam Cooke was brutally murdered under circumstances that remain mysterious. After so many dizzying highs, Curtis greeted 1965 mourning both his brother and his hero.

It was a harbinger of things to come.

6

People Get Ready

"What has happened, what has caused this to be?
Have I become insane or is this true reality?"
—"I've Found That I've Lost"

February 21, 1965, Audubon Ballroom, Manhattan—Malcolm X knew the men who came to kill him. Standing before a large crowd of Negro Muslims, he prepared to give his remarks on his new Organization of Afro-American Unity. Before he could start, a man walked to the stage, raised a sawed-off shotgun concealed under his coat, and pulled the trigger. On cue, two other men stood up and emptied handguns into Malcolm's body.

The months leading to Malcolm X's assassination marked the most intense and fractious period since the movement had begun. As his biographer Manning Marable wrote, "The fragile unity that had made possible the great efforts in Montgomery and Birmingham was showing signs of strain. The arguments between so-called radicals like John Lewis and more mainstream black leaders like King and Ralph Abernathy had not abated, and as long-desired goals finally came within sight, they had the peculiar effect of further splintering the movement."

Watching the movement unravel around him, Dad found solace, as always, in his guitar. In what he called "a deep mood, a spiritual state of mind," he put together the follow-up to "Keep On Pushing." He showed the song—a breathtaking ballad called "People Get Ready"—to Johnny in his normal way. "Curtis would usually bring me the material on a cassette tape," Johnny said. "When he brought me the songs, it was nothing but guitar and voice. Generally, with Curtis, he would have no idea what the arrangement was going to sound like until we got to the session. We never had the opportunity to sit down and work out an arrangement together. He would bring me the basic tape, and at that point, he'd get back with Fred and Sam, they would work out the harmonies, and then we would hit the studio."

Fred and Sam learned the song, but before hitting the studio, they had a run of shows with the Temptations, Smokey Robinson and the Miracles, Martha and the Vandellas, and the Marvelettes. At the Uptown Theater in Philadelphia, they gave the audience a tantalizing hint of what was to come.

During the show, they got into a singing battle with the Temptations. Fred recalled, "The Temptations went out and did one of our songs, 'Gypsy Woman.' So when it was time for us to go on, we went out and did one of their songs, 'The Girl's Alright with Me.' And then, it was on. We would do a song; they would do a song. The host of the show was Georgie Woods, and he just let us go at it."

After the third or fourth encore, the Impressions stood backstage caught in a bind. They'd run out of songs, but the audience screamed for more. My father said, "Well, we got 'People Get Ready.'" Sam nervously spoke up: "Are you sure we can do this song? We just learned it." My father replied in his customary seat-of-the-pants way, "Sure, let's give it a try." They returned onstage to a chorus of cheers, and Dad plucked the opening chords. "You could almost hear a pin drop in there," Sam said. "It was so soulful, man, it just knocked these people out."

It knocked Johnny out, too. "The song touched me quite a bit," he said. "I listened to the lyrics, I listened to the melody, and I thought, 'This could be a big, big song,' because of the message that was involved, for one thing, and because of the way Curtis was delivering it. You could tell he was bringing something really that he felt." They cut it immediately after the tour ended, and ABC released the single just after Malcolm's assassination.

––––––––––

"People Get Ready" plays like a meditation, a hymn, a love letter to the fathomless strength and endless struggle of Negroes in America. It opens with a haunting, hummed melody that sends chills up the spine. Johnny's arrangement is masterful—pizzicato strings and lilting violin lines weaving around plinking chimes. Once Curtis begins singing, it is clear he'd found a way to merge the movement's vast hope with the fierce sadness and pain Negroes experienced trying to make that hope a reality.

My father intended "People Get Ready" to reach far back in history, even as it kept an eye on the future. His lyrics brought the coded messages of old Negro spirituals into the turbulent '60s. When he sang about a train to Jordan, everyone fighting for their rights in Mississippi, Alabama, Florida, and Georgia knew what he meant. Everyone who had migrated to Chicago, New York, Baltimore, Philadelphia, and California knew it too.

It was the same train that formed the Underground Railroad during slavery; it was the train that brought Annie Bell and millions like her to northern cities during the Great Migration; it was the movement train my father's generation boarded, determined to get to a better place or die trying.

Like "Keep On Pushing," the song had heavy gospel roots. "Lyrically you could tell it's from parts of the Bible," Dad said.

> "There's no room for the hopeless sinner who would hurt all mankind just to save his own / Have pity on those whose chances grow thinner, for there's no hiding place against the kingdom's throne." It's an ideal. There's a message there. I couldn't help myself for it. And it was also my own teachings, me talking to myself about my own moral standards. As a kid, sometimes you have nobody to turn to. I could always go back to some of the sermons and talk to myself in a righteous way. I had heard preachers speak of how there is "no

hiding place." If you've been around enough preachers, you'll see
how their words are in the song in one form or another. I wanted
to bring a little gospel into the drive for reality with the song, and
it also lent a pride to those who were oppressed and trying to define
themselves on another level.

Annie Bell left her imprint on his music once again, evoking his most
powerful poetry yet. In a way, he sang directly to her as she boarded the
Panama Limited with Mannish and Mercedes almost forty years before:

> *People get ready, there's a train a-comin'*
> *You don't need no baggage, you just get on board*
> *All you need is faith to hear the diesels hummin'*
> *Don't need no ticket, you just thank the Lord*
> *So people get ready for the train to Jordan*
> *Picking up passengers coast to coast*
> *Faith is the key, open the doors and board 'em*
> *There's hope for all among those loved the most.*

The single shot to number three R&B and number fourteen pop,
and the album hit the top spot on the R&B album chart. It was the only
Impressions album to rise that high, and the song remains one of their
most famous and recognizable works. After "People Get Ready," my
father became the foremost social commentator in pop music. He now
understood that the songs of his that contained conviction—dripped
with it, actually—tended to be ones that were *about* something.

Music had given Dad power to fight and sometimes defeat the
personal challenges that haunted him. He now saw music as a way to
combat another source of powerlessness in his life—being a Negro in
America. Only this time, everyone could benefit from his fight.

Songs like "People Get Ready" and "Keep On Pushing" didn't come
from his head whole cloth, though. Rather, they were works of journal-
ism, expressing the thoughts, feelings, and actions of his community in
a way the evening news never could. "I was observing things, what hap-

pened politically, what was in the paper, what was on television," he said. "Asking what things were wrong that oughta be right."

As the movement inspired my father to create these songs, he also inspired it. "'People Get Ready' was one that we used," said Andrew Young, one of King's partners. "None of us had great voices, but this was music that everybody could sing. You couldn't do Curtis Mayfield's falsetto, but we had kids who could. He was always one of the heroes of the Civil Rights Movement."

Shortly after the song became a hit, Chicago churches also began using "People Get Ready" in their services. Some churches changed the final couplet, "You don't need no ticket, you just thank the Lord," to "Everybody wants freedom, this I know."

———

People Get Ready featured lighter fare as well. "Woman's Got Soul," a great party/love song, charted at number nine R&B. "Can't Work No Longer" hit number six R&B later in the year for Billy Butler, and "We're in Love," "Get Up and Move," and "Just Another Dance" all had upbeat rhythms and simple messages about young love.

But as catchy as they were, these songs didn't approach the effect Dad's message music had on his fans. "I can remember ['People Get Ready'] just making people listen," he said. "It was so different from what was looked upon as a hit." He now knew his greatest strength as a songwriter came from the strength of his soul. After "People Get Ready," his fans expected him to put something heavy on their minds, and he embraced the role. "I'm not totally about being just an entertainer," he said. "It means a little bit more to me than that."

After the release, the Impressions began two months of constant touring and television appearances. For some reason, when they appeared on Dick Clark's *Where the Action Is*, they lip-synched "People Get Ready" as they rode a pleasure boat in Los Angeles's MacArthur Park. The visual clashed with the song's somber tone, but it was good exposure nonetheless.

On tour, "People Get Ready" added tremendous weight to the Impressions' style of performing. "When we came out, it was like we were in church, that's how the audience turned over," my father said. "They could just be screaming and hollering and getting down and boo-gieing with one artist, but when the Impressions came out, they would respectfully be quiet."

Sometimes, other artists on the bills would exit the stage mystified at the Impressions' static power. Fred said, "We did a lot of shows with James Brown, Jackie Wilson, and they said, 'Good Lord, you cats come back just like you went onstage.' James Brown said, 'Man, how can y'all go out there and don't sweat and don't do nothing but just sing and the people just go crazy? I have to go out there and work my butt off.' But, we had to rely on our voices because we couldn't dance."

Perhaps no one underscored how little the Impressions moved onstage better than Otis Redding. "We were doing a show with him at the Regal Theatre in Chicago," Fred recalled. "Otis came on before we did, and the stage was dirty. He was out there stompin', and sweatin', and stompin', and dust was flyin' all up, and when he was coming off, we were standing in the wings getting ready to come on behind him. He had dirt all up on his pants. It looked like he had been swimming. When he got to us, he looked at us, and we were nice and clean, and he said, 'Man, [you're] the only group I know that can do a show here for a whole week and don't have to change their shirt.'"

As my father said about his guitar playing, when you can't do something, you find a way not to need it. The Impressions couldn't dance. Instead, they relied on dazzling harmonies and stone-heavy messages to get over.

———

Traveling the South, my father saw how much his message songs were needed. He witnessed firsthand the hope and terror coursing through places like Alabama, where a few weeks after *People Get Ready* came out, King and the SCLC joined a march from Selma to Montgomery. With the Civil Rights Act still facing violent resistance, the marchers planned on demanding voting rights at the state capital.

The first attempt, on March 7, became known as "Bloody Sunday" after state and local police brutalized the marchers with clubs and tear gas as white spectators cheered and whistled. After a second attempt ended in failure—without violence this time—President Johnson addressed a nationwide television audience. Seventy million people watched Johnson say, "It is wrong—deadly wrong—to deny any of your fellow Americans the right to vote in this country." He ended by quoting the movement's slogan, vowing, "We shall overcome" America's "crippling legacy of bigotry and injustice." Never before had the movement received such strong federal endorsement.

The day after Johnson's speech, events in Montgomery foreshadowed the new direction the movement would take. That day, a group of Montgomery sheriff's deputies attacked a crowd of Student Nonviolent Coordinating Committee workers with nightsticks. Witnesses reported hearing the sound of the sticks cracking against skulls up and down the block. After the attack, SNCC's James Forman told the crowd if Montgomery was unwilling to let Negroes sit at the table of government, then SNCC would knock the "fucking legs" off the table.

Forman wasn't alone in advocating "violent overthrow of the government." Stokely Carmichael, a young movement worker who had been active since the early freedom rides, ascended the ranks of SNCC and thrust the organization toward militancy. Like Forman, Carmichael demanded a policy of freedom by "any means necessary." His ideas would soon father the next phase of the movement.

Around the time Curtis returned home from tour, King announced the SCLC would target Chicago as the first city in its northern campaign. King desperately needed to succeed in Chicago. For all his gains in the South, he knew life had barely changed for the vast majority of Negroes around the country. Even when it did change in places like Birmingham and Montgomery, it often went right back as soon as the SCLC left town. It seemed the future of the nonviolent movement, already teetering, would be decided by what happened in Dad's hometown.

King faced formidable odds in Chicago. The organizations he once counted on as allies were in the midst of power struggles between the old guard and a younger, angrier faction. James Farmer lost control of CORE to Floyd McKissick, a Malcolm X devotee. SNCC fractured from within as the pacifist Bob Moses fought for control with Carmichael, who had just about run out of patience with the nonviolent movement.

————

As King prepared for the Chicago campaign and *People Get Ready* struck a chord with movement workers, my father continued writing for OKeh. He gave Major three hits—"Sometimes I Wonder," "Come See," and "Ain't It a Shame"—and wrote "You Can't Hurt Me No More" and "I'm So Afraid" for the Opals, a girl group modeled after the Supremes. Gene Chandler remade "Rainbow" as "Rainbow '65," and took it to number two on the R&B chart. Meanwhile, the Impressions had eight songs on the charts and a number-one album. "We were so hot," Fred said. "I never will forget, I was looking in *Billboard* and they had Sam, Curtis, and myself standing in a big skillet, flames shooting up around us, because we were just so hot."

It is hard to think of any songwriter with more hits at one time than Curtis during this period, let alone the number of hits he'd written over the past three years. His songs had built OKeh into a first-rate label. They'd made Major Lance, Gene Chandler, Billy Butler, and half a dozen others into stars and took the Impressions from one-hit wonders to premier social commentators and legends in the making.

Dad knew he was good. He proved it relentlessly with hit after hit. His success was a resounding answer to everyone who wrote him off because of his poverty, stature, or looks; to everyone who had hurt or mocked him as a child; to every record label that rejected him because they didn't like his songs or his voice. As Eddie says about Vee-Jay, "They thought they had the cream of the crop, which was Jerry Butler. They had no idea they were throwing away the greatest songwriter I've ever known in this business. The cream of the crop was Curtis Mayfield." They paid for it, too, as my father gave ABC and OKeh his constant stream of hits and the untold millions of dollars they earned.

————

In mid-1965, Diane told Curtis he'd soon have a second son—me. The news came at a point when their relationship had started showing signs of strain. My mother had difficulty dealing with my father's idiosyncrasies, and they fought often. When they first met, she noticed the loner in him, but she didn't realize he was a borderline recluse. On tour, he preferred to stay in his hotel room; at home, he felt most comfortable in his den with his guitar. "We would go to friends' houses, either a party or Jerry Butler's house, but he never wanted to stay very long," she says. "He'd say, 'Either leave now or figure out how to get home.' And sometimes I'd leave and sometimes I'd catch a cab. But he was never a social person. His mother was kind of a loner. He was kind of a loner. He could go in the den, play his music, be creative. He didn't need to be around people."

He'd always been that way. It helped him handle the pressures of life, and with the added pressures of fame, he needed the solace of his guitar more than ever. It was his shield against the outside world.

My mother also discovered a tempest churning beneath his cool demeanor. "He seemed like butter wouldn't melt in his mouth—real easygoing," she says. "But that was his facade in front of people. He was moody, so it would just depend on his mood." His mood could swing from loving and affectionate to dark and brooding at a moment's notice. It was the Gemini in him. His mind changed as fast as his mood—he often made last-minute plans to go to the Bahamas or Bermuda, and it had to happen *now*. The longer it took to leave, the more likely he'd change the plan or scrap it altogether.

She also had learned about his intense need for control. "He picked my friends," my mother says. "When I was trying to be friends with the lady down the street, and I wanted to go to a movie with the kids, he said no. He didn't know her, so I couldn't go with her." Dad's controlling nature seemed to contradict the way he worked as a musician. Everyone who played for him knew him as easy and free in the studio. Only those closest to him saw the truth—beneath that laid-back demeanor lurked a man who needed control and almost always had it.

That need came from growing up in treacherous circumstances. Childhood in the White Eagle taught him what happened when you didn't control your finances, your relationships, or your life. His mother couldn't control those things, and as a result, his family starved and suffered. The lesson was sewn into his sinew and bone. Music gave him the power to overcome. It gave him control over himself and his family. It let him lift his friends from the ghetto with the power of his songs. He could never have total control, though. He couldn't control racist radio programmers who put a lid on the success his songs could achieve. He couldn't control which songs hit and which flopped. He couldn't control his own insecurities. He couldn't always control my mother, either, especially with her fiery demeanor.

Pursuing total control worked in the studio, where success was the only rule. It did not work in a romantic relationship. Even though he loved to buy my mother things—especially jewelry, including three wedding rings, though they never officially married—that didn't make up for his shortcomings as a husband. "He was a better father than a husband," my mother says. "He spoiled the kids, where I was more frugal. But with his schedule, a lot of times, I'd cook dinner, he wasn't there. He'd come home, eleven or twelve o'clock at night, expect me to heat it up or fix him something to eat. And sometimes it was OK and sometimes it wasn't. When he was in the studio, I'd understand. But you don't know if they're always in the studio."

My mother's fears were justified. Once the Impressions became famous, Dad had never been faithful to any woman. "Because of who he was, there were always women after him, and that makes it hard for a man, I guess, to say no," my mother says. "I think he was addicted to sex."

They'd fight often about lipstick on his collar and other indiscretions, and even though my mother was a louder and more forceful arguer, Dad didn't end his affairs. It became a constant issue, harder to deal with given his expectation that she only socialize with people he picked for her. He wanted a woman who bent to his wishes. My mother was no such woman. Growing up, it often seemed strange to me how they came together at all.

Dad's obsession with control could be both dark and comical. For instance, in the late '60s, he and my mother moved into a house in Pill

Hill, and my mother received an offer to model. My father's half sister Ann came to watch Tracy and me on the day the modeling gig was to take place. On a break at the studio, Dad called the house and found out about the modeling gig from Ann. He jumped in his car and sped home, screeching into the driveway before my mother could leave and demanding she stay home. She yelled, "I want to work! I want my own money!" He shot back, "You want money?" Then he snatched a wad of cash from his pocket and threw it at her. It caught the wind and blew all over the street. As my mother peeled out of the driveway, she watched him recede in the rearview, scrambling to gather the money he'd thrown to the breeze.

Like many a self-conscious man in love with a beautiful woman, Curtis wanted to control Diane's every move. He couldn't give her the space to make her own decisions—it felt too dangerous, especially when she decided to do something as fraught with sex appeal as modeling. As in most things, he was capable of the grand gesture—whisking her away to the islands, buying her the three wedding rings—but he couldn't do the small things necessary to keep their relationship alive. Things like supporting her ambition to earn her own money, or helping around the house, or pitching in with the grunt work required to raise Tracy and me. He did love her, but his love often came from a place of insecurity. Inside, he was still the little boy called Smut, the one pretty girls laughed at or ignored.

That insecurity was wearing off in his professional life. He'd grown accustomed to others complying with his wishes when it came to business, and no one challenged him in the studio. With each new hit, he became more confident. He trusted his instincts, and if a musician didn't see things his way, he found someone else who did. Even Fred and Sam followed his lead. He expected the same from his personal life, and his temper sometimes flared when he didn't get it.

———————

While my parents prepared for my arrival, Dad decided to leave OKeh. He couldn't continue to supply hits to the label's entire roster while also writing, touring, and promoting for the Impressions. "He was always up late writing," my mother recalls. "I could hear him playing the guitar. He was always taping songs and going back over them. That was his main focus: writing, writing, writing."

For a while, he tried focusing only on the Impressions, but true to his nature, he could never limit himself to one project. By the time King got to Chicago in July, Dad was in the studio with the Impressions working on two albums simultaneously. *One by One*, the first to be released, showed just how tired he was creatively. It had only three original songs out of twelve. The other nine were covers from a bygone era, such as "Mona Lisa" and "Nature Boy," both made famous by Nat King Cole when my father was a child. The lead single, an original ballad called "Just One Kiss from You," marked the Impressions' first flop in two years.

Both the single and album seemed inconsistent after the triumphs of *Keep On Pushing* and *People Get Ready*—even more so considering what King was doing in my father's backyard. Just before *One by One*'s release, King led a march down State Street to Madison Avenue in downtown Chicago. Traffic halted when the marchers reached Madison, a pocket of them singing the Impressions' "Meeting Over Yonder." By the time the procession reached city hall, the crowd had swelled to almost one hundred thousand bodies sweating in the sweltering heat.

As King spoke that day, there was serious dissension within the SCLC about the Chicago campaign. Tom Kahn, a movement activist close to both King and northern civil rights activist Bayard Rustin, recalled, "King had this naive faith that he could do in Chicago what he had done in the South, that he could reach down and inspire them, mobilize them, and so forth. And Bayard kept saying, 'You don't know what you are talking about. You don't know what Chicago is like. . . . You're going to be wiped out.'"

King expected to face white opposition, especially from Mayor Daley, and Daley delivered, setting his infamous political machine into action. Businessmen who backed King suddenly encountered trouble with garbage collection and city permits. Church leaders who offered

King support found city inspectors knocking at their door, threatening to condemn the church's property.

What King didn't expect was the resistance he would face from his own people. Many Negro ministers and politicians told King to go back where he came from—they benefitted from the racist structure in Chicago, though they wouldn't admit it. People on the street were just as hard to reach. After meeting with a group of Chicago Negroes, King's close friend Hosea Williams said, "I have never seen such hopelessness." Even King commented to an aide, "You ain't never seen no Negroes like this, have you? . . . Boy, if we could crack these Chicago Negroes we can crack anything." Despite the battle raging in his hometown, my father didn't specifically comment.

On August 6, a month after *One by One*'s release, Congress passed the Voting Rights Act, outlawing discrimination in voting. It didn't affect Curtis since he didn't vote—a fact that always puzzled me, although it seemed he felt most comfortable (and perhaps most effective) dealing with politics in his music. Regardless, the movement scored another huge victory. As if on cue, a week later police brutality in the Watts neighborhood of Los Angeles ignited a massive riot there. For six days, columns of fire shot into the sky as Negroes in Watts destroyed everything in sight. They were sick of reading about King's successes down South while they suffered in desperate poverty. They didn't care about the Voting Rights Act or the Civil Rights Act as long as the police continued to harm them without repercussions. The riot caused 34 deaths, 1,032 injuries, 3,438 arrests, and over $40 million in property damage. It was just the beginning.

———

As the year ended and my mother neared the end of her term, the Impressions put the finishing touches on their next album, *Ridin' High*, and released an EP, *Soulfully*. Yet again, though the movement now battled racism in his own city, Dad made no public comment. He still cared about the movement, but he was not a political man. He didn't write made-to-order messages to inspire people; it had to come from his soul.

For whatever reason, he didn't seem to feel that soulful inspiration while King stayed in Chicago.

In fact, he seemed to be running low on inspiration in general. *Soulfully* featured the single "You've Been Cheatin'," a song that borrowed its DNA from Motown and returned the Impressions to respectable chart positions. The next several singles bombed, and *Ridin' High* didn't fare much better than its predecessor. The album features several love letters to Motown, cribbing their insistent tambourine-backed beats and punchy horns.

Dad never wanted his music to sound like anybody else's. He rarely listened to the radio or played another group's records. When he did, he approached it scientifically, seeking to understand his competition. He remained that way throughout his life—Tracy recalls getting a lecture in the early '70s about the dangers of listening to the radio, which seems ironic given how big a role radio played in Dad's childhood.

Yet, despite his desire to forge a unique sound, Dad's music became less and less original during this period. His most complete copy of Motown came with the single "Can't Satisfy," which borrowed heavily from the Isley Brothers' "This Old Heart of Mine," and led Motown to sue for publishing rights. They won. "[Curtis] just kind of lost his way there for a moment," Fred said. "The ideas kind of dried up. It just went dead."

Ridin' High didn't revive anything. For the second straight time, the Impressions failed to hit the charts or fit the times. In 1966 drugs came to the fore of youth culture and the psychedelic revolution swept the nation. Pop music took incredible strides into the unknown with albums like the Beatles' *Revolver*, Dylan's *Blonde on Blonde*, and the Beach Boys' *Pet Sounds*. James Brown was busy inventing funk with the monumental success of the previous year's "Papa's Got a Brand New Bag" and "I Got You (I Feel Good)." Motown scored seemingly endless number-one hits, including genre-defining tunes like the Four Tops' "Reach Out I'll Be There" and the Supremes' "You Can't Hurry Love," both of which rode the heels of the Temptations' game-changing "My Girl." For the time being, it seemed Curtis couldn't compete.

Perhaps the strains of his personal and professional obligations became too much. When I was born in February 1966, my father was on tour. He wouldn't see me for more than a week after my birth. A woman named Annette kept my mother company during that time and helped navigate the stresses of a newborn baby. Annette had two children with Lenny, the bass player in the Impressions' band, and for a while my mother felt close to her and confided in her. Then, she learned my father was sleeping with her.

Two months later, Dad founded his own record label, Windy C, distributed by Cameo Parkway in Philadelphia. The label focused on a family band called the Five Stairsteps, who had won a talent contest at the Regal Theatre in Chicago. In the spring of '66, the Five Stairsteps released "You Waited Too Long" on Windy C, which climbed to number sixteen R&B. In Chicago, even the B-side—a song of my father's called "Don't Waste Your Time"—became a hit. Perhaps the most important aspect of their success was the fact Curtis didn't have to write hits for them. After the exhaustion of his days as a one-man hit factory at OKeh, it was a relief to have a group that could develop their own material.

With Windy C up and running, he launched Mayfield Records. The label became a vehicle for the Fascinations, a girl group in the mode of the Ronettes. True to their name, they had a fascinating story. The Fascinations formed in 1960 with two young girls named Shirley Walker and Martha Reeves at the helm. After a disagreement, Reeves left and rejoined her old group, the Del-Phis. The Del-Phis signed to Motown, changed their name to Martha and the Vandellas, and became one of the biggest groups in the world.

The rest of the Fascinations signed to ABC-Paramount in 1962, where they met Curtis. He produced their first single, "Mama Didn't Lie," the song he'd written for Jan Bradley that almost led him to a job with Chess Records. After failing to hit at ABC, the Fascinations kicked around until my father signed them to Mayfield.

The Fascinations didn't write their own material, so in August my father gave them "Say It Isn't So," a tune that, with Johnny's arrangement, captured the sound of the day. It cracked the top fifty R&B. A few months later, he wrote "Girls Are Out to Get You," which went to number thirteen R&B.

The success of these songs helped position Dad as one of the premier writer/producer/executives in America. Unlike his previous work for other artists, the singles he cut on Mayfield Records left no doubt who deserved the credit. On "Girls Are Out to Get You," for example, the name Mayfield was stamped on the 45's label four times—"Mayfield" was written in big block letters across the bottom, "Curtis Mayfield" appeared in parentheses below the title as the writer, "Prod. By Curtis Mayfield" appeared in the production credit below the group's name, and "Mayfield Records distributed by Calla Records Inc." appeared on the label's edge. The effect was overwhelming. No longer was it ABC, OKeh, or Vee-Jay. Now, it was Mayfield, Mayfield, Mayfield, Mayfield.

He also signed another group to Mayfield featuring two young musicians who would have an impact on his career and life over the next few years—Donny Hathaway and Leroy Hutson. Perhaps to get in good with the boss, they renamed the band the Mayfield Singers. They didn't need that extra touch; my father already respected their artistry. About Donny, he said, "This fella, you could just talk to him over the phone and play him a piece of music, and he could call out every chord and every movement and where the fifth was and the augmented and tell you what key it was in. He really baffled me. I always admired people that could do that because I never had that kind of learning." Dad could already see how Donny would come in handy as a multifaceted weapon—producer, arranger, writer, performer. The same went for Leroy, who studied music in college.

Along with his new labels, Curtis created two new publishing companies—Chi-Sound and Camad. So much for focusing on the Impressions. He couldn't help trying to take on more than one man could handle. Perhaps it was the duality of his Gemini nature surfacing again. Never satisfied with being one thing, he wanted to be both an artist and a businessman. The struggle between business and creativity would continue to tear at him.

As Mayfield and Windy C struggled to get off the ground, serious changes wracked the movement. While the Fascinations rode the charts, Carmichael finally took over SNCC. In early June, after a white racist shot James Meredith during Meredith's March Against Fear from Tennessee to Mississippi, Carmichael joined King, Floyd McKissick, and others to complete the march. Cops arrested them en route. After their release, Carmichael gave a speech that set the terms and language for the new movement. Much like King did with his "I Have a Dream" speech, Carmichael took a feeling that had been in the air for a while and crystallized it. "This is the twenty-seventh time I have been arrested. I ain't going to jail no more!" he bellowed. "The only way we gonna stop them white men from whuppin' us is to take over. What we gonna start sayin' now is Black Power!"

The crowd took up the chant—*Black Power!* . . . two words . . . *Black Power!* . . . an old idea that finally found its time . . . *Black Power!* . . . and a new movement was born.

As Black Power resonated across the country, Negroes went through a symbolic process of renaming. No more would they accept "Negro"—a word descendents of slave owners had forced upon them. It wasn't Negro Power; it was *Black* Power. Black Power was angry and impatient. Black Power was fed up with festering in the ghetto. Black Power was a short-fused keg of dynamite, and white America held a burning match just above it.

My father supported Black Power in theory. He was all for black pride and empowerment, and he'd remain that way to his death, but he had a harder time backing the violent streak coursing through the new movement. Shortly after Carmichael's speech, riots raged through Cleveland and Atlanta.

Curtis wouldn't comment on the violence and anger for a few years. He couldn't help but notice it growing, though. As the riots died down, two young black men named Huey Newton and Bobby Seale formed the Black Panther Party for Self Defense. It would soon become one of the most militant groups in civil rights history.

For many black people, militancy was the only answer. They had tried nonviolence, and it didn't seem to work—not even for King. On August 5, King marched against segregated housing in Marquette Park on the city's southwest side. As he marched, a jeering crowd of whites mounted a counterdemonstration. One man proudly hoisted a sign that read, "The only way to end niggers is exterminate."

When King passed the crowd, someone hurled a rock as big as a fist at his head. He fell to his knees, and as he tried to get up, the mob let loose with bottles, eggs, firecrackers, and more rocks. "I have seen many demonstrations in the South," King said. "But I have never seen anything so hostile and so hateful as I've seen here today."

King saw the worst of the worst in the South. White southerners beat him and jailed him, firebombed his house, and threatened his family. The fact that Chicago's situation seemed worse to him than those tragedies speaks volumes about racial tensions in my father's hometown. It also helps explain why Dad felt so driven to write songs to inspire his people. He grew up in a place where black people suffered extreme hatred, violence, and degradation—perhaps worse than in Birmingham and Selma.

———

Throughout this period, as King spent part of his weeks in Chicago and the rest crisscrossing the country, my father played out a similar script in reverse. He toured with the Impressions part of the week and returned home to work and spend time with Tracy, Mom, and me whenever possible. Traveling the country, he watched fury and despair replace peace and hope in the movement. In the studio, he didn't know how to deal with it. Neither did King. "I don't know what the answer to that is," King said. "My role perhaps is to interpret to the white world. There must be somebody to communicate to two worlds."

My father had already shown he could communicate with both worlds, but it seemed as if he had stopped trying. Or, perhaps his focus was drawn elsewhere. He no longer faced many of the problems King fought in Chicago. He had enough money to buy a house wherever he wanted—although racism still barred him from some areas. He also had the Impressions and two independent labels to think about, as well as the demands of a family to worry about.

As 1966 ended, Curtis took solace in work, returning to the studio to cut the next Impressions album, as well as new material for the Fascinations and the Stairsteps. Meanwhile, by the beginning of '67, it was clear King's Chicago gamble would not pay off. "We raised the hopes tremendously but . . . we were not able to really produce the dreams and the results inherent in that hope," King said. "We as leaders lifted the hope. We had to do it. It was a fine thing to do. But we were unable to produce."

The greatest successes of the movement in Chicago belonged to Jesse Jackson and his Operation Breadbasket. As for King, the time in Chicago changed his mind—not about nonviolence, but about the true depth of racial problems in America. "For years I labored with the idea of reforming the existing institutions of the society, a little change here, a little change there," he said. "Now I feel quite differently. I think you've got to have a reconstruction of the entire society, a revolution of values."

As he moved the SCLC toward the popular militarism of the Black Panthers and SNCC, King's power over the movement reached its lowest point. One journalist pointedly predicted that King's work in Chicago marked his final moments as the country's preeminent civil rights figure. "Both his philosophy and his techniques of leadership were products of a different world," the writer said, "of relationships which no longer obtain and expectations which are no longer valid." King "had simply, and disastrously, arrived at the wrong conclusions about the world."

––––––––

The past two years had seen the movement's most dramatic showdown with entrenched racism in the North—a showdown King and his followers lost in Chicago—yet my father still did not feel inspired to comment on it. The next album, *The Fabulous Impressions*, did worse on the pop chart than any Impressions album before it and was their worst showing on the R&B chart in three years. It was, however, their strongest album since *People Get Ready*. The lead single, "You Always Hurt Me," was my father's most rhythmically insistent song yet, opening with an organ glissando and conga pattern—sounds he would use to great effect in later years. He also gave majestic guitar showcases on "Love's A Comin'" and "I Can't Stay Away from You."

But *The Fabulous Impressions* had clunkers like a cover of "100 Lbs. of Clay," which showed how far the group had fallen from the mainstream. It also contained a virtual copy of "Gypsy Woman" called "Isle of Sirens," which featured some of the Impressions' most haunting harmonies but didn't sound new or current.

Curtis seemed stuck between eras while music in 1967 had another watershed year. The Beatles released their magnum opus, *Sgt. Pepper's Lonely Hearts Club Band* as well as a trippy EP/film called *Magical Mystery Tour*, Aretha Franklin reached down and pulled up some gut-bucket soul with the stunning *I Never Loved a Man the Way I Love You*, and James Brown added new levels to his funk with *Cold Sweat*. Then, there was a new cat on the scene named Jimi Hendrix—the same kid who had backed the Impressions a few years before, now reinvented as a flamboyant frontman. He threw down the axe, literally and figuratively, with *Are You Experienced*, forcing every other guitarist in the world to bow down in his wake.

Hendrix's appearance on the scene during the lull in the Impressions' career is even more interesting because Curtis influenced his playing so much. Hendrix even played a Stratocaster like Curtis, which wasn't typical for blues or rock music. As musician Bob Kulick recalled from his days of jamming at the Cafe Wha?, "I asked Hendrix who his biggest influence was, and he said Curtis Mayfield." Hendrix's drummer, Mitch Mitchell, remembered him the same way: "I really like Curtis Mayfield & The Impressions, and I was astounded that [Hendrix] knew that style really, really fluently."

The influence came out in bits and pieces on songs like "Remember" and "The Wind Cries Mary," but when Hendrix released his follow-up later that year, *Axis: Bold as Love*, my father's imprint was impossible to miss. Listen to "Wait Until Tomorrow," "Little Wing," "Castles Made of

Sand," "One Rainy Wish," and "Bold as Love," and you'll hear Curtis interpreted through a haze of LSD and a lefty playing in standard tuning. That's not to say Hendrix brought nothing new to his style—many consider him the greatest guitarist to bend a string—but my father's playing was a strong influence. He translated it to the psychedelic age with fuzz and wah-wah pedals, phasers, flangers, and a whole host of other effects, taking it to a place Dad was not yet ready to go.

Ironically, as mainstream radio programming left my father still struggling to connect with a pop audience—which meant a white audience—Hendrix struggled to reach a black audience because his music did not fit R&B radio programming.

———

The summer of 1967 laid bare the chasm between white and black America. For white people, it was the Summer of Love—bellbottoms, acid rock, free love, and flower power. For blacks, it was a summer of agony. White people turned on, tuned in, and dropped out as the Beatles sang "All You Need Is Love" on the first live, international satellite broadcast in history. Black people had nowhere to turn, little to tune into, and nothing to drop out of; they'd never been included in the first place.

White people protested the war in Vietnam. Black people fought wars in their own neighborhoods. Riots tore apart ghettos in Newark, Detroit, Milwaukee, Minneapolis, Birmingham, New York City, Rochester, Atlanta, Boston, Cincinnati, Buffalo, and Tampa. By the end of the summer, 159 riots had broken out all over America. The seeds for the summers of rioting had been planted decades before, back when Annie Bell first came to Chicago and Negroes were shunted into stifling ghettos.

Making matters worse, the rate of black unemployment was twice that of whites. These problems went untouched by the Civil Rights Act, the Voting Rights Act, or anything King had done in the South. Negroes in northern ghettos were like teakettles over a fire, and by 1967, nothing could stop them from boiling over.

With each new riot, my father watched the hope he had tried to inspire with "Keep On Pushing" and "People Get Ready" crumble, burn, and shatter like so many ghetto tenements. Even King said, "There were dark days before, but this is the darkest." Chicago militants tipped King off to further violence planned for Cleveland, Oakland, and Philadelphia. They also let him in on the plans for Chicago. "They don't plan to just burn down the west side," an FBI wiretap recorded King saying in a phone call. "They are planning to get the Loop in Chicago."

The Loop was, and still is, the heart of Chicago. Crippling it would have crippled the entire city—the political structure, the financial structure, the business structure, everything. The riot didn't quite go off as planned, but for King, the rebuke was personal and total. He had spent two years living with blacks in Chicago fighting for the idea of peaceful protest, and in response those same blacks had planned the worst violence in a summer full of carnage. King was warned that Chicago would break him, and it did. His wife, Coretta, watched as he slipped into a deep depression. "I have found out that all that I have been doing in trying to correct this system in America has been in vain," King said.

At the same time, the military continued drafting hordes of young soldiers, including thousands of black men who were asked to die for a country that refused to protect them at home. The Vietnam War now concerned my dad, too. In early May, Uncle Kenny enlisted in the army, and when the fighting broke out in the concrete jungles of America, he was halfway around the world with fatigues, combat boots, and a gun, fighting in a real jungle. He was only seventeen.

———

The end of 1967 was a mixed bag for my father. His first two independent labels, Windy C and Mayfield, collapsed. The Impressions neared the end of their contract with ABC, and my parents' relationship continued to erupt in fits of infidelity and anger, even though my mother was pregnant with my sister Sharon. All the while, my father lived in anxious fear he'd never see his brother again.

At the same time, he'd proven his worth to the world. He was more than a ghetto child, more than another faceless black man withering under American racism—he was a genius, a businessman, a celebrity, and a messenger. To prove it yet again, he dipped his pen back into movement ink and wrote an excellent new song called "We're a Winner."

"That song came to me in a dream," Dad said. "I ran down in the basement and put enough down that I would remember; that was one of the few times I knew I had a smash. Maybe not a charted smash that would earn more money, but the lyrical content of equality and freedom needed for somebody to 'Say it loud, I'm black and I'm proud.' We needed to come from crying the blues to standing tall." The Impressions recorded the song with a live audience in the studio, and it begins with Eddie's first wife, Audrey, saying almost inaudibly, "Have you seen Diane? Hey!" then shouting, "All right now, sock it to me baby!" as the song kicks in. It was the funkiest, and frankly, the blackest song the Impressions had ever recorded. The bass drum booms like the makeshift bombs exploding in riot zones across America, and my father's singing is more rhythmic and nuanced than ever before.

"We're a Winner" spoke to Black Power in a way pop music had never done. My father had been absorbing the world around him even during his years of silence on the movement, intuiting the shift from the gospel foundation represented by King and the SCLC to the secular, inner-city vibe of Carmichael and the Black Panthers. "We're a Winner" is the result of that absorption.

With his fourth movement anthem, my father made an important lyrical shift away from the dual-voiced poetry of Dunbar. "We're a Winner" was his boldest attempt yet at speaking to a black audience in a single voice. As he said, it was "a message to all, and yet basically to the black masses of people. It is an inspiring song. I believe everybody once in a while should sing in terms of trying to keep the movements going, even though sometimes things are tough. Things move slowly sometimes, but with the movement we truly are a winner."

In explaining the lyrics, he showed his growing awareness of all sides of the movement. "I was listening to all my preachers and the different leaders of the time," he said. "You had your Rap Browns and your Stokely Carmichaels and Martin Luther Kings, all of those people right within that same era."

There was another side to the lyrics that his audience wouldn't know about for a few years. Sam recalled, "Curtis had written some real tough lyrics on this song. One portion says, 'The black boy done dried his eyes,' and then it said, 'There'll be no more Uncle Tom, at last that blessed day has come, and we're a winner.' We started fooling around in the studio with Johnny, and we start singing it that way, and Johnny jumped up and said, 'Cut! Cut! Cut! Cut!' He leaned out the door and said, 'Curtis, come here a minute.' Curtis was laughing, and Johnny said, 'You can't use those words. That's too harsh.'" They all knew ABC wouldn't put out a song with such heavy lyrics, so my father softened the words, singing, "We have finally dried our eyes," and "At last that blessed day has come, and I don't care where you come from."

It came as a surprise when several radio stations across the country banned "We're a Winner" anyway, including the top station in Chicago, WLS. "They thought that we had become militant," Sam said. "All we were doing was telling it like it was. They picked out a couple of lines in the song to say why they wouldn't play it. They said, 'Like your leaders tell you to,' but we got white leaders and black leaders. That's what the song was about. Everybody can be a winner. All you have to do is stand up and be counted."

My father felt angry about the censorship. "I've run into frustrating obstacles, such as will a certain radio station play my records," he said years later. "But that is his or her choice, as to whether they want to mix in or take on new music such as 'We're a Winner' and put it in with the typecast of the old R&B or rock & roll music. I knew where I was going."

The refusal was even more surprising because my father had never written a more immaculately constructed song. It was a supreme blend of ear candy and message music, and it was so strong, the radio ban didn't hurt it. The single stayed on the charts through the beginning of 1968, and it reached number one R&B and number fourteen pop by the beginning of March, just days after Sharon's birth.

It seemed 1968 would bring Dad great things. He had his first baby girl and a number-one single. He also formed a new label with Eddie called Curtom, distributed by Buddah Records. "I wasn't a quitter," he said of his decision to start a new label. "Sometimes these things are like marriages. You don't give up wanting to be in love and having the best you can expect, just because your marriage fails."

His influence was still growing a decade into his career, something few musicians ever achieve. My father's success, especially with "We're a Winner," helped open a niche within pop music where blacks could succeed on a significant financial level while remaining true to their people, using their rhythms, their slang, and their ideas. Soon after, James Brown released "Say It Loud—I'm Black and I'm Proud," Sly Stone released "Don't Call Me Nigger, Whitey," and it seemed everyone wanted in on the game.

Black performers were stepping off the tightrope my father first discovered during his debut at the Apollo. Acceptance by the white world no longer meant as much as staying true to one's blackness, and Dad's music played a huge role in that shift.

Unfortunately, he couldn't get out of his own way long enough to enjoy it, as infidelity clouded the happiness he'd earned. First, my mother learned he'd impregnated someone else. Then, she came home and caught him in the act with yet another woman. Then, the pregnant woman called saying she'd lost the baby. Many times my mother knew these women. Sometimes she confronted them. Tracy recalls one such moment. "Mom would take us to some lady's house that I think Dad was messing around with," he said, "and I remember Mom picking up one of her friends, and her friend confronted the lady. I remember looking out the back window to see what was going on. I did know there was some turmoil."

Despite marital difficulties, Dad had terrific momentum as the Impressions finished their contract. ABC offered them $500,000 to stay with the label, no small sum for a poor kid from Cabrini-Green. The guys had many serious discussions about what to do—Dad always dreamed of running an enterprise like Motown, and he had a chance with Curtom.

Still, leaving a heavyweight like ABC to make it on his own represented a great risk. That risk extended not only to his livelihood and career, but also to Fred and Sam.

Ultimately, Dad felt the risk was worth it. He wanted to own himself more than he wanted half a million dollars. After some back and forth, he convinced Fred and Sam to turn down the money and jump ship for the new label. According to Fred, that decision came with the understanding they'd each own a share of the Curtom label. They knew my father well enough to know he didn't share when it came to business. Perhaps they thought he'd treat them differently.

As the Impressions left ABC, my father knew he could make it on his own. Over the past seven years, he'd scored twenty-two hit singles on the pop and R&B charts with the Impressions, including four R&B number ones, and a dozen charting albums. He'd written more than forty hits for other artists, toured the world, and become a major voice of his generation. He had fought and clawed his way to something only a handful of black musicians had ever attained in the business—autonomy. He felt strong, important, and optimistic. Self-assurance and confidence began to replace the insecurities that once plagued him.

Even as King's nonviolence fell out of vogue, Dad still believed in him. Despite three consecutive brutal summers, he did not succumb to the ghetto rioter's despair. He still believed the key to success for black people was to "keep on pushing, like your leaders tell you to." He hadn't lost hope in America or the movement.

The coming bloodshed would take care of that.

7

Curtom

> "We're killing up our leaders,
> It don't matter none black or white,
> And we all know it's wrong,
> But we're gonna fight to make it right."
>
> —"Mighty Mighty (Spade and Whitey)"

April 4, 1968, Lorraine Motel, Memphis, Tennessee—Martin Luther King walked onto the balcony outside his room to get some air. He'd just finished a pillow fight with Andrew Young and several other top SCLC aides, a rare moment of levity for a man engulfed by despair. Seconds later, a loud crack shattered the silence. King fell flat on his back, blood gushing from a wound in his jaw. Abernathy rushed over to him. "Martin! Martin! This is Ralph," he said, panicked. "Do you hear me? This is Ralph." King's friends watched in agonizing impotence as he met the violent end he had so often predicted.

King's assassination crumpled the movement. His tactics might have fallen out of fashion with the younger, militant crowd that had taken the reins over the last three years, but for the majority of black people—and whites who felt sympathy with the movement—King still represented the best hope. The bullet that ended his life also ended his dream, at least for the foreseeable future.

The news hit my father hard. He knew the Lorraine Motel well. It was a safe haven for black performers on the chitlin' circuit, and the Impressions had stayed there many times. As Eddie says, "That's one place that anybody could find you if you were playing Memphis. They knew you were going to be staying at the Lorraine Motel. We heard about King, and we were just totally dismayed. It hurt everybody."

For the moment there seemed little reason for hope. As my father said years later, "How are young people supposed to feel when they see that many of the respected leaders were destroyed, and many who weren't respected got rich? Seeing your political leaders making dramatic mistakes, people being rewarded for stealing billions, while you go to jail for stealing an apple. You look around you and it's easy to think, 'I'm living, I'd better get mine now,' because all your values may come to nothing, and there's too many people to fight." That statement reflected his deep understanding of the angry forces that had taken over the movement.

He wasn't ready to give up, though. With a broken heart, Dad wrote a poem with instructions for the path forward and a message of healing for what had passed:

> *Another friend has gone and I feel so insecure*
> *Brothers, if you feel this way, you're not by yourself*
> *We have lost another leader, Lord, how much must we endure?*
> *If you feel this way, you're not by yourself*
> *But if they think we have no one to lead us*
> *That then we've lost the fight and every night no one can breed us*
> *They don't know every brother is a leader*
> *And they don't know every sister is a breeder*
> *And our love, you see, is gonna help the world be free*
> *We're going to move at a scarlet pace*
> *Keep every brother on the case*
> *They don't know, to help a sister help themselves*
> *We cannot let our people be until we're all out of poverty.*

He molded those words to a melody as the news of King's death shot around the country. Stokely Carmichael said, "Now that they've taken

Dr. King off, it's time to end this nonviolence bullshit," but after the past three summers of riots, no one in the ghetto needed instructions on what to do. They razed Baltimore, DC, Louisville, Kansas City, and Wilmington, Delaware. They also set buildings ablaze in Cabrini-Green and Lawndale.

Plumes of black smoke towered so high over the ghettos in Chicago that people could see them from the Loop a couple of miles away. Dad watched those dark clouds threaten the horizon. He now lived far from the carnage, in a Hyde Park townhouse with my mother, Tracy, Sharon, and me. Hyde Park was an integrated neighborhood of middle and upper-middle class families near the University of Chicago. In terms of social status, he'd moved far from the riots. But in terms of his heart and spirit, he couldn't separate himself from the despair roiling Chicago's black community. One day, he and my mother traveled to the West Side to witness the destruction there. They saw a hellish scene. This was no mere disturbance; it was a war zone.

Many of my father's acquaintances still lived in the West Side and Cabrini ghettos. They were trapped in the violence. A woman named Lillian Swope, who used to let Curtis practice in her row house on Hudson, said, "A truck came through here—right down Oak Street . . . The young men actually pulled the driver out of the truck, and emptied the truck and just took all the man's stuff out and they was beating him so bad that they almost killed him."

Rioters destroyed the stores on Oak Street, close to where Grandma Sadie lived, and they wrecked Del Farms and Pioneers grocery stores. They beat random white people with bricks. A melee erupted in the cafeteria of Curtis's old high school as black students threw food and smashed their plates.

The National Guard stormed Cabrini to restore order by any means necessary. Soldiers in tanks plowed down the small streets. Others drove in Jeeps, clutching rifles with bayonets affixed to the barrels. The Guard set a curfew and patrolled the streets at night, sweeping the neighborhood with piercing lights. Meanwhile, all day and night police traded gunfire with roving gangs that were trying to impose their own sort of order. Shootouts, broken windows, crumbling structures, fires, violent deaths—these now defined the project. It would never again be the idyllic place my father once knew with gardens, parades, and doo-wop groups on the corner.

Cabrini resident Zora Washington recalled the hopelessness she felt when at last the violence and destruction subsided. "Black people had torn it up and the powers that be were not going to fix it up," she said. "You knew that. It was a scary time. It gave you a scary feeling. How could you help not being depressed? It was like we lost hope. The person that could do it for us was gone. It was a terrible time."

―――――――

Watching his city burn, Curtis kept on pushing. He bought a small brick building at 8543 Stony Island Boulevard in South Chicago and opened the Curtom studio and offices. He began auditioning and signing acts with Eddie, including June Conquest, who had released a single on Windy C. Her single "What's This I See" was Curtom's first release. It became a hit in Chicago as the riot's flames died down, although it didn't make noise nationally.

The Five Stairsteps also joined Curtom, as did the Symphonics, a band from Philadelphia. Eddie recalled auditioning the Jackson 5, but my father passed because Curtom already had a family band. Needless to say, that wasn't his best business decision.

He was right to have high hopes for the Stairsteps, though. They'd prove that in 1970 with the smash single, "O-o-h Child," which rose to number eight on the pop chart, and has since inspired more than twenty covers and earned a ranking on *Rolling Stone*'s 500 Greatest Songs of All Time. Unfortunately, they recorded the song for Buddah, not Curtom. They switched labels after my father's workload became too much for him to give them the attention they needed.

Dad made another good choice in signing Donny Hathaway, but he couldn't make that work either. "Donny could do everything," Eddie said. "Sing, arrange, produce, play keyboards, write songs—many talents. But, he butted heads with Curtis a lot. Both men had equal skills yet had very strong and stubborn personalities. Curtis wouldn't do things Donny's way and vice versa."

My father's need for control didn't allow Donny the space he needed to create, so Donny asked to get out of his contract, saying he no longer wanted to make music. When he later began talks with Atco Records, Dad cut all ties with Donny and forced my mother to do the same with his wife, Eulaulah. Curtom suffered as a result. In the end, Donny did his most important work with other labels, including two gold albums with Roberta Flack for Atlantic.

Rounding out Curtom's first lineup—and providing another frustrating missed opportunity—was the Impressions' old road band, the Winstons. They cut only one single on Curtom before changing labels and releasing the Grammy Award–winning "Color Him Father" on Metromedia Records.

The Winstons hold an extraordinary place in music history. The B-side to "Color Him Father" was an up-tempo, instrumental version of "Amen" called "Amen, Brother." It contained a six-second drum-break that became the underpinning of hip-hop. In the 1980s, dozens of artists used the "Amen" break as the basis for their songs. Listen to N.W.A's "Straight Outta Compton." That's the "Amen" break. It has appeared some thirteen hundred times throughout hip-hop history. Hundreds of artists—from Salt-N-Pepa, to Tupac Shakur, to Jay Z, to Tyler the Creator—have used it.

Its influence goes further still. As hip-hop gained steam in the '80s, the "Amen" break crossed the Atlantic Ocean where it became the foundation for techno, raga, jungle, and drum-and-bass music in the United Kingdom. An entire culture formed around six seconds of a drumbeat from a group my father lifted to fame, playing their version of a song the Impressions made popular.

Curtom missed all these opportunities. It is hard not to imagine the possibilities had my father signed the Jackson 5, kept the Stairsteps and the Winstons, and given Donny free rein. Music history itself would be different, and Curtom might very well have reached Motown-like heights. But for better or worse, Curtom's fate rested in my father's hands.

———

As spring turned to summer, Eddie got Curtom running at full speed
using everything he'd learned in a decade turning Curtis's songs into hits.
"One thing you knew, you knew the DJs," he says.

> You knew the record stores—the Mom-and-Pop as we called them,
> they're the ones that report to *Billboard*, they report to *Cashbox*.
> You knew the distributor for the record itself. Between maybe three
> distributors in Chicago, they together had all the product coming
> in. So now you got to pick a company that is strong enough to
> distribute your record. Curtis and I shopped around and went with
> Buddah Records. Whatever door they had open, we were going
> through the same door. They had the Village People, they had
> Casablanca, which was a big, big label back in those days. They
> were smokin'. We had a free ride.

The more Curtom gained its footing, though, the further my father
grew from Fred and Sam. When they learned he wasn't going to give
them shares in the label, they questioned the wisdom of passing up half a
million dollars at ABC. My father harbored no such apprehensions. With
each new success, he became more self-assured. He was only twenty-
six years old and had already led one of the most successful careers in
popular music history. With Curtom, he stood at the helm of his own
emerging empire. More than ever, he was master of his fate. As he told
Jet magazine, "With my own label, I control myself." He used his control
to help his family again, moving his mother out of Cabrini. Within a few
years he'd provide housing for her, Grandma Sadie, and Judy.

He felt proud of these accomplishments, and that pride began to
eclipse his insecurities. At the same time, he remained a complex man
occasionally haunted by his past. He went to a dentist to get his teeth
fixed, but that didn't fix his mind. He still remembered the taunts of
Smut and the poverty he'd escaped. Sometimes these issues drove him in
positive ways, helping him achieve great things. Other times, they hurt
him and those he cared about. Nowhere did they cause more trouble
than in his relationship with my mother. He felt himself losing her, and

it scared him. He could write about it movingly, as he did on *We're a Winner*'s "I Loved and I Lost"—"She was so beautiful like flowers full bloom in May / Her kiss was like the roaring wind, it left me speechless, with nothing to say / I loved and I lost." He couldn't do the one thing that might have kept her—remain faithful.

The temptations he faced only grew as he gained more power, confidence, and influence. His songs had already made him an icon; Curtom made him a titan. He'd done what a black man in America wasn't supposed to do—snatched control from a system designed to subjugate him. As a result, more people wanted a piece of him than ever.

Running Curtom put him under incredible pressure, and deciding whom to trust became an issue of dire importance. He and Eddie now had to handle business concerns they knew little about—accounting, office management, record pressing. For months, they had no hits, which worked well since they didn't have the capability to print enough records to meet the demands of one. My father struggled in a situation that didn't play to his strengths. He never had a mind for mundane day-to-day tasks. Big-picture ideas, like starting his own label, he could handle. When it came time to run the label, he needed help.

Rather than folding under the pressure, he did what he'd always done—relied on his guitar. While Eddie arranged distribution with Buddah, Dad began cutting Curtom's first full-length albums for the Impressions and the Stairsteps. His confidence soared.

———

At the same time, the 1968 presidential race heated up. Three days before King's assassination, Johnson announced he would not seek another term, and Robert Kennedy became the frontrunner to win the Democratic nomination and the presidency. Republicans threw their fate in with Richard Nixon, Eisenhower's vice president, who had lost to JFK in 1960. Nixon showed no signs of sympathy for the movement.

While JFK had aligned with the movement in the early '60s, RFK's speeches on the campaign trail made him look even more exciting and progressive. It seemed he could take the scattered ashes of a once great coalition and gather them around the mantle of his slain brother in the wake of King's death.

The script was all but written—RFK was young, good looking, popular, and sympathetic to the issues of the moment. On June 4, he won Democratic primaries in California and South Dakota, and just after midnight, he celebrated his victories in a speech at the Ambassador Hotel in Los Angeles. The Democratic National Convention was scheduled for Chicago in two months; "On to Chicago," he said. As he walked through the crowd, shaking hands with his supporters, a man approached with a gun and opened fire. Kennedy collapsed on the floor with a bullet in his head and several more scattered throughout his body. He died the next day.

———

While the years of success and fame changed my father emotionally, making him more confident in the present and less concerned with the hardships of the past, the years of assassinations and violence changed him creatively. For the first time, anger seeped into his lyrics—the anger of seeing his childhood home destroyed, his heroes murdered, and his hope trampled as the brutal deaths of JFK, Malcolm X, MLK, and RFK effectively ended the movement. As Robert Kennedy's slaying played out on the news, Dad wrote "This Is My Country," which shares a title with a patriotic folk song from the 1940s. Unlike that old folk song, my father's lyrics seethe with sadness and militancy:

> I've paid three hundred years or more
> Of slave driving, sweat, and welts on my back
> This is my country
> Too many have died in protecting my pride
> For me to go second class
> We've survived a hard blow and I want you to know
> That you'll face us at last
> And I know you will give consideration
> Shall we perish unjust or live equal as a nation?
> This is my country.

The repeated lyric, "This is my country," was a subtle rephrasing of Black Power. My father was saying black people had built America with their sweat and blood, with each lash of the slave driver's whip, with hundreds of years of forced labor; that they'd battled titanic forces to receive the benefits America offered everyone but them; that they'd been tortured, lynched, assassinated, humiliated, and rejected every step of the way, and yet they never stopped fighting for what was theirs. He'd never written more straightforward lyrics. Ditching the dual voices of Dunbar for good, he sang in the single voice of a people who had been owed something for a long time and now demanded payment in full.

The song marked a major shift in his thinking and reflected the militant shift in the movement. Yet, as personal as these lyrics were, he still never took credit for his messages. "I only look upon my writings as interpretations of how the majority of people around me feel," he said. "I would only take credit for being able to put what they think into lyric form . . . I'm not singing protest; I'm only singing happenings; the actual reality of what's going on around us, whether we'll admit it or not—it's there." These songs were more than messages. They were a kind of therapy for people who had just experienced the latest in a long parade of traumas.

My father experienced other changes as he wrote the new album. He latched onto the fashion of Black Power. He couldn't wait to get rid of the suits and ties the Impressions had always worn and slip into something hipper. "The style, the clothes, the wide pants, and the long German coats," he said. "Everything sort of fell in, and it hit a real nice fashion. To be fly was to *be*." These changes led him somewhere the Impressions had never been—and might not be able to go.

On top of those changes, he was responsible for running a business. Working for OKeh and ABC simultaneously seemed easy compared to the toil of running Curtom, where he was head writer, producer, A&R man, CEO, president, and leader of the most important act on the roster. Once again, he demanded more of himself than one man could accomplish.

He wanted Curtom to succeed on Motown's level, but an insurmountable obstacle stood in the way of that dream. Motown had a stable of talent—Lamont Dozier, the brothers Eddie and Brian Holland, Marvin Gaye, Smokey Robinson, Stevie Wonder, and half a dozen more who could write, arrange, and produce. Curtom had one horse. Of the twenty songs on Curtom's first two album releases, my father wrote sixteen of them outright and collaborated with Donny on one. He found himself under more creative pressure than ever. Unlike ABC, Curtom couldn't survive if Curtis didn't write hits.

Soon, his recording habits changed. He spent more time as a producer in the control room, mirroring his work with OKeh in the early '60s, and less on the floor cutting with the musicians. "It's hard work running between the studio and the control room," he said, "and now that over the years I have found musicians who can constantly create the sound I want, I spend most of my time in the control room where I can get a better idea of what the song will sound like when it's been recorded."

———————

As Dad cut the new Impressions album, one of the most infamous moments in American political history unfolded just a few miles away. On August 28, 1968, ten thousand protesters held a rally outside the Democratic National Convention in Grant Park. A disturbance erupted when a young boy lowered the American flag and cops began beating him. The crowd retaliated, hurling rocks and chunks of concrete at the cops while chanting, "Pigs are whores." The cops doused the crowd with noxious billows of tear gas, and when it was over, a huge tear-gas cloud crept down the street to the Hilton Hotel, where it reportedly disturbed Vice President Hubert Humphrey in the shower. For seventeen minutes, live television broadcasted the whole gory thing. The protestors shouted, "The whole world is watching."

While the whole world indeed watched, so did conservative white America, and it had finally had enough of youth movements, riots, and radical social makeovers. Come November 4, Richard Nixon celebrated a decisive victory over Hubert Humphrey. That same November, Curtom released *This Is My Country*.

After the release, Eddie hustled to make the album a hit. "When you get your record on the radio station, that's first," he says. "That's when you really gotta start running. You got to go to the stores, give the guy four or five copies, and say, 'I got this new record out, here's the name of it, order it for me or push it for me.' You got to do all of those little stops. You burn up a lot of rubber. You got to go to the nightclubs where the DJs are spinning the records. It never ends to get it going."

His hard work soon paid dividends. *This Is My Country* hit number five R&B, and the eponymous single went to number eight R&B. It was the Impressions' best work in three years, and it put Curtom on the map. Curtis and Eddie could relax. "Half a million start selling," Eddie says, "then you can sit back in your chair a little bit and say, 'Man, we did it. We got a $90,000 check coming in from the publisher, our royalties.'"

It came at the right time too—1968 had been another momentous year for music. Just one month before *This Is My Country*, Hendrix released his most successful album, *Electric Ladyland*. The title track featured Hendrix singing in a warbly falsetto, playing lyrical guitar licks he nicked from my father's style.

Put alongside songs like "Gypsy Eyes" and "Long Hot Summer Night"—cross referenced with the Impressions' "Gypsy Woman" and "Long Long Winter"—it is hard to miss my father's thumbprint on *Electric Ladyland*. Hendrix never tried to hide it, either. In fact, he often performed a cover of the Impressions' "Sometimes I Wonder" in concert.

On *Electric Ladyland*, Hendrix recorded his only message song, "House Burning Down," which dealt poetically with the recent riots. In fact, it seemed everyone felt the need to address the bloodshed of the past few years. Even the Beatles—who just the year before sang "All You Need Is Love"—now sang about revolution. On their self-titled double album, released at the same time as *This Is My Country*, John Lennon captured the ambivalence many felt about the use of violence, singing, "When you talk about destruction, don't you know that you can count me out and in?"

Unlike previous years, which saw my father lose touch with the continuing social upheaval, with *This Is My Country*, he reclaimed his role as the movement's musical conscience. He turned his ode to Martin Luther King into a song called "They Don't Know," which married the Chicago Sound to the gut-bucket soul of artists like Aretha Franklin, who had just released *Lady Soul*, and Otis Redding, who had died in a tragic plane crash the year before but continued to direct the course of soul music from beyond the pale with the posthumously released *The Dock of the Bay* and *The Immortal Otis Redding*.

Dad had something Redding and Franklin never had, though—his own label. It wasn't unheard of for a black man to run a record label at that time. Ray Charles had done it with Tangerine Records, Sam Cooke had SAR, the Isley Brothers had T-Neck, James Brown had Try Me, and of course, Berry Gordy had Motown. However, it was still an anomaly in a country where many black people struggled to eat, let alone start a successful business.

With "They Don't Know" and "This Is My Country" coming out on his own label, Dad became a symbol of black accomplishment. He had also put two message songs on the same album for the first time, taking a chance few other artists dared take. Even James Brown surrounded his paean to black pride, "Say It Loud—I'm Black and I'm Proud," with unthreatening pop fare. My father had done the same thing on previous albums like *Keep On Pushing*, *People Get Ready*, and *We're a Winner*. But as he reacted to the recent violence and despair, he knew his audience looked to him to put heavy truths in his songs. He'd given them so much food for thought, they began to expect it from him. They wouldn't accept it the same way from anyone else.

Though his fans accepted it, Dad took a double risk with those songs. While they maintained a positive outlook, their lyrics held his most pointed critique yet on America's problems and who was responsible for them. It was a sign of the direction he wanted to go, and the public's acceptance told him he'd found the right track. Not only could he sustain his fan base with harder messages, he could also grow his business.

———

As the Impressions toured to support the album, the movement entered its final phase as the forces for and against it moved further toward their respective fringes. Nixon was the emblem of conservative white America, which wanted to take back as much ground in the name of traditional values as possible. Upon assuming the Oval Office, Nixon slowed federal spending for the advancement of black people and poor whites, saying in his first State of the Union address, "It is time for those who make massive demands on society to make minimal demands on themselves." He tried to placate alienated whites by nominating southern conservatives for the US Supreme Court and keeping black congressmen waiting months for a reply to their requests for an audience.

On the other side, the Black Panthers filled the void left by King's death. From the beginning, the Panthers were one of the most misunderstood civil rights groups in history. Part of it was their desperate situation. As Huey Newton wrote in the *Black Panther*, "We've been pushed into corners, into ghettos, you dig it?" That cornering left them little choice but to lash out, especially after King, the paragon of nonviolence, was murdered.

Part of it was the Panthers' fault—they realized the more violent and incendiary they acted in public, the more media coverage they got. Satellite television had just been invented, and the rush of news from around the world roared with the force and noise of a white-water rapid. Amidst that din, the Vietnam War roared loudest. No longer did folks back home read about yesterday's battle in the newspaper. Now, they watched it on television as they ate dinner. The Panthers shrewdly realized meekness wouldn't get them featured on the evening broadcast.

Part of it came from Stokely Carmichael, who had just joined forces with the Panthers. He called Black Power "a movement that will smash everything Western civilization has created"—a statement incendiary enough to get plenty of news coverage.

Though polls at the time showed only 15 percent of blacks identified as separatists, the Panthers had taken control of the public discourse by making more noise. Still, as Huey Newton, Eldridge Cleaver, and Bobby Seale pushed the violent side of the Panthers, they also developed another side to the organization, starting community projects including a free healthcare clinic and a free breakfast program for schoolchildren.

My father supported many of the Panthers' goals, but he couldn't get behind them the way he got behind King. "They aren't a national organization," he said. "They don't have the muscle." The Panthers would continue to gain influence, but they'd never reach the level of the SCLC, SNCC, CORE, or other groups that preceded them. Constant confrontations with police, disruptive tactics by the FBI, and vicious infighting made sure they never cohered as a unit.

———————

With so much fighting going on at home, my father still worried about his brother fighting in Vietnam. Uncle Kenny was scheduled to finish his tour at the end of 1968, but he says:

> They had a thing going on back then that they could not send two brothers to Vietnam at the same time, and I knew the government was still trying to draft certain people, so I extended another year to make sure that if my brother did get drafted, he wouldn't come there. So, that's why I took my extra year in Vietnam. Plus, when I got ready to leave Vietnam, they wanted to send me to Germany, and I refused that because at that time, they were still having racial problems. Any place they were having racial problems, I tried to avoid, because I'm outspoken. It's hard for me to get mad, but when I do get angry, I'm not in control of myself, so I kind of tried to avoid that, and I guess that's why I've always been a loner.

It's no surprise Uncle Kenny was a loner, coming from a family of loners, but he found solace hearing his brother's voice in Vietnam. "A lot of Curtis's music reached way over there," he said. "My favorite one was 'Choice of Colors.' Then you had 'We're a Winner.' If you sit down and listen to it, it was inspirational, trying to build you up, trying to make you feel like you were somebody, trying to make you feel like this is my country."

Even though he risked his life for America, Uncle Kenny didn't feel he had a country. Like many black soldiers, he followed the tragedies in America as news trickled into Vietnam, and he knew his prospects would be bleak upon returning home. "Here I am over [in Vietnam] fighting for somebody else's freedom that I didn't even have, but with what was going on in the country here, I didn't want to come back," he says. "I didn't know where I was going, but I just didn't want to come back."

He still faced racism, even in Vietnam. "I'll never forget it, I got off the boat in Danang, loaded down, had an M-14 automatic weapon, and this little Vietnamese guy come up to me and called me a nigger," he says. "I took the butt of the weapon and I hit him with it." His feelings fit perfectly with the movement's direction back home, both nonviolent and otherwise.

Around the time Uncle Kenny enlisted, the Defense Department had launched Project 100,000, which lowered standards for draft requirements, making one hundred thousand former rejects acceptable for induction. As a result, a disproportionate number of black soldiers ended up on the front lines. Black soldiers served as cannon fodder, suffering a higher casualty rate than white soldiers.

King had spoken against the war before his death, but SNCC, CORE, and the Panthers now made the war a major part of their rebellion. Carmichael and others trolled college campuses passing out flyers playing on army recruitment propaganda. "Uncle Sam wants YOU nigger," the flyers read. "Become a member of the world's highest paid black mercenary army! Support White Power—travel to Viet Nam, you might get a medal! Fight for Freedom . . . (in Viet Nam). Receive valuable training in the skills of killing off other oppressed people! (Die Nigger Die—you can't die fast enough in the ghettos)."

Even the Viet Cong exploited American racism. At least one sign posted in Vietnam read, "U.S. Negro armymen! You are committing the same ignominious crimes in South Vietnam that the KKK clique is perpetuating against your family at home." Perhaps no one summed up the situation better than Muhammad Ali, who put an exclamation mark on the black resistance to the draft when he issued his heartfelt but incendiary reason for his refusal. In an often misquoted statement, he said, "My conscience won't let me go shoot my brother, or some darker people, or some poor hungry people in the mud for big powerful America. And shoot them for what? They never called me nigger, they never lynched me, they didn't put no dogs on me, they didn't rob me of my nationality, rape and kill my mother and father. . . . Shoot them for what? . . . How can I shoot them poor people? Just take me to jail."

My father noticed all these developments. He and Ali were friends—my mother remembers the bombastic boxer visiting them at home—and Uncle Kenny still fought the war Ali resisted. Dad had never written an antiwar song before, and he wasn't ready to yet. The idea germinated in his mind, though. Perhaps he wanted to wait until his brother came home.

In 1969, Curtis celebrated a decade in the music business. Within those years, he'd gone from being Jerry Butler's sideman to one of the most powerful voices in popular music. He now stood on the cusp of even greater success, as he continued adding acts to the Curtom roster, including Baby Huey and the Babysitters. Baby Huey, real name James Ramey, was a hulking 350-pound man with a hell of a voice and one of the most popular live bands in Chicago. By the late '60s, he'd taken Sly Stone's lead and turned the Babysitters into a psychedelic soul act, electrifying audiences with R&B freak-outs amplified by his ample Afro and the trippy African robes he wore to cover his heft. In early 1969, the Babysitters' manager, Marv Heiman—also known as Marv Stuart—invited Donny Hathaway to watch the band at the Thumbs Up club in Chicago. Donny left so impressed that he had my father come with him the following night. Dad saw a star in Ramey and signed the band that night. Not long after, Baby Huey and the Babysitters released their first single on Curtom, a cover of the Impressions' "Mighty Mighty (Spade & Whitey)," renamed "'Mighty' 'Mighty' Children (Unite Yourself This Hour)."

Signing the Babysitters changed my father's life and career in major, unforeseen ways. Their manager, Marv Stuart, became a fulcrum that pushed Dad into the next phase of his career. Marv was a hustler in every sense of the word. He'd already booked Baby Huey on Della Reese's talk show, *Della*, as well as *The Merv Griffin Show*, which even the Impressions couldn't get. He also booked them at the Whisky a Go Go and several other major clubs across the country. All this without a hit to their name.

Marv hadn't spent as much time in the music business as my father and Eddie, but his track record was so impressive that when the Impressions released their second album on Curtom, *The Young Mods' Forgotten Story*, Dad asked Marv to act as the group's manager. Dad liked Marv, frankly, because he was white and Jewish. As much as he believed in solidarity among black people, he also said, "My face during those years would not allow doors to open for me. As a black man, you don't get an invitation." He thought Marv's face would open those doors, so he put his trust in a man who hadn't earned it.

Marv began booking the Impressions on television shows to coincide with an upcoming California tour. According to Marv, when he asked the producers why they never had the Impressions on the shows before, they said no one ever asked. He also took a hard look at Curtom's books. "There was one guy in charge of all the accounting, royalty collecting, bookkeeping," Marv says. "According to the books, Curtom was broke and they weren't receiving the royalties they were due. Curtis said, 'Is someone stealing from me?' I said I didn't think so—they just weren't able to handle the volume of work." Marv hired an accounting firm to handle the books and Curtom quickly raked in roughly $600,000 in unclaimed royalties. From that point on, he was in.

Of Marv, my father said, "As green as he was, he was very ambitious. I taught him the record business and how to relate to people. Through his own know-how and his own go-gettingness, he learned. He was able to find weak spots in Curtom, and he turned them around." Fred, Sam, and Eddie didn't share Dad's excitement, and the Impressions grew further apart.

Marv came onboard as Curtom took its biggest step toward legitimacy. The leadoff single from *The Young Mods' Forgotten Story*, another message song called "Choice of Colors," shot to number one R&B. No stranger to the top of the chart, my father had now done it with his own label for the first time. With "Choice of Colors," he retreated a bit from the edge of "This Is My Country" and offered a song more in the mold of his positive, food-for-thought, mid-'60s message songs. One main differ- ence—"Choice of Colors" took on the issue of race directly. He sang, "If you had a choice of colors / Which one would you choose, my brothers? / If there was no day or night / Which would you prefer to be right?"

Dad held out hope for America longer than many black people around him did. "Choice of Colors" contained lyrics such as "People must prove to the people / A better day is coming," and "With just a little bit more education / And love for our nation / Would make a better society." But those sentiments, which once helped give the old movement direction, now put him at odds with the new movement's goals and mindset.

The Young Mods' Forgotten Story also contained a second message song, though, and it showed that even my father's hope for America had begun to erode. Tucked at the end of the album, "Mighty Mighty (Spade & Whitey)" warned about the dangers of "black and white power," and it was clear when he sang, "We're killing up our leaders," that King's death still weighed heavily on his mind. Unlike any song he'd yet writ- ten, this one played like a conversation about his feelings on where the country stood:

> *Everybody's talking about this country's state*
> *We give a new power every hour, just about with every Christian fate*
> *We're killing up our leaders, it don't matter none black or white*
> *And we all know it's wrong, but we're gonna fight to make it right*
> *And mighty, mighty Spade and Whitey*
> *Your black and white power is gonna be a crumbling tower*
> *And we who stand divided, so damn undecided*
> *Give this some thought: in stupidness we've all been caught.*

It was his most honest song yet. It wasn't about hope; it was about reality. It seemed he couldn't write about hope when no one around him felt any. He knew he had to start speaking a different truth—a harder truth—but he didn't know if the Impressions were the right group to deliver the message.

––––––––––

While "Choice of Colors" rode high on the charts, the Impressions stayed just as high in demand. They began another sprawl across a country in terrible turmoil, and although my father grew tired of touring, saying, "The road wears a man down after twelve years," he also knew the road made him who he was. "There's nothing else I want to do," he said. "There's nothing else I could do anyway, but if I could do something else I wouldn't want to do it because this life, if you live it in such manners, can be beautiful for you." It was beautiful for Curtis. The road gave him an escape from the poverty of his childhood. Since he had become a traveling musician, Dad was too busy, too free—and eventually too rich and famous—to be backed into the ghetto's corners anymore.

Like much about the late '60s, though, what once seemed beautiful turned tragic. During a show with Jackie Wilson in Grenville, South Carolina, a switch broke on the Impressions' sound system, and they had to go to Atlanta to get it fixed. My father's quiet voice made the special sound system necessary for the tour to continue. In the studio, they could rely on studio tricks to pump up his volume, but on tour they'd bring their own speakers—four for Fred and Sam, and four just for Curtis. Otherwise, Fred and Sam would drown him out.

They had time before the next show, so the backing band threw the broken gear in the trailer and took off to Atlanta, as Dad, Fred, and Sam sped away in their sports cars. The next morning, Fred called home and heard the news. The band was dead. "They were coming down a big double highway to a bridge," Fred said. "The bridge had this curve in it and it went over this river. They must have been doing ninety or a hundred miles an hour and they just never got across that bridge. They just went through that rail and they went two hundred and ten feet in the air clear across the river and hit the bank on the other side. A farmer found them about eight o'clock the next morning."

The tour couldn't go on. My father drove to the morgue with Fred and Sam to identify the bodies, and when they finally summoned the courage to go in, a gruesome scene awaited them—the guitarist and drummer lay mangled on the floor while the bass player was stretched flat on the embalming table. "They was messed up," Fred said. "The guitar player had his arm all twisted . . . The Lord must have been telling us something. We all used to have sports cars. In '63 Curt had a Jag and Sam and me had Corvettes and that Jag wasn't fast enough, we used to run away from it. So Curt got a 427 Cobra, and then we got 427 Corvettes. We used to run 150 miles an hour every day. We used to drive a lot, especially during the summer. Drive, drive, drive. None of us liked to fly, and we'd drive to concerts all over the Midwest and the South. After that accident we sold the Corvettes right then."

Around that same time, my father wrecked his Cobra. After the wreck, my mother recalls, "He had the guy at the body shop to fix it, and you know, Curtis was gone, and it had something to do with money, and Curtis didn't want to pay the guy for storage or something, and the guy kept the car. I'd say, 'Why aren't you going to get the car?' 'Well, they want money.' 'Well then, pay him!' You know that car cost a lot of money. And the man ended up keeping that car."

After the band deaths, he no longer wanted a sports car. Still, it didn't make sense to abandon an expensive car just because he didn't want to pay the mechanic's storage fee. He ended up giving away a collector's item worth hundreds of thousands of dollars today. That was my father, though. His stubbornness often got the best of him, and his strong Gemini traits meant he could be two people at once—shrewd and blind. As Curtom demanded more of his attention, those tendencies left him open to predators. He remained a man of few friends, and he began trusting the wrong people. Crooked accountants could easily cook books without him knowing it. He also gave Marv more control over his finances than he had allowed anyone in his life.

These events exacerbated the mounting friction with Fred and Sam. They felt Curtis and Marv were forming a cabal with the intent of pushing them to the side. Fred said, "I think they just didn't think that Sam and I really mattered at that point, and that's why it just kind of escalated. Why did he trust [Marv] so much? I don't know to this day. I've had some people that's very close in his family ask me the same thing and I just don't know." Figuring out why my father trusted Marv became a parlor game for family and friends. None of us have come up with a definitive answer.

Dad never explained it either, but it makes sense looking at his life as a whole. He'd been fighting for control from childhood. It seemed every circumstance tried to keep him down—his skin, his looks, his poverty—but he fought to overcome them all. Though he fought for his family and his friends and even for his people as a whole, ultimately, he fought mostly for himself. He had little choice but to grow up that way. His father refused to look after him, and his mother didn't have the means to do it properly. He learned at an early age to rely on himself, and he'd proven to himself beyond a doubt that he could meet any challenge. The mere fact that he had risen beyond humble beginnings to run his own label proved he was not a man to be trifled with.

By looking out for himself, he earned control over his life and power over his circumstances. He didn't mind sharing that control and power with Fred, Sam, and Eddie as long as doing so aligned with his business interests. But if he saw something that could help him better extend that control and power—a different business partner like Marv, for instance—he'd run with it and not look back.

He believed Marv could make him more money. More money gave him more power and control. In the end, his trust may have had more to do with that than anything else. He didn't want money for its own sake. As he said, "Now that I have money I spend it less than I used to." He wanted it because it made him feel secure, assuring him he'd never suffer again like he did in the White Eagle.

If Eddie didn't like it, if Fred and Sam couldn't take it, too bad for them. They couldn't change his mind. There again came his duality as a Gemini—he could be deeply in tune with his community and at the same time selfish to the point of hurting his closest friends. Despite Dad's growing confidence, which became stronger than ever with Curtom's success, the scars from his childhood ran deep—as deep as the sense of worthlessness society taught him to feel. He had to escape it by any means necessary.

———

Tensions within the Impressions remained beneath the surface as they began piecing together a new backing band. They had a hard time continuing in the face of such tragedy. "That was a heavy blow because we all were close," Curtis said. Fred agreed: "That was one of the hardest and the saddest periods of our life."

Still, the show had to go on, so they hired new musicians, including Sam's nephew Joseph Scott. Everyone called him Lucky, and as Sam said, "He didn't read music, but he had the best ear you wanted to hear, because he could go into the studio and record anything that you want to record." My father felt happy with the choice, since he'd known Lucky his entire life. "When we came out in 1958, Lucky and his brother were in diapers," he said. "Lucky grew up seeing us doing our thing and somehow he picked up a bass and he worked himself to a point where when the time came we had to bring him in."

Lucky became the bandleader as the Impressions went on a critical swing through California, taking them to the Fillmore West and Dick Clark's *American Bandstand,* among other places. A *Rolling Stone* reporter followed them on that trip and gave a fascinating insight into life on the road for the Impressions and how Marv's influence had grown.

Without knowing it, the reporter was also witnessing an end for Curtis, Fred, and Sam.

8

Now You're Gone

"Ain't no hard feelings,
I won't worry my mind with such dealings."
—"So You Don't Love Me"

The San Francisco Hilton, early 1969—*Brrrrrrrrrring!* went the phone in Fred's room. "Hello?" Fred mumbled into the phone. Then, exasperation creeping into his soft Chattanooga drawl, "Baby, I'm not going to give you any money, understand? I'm sorry, but no. Good-bye." He hung up. "It was this girl who tried to see me yesterday," he told Michael Alexander, the reporter from *Rolling Stone* who accompanied the group on their California jaunt. "I don't know how she knew I was here. She says her mother works here. She wants money! Says she has to visit her grandmother or something. We don't get hustled like that very often. I can count the girls like that on one hand. We don't hang around with that kind of people."

Fred wasn't being completely honest—like Curtis and Sam, he was no stranger to road affairs. As Eddie says, "The girls would all line up backstage. You'd say, 'You two come with me, you three come with me.' That's the way it was." With a wife at home, however, Fred couldn't go trumpeting that news to a major music magazine.

Preparing for the first Fillmore show, Fred sent out for Leonard's Hickory Pit barbecue and called room service for a Coke. After eating, he showered and shaved, singing along with an Impressions record on a battery-powered phonograph. Then, he dressed, burning loose threads off his new shirt with a cigarette. Fred couldn't stand loose threads.

Just from the Impressions' stage clothes, it was obvious how much the world had changed since they bought suits at Maxwell Street Market in 1958. Fred and Sam followed Dad's lead and ditched the tuxedos they once sported. Instead they wore the hip mod style of the time—colorful leisure suits, black ankle boots, and German coats, as featured on the *This Is My Country* album cover. Marv made a special point of instructing road manager Robert Cobbins, "Street clothes, no suits or ties. And nobody shows up in a tuxedo." This represented more than just a stylistic choice. It was a statement of Black Power told through clothing. Black performers didn't dress up for the Man anymore.

Finally, show time. Curtis, Fred, and Sam, tired from the press party at Basin Street the night before, took the stage at the Fillmore West alongside Santana and Ike and Tina Turner. They still didn't feel comfortable performing—losing their road band in the accident meant making do with new guys who only knew the hits, and they were fed up with their current drummer. Regardless, they were seasoned performers and did their best to get over to the crowd. Sweating through their hip getups under the spotlights, they ground out old classics like "Gypsy Woman" and "Keep On Pushing" along with "Choice of Colors" and other new hits. Unfortunately, the largely white rock crowd that packed the Fillmore gave the Impressions a tepid welcome. Despite years of toil, they hadn't crossed over to the pop market in a meaningful way.

After the set, a black man with an Afro accosted my father backstage. The lyrics to "Choice of Colors" had him upset.

If you had a choice of colors
Which one would you choose, my brothers?

Curtis as a newborn, Chicago 1942.
AUTHOR'S COLLECTION

From left: Curtis's grandmother Annie Bell;
his father, Mannish; his aunt Mercedes's son
Junior; and Mannish's wife Rosie, Chicago,
date unknown. *COURTESY JUDITH MAYFIELD*

The White Eagle Hotel, Chicago, where Curtis and his family lived in the late 1940s.

Curtis in Chattanooga in 1958 after the release of "For Your Precious Love." He would soon lose the processed hair look.
AUTHOR'S COLLECTION

MAY · 59

Curtis in his family's Cabrini-Green row house, May 1959.
AUTHOR'S COLLECTION

urtis at age eighteen with his first car, a 1952 Mercedes, at Cabrini-Green in 1960.
JTHOR'S COLLECTION

Curtis's mother, Marion, outside the family's
Cabrini-Green home, Chicago 1963.
AUTHOR'S COLLECTION

Curtis at the Apollo Theater in New York City,
performing with the Impressions circa 1959.
AUTHOR'S COLLECTION

The Impressions rehearsing in the studio, Chicago circa 1965. *AUTHOR'S COLLECTION*

Curtis and Jackie
Wilson, circa 1967.
AUTHOR'S COLLECTION

Curtis and Todd Mayfield, Chicago 1968. *AUTHOR'S COLLECTION*

The Impressions in
Los Angeles circa 1969.
AUTHOR'S COLLECTION

Curtis at the Miss Black
America pageant 1969.
AUTHOR'S COLLECTION

Backstage before a concert,
circa 1973. From left: Curtis's
partner Diane and her son Tracy;
Curtis, daughter Sharon, and
son Todd; and Grandma Sadie.
COURTESY DIANE MAYFIELD

Curtis at the Berlin Hilton,
West Germany circa 1973.
AUTHOR'S COLLECTION

Curtis in London circa 1973. *COURTESY MICHAEL PUTLAND*

Curtis at the Montreux Jazz
Festival 1987, Switzerland.
AUTHOR'S COLLECTION

Curtis on the Impressions'
1983 reunion tour.
COURTESY MICHAEL PUTLAND

Curtis and Todd after
1994 Grammy Awards.
Curtis received the
1994 Legend Award.
JIM MCHUGH

"We *don't* have a choice of colors," the man said. "We don't. We don't have a choice at all." My father listened patiently and tried to explain his side. "You aren't listening to the words," he said. He repeated them, a tinge of annoyance creeping into his soft, measured voice. "You listen to that song again," he said. "If you still don't understand it, we can talk about it again tomorrow night." Few celebrities would have invited a fan to engage in such a deep discussion about lyrics, and though Dad never saw the kid again, it showed how much he wanted people to understand him.

While "Choice of Colors" hit the top of the R&B chart—the Impressions' fifth number one—the young man put a fine point on a feeling Dad had sensed for a while. His audience had changed. Lyrics like "How long have you hated your white teacher?" made sense in his head, but perhaps they didn't make sense to his listeners. Even the term "white teacher" had paternalistic undertones that didn't fly with the young, militant, urban blacks that had taken over the movement. For these young kids, the white man was the problem. My father often complained about "Whitey" and "crackers," but he still believed the biggest problem was "ourselves." "'Choice of Colors' isn't for Whitey, it's for us," he said. "We have to get together. If we united behind our leaders we'd be much stronger. Martin Luther King had the biggest following and it was too small. There's twenty million of us and that's not enough." Of course, my father understood the young man's position. "That doesn't mean you just lay down all the time," he said. "You should be pushing, even scaring, sometimes." Still, he didn't see Black Power as any more viable in the long run than White Power.

The young man walked away from the conversation unsatisfied. Dad did, too. He always wrote songs based on what he heard from his community, and now he heard anger like never before. At the same time, his main concern was selling albums, and while conciliatory songs like "Choice of Colors" didn't sit right with some militant young blacks, songs with harder edges like "This Is My Country" alienated many white listeners. Sam recalled when they played white college dates in the South, they had to stop performing the latter song. "People didn't like it too much," he said, "especially down South when you're talking about 'whips on your back.'" It put my father in an impossible situation. He couldn't please every listener, and he had too much integrity to sell out his ideals in trying.

———

At eleven o'clock the following morning, Curtis, still in a robe, opened the door of his sixteenth-floor room. He'd come a long way from the days of being chased out of a white hotel because Sam tried to get some ice. In making his living as a traveling performer, he'd seen the worst segregation had to offer. He knew about staying in seedy motels because no hotel would take him, eating in grimy back alleys because no restaurant would seat him. Now in his fancy San Francisco hotel room, he finished a room-service breakfast—steak and fruit cocktail—slipped out of his plush robe, and got dressed.

That day, the Impressions planned to find some hip West Coast clothes before another late night at the Fillmore. As my father dressed, Marv entered the room. "Are you doing any writing?" he asked. "I haven't had any time," my father said. "All this moving around, trying to get the band into shape. There's no time to write." That represented another major change from years past—years when Dad could knock out chart-busting songs in between sets on tour, or in the car speeding from gig to gig. It frustrated him. Writing was like breathing, and the road felt increasingly suffocating.

Touring wasn't all a grind, though. As the Impressions drove to the fashionable stores on Polk Street, they talked about the Playboy Club, where they had dined after the Basin Street press party two nights before. They still couldn't quite believe it. Bunnies brought them gourmet food, and the manager personally welcomed them. It seemed like everyone in the place tried to make them feel pampered, including a bevy of beautiful women. Just think of it, that whole production for three guys from the South Side of Chicago.

At the store, they browsed the racks with my father complaining, "I can't get into anything. It's my ass, sticks out and throws everything out of whack." He still didn't feel comfortable with his body. He picked out a few things, stuck a Napoleon hat on Marv for giggles, paid with a hundred dollar bill, and the band headed back to the Hilton to prepare for the second show and the week ahead.

————

The day after the second show, the Impressions had a spot on KDIA, a local R&B station, where the interviewer leveled a serious accusation: "You try to present yourselves as ordinary people, but you're not ordinary," he said. My father replied, "Well, we're just simple people. Just down to earth." The interviewer pressed to find the big ego somewhere. He asked the Impressions about making themselves spokesmen for their people. "I like to call these songs of inspiration, songs of faith," Dad answered, deflecting the question. "We don't try to be spokesmen, although we speak our minds. We're entertainers. We're complimented that they look on us as spokesmen, but we just think we're singing what all the brothers feel." Sam added, "The black performer isn't a shuffler anymore." Fred picked up on the theme and said, "James Brown wouldn't sing about pride three years ago." What Fred tactfully left in the subtext of that statement was that the Impressions had played a major role in creating a world where Brown could sing about pride.

They had precious little time to pause and reflect on these things. The week after the last show at the Fillmore, the Impressions appeared on a local television show and played four nights at Basin Street. The next week, they traveled to Los Angeles, where Marv had booked a radio spot, five television guest appearances including *American Bandstand* and *The Joey Bishop Show*, three nights at the Troubadour, and a Saturday night concert at the Hollywood Palladium. Dad always found the road exhausting, but with the extra weight of Curtom on his back, he couldn't bear it much longer.

Despite the increased demands on his time, the Impressions were freer than ever. They could dress how they wanted, sing what they wanted, and express unabashed pride in their blackness. Most of that freedom came from my father's songs and his decision to start Curtom, which allowed the Impressions to call their own shots in ways that were impossible at ABC. Marv also added to their freedom, booking slots on TV shows they'd never played before and giving them a stronger connection than ever to the white pop market. The freedom also hurt the group, though. It moved Dad further into his own world—a world where he saw himself standing on his own, free from the monotonous slog of touring.

————

During the Impressions' run at the Fillmore, the Four Tops had an engagement just down the street in the Crown Room at the Fairmont Hotel. The Tops played to a white supper-club audience and made a killing. One night after their show, they dropped by the Impressions' dressing room. Even though it was two in the morning, even though they were all exhausted, even though the road had ground them down physically, mentally, spiritually, the room exploded with, "How you *doin'* brother?" and hands shaking, hands slapping, everyone laughing, exchanging their newest road stories, talking about whose band was hot, who had the tightest rhythm section.

Dad got the scoop from the Tops on playing the white supper-club scene and how much money he could make there. Then, Levi Stubbs of the Tops asked about the audience at the Fillmore, and the Impressions—who just moments before onstage had been three men with one voice—all began talking at the same time. "You wouldn't be-*lieve* that smoke when you walk out there it's like to knock you *over*. There's cops standing right there next to it and I think *they's* high *too*."

Fred and Sam shied away from drugs, but my father had begun experimenting with marijuana. "I wasn't dropping acid, but I guess it's safe for me to say that I too smoked herb," he said later. "It was no big deal. I didn't do nothing until I was twenty-seven years old, and smoking herb didn't seem like a heavy cost to pay to cure my curiosity." Still, he never performed high, and even he felt surprised at the level of drug use in the audience. By 1969, it seemed few remained immune to the siren song of mind expansion.

The next night at Basin Street, a young drummer named André Fischer—who would go on to play in the band Rufus with Chaka Khan—caught the Impressions' set. André had met my father a few times before, so he stepped backstage after the show and said hello. "What are you doing here?" my father asked, a little surprised. Every time the two had met, it had been in a different city. André explained he was drumming for *Big Time Buck White*, a Black Power play down the street. Then, he started talking with organ player Melvin Jones. "Man, we can't stand this drummer," Jones said. "We're looking for another one."

The next day, André stopped by the Impressions' sound check at Basin Street. The Impressions didn't invite their current drummer in order to give André a shot. Turned out the kid had big ears. He knew their records and had seen the show the night before, so he could play all the parts. No one wanted him to leave. He didn't.

Upon learning the band made $250 a week with no per diem, he asked for $300 and a per diem. He got it. It pissed off the band, so André made them see it as an opportunity to increase their own pay. My father grudgingly agreed to the raise. If he had trouble sharing stakes in Curtom with Fred and Sam, he certainly didn't want to give away money to his backing band, even though he needed them, too.

Hiring André proved fateful, leading my father to a musician who would influence his direction in coming years. When the Impressions sought a second guitarist, André called his friend Craig McMullen, who was fluent in jazz, psychedelia, soul, and R&B. At the time, Dad was searching for new textures to add to his sound. Craig, with his guitar effects pedals and jazzy chord changes, helped point the way forward.

The new members locked in with Lucky as their leader. My father loved Lucky—everyone did—but he learned Lucky was a peculiar man. On stage, he'd wear a Nehru jacket long after that style had passed, along with black dress pants that had been pressed so often they were shiny as glass, and he'd pull them up too high, leaving the cuff several inches above his shoes. He wore fake silk socks and Stacy Adams dress shoes. While he played, a Marlboro cigarette dangled from his lips, and he bit the filter, shooting a steady stream of smoke into his face. He'd squint his eyes through the smoke and violently thrust his hips, appearing to hump his bass guitar.

Lucky's idiosyncrasies went beyond dress and stage presence. He carried a briefcase on tour, and everyone assumed he had gear or sheet music in it—until he opened it. His briefcase was custom designed to hold a liquor bottle and shot glasses. Next to a bottle of J&B scotch, he kept a bottle of hot sauce, a Polaroid camera, and a huge picture collection bound by rubber bands. Each picture showed an overweight old woman wearing skimpy lingerie, striking a sensual pose. Lucky liked older women and often joked, "If you see me with a younger woman, I'm holding her for the police." But the man could play a bass into submission, and that was enough for my father.

———

In an era with few television outlets, performing on a late-night network talk show gave them precious exposure to the pop market. So in 1969 the Impressions were fortunate to book an episode of ABC's *The Joey Bishop Show*. As with radio, however, television came with its share of racism and conservatism. While the Impressions rehearsed "Choice of Colors," Bishop's producer loomed nearby. "You won't be able to do that song on this television show," he said. "It isn't right for the format, and it won't work on a national televised audience." Tense moments passed as my father considered leaving the show rather than submitting to unfair censorship. Bishop noticed the problem and walked over to discuss it. "What's going on?" he asked. My father explained the situation. Bishop thought for a second and said, "Hey, if this is your hit record, go ahead and do it."

Though they won the showdown with Bishop's producer, it seemed the country's problems followed the Impressions wherever they went, all the more so because Dad bravely put himself and the group in the middle of those problems. Racism, revolution, and riots hung heavy in the air. Everyone had to deal with them. Some, like Bishop's producer, tried to ignore them until they went away. Others, like the Impressions, confronted them fearlessly. Yet, the more fearless my father became with his songs, the more he worried for Fred and Sam. He didn't mind taking chances by himself—chances that could end in radio bans or worse—but he didn't feel comfortable putting Fred and Sam and their livelihoods on the line. Dad wanted to confront society's ills more powerfully than ever before. He also wanted to stop touring. Somewhere deep within, he knew he couldn't achieve those desires with the Impressions.

———

After finishing their work in California, the Impressions drove back to Chicago's stinging cold, and Curtis found his grandmother in the hospital. Annie Bell died on March 13, 1969, of pneumonia and congestive heart failure brought on by diabetes. The next day, Uncle Kenny returned safely from Vietnam. Annie Bell told Uncle Kenny she'd wait for him to get home. She almost made it.

Of all the tragedies over the past few years, losing Annie Bell hurt Dad the most. He'd already put his brother Kirby in the ground, and he'd seen five of America's greatest leaders slain. Now, he said goodbye to the woman who had done more to shape, guide, and inspire him than anyone but his mother. Annie Bell helped lead him to music. Her voice echoed in his lyrics. Her sermons gave his songs direction. Because of her, he met Jerry Butler. Because of her, he joined his first vocal group. Because of her, he fell in love with the life of a traveling musician. Without her, nothing else he'd achieved would have been possible.

Amidst this emotional upheaval, Dad struggled with a romantic relationship on the brink of failure. My mother's patience for his cheating wore thin, but he couldn't stop. He set up a mistress in an apartment on the North Side, and he lived two lives, splitting time between our home and her apartment.

It's amazing he found time for a mistress. He had four children, his own label to run, a successful album to promote, and a fiery partner at home who inched closer to leaving him. On top of all that, after the tour ended, my father booked time in the studio to recut most of the Impressions' catalog because ABC-Paramount owned his old masters. In shrewd businessman style, he wanted to record the songs again so whenever anyone wanted to license them, they would license his masters, and all the money would go to Curtom. André, Craig, Lucky, and Melvin remained close during this period because my father, unlike many artists, recorded with his road band whenever possible. Lucky stayed with André in a motel on Stony Island Avenue, sharing a room about five minutes from Curtom's offices.

After a long day of recording old Impressions material, Lucky would return to the hotel and eat barbecue ribs or pizza for dinner. He'd ruffle through the briefcase, pour a nip of J&B scotch, douse his food with hot sauce, and wash it down with red soda. After a few weeks, his fingertips began to turn yellow. He thought he had jaundice, so he and André hopped in a cab and found an emergency room. The doctor said Lucky had elevated blood pressure and asked if he ate large amounts of canned-tomato products. As it turned out, between the acid from the hot sauce and the trash he ate, his hands had become discolored. The doctor told him his lips would turn yellow too if he didn't lay off the hot sauce and pizza.

Lucky would have little choice but to diversify his diet on the road as they set out for ninety days of one-nighters through places like Mississippi, Louisiana, North Carolina, and Georgia. As the Impressions toured, *Young Mods* threw "Seven Years" high on the R&B chart to keep "Choice of Colors" company. The new single continued the album's success and kept Curtom moving forward.

Success or not, touring continued to drain my father physically and mentally. "Sometimes we'd drive five or six hundred miles," André says, "and sometimes a couple of the gigs would be canceled and we'd have to drive all the way back." It also exhausted Dad emotionally, especially because integration remained a sore subject in the South. At a show in Natchez, Mississippi, the Impressions were escorted to their dressing room and weren't allowed to leave until showtime. As soon as they finished performing, a group of white highway patrolmen told my father they couldn't stay the night. Weary as usual, the band piled into the bus and set off for the next stop. It stung, but at least in the South they'd let you know why. The same thing would happen in the North, but they'd do it with a smile, never admitting the real reason. "Your services were welcome, but you as a person were not welcome," André says.

Touring was harder on the band than the Impressions. My father, Fred, and Sam never rode the bus—they sat in the comfort of their Cadillacs. Band members could ride with them, but the rule was they had to drive. So, it was either driving all night in a Cadillac, or jostling on the bus, where sometimes the heat would break and they'd freeze their balls off, or they'd all be sick, sneezing, and coughing, or the driver wouldn't stop when they needed a bathroom so they'd have to piss in coffee cans.

Even in the comfort of his Caddy, Dad was worn out. He'd traveled the country nonstop since he was a child with the Northern Jubilee Singers. "I shouldn't even be traveling, in this tax bracket," he said. Fred was tired too. "We'd get up at eight or nine in the morning and do four or five shows, man, and work to two AM, and then get up the next morning at eight or nine again and do it for seven days," he said. "It wears you *out*."

Touring also left them with very little time to pursue other interests. Fred started a beauty salon in Chicago and wanted to open several more, but, as he said, "I have to be there for that." Sam dreamed of playing professional baseball—a chance he'd passed up for a life of singing. "I still play semi-pro baseball," he said. "I had an offer from the Chicago Cubs back in 1959. At that time, we had a hit record. And I thought the guy wasn't coming back, so I stayed with the group. But I'd rather play ball right now, rather play than sing. It'd keep me in better shape."

My father, as usual, had too many interests at once. Constant traveling inhibited his creativity. "I used to write all the time," he said. "I'd never sit around like this, especially on the road. I want to write stories, too. Once for a week I had dreams every night that were complete stories. They were like movies—I could see the things." He'd never find time to write those stories.

He also struggled navigating the pressures of family life. He had children, he said, "which means responsibilities, securities, college for the children and a place to try and finally lay out for them. As well as our own selfish pleasures, y'know, sports cars and big time, but no more than anybody else."

Dad didn't want out of the game; he just wanted to change its rules. The old model—write an album, cut it, promote it, tour it, come home, repeat—no longer made him happy. "Being an entertainer, even though it's beautiful and it's nice in the public's eye and to have people gawking at you, it has its hangups," he said.

> We don't have as much privacy as we would like. I resent it, but I find my resentment's in vain simply because I brought it to be. I wanted to be successful, I wanted the money, I like doing what I'm doing, I wanted to be just what I am. Now I've got to give up some of those other things. There's other stars who've got to be even more hungup whether they realize it or not—James Brown, the Beatles, some of the bigger acts—they can't do *nothing*. At least in most places, even though I may be Curtis Mayfield, I can mix in the crowd, where a lot of people can't do that.

My father often tagged along with the road band on days off, while Fred and Sam generally stayed to themselves—a reversal of the way they usually acted on tour. As a result, André and Craig introduced him to the cutting edge of music, taking him to see people like Carlos Santana, who was a big fan of the Impressions. "When Curtis Mayfield would sing, he would remind me of my totality," Santana said. "He reminded me that I am part of Martin Luther King. I am part of Cesar Chavez. I am part of Bobby Kennedy. It transcends white, black, Mexican, or whatever. He resonated with me because I identified with something bigger than a nation."

Watching artists like Santana, Dad began hearing different possibilities—rhythmic and harmonic grooves he couldn't do with the Impressions. Craig taught him how to use effects pedals and write with chords outside normal blues or gospel changes. My father trusted Craig and learned from him. Their relationship became so close, an unwritten rule developed—no one touched Curtis's guitar, even to tune it, except Craig.

As the camaraderie grew, the road band spent downtime joking with my father, maybe asking what new songs he was working on or just hanging out in his hotel room. They had nicknames for each other—André was "College Boy" because of the erudition of his speech, my father was "Bucky Beaver" because of his big teeth, and Melvin was "Fattenin' Frogs for Snakes." That last one was a favorite of road manager Robert Cobbins. Melvin always had his eye on a girl at each show, but every time he tried to bring her in the dressing room, Lucky would say, "No, you have to leave the girl outside. Talk to her after you change your clothes." Lucky would hurry up and get dressed, and by the time Melvin came out, Lucky would be gone with the girl. Melvin would shake his head and say, "Fattenin' frogs for snakes." Every time Robert saw Melvin, he'd say, "Here comes Fattenin' Frogs for Snakes." The camaraderie wasn't constant though, and many times my father would find a girl of his own and disappear.

Still, the band gelled. "Curtis was not hard to work for at all, but you definitely had to know your part," André says.

> You couldn't do something obviously wrong, and there had to be dynamics. The rule was if you couldn't hear the vocals, you were playing too loud. At the time, there weren't sound crews and semis pulling up. It was tour buses and tired musicians setting up their own equipment. The sound systems weren't great, and sometimes you couldn't hear properly. There would be no monitors on stage, and you'd hear the echo back of the house speakers, which was disconcerting if you're trying to play time. What happens is, you didn't spread yourself out too far on stage. You set up close to each other to play like an ensemble. Even when you saw James Brown, they wouldn't set up far apart. They'd be like an arm's length away from each other. That's for communication. That was very special for Curtis.

―――――――――

As the year wore on, more heavy changes came over the world. In July, humanity broke its bond with Mother Earth and put its first footprints on the moon. In August, the biggest gathering of peace-loving hippies in history took place on Yasgur's farm near Woodstock, New York. The Woodstock concert marked the climax of the 1960s. Thirty-two of the decade's most influential acts performed for four hundred thousand people, and the concert was captured in a film that encapsulated the spirit of the times—the escapism into drugs, the belief that music and love could stop war, the certainty that the youth (at least, white youth) would change the world.

Hendrix closed the festival with a new band he called Gypsy Sun and Rainbows, later shortened to Band of Gypsys. On a cold Monday morning, he ripped into a version of the "Star Spangled Banner" that became a haunting epitaph for the era. He put every moment of the brutal, wonderful decade through his guitar, making the national anthem by turns tragic, gorgeous, and jarring—sometimes it sounded like war, like sirens wailing and bombs dropping; sometimes it sounded like rock 'n' roll, like hallucinogenic drugs and free love; sometimes it sounded like chaos, like riots and assassinations.

The next month, the Chicago Seven went on trial for inciting the riot at the DNC the year before, and a new group called the Weathermen committed acts of terrorism intended to cripple the American government. Meanwhile, the movement remained without leadership except for the Panthers, who crumbled under pressures from within and without.

Anger in the militant black community surged as conservative white America became more entrenched against it. The pendulum King had started swinging to the left in the late 1950s, toward black people's rights, toward equality, now swung almost all the way back. The Panthers' violent image only helped it swing faster. Even liberal whites began distancing themselves.

––––––––––

My father tuned into these events as closely as he tuned into the radio as a child. They affected him just as much. He despaired at watching the peaceful movement he had once believed in suffer a bitter, violent death. He never felt his job was to keep that peaceful movement going; rather he felt called to reflect what the people around him felt and experienced. These people felt increasingly furious, paranoid, depressed, abandoned. Dad needed to write about these changes, but he didn't feel right doing it with the Impressions. He needed to get something new across. He hinted at it with "We're a Winner," but he had to censor himself while recording that song so ABC would release it. He needed to grow, but he also needed Curtom to grow. One way to increase sales without adding new acts was to do what record companies had been doing to singing groups for decades. It was the exact thing Vee-Jay did to the original Impressions—pull the lead singer from the group and give him a career of his own while the band continued without him.

Marv had long been in my father's ear about that. "Everyone makin' it [is] a singer-songwriter," he repeated, over and over again. "You're an artist, you should go out on your own." Marv angled for more control, and Dad wanted to make him vice president of Curtom. Eddie disagreed, feeling Marv should work his way up the ranks. Dad leaned toward Marv, driving a bigger wedge between him and Eddie. "I suggested to him that he just focus on producing and writing," Eddie said. "Marv told him that he should start a solo career . . . I feared that Curtis would burn out in short time." It was a difficult decision, but my father went with the advice of a man he hardly knew over that of his closest friend and business partner.

———

As the ninety-day tour for *Young Mods* wound down, the Impressions arrived at Madison Square Garden for one of the last shows of the year. The bill that night in New York included Jerry Butler and the Four Tops. André had left the group to play with Jerry, but since the Impressions hadn't found a solid replacement, he stayed on the stage and performed two sets. The next day Jerry had off, so André went with the Impressions to a gig in Buffalo, New York. It was the dead of winter; the year was dwindling to a close. When they arrived in Buffalo, five feet of snow blanketed the ground. The gig went off, but afterward, the Impressions were mad as hell about something and left Lucky, André, Melvin, and

Craig at the auditorium. They had no way to the airport and the theatre was locked, so they stood in the middle of Buffalo, snow up to
their chests, facing the prospect of lugging their equipment to God knew
where. By some miracle, a man with a station wagon who had seen the
show offered them a ride. On the way to the airport, he asked if they
wouldn't mind stopping by a club.

They wound through the snowy Buffalo streets until they stopped at
the club—a real down-home type of place where a local band sweated it
out on a small stage. The station-wagon man talked to the locals, said he
had the Impressions' band in the club, and before they knew it, the guys
were on stage playing. They jammed from eleven at night until four in
the morning. They played every song they knew, made things up on the
spot, and brought the roof down.

As the night petered out, leaving a few stragglers nursing their beers
in the hazy predawn, Lucky, André, Melvin, and Craig crammed back
into the station wagon and rode to the airport. They gave the man some
money, walked inside dead tired, and each boarded a plane to a different
city. It was the last time they'd perform together as the Impressions.

———

It was a time of endings. The decade sputtered out in a grotesque spasm
of bitterness and violence. Free love, flower power, Woodstock, moon
landings, marches, movements, assassinations, drugs—the whole vicious,
beautiful thing was unraveling. Life was unraveling for my father too.
Around this time, my mother finally decided to leave. She tried to put
the house up for sale, only to realize her name wasn't on the deed.

My father also grew further from Fred and Sam than ever. These
were the most important relationships of his life so far, and the longest
lasting. Indeed, he might have spent more time with Fred and Sam than
he did with my mother or any woman he'd ever known. Somewhere in
his mind, though, he knew he needed to leave the group. He didn't say
anything yet, but as 1969 came to a close, he felt the need to free himself,
to reinvent himself, to speak his mind like never before.

When the story about the Impressions' West Coast tour appeared in *Rolling Stone* near the end of 1969, Alexander ended it by saying, "[Curtis] is writing the songs of the coming black middle class. The songs of aspirations. A good home, a nice car, decent neighbors, money, educated kids, travel, security. You can't knock it until you've had the opportunity to reject it."

In his defense, Alexander couldn't have known what my father was about to do. And he was right—the Impressions' music was aimed mostly at the "coming black middle class." It was about pushing, and moving, and creating a better tomorrow. But my father's mind had moved somewhere else.

At twenty-seven years old, he was about to change the game again.

9

Move On Up

"Top billing now is killing,
For peace, no one is willing."
—"(Don't Worry) If There's a Hell Below, We're All Going to Go"

Chicago, 1970—The decade dawned under dark clouds. Nixon, swept into office with promises of a return to law and order and an end to the Vietnam War, delivered neither. The year turned foul almost immediately. In February, the Weathermen hurled Molotov cocktails all over New York, the Black Liberation Army allegedly bombed a police station in San Francisco, and racists in Colorado bombed school buses that were being used to desegregate a Denver school. Three months later, race riots broke out in Georgia, the Ohio National Guard killed four students at Kent State, and police killed two students during an antiwar rally at historically black Jackson State College in Mississippi. In the music world, Motown's Tammi Terrell died of brain cancer in March, the Beatles disbanded in April, and Diana Ross released her first album without the Supremes in May. Meanwhile, boys in body bags came home in heaps as the death toll in Vietnam mounted.

Amid the carnage, my father wrote, produced, and fronted his final Impressions album, *Check Out Your Mind*. The title track foreshadowed the new direction of his writing—dark, rhythmic, driving. It matched the paranoia eating away at Dad's generation. The new sounds benefitted from a subtle shift in personnel. Johnny Pate had moved to New York to work for Verve Records, and now my father brought in two other arrangers, Riley Hampton and Gary Slabo.

Hampton was known as *the man* in Chicago for scoring strings. He did extensive work for OKeh during Curtis's tenure there as staff writer and producer, and he worked for Vee-Jay, the Impressions' first label. Hampton also arranged for Motown, and most famously, he worked with Etta James at the pinnacle of her career. His arrangement on her version of "At Last" remains one of the most famous string scores in pop music history.

Hampton tended toward languid, pretty string lines. When those lines mixed with Slabo's punchy, insistent horns, the effect became eerie and schizophrenic. It still had the Chicago Sound, but instead of the jazzy swing of Johnny's arrangements, it was more straightforward, funky, and gripping.

The sound complemented the times perfectly. Soft drugs like marijuana and psychedelics like LSD had fallen out of fashion; heroin and cocaine now dominated the scene. These drugs had teeth in a way the peaceful drugs of the '60s didn't, and they devastated the black community. Many a black soldier copped them in Vietnam and brought them home, where mind-numbing substances helped cope with the haunting specter of war alongside the soul-crushing despair of the ghetto.

Uncle Kenny never got into that scene, but he recalls the brutal mixture of war and drugs he encountered in Vietnam. "Over there you could get the purest stuff," he says. "You could always tell when you were going to get hit because you could smell the opium in the air. I have shot somebody with a fifty-caliber machine gun, half his body's gone, and he's still trying to get to me. I've seen guys get so high, they watch a man come in to kill them."

Black soldiers like Uncle Kenny had to deal with double rejection on their return home. Not only did the militant antiwar crowd greet them with hateful sneers, the country for which they risked their lives still refused to accept their humanity and respect their basic rights. Five

heavy years had passed since the Civil Rights Act, and it seemed nothing
had changed but the law. Reality remained rigged against black Americans. Many retaliated.

A *Time* magazine poll in 1970 found that more than two million
black Americans counted themselves as "revolutionaries" and believed
only a "readiness to use violence will ever get them equality." The poll
also showed that the number of those who believed blacks "will probably have to resort to violence to win rights" had risen 10 percent since
Malcolm X's assassination. Meanwhile, the Black Panthers continued
gaining support even as their organization fractured. Newton said,
"Every one who gets in office promises the same thing. They promise full employment and decent housing; the Great Society, the New
Frontier. All of these names, but no real benefits. No effects are felt in
the black community, and black people are tired of being deceived and
duped."

Check Out Your Mind hinted at the way my father would deal with
these depressing changes. The album pushed the Impressions further
into funk than they'd ever gone with the singles "(Baby) Turn On to Me"
and "Check Out Your Mind," which hit numbers six and three, respec-
tively, on the R&B chart. The album was a good effort, although it only
rose as high as twenty-two R&B and missed the pop chart. Still, it sold
based on the power of the singles. Curtom had another hit to its name.

The album's release deepened fractures within the group. While Fred
and Sam always stood behind Curtis's songs, neither liked "Check Out
Your Mind." Fred, who spent so many late nights listening to my father
pluck out new songs in his hotel room, saying, "Curtis, you just wrote
us another hit," couldn't say the same about "Check Out Your Mind."
"That was a tune that I didn't really care about," Fred said. "I don't know
what he was thinking where writing that song was concerned. But it
never killed me."

That particular track also illustrated the musical reasons my father
needed to go solo. Having to account for three voices didn't give him
room to do much but sing on the beat. He couldn't deliver lines in idio-
syncratic ways that came to him spontaneously because he had two other

guys whose job was to follow his lead. As a result, it changed the sub-text, the attitude, and the meaning he could imply behind his lyrics. He needed to be funkier, freer. While the interplay among the three voices added power to a song like "People Get Ready," it detracted from the funky grooves Dad wanted to explore.

He felt ambivalent. On one hand, he said, "Of course, the Impressions were just the perfect bunch of fellas to be able to express yourself." On the other, he said, "Not being with the Impressions allowed me, in my mind, to be more free about things I felt I had to say. It was more risky for the Impressions to sing songs like 'Choice of Colors' and 'We're a Winner.' For getting airplay, that wasn't the norm. I didn't mind taking those chances myself, but I was always concerned of the fellas' feelings."

—————

As the Impressions finished recording *Check Out Your Mind*, Dad decided to leave the group. He didn't say anything, but he began writing songs for his first solo album, more self-confident than ever, and conscious of the anger fueling the militant surge in black culture. He was also conscious of another feeling in himself—after touring *Young Mods*, he wanted to focus on building Curtom. The constant slog of touring always weighed heavy on him, and by focusing on the label, he saw a way to shuck that weight while keeping his career moving forward. As he said, "I've been on the road for twelve or thirteen years now and I can't recall living in my hometown for any more than three months at one time. I've never been in Chicago for one whole year since I've been in the business. You know, I'm born under the star Gemini and they are supposed to be very changeable people. So I'm making a change to try to do other things."

Midyear, he made his break. Nothing happened to force his hand, no dramatic falling out or heated argument. In his customary seat-of-the-pants way, my father simply picked up the phone one evening, called Fred, and said, "Fred, I'm going to try to go on my own and see what I can do. You and Sam can do the same thing. Y'all go on your own and see what you can do." Fred called Sam and told him the news, and that was it. My father left the group.

Fred, Sam, and the Impressions, three of the most important forces in Dad's life for more than a decade, no longer occupied his mind. The boyhood dreams, the endless miles traveled in the green station wagon, the lonely nights trying to steal sleep in motel beds, the harmonizing and fraternizing all came to an end. Dad struggled with the decision. "Leaving the Impressions was a lot like leaving home," he said. But he knew he was right. "When the time is right, you have to go. You need to make it on your own."

Even though their split had been building since the dissension over owning shares of Curtom, it still stung. Fred said, "I felt bad for a simple reason: I had a family, Sam had one, and we always looked to Curtis—he was a great writer, and you've lost that now, so what do you do? You can't never replace a Curtis Mayfield."

For years, Curtis, Fred, and Sam were so close that if you saw one of them, you usually saw the other two. They spent more time with each other than they did with their own wives. Yet, as he'd already shown, my father had the ability to turn off his emotions and make cold, calculated business decisions when he felt it necessary.

Recalling this side of him, Tracy says, "You saw a good and evil. The evil part came out when it was about business. I always separated the parent from the businessperson. Because the parent was very nice, soft, sweet, but when he puts his business hat on, you've got a different animal there. He becomes something that you don't want to be around. When it came to business, he was about business. If he's making the money, he wants all of it."

Fred and Sam decided they wanted to keep the group going, so they auditioned lead singers and found a replacement in Leroy Hutson, former vocalist in the Mayfield Singers. To the press, my father painted it as brightly as he could. "The Impressions are still the Impressions," he said. "One brother doesn't stop the show. I'm sure [Leroy will] live up to whatever I was with the Impressions." He must have known that was impossible, but that was a problem for Fred and Sam, not Curtis.

———

Soon after the split, my father put the final touches on his first solo album. After more than a decade of writing with others in mind—either the Impressions, Jerry, Major, Gene Chandler, or countless others on OKeh and Curtom—he now thought solely of himself. No expectations hung over his head. He could paint his songs with all the darkness and pain that lurked in the ghetto. His pallet was wide as the world. He also had a tight band to match the material, including "Master" Henry Gibson, whose percussion would come to define much of Dad's solo career.

He toiled through July and August, even putting in a marathon forty-eight-hour session to finish the album on time. Eddie recalled dozing off in the studio as my father polished and perfected a song. Curtis would then shake him awake and ask, "What do you think, Tom? What do you think we should do with this?" Eddie would answer with something like "Well, we should bring the horns down a little bit here," and then fall back asleep as Curtis kept working.

Curtis came out in September, just weeks after Dad performed his final concert with the Impressions at Chicago's High Chaparral. It marked a bright moment for him, but it came amid more darkness. Days later, Hendrix choked to death on his own vomit. Saddened by the loss, my father connected himself to Hendrix in clearer terms than ever before. "There were movements sometimes that he brought to his music that would make you immediately think of [me], where he actually does a little falsetto with his voice and makes a few Curtis Mayfield chord structures," he said. "Every once in a while I have a need to hear that, Jimi and Buddy Miles and Billy Cox, just those three musicians lock in so well."

That was high praise coming from a man who rarely listened to his contemporaries. There was little time to mourn Hendrix, though. A month later, Janis Joplin overdosed on heroin and Baby Huey fell dead of a drug-related heart attack in a Chicago motel room. Times were strange, dark, deadly. *Curtis* captured it all.

No one could have been prepared for the album except my father and those who helped him make it. It starts with the sinister opening strains of "(Don't Worry) If There's a Hell Below, We're All Going to Go." Lucky's bass growls menacingly as a woman exhorts the book of

Revelation, and my father, with a heavily processed voice, shouts, "Sisters! Niggers! Whities! Jews! Crackers! Don't worry. If there's hell below, we're all gonna go." Then, he lets out a demonic howl as Slabo's horns and Hampton's strings ride atop the bass, drums, guitars, and percussion, laying down a wicked backdrop for some quasi-apocalyptic soothsaying. While Sly Stone had recorded a song that said "nigger" several years before, "Hell Below" was among the first mainstream recordings to use the word, setting the scene for both the unflinching honesty of my father's solo career and the hip-hop age it helped spawn.

As the song progresses, my father's obsession with producing different sounds in the studio—assisted by his newfound love for weed—takes off like a V-2 rocket, with trippy guitar and vocal effects that sweep across the sonic field, sounding like the haunted hangovers of a nightmare. The drilling bass, the urgent string arrangement, the pounding rhythm section, and the fuzz guitar intertwine in cascading crescendos. Curtis didn't just have his finger on the pulse of the new decade; he was in the bloodstream.

Clocking in at almost eight minutes, the song played more than twice as long as anything he'd done with the Impressions. It focused on the groove, with few chord changes. Part of that came from his new recording habits. Instead of handing Johnny a demo tape and waiting until the session to hear the arrangement, now he locked in the rhythm beforehand with Lucky, putting more emphasis on the bass guitar than ever before. "He used to sit down with Lucky and they just would do rhythm," Sam said. "They'd sit down and learn songs. Lucky would listen, and they would play along with what Curtis was playing, and learn the songs, so that when they went into the studio, he knew exactly the way the song was going."

The heaviness of the groove meant the melodies had less room for complexity, something critics would disparage my father for on much of his solo work. It took critics years to understand that Dad had a hard message to deliver, and he needed a solid musical platform to deliver it. Too many chords would have impeded the message. He knew what he was doing, and he didn't have time to wait for critics to catch up.

With his new lyrics, Dad became a true street poet in the vein of Gil Scott-Heron and the Last Poets, who had recently debuted with politically charged, nationalistic poetry set to music, aimed at raising the consciousness of black people. He now used the dialect of the street and the terror of the times to create something as devastating as a shot of heroin to the vein.

His phrasing is almost that of a rapper as he sings:

> *Sisters, brothers, and the whiteys*
> *Blacks and the crackers, police and their backers*
> *They're all political actors*
> *Hurry, people running from their worries*
> *While the judge and his juries dictate the law that's partly flaw*
> *Cat calling, love balling, fussing, and a-cussing*
> *Top billing now is killing, for peace no one is willing*
> *Kinda make you get that feeling*
> *Everybody smoke, use the pill and the dope*
> *Educated fools from uneducated schools*
> *Pimping people is the rule, polluted water in the pool*
> *And Nixon talkin' 'bout don't worry, he say don't worry*
> *But they don't know, there can be no show*
> *And if there's Hell below, we're all gonna go.*

By the end of the song, as Hampton's nervous string line meanders around the hard groove, Dad takes a moment to question himself, to hope there might be some light within the bleak picture he has painted. He sings:

> *Tell me what we gonna do*
> *If everything I say is true?*
> *This ain't no way it ought to be*
> *If only all the mass could see*
> *But they keep talkin' 'bout don't worry.*

In the second track, the light is nowhere to be found. "The Other Side of Town" contains some melodic traces of the Impressions' "Choice of Colors," but the message is much tougher. Curtis's confrontation with the Afroed man in San Francisco and his observations of the increasing violence tearing through his community gave him license to bare his teeth. While "Choice of Colors" pulled a few punches, "The Other Side of Town" plays like a fist to the throat. "The need here is always for more," he sings. "There's nothing good in store / On the other side of town." Instead of placing the burden of change on his black audience, my father described the stark reality of what they faced in cramped ghettos, forcing the grim picture onto the long-averted eyes of white America. "I'm from the other side of town / Out of bounds," he sings. "Depression is part of my mind / The sun never shines on the other side of town."

Anger shows through in his reading of the lines "Ghetto blues showed on the news / All is aware, but what the hell do they care?" He had never delivered a lyric with such accusation, pointing directly at the side of town where the sun did shine.

Next, the mood lightens briefly on the gorgeous ballad "The Makings of You," which shimmers with Hampton's fine orchestration. It remains one of my father's most beautiful love songs, and it was the first song from the album he performed on television, in Cleveland on Don Webster's *Upbeat* show.

But the focus goes back to the message on "We People Who Are Darker Than Blue," by which point Dad had already presented three of the best songs he'd ever written. "Blue" blew them out of the water. It starts as a slow blues, as he confronts society's expectations of black people. "We're just good for nothing they all figure," he sings, "A boyish, grown up, shiftless jigger." (As Andrew Young said, "It's 'jigger' but he meant 'nigger.'") He confronts black people's feelings of self-worth relating to skin color, singing, "High yellow girl, can't you tell / You're just the surface of our dark, deep well?" Perhaps most powerfully, he confronts the white world's version of history, singing, "Pardon me, brother, as you stand in your glory / I know you won't mind if I tell the whole story."

Then, the song stops and shifts abruptly. Master Henry's congas take control as the rhythm section pushes into fast, syncopated funk. And when my father sings, "If your mind could really see / You'd know your color the same as me," it is clear how far he'd grown beyond his work with the Impressions. No longer was there a choice of colors; now there was only one. Black.

He even pointed to the song as evidence of why he chose to go on his own. "Songs like 'We People Who Are Darker Than Blue' transcended the roster of the Impressions," he said. "[It was] more of what was in my head during those times." The polyrhythmic, Latin-tinged breakdown highlighted another aspect of his music that transcended the Impressions. "It was the '70s," my father said. "Time to get away from just R&B and be freer as to the happenings around me."

Sam and Fred were surprised by the power of the new songs. To this day, they debate the meaning of "We People Who Are Darker Than Blue." In an interview in 2008, Sam said, "I took it as a person that was very, very angry . . . The thing I got from it was, 'Are you going to let them do it to you?' Who? Are you going to let *who* do it to you?" Fred, providing the obvious answer: "At the time, he was talking about white folks . . . He ain't talking about black folks. Get up, go out, do something for yourself. That's what I took that meaning as."

My father's audience was equally surprised. No one had made an album like this before, least of all the Impressions. Sure, socially minded songs formed a major part of the movement, but to put so much on the A-side of a record—and in such a personal manner—was bold and new. It was the work of a man who knew exactly who he was and what he wanted to say. He'd commented on society before, but now he climbed in its skull, poking around the demented mind of a decade that would witness the death of free love and the advent of mass paranoia.

As fans digested the A-side, they learned the new Curtis brought nothing but straight truth. No longer was it a message song or two surrounded by love songs. Now he held a mirror to the realities of ghetto life and forced his audience to look into it, song after song after song. As he described his motivation, "The latter part of the '60s and the early

'70s brought about a feeling in me that there need to be songs that relate not so much to civil rights but to the way we as all people deal with our lives."

If my father proved he could be an incisive commentator on the first side, he proved he could still be a damn good motivator with "Move On Up," the opening song on the second side. Rhythmically, it is perhaps the most complex song he ever wrote, and it contains a drum break that predicted the rise of hip-hop in the next decade. Two other things are especially important about the song. One, he chose to put it on the B-side and start his first solo album with the super-heavy, brutally honest "Hell Below." The decision showed Dad's guts and merit as an artist. From a commercial point of view, it would have made more sense to hook the listeners first with the positive, infectious ear candy of "Move On Up" and then lay down the dope. My father decided that his message was too important and put it up front. And two, he went even further by releasing "Hell Below" as the first single, instead of "Move On Up." Again, the message came up front, and the audience responded. "Hell Below" went to number three on the R&B chart.

"Move on Up" also bore ties that still bound him to the Impressions. The song was slated for *Check Out Your Mind*, but my father kept it for himself. At the same time, he put "Miss Black America" on the *Curtis* album, which the Impressions recorded for a beauty pageant of the same name in 1969. With Fred and Sam on backing vocals, it belongs more to the Impressions than Curtis. But in the context of *Curtis*, it takes on political and even feminist overtones, confronting society's standards of beauty and skin color as they related to black women.

The album finishes with "Give It Up," which, despite triumphant orchestration, plays more like a heartbreaking farewell to my parents' ending relationship. Even though they still made room to raise us together respectfully, my mother had left, and on some level, they knew their problems had no solutions (although they'd try a few more times). "No matter how much we try / Our indifference would still show," my father sings. "Now we've got to give it up." It was a bittersweet way to end the album, and it marked a major shift in our lives. Sharon, Tracy, and I moved with Mom, and our family was now shared across two homes.

———————

Dad made a point of remaining a strong presence in our lives despite the split, but the wild success of *Curtis* put new demands on his time. The album became a mammoth, hitting the top twenty pop and selling at a furious pace, instantly justifying his decision to go solo. It stayed on the charts for months, and by April of 1971, *Curtis* would take the top slot on the R&B album chart. "It just wasn't my plan," Dad said. "I thought I'd go home and be a businessman. I guess it just hit me by surprise. Of course, we were very serious towards the recording and the music and I hoped we'd maybe sell 25,000–50,000 albums, which, of course, would have been an asset to help the company. But I guess I just didn't realize that we did have so many beautiful people out there."

That such a race-conscious album did so well on the pop chart showed the power of music to change attitudes, and it showed my father that the masses were ready to hear even the hardest truths. But racism in radio still prevailed. At the same time as *Curtis*'s rise, a white singer named Brian Hyland cut a version of "Gypsy Woman" that sold three million copies, outselling the Impressions' original nearly ten times over and rising far higher on the pop charts. It was a story almost as old as recorded music—white artists made the money even when black artists made the songs. Curtis was among the only black artists to change that story by keeping as much of his publishing as possible, which meant he made good money from Hyland's cover, but the business was still rigged against him.

The music business had changed for the better, though, and my father played an integral part in that change. So did Curtom and *Curtis*. The album also changed his image. The iconic cover photo of him sitting in his yellow chamois-cloth suit, and the gatefold images of him surrounded by me, Tracy, Sharon, and Curt Curt showed a man who had come into his own. He'd even grown a beard, further separating himself from the clean-cut look he sported with the Impressions. My father claimed he never intended to leave the Impressions forever, but *Curtis* showed him that Curtom now had two artists that could bring in major sales. He never looked back.

———

After *Curtis*, the press trumpeted my father's new direction while speculating on the permanence of his split with the Impressions. In England, where he had a devoted underground following but hadn't yet broken on the charts, the album raised his profile. When John Abbey, founder of England's *Blues & Soul* magazine, interviewed him just after the album's release, my father spoke of his duties at Curtom as the main reason for the split. "My thoughts were that if we were to make a success of the label in the way we wanted, I would have to devote more time to the creative end of it," he said. "So that's why I made the decision. This way, I'm not holding the Impressions back as far as their personal appearances are concerned . . . You see, we are all aware that there can be no Impressions without a Curtom and so we all have to take care of business first and foremost."

Dad also discussed plans to jumpstart Major's career again and to release a posthumous album on Baby Huey. Abbey ended the interview by asking, "Now, when do you expect to come to Britain?" As it turned out, John would play an instrumental role in bringing my father to Britain, even chaperoning him on his trip.

Dad had achieved moderate success with the Impressions overseas, but with John's help, he became a star there during his solo career. When he went to the United Kingdom after *Curtis*, he didn't go on tour per se. "What we did in the UK was more promotional," John says. "Back in those days, black music was only just catching on over there in Europe."

Even with only a few appearances, Dad's popularity skyrocketed as European fans thrilled to his live show. "Move On Up" soon became his first hit overseas, reaching number twelve on the British chart. As John recalls, "Him being there, in my opinion, was the thing that pushed that track over. But initially, it was because of the music, rather than the lyrics. It was quite danceable. Then people started to pick up on some of the lyrics, and I think it took him to a new place. He found a new kind of audience. He found a broader audience. It wasn't people who just cared about R&B music. I think he found people that respected the poetry value, the lyrical value, the message he was trying to get across."

Spending so much time together traveling through the United Kingdom, my father kindled a friendship with John that would last until the end of his life. During that time, John learned the intricacies of Curtis's personality. "It was misleading sometimes," John says, "because he was always so quiet and laid-back, a lot of people didn't realize the sort of passion that was actually running through his blood. He was much, much deeper than I think people even realized. When you read his lyrics, you can see right there. This is not your everyday guy."

Watching him work, John came up with a nickname that followed Curtis for the rest of his life—the Gentle Genius. "He was a very genuinely kind man," John says. "I'm not going to lie and say I agreed with everything he did in all the years that we worked together. There were lots of times that we saw things differently. But there was never any animosity. He was always willing to listen to what you said, even if he disagreed with it. There was an aggressive side to him, and sometimes you may be having a passive conversation with him and laced inside that passiveness, there was an aggression there. He knew how to bite. But I didn't really get to see that side of him too much because I was on his team."

The side of my father John did see knew how to charm and disarm. For all his loner tendencies, Dad had no problem amping up his personality when needed. He could sparkle as well as he could sulk. In public, he often seemed like the star of one of those old E. F. Hutton commercials, everyone in the room crowding around him just to see what he'd say next. People loved him, and he loved them back. He felt more confident than ever.

———————

As 1970 limped toward its merciful end, my parents worked out the details of their split. "[Curtis] wanted me to move into an apartment and

I told him he has got to be out of his mind," my mother says. "He said, 'Well, you were raised in an apartment and so was I.' I said, 'Yes that's because our parents couldn't do anything, but we can do better. And my children are going to be raised in a house.' He said, 'Well, I don't want to get you another house. And I said, 'Well, I'm not moving [to an apartment]. Because my children are going be in a house.'"

Finally, my father agreed to get another house, buying a nice little place at 9121 South Luella. He also bought a three-flat house at 9225 South Cregier Avenue, just down the way from our new house, where he lived in the basement apartment. He decked it out with a waterbed, some funky artwork on the walls, and thick shag carpeting. Aunt Judy moved into the second floor, and Marion moved into the top floor. The neighborhood at that point had become mostly black, as white flight changed Chicago's complexion. Carl Davis lived on the opposite corner, and Mr. Cub himself, Ernie Banks, lived down the street.

Living so close to my father meant we saw him often. All we had to do was ride our bikes a few blocks to his house. When he wasn't on the road, we spent many weekends with him. That proximity also made it difficult for my parents' relationship to end, and they'd go back and forth for the next two years.

Still, their split surprised no one—except maybe my father. Even as a child, I couldn't understand how they got together in the first place. They possessed opposite personalities. My father was reclusive and seemed to prefer submissive women—another area in which he demanded control. My mother is outgoing, outspoken, and anything but submissive.

Perhaps their insecurities drew them together. In Diane, my father had a woman so beautiful she was offered modeling gigs, which might have calmed parts of him that still heard echoes of "Smut" in his mind. In Curtis, my mother had a man who earned good money and took care of her, which might have calmed the part of her that still feared she'd never escape her childhood in the ghetto. If these things brought them together, though, they couldn't keep them together.

As *Curtis* reverberated around the world, Dad's influence echoed again from Jamaica when Bob Marley and the Wailers released *Soul Rebels*, their first record with international distribution. The Impressions had followed Marley's career with great interest. "They were calling them the 'Jamaican Impressions,' and it was a *very* big compliment for us," Sam said. "Of course we knew things that he was doing. New music; that's the only way we related to Bob was through music." With *Soul Rebels*, Marley and the Wailers seemed closer than ever to breaking out on the world stage. They wore their influences on their sleeves—the song "Rebel's Hop," for instance, featured the Wailers mixing together snippets of popular American R&B, including the Impressions' "Keep On Moving" and the Temptations' "Cloud Nine."

At the same time, Dad rehearsed a new band for a tour that would include a jaunt through Europe, with John Abbey's help, and a show at New York's Bitter End. To escape the Chicago winter and the Hawk—and the bitter cold of a failed relationship—he brought the band to the house in Atlanta he'd bought in 1968. It was a nice place with a swimming pool out back. The whole thing felt like a big sleepover party—just my father, Craig, Henry, Lucky, and a new drummer named Tyrone McCullen, hanging around the house jamming.

They worked on old Impressions' material, learned several songs off *Curtis*, and fleshed out a few new ideas my father brought in, including the excellent cuts "I Plan to Stay a Believer" and "Stone Junkie," which he'd written in the midst of a doughnut binge. "Me and [Marv] were driving into Chicago eating a box of glazed doughnuts," he said. "I don't know how we got hooked on 'em . . . We got into a conversation about junkies, and before we got downtown, I had written 'Stone Junkie.'" My father often said every conversation could end up as a song, and "Stone Junkie" showed just how true that was. He didn't need much. Just a word or two, and his imagination would set off running.

As the year turned, he told the guys why they were rehearsing so much. "We're going to cut a live album," he said. He made the decision after talking to Marv and Neil Bogart, who worked for Buddah, and realizing the Bitter End would make a great place to tape. Craig reacted with apprehension. "For real?" he said. "Man, I don't even know the names of these songs." My father reassured him. "Don't worry about it," he said. "I might not even know them myself, but let's go do this."

Craig still felt nervous. The band had never performed together, and now they learned their first performance would appear on a live album. That was my father, though. He'd get an idea and have to do it *now*. Otherwise, his inner Gemini would kick in, and he'd change his mind.

The camaraderie in the band kept everyone's spirits high as they arrived in New York in January 1971 to find the Big Apple frozen and frigid. The youthful exuberance of the rehearsals followed them to Greenwich Village, and though winter had hit with particular severity, it didn't stop Craig from taking on an ice-cream challenge. The Bitter End served enormous ice-cream sundaes meant for two or more people. Craig boasted he could eat one by himself, so the club's management offered him a deal: if he could finish a sundae by himself, he could eat free for the group's three-night run. "Curt, watch this," Craig said. He proceeded to eat several sundaes, gorging himself on sugar. Those were the kinds of antics that made touring bearable. It impressed my father so much, he mentioned it when introducing the band, and it made the final pressing of the album.

They gave twelve performances at the Bitter End, from which my father put the album together. "We were fortunate enough to find a studio that knew what they were doing," he said, "and it was really as though we weren't recording at all—until you walked out of the place and saw this thing that looked to me like a little milk truck." The studio they found was none other than Hendrix's brainchild, Electric Lady Studios. After the recording, Dad edited the tapes with Hendrix's old engineer, Eddie Kramer.

———

A live album is meant to capture an experience that is impossible to capture, because while the music can be recorded, the magic of seeing a concert in person cannot. Perhaps because the Bitter End is the size of a matchbox, or perhaps because the crowd each night was riveted to the music, or perhaps because the band shared such a tight bond, or perhaps for some indefinable, mysterious reason, *Curtis/Live!* succeeds in a way few live albums do. Embedded in the grooves on the record is the feeling the listener is sitting at one of the little wooden tables amid the ninety or so people in the mixed-race audience, watching the band on the soapbox-sized stage.

The album kicks off with "Mighty Mighty (Spade and Whitey)," which had taken on new life in the two years since the Impressions cut it. My father's phrasing is funkier, looser, and he takes the song a step further than he did with the Impressions. On the original version, he sang, "I'm gonna say it loud / I'm just as proud as the brothers too." Now, he puts extra muscle in it, singing, "I got to say it loud / I want to say it loud / I got to say it loud / I'm black and I'm proud." In the intimate setting, the crowd's delighted reaction is palpable.

Next, my father eases into the deep groove of "I Plan to Stay a Believer," which features heavy lyrics like "Why don't you look around? / Haven't you found that the judgment day is already in play for the black / And now come time for the ofay?" He had now brought three racial slurs into pop music's lexicon on his first two albums—"nigger," "cracker," and "ofay." After singing a verse about the American Indian civil rights movement, which had just flowered, he ended with more excellent wordplay:

> *We're over twenty million strong*
> *And it wouldn't take long to save the ghetto child*
> *If we'd get off our ass, ten dollars a man yearly, think awhile*
> *Twenty million times ten would surely then set all brothers free*
> *What congregation with better relations*
> *Would demand more respect from society?*

The crowd applauded this formula, even though some album reviews singled out that line as symptomatic of my father's downfall as a writer (today we'd call such people haters).

For his part, he explained the change in his lyrics like this: "Lately my lyrics have been more conscious of surroundings, of minorities. They're designed to try to motivate minority groups, to make them keep on pushing and see that they do belong . . . Right now, there's a growing audience of all kinds of people looking for music like that. They want to get down to some heavier music that relates to actual happenings in the world."

After "I Plan to Stay a Believer," the band kicks into "We're a Winner." The song injects crackling energy into the crowd, which replaces the missing Impressions, supplying backing vocals on the chorus. Through the people clapping, hollering, shouting, cheering, and testifying, it's easy to tell how much my father's music meant to his audience and how deeply they felt his message.

Then, in the middle of the song, he breaks it down. "You know, you might recall reading in your *Jet* and Johnson publications, a whole lot of stations didn't want to play that particular recording—'We're a Winner.' Can you imagine such a thing? Well, I would say, as I'm sure most of you would say, 'We don't give a damn, we're a winner anyway.' Right on?"

Met with cries of "Right on!" and "Preach, baby!" my father feels the audience. "We got a little strength out there tonight," he says, laughing. "Putting the fire under us. Outta sight." Then, he sings the original version of the song, the one Johnny made him change in the studio because of its incendiary lyrics. "We have just another version we'd like to lay to you about here," he says, "believing very strongly in equality and freedom for all, and especially we people who are darker than blue. We'd like to just lay another version to you, trying not to offend anyone but basically telling it like it is."

If radio stations didn't want to play the song in 1968, the live version might still be considered too risqué for radio today. To the already political lyrics he adds the original lines "No more tears do we cry / The black boy done dried his eyes," and, "There'll be no more Uncle Tom / At last that blessed day has come." Radio might not have been with him, but the crowd was there one hundred percent.

———

Curtis/Live! dropped in May 1971, a month after *Curtis* took the top spot on the R&B charts. It spent thirty-eight weeks in the top one hundred pop, hit number three R&B, and created renewed interest in *Curtis*.

Critical reception was mixed, many writers complaining my father didn't sound as good without the Impressions, but time has rightly judged the album a classic.

One complaint voiced by many critics deserves special note—the claim my father's voice sounded thin in comparison with the new music. Of course, it would have been impossible for him alone to equal the power of a three-man group. But what the critics mistakenly bemoaned was in fact a refining of his vocal style. It takes a mature artist, a master, to understand that sometimes the best way to make something louder is to make it quieter. My father used the thinness of his voice, the imperfections, the subtle warbles, to draw the listener closer. By pulling back, he invited his audience to lean in and pay intimate attention to what he said. It worked because his words were so powerful, so uncompromising, so true. If the audience missed the Impressions, they didn't show it. With two blockbuster albums in the span of one year, Curtis was undoubtedly a solo artist.

On these first two solo albums, Dad moved his message far beyond what any other artist of the time had done, retaining his crown as the premier social commentator into the new decade. But at almost the exact moment of the release of *Curtis/Live!*, two developments changed the cultural landscape, outpacing my father and driving him to go further with his music.

In April, as Dad performed with B. B. King and the Last Poets, the film world went through a major shift with Melvin Van Peebles's *Sweet Sweetback's Baadasssss Song*, the first so-called blaxploitation film. Blaxploitation movies were the first in Hollywood history made almost entirely by black people. They depicted gripping tales of inner-city life that either glorified drugs and violence or simply showed the world the reality of the ghetto, depending on one's politics.

Sweetback launched a movement and spoke to black people in a way no movie had before. As actor John Amos said, "[Melvin] went out and made a movie that generated so much revenue against the production dollar spent that it literally made the industry sit up overnight and say, 'My God, there's an audience of black people out there that will pay to see movies about black people.' Now, how they managed to overlook that for all the years since the inception of the business remains to be explained."

Blaxploitation movies served another important psychological function. They were the first to feature black actors—mostly men—as heroes, central characters, and eventual victors. This marked a major shift. As Huey Newton wrote, "As I suffered through Sambo and the Black Tar Baby story in *Brer Rabbit* in the early grades, a great weight began to settle on me. It was the weight of ignorance and inferiority imposed by the system. I found myself wanting to identify with the white heroes . . . and in time I cringed at the mention of Black." Newton noted that this "gulf of hostility" led to the surge of anger and militancy that had taken over the movement. "We not only accepted ourselves as inferior; we accepted the inferiority as inevitable and inescapable . . . Rebellion was the only way we knew to cope with the suffocating, repressive atmosphere that undermined our confidence." That rebellion was at the heart of the blaxploitation genre.

Music was also a major part of that shift. A month after *Sweetback*, Marvin Gaye dropped his seminal album, *What's Going On*, which invented the format of concept-album-as-social-commentary. It one-upped even *Curtis* in terms of straight truth. My father had never done anything like it, and he knew it. "When I first heard *What's Going On* I felt like Marvin had said everything there was to be said," he said. "The album had such qualities and the timely release was perfect. The clarity with which he expressed himself left you wondering whether there was anything left to write about; it seemed to me that he really had said it all." Of course, there was plenty left to say. It wasn't until July brought Gordon Parks's *Shaft* that my father began considering just how much.

Shaft became the emblem of the blaxploitation genre and is still the most famous of its ilk. A huge part of its success came from Isaac Hayes's soundtrack, which won a Grammy Award for Best Original Score (*Sweetback* also had an excellent score by the then-unknown group, Earth,

Wind & Fire). The Grammy legitimized the genre's commercial pull and created a new business model. Soon, just about every black artist wanted to write a film soundtrack, my father included. He had been interested in working on films ever since he'd been asked to contribute two songs to a disaster of a movie called *Krakatoa, East of Java* in '68. Now, he just needed the right movie to score.

Throughout 1971, the band toured sporadically, including my father's first full solo tour of the United Kingdom, where his popularity with critics still skyrocketed. "A year ago, I'd have been pleading with you to listen to him," one British journalist wrote. "Now I don't need to because [he's] going to take it for [himself]." Part of that surge in popularity came from "Move On Up," which remained on the charts.

In early July, Dad appeared at the Speakeasy Club in London, and *Blues & Soul* writer David Nathan painted a convincing picture of his growing popularity. "The all-too-brief, spur-of-the-moment appearance of Curtis Mayfield at London's Speakeasy club must surely rank as a historic event in the history of soul music in this country," Nathan wrote. "Historic because it was the first time Mr. Mayfield had played in front of a British audience (albeit a totally unrepresentative one) and historic because it proved that if the term 'superstar' still has any meaning . . . . Curtis Mayfield is already there."

Nathan's reference to the brief appearance referred to the fact that my father played almost exclusively at army bases overseas, where an American audience familiar with his music greeted him. This was largely a matter of necessity—British audiences still hadn't come around to his music in significant enough numbers to support a full tour.

Nathan also noted Dad's lyrical prowess, writing, "Probably the most significant factor about Curtis' work is his lyrical genius. Apart from his obvious musical talent as a vocalist and guitarist of the first order, his lyrics are profound, honest and never trite." And Nathan set him atop the pantheon of socially conscious soul men of the era: "It has often been implied that Motown's Smokey Robinson is 'the greatest living poet' (the

quote is reputedly from Bob Dylan!), but, when it comes down to dealing with today's problems, Curtis must come tops."

Interestingly enough, Nathan also mentioned that the group encored
with a new song called "We Got to Have Peace," and my father told the
audience that they'd hear it on an upcoming release. True to form, he
already had songs ready for his next album.

———

They stayed one week in England, where the band grew tighter still. Curtis and Craig made little wagers on who would make the most mistakes
during the performances. Everything felt loose, fun, fluid, despite the
mood back home in America.

In May, a race riot had exploded in Brooklyn, cops arrested 13,000
antiwar protestors across the country, and Nixon rejected sixty of the
Congressional Black Caucus's demands. June had seen Ed Sullivan's last
broadcast and the publishing of the Pentagon Papers, which detailed a
vast campaign of deception by the US government about the Vietnam
War. July had found Doors front man and cultural icon Jim Morrison
dead in a bathtub in Paris.

The country's humor soured as hippies entered adulthood to find
their heroes dropping as fast as soldiers in Vietnam. Trust in the government hit a critical low point as sordid details from the Pentagon Papers
sifted through the news. Perhaps for the first time, even white Americans
lost trust in most basic institutions. For much of black America, that
trust never existed, nor was it soon to come. In April, the Supreme Court
had upheld busing to achieve desegregation in schools, which meant seventeen years after *Brown*, major challenges to desegregation still existed.

Between tours, the band returned to Chicago to record *Roots*, Dad's
second solo album. *Roots* opens with "Get Down," the most sensual song
he'd yet recorded. The Impressions had done love songs galore, but none
of them came close to touching the raw sexuality of "Get Down." Dad
wrote the song after hanging out at nightclubs watching people dance.
"If you've ever walked into a large hall or a place where a lot of kids are
dancing and you're hearing some funky music, there are several things

you'll immediately observe and take in," he said. "Those are the feelings and the hard breathings of one dancing, and the stomping, and you take all of this and all of a sudden it hits you—everybody's doing their thing."

He also tried to ring some hopeful, motivating notes on *Roots*, especially on the excellent cuts, "We Got to Have Peace" and "Keep On Keeping On." The former was his first song about the war. In it, he wrote some of his most brilliant poetry and wordplay, especially the lyric, "We got to have peace / To keep the world alive and war deceased," where he proves a master of inner rhyme, assonance, and alliteration. It is among his most infectious, upbeat songs. "I don't think we should stop demanding it until we actually get it," he said about pushing the peace banner even after reality had become so dire. "Though it might be a little repetitious because so many people have been singing about it, peace is something we really need, and I feel, like love, it should be expressed over and over until everyone gets the message."

"Keep On Keeping On" boasts one of my father's best melodies and became one of his most beloved anthems. He felt partial to its message, saying, "If ever you could gather up a bunch of kids, sit them down, and sing just one song, this is it. You would not be there as an entertainer. You would be instilling a message in our young. Within the song is life's story—the hopefulness . . . the sweetness—and the bottom line to keep on keeping on." With four children of his own, Dad felt the need to speak to the next generation.

The song is also fascinating in comparison to his earlier work. It spoke to the times just like its corollary, "Keep On Pushing," saying, "Many think that we have blown it / But they too will soon admit / That there's still a lot of love among us / And there's still a lot of faith, warmth, and trust / When we keep on keeping on." It was a recognition the movement had faltered, and it represented a subtle and important shift in my father's message. No longer was he exhorting his people to keep on pushing. With everything that went down since the Impressions' first message song in 1964, simple survival now became his main message.

With good reason, too. Darkness and confusion ruled the day, which my father dealt with powerfully in "Underground," a song that plays like a love letter to *What's Going On*. The song also expressed an expanding notion of the world's problems and a determination to go beyond race into issues like the environment. "Everyone knows we have a pollution problem and knows it's going to get worse, this is what brought the whole idea of the song 'Underground' to life," he said. "The song speaks in terms of what might just happen if the pollution got so bad that everyone had to live underground; it gives my impression of how it would be in the dark down there; we wouldn't be able to see who is black and who is white so there wouldn't be any discrimination. As the song says, 'We'll all turn black, so who's to know, as a matter of fact color, creed and race must go.'"

One of the most surprising songs on the album was a sultry blues number called "Now You're Gone," which Dad wrote with Lucky. Though he grew up in the home of electric blues, my father had taken his music down a different path from the beginning. But with "Now You're Gone" he paid homage to the greats like Muddy Waters and Buddy Guy. "I was never crazy about my ability to sing the blues," he said. "Even though I could write it, I think other people could sing it better. The music and the arrangement were much stronger than the vocals. It needed someone with a growl! I tried it, but I always understood that every song I write isn't meant for me."

While such honest self-criticism was laudable, my father might have been too hard on himself. He gives a fine vocal performance, perhaps spurred on by his failed relationship with my mother. Like everything else about him, though, his love life was never just one thing, which he proved on the closing track, "Love to Keep You in My Mind." "I was in love with this particular lady," he said, "so that song came easily." The lady in question was Toni, a woman my father met in Cleveland. *Rolling Stone* would mistakenly identify her as his wife the next year.

Overall, *Roots* is a continuation of the sounds explored on *Curtis*. Cuts like "Beautiful Brother of Mine" and "Get Down" could have fit right next to "Hell Below." The album sold well on its release in October, hitting number six on the R&B charts. Dad's decision to go solo had now produced three of the biggest records of his entire career. "I believe

my vocal is stronger and certainly that the material is better than anything I've written," he said of *Roots*. "I must admit, I wanted to change
the name at the last minute but Buddah had already printed 50,000
sleeves, so I was too late." The cover photo featured him sitting in front
of an upturned tree in Chicago. My father liked the image because he felt
his own roots were in Chicago. Five years later, writer Alex Haley would
pen a hugely successful book and TV miniseries of the same name, giving the concept of roots a deeper meaning in black culture.

Though my father had a different image in mind when he called the
album *Roots*, his songs were just as focused on the black experience. He
continued to speak about that increasing focus in his songs, saying, "I
think my music is aimed at a general audience. However, at home, the
biggest concerns that I express are mainly those of the black community.
The community in which I grew up."

At the same time, my father's white audience had never been bigger,
and he knew it. "Those concerns are not just black problems," he said.
"Most of my songs are songs that I'm sure relate to the majority of people's everyday life. But attitudes in the world are constantly changing.
The subjects and moods of my songs reflect what concerns me, what I
am currently thinking about. My songs attempt to break it down—communicate my theories to people of all kinds. I'm very happy if my songs
hit home with a wider audience—as they seem to be doing right now."

As soon as the album hit the streets, so did he. The band played the usual
places, including a date at the Apollo in September. They also did something my father had never done before—perform with a live orchestra.
At a show in Dallas, the seventy-piece Dallas Symphony backed him,
providing what must have been a jaw-dropping performance.

He also toured Europe again with John's help. Throughout the trip
he exchanged letters with my mother, and he found himself in the agonizing position of trying to save his relationship from across the sea.
Though he'd gotten serious with his new girlfriend Toni, he still hadn't
accepted losing Diane.

Preparing to come home, he composed one final letter to my mother. In it, he poured his passion into beautifully poetic passages; he made passive aggressive threats, then backed off with conciliatory words; he played the part of a spurned lover, though he never remained faithful; he slipped in guilt trips. Then, as if unsure that his message had gotten through, he added a passive aggressive ultimatum, signed with only his initials. In all, he sounded like a desperate man trying every tactic he can think of to keep his woman by his side—which he was. He wrote:

Dearest,

Tho I slept well last night all the way thru until about six my mind was once again fallen to the thought of yourself and I. I want so badly to call you but realizing it to be late you wouldn't understand . . . Not seeing you as I would like to, I am afraid that we are now entirely beyond each other. I have seen nothing more than friendly gestures of intention toward me as you would do any male friend . . . At this moment I am very tense partly from fear that your tender statements of love to me in the past week may truly be what you want, feeling that it is right. And yet you still seem resistant as in what you really want. You have said these things many times before. I have found you not to be sure really as to what you want where I may be concerned. As you have always said, actions speak louder than words . . .

I am very happy that you won't receive this letter until you have come back from your trip. Altho this is very intimate to me I am sure you will find reasons to share this letter with your companion. It is good to know that you have someone whom you enjoy spending your life and time with. I wish not to interfere, just unhappy that I don't play a part of such confidence and intimacy of you two. But maybe this is a blessing to both of us in disguise. In the letter prior to this one I tried not to be too mushy with words of love knowing that is really not your bag and not wanting to sound like I'm rapping.

I have been very sincere with my feelings for you and of you, and have often said times before that I want you and ours together.

That has not been the wish of both of us and decisions have been most permanent and clearly stated. Have you come to change your mind? How do you come to say your love when you often stated having no feelings at all as well as having clearly shown me that I am not needed? How do you look upon me? Diane, surely not as a companion, lover, buddy, nor really a friend. Then what am I needed for in your life? What is there you want that I may be able to give you other than financial support?

Without love there can be nothing else, although through loving you I have wanted to give of myself in every possible way but you have turned me out to deal with my needs and desires of love, only from the streets. I am sorry to say that Mrs. Diane Mayfield has truly become Miss Diane Mayfield as to your preference. But I have no love from the latter. It is not in me anymore to have to buy of love, companion[ship], and intimacy. The price is much too high. As always love knows not its own depth until the hour of separation. It is not necessary for you to come to Atlanta as I do not wish to be part of your summer fun tour only to see it die come fall when the need of warmth shall truly prove upon us. Before there is anything more let us truly find the respect that has been lost. Only then can there be a true happiness . . .

Always,
Curtis

This is my final proposal of love and life with the two of us. As the years are rapidly moving I am eager to build all that has been torn down with or without—CM.

He'd have to go without. It stung, but like always, he had piles of work waiting for him when he got home in December. He planned on producing two new Curtom artists—Patty Miller and Ruby Jones—and he also had begun writing the next Impressions album.

Curtom also had its sights on the singer, playwright, musical writer, actor, and movement activist Oscar Brown Jr. Dad kicked around the idea of writing a musical with him. It never happened—Dad was over-committed already, including an upcoming trip to Europe in January to appear at the MIDEM Festival in Cannes, France. "With me running cross country we figured we might be overloading," he said.

Though the Brown deal fell through, Curtom had cobbled together Baby Huey's attempts at making an album, resulting in the posthumous *The Baby Huey Story*. Ruby Jones also put out her self-titled debut album, on which she covered my father's "Stone Junkie." At the same time, several other Curtom releases were selling at a fast pace, including a single released in July of the previous year by Moses Dillard and the Tex-Town Display, featuring a young Peabo Bryson. That single, "I've Got to Find a Way (to Hide My Hurt)," sold a quarter million copies.

Everything was working. Curtom was flush with money.

———

After Dad finished touring *Roots*, his feelings on the album changed, due in equal part to his mercurial nature and his insatiable need to create something new and better. "It's sort of funny," he said, "but I guess as a writer I have to be a good critic as well and though I am pleased with it and people tell me they feel it's one of the better things I've done, I kinda feel I would like to try it one more time and come up with something fresher and stronger. But that's just the way I work, I have to keep on writing so by the time the album was out some of the stuff seemed stale to me."

Roots was old news. He'd thrown himself into rehearsing new songs for the Impressions. While at Fred's house one day, he gave an interviewer a taste of what to expect, saying, "We're working on several new things, new ideas and concepts for a fresh new album for the group. It will be a somewhat 'down' album and the tunes will include timely things relating to what's happening around us as well as love tunes. There's another 'Stop the War' song, which is nothing new and something everyone has already said, but I feel it's an important message; and there's a tune called 'Potent Love' which I think might prove to be a single. It's a love song and a very tasteful track."

With such constant writing, my father pulled off the staggering task of creating an entire record label's worth of music by himself. Perhaps he knew that no one could keep up such a workload forever, but for the time being, his songs gave him total control over the fate of his Curtom family, the same way they had given him control over his own fate and that of his actual family. After so many years of success, his decision to go solo had catapulted him to a level he'd never imagined.

As the label grew, so did Marv's influence. It remained a source of friction between Curtis and Eddie as they split further apart, their fifteen-year friendship and partnership fraying. "I told Curtis, 'If we want Marv Stuart in our company, we could put him in here as an advisor, pay him what he earns, and leave it at that point so that we can watch everything that's going down,'" Eddie said. "But Marv had really done a job on Curtis—nothing I could say or do to change him."

My father called a meeting with his two partners and said he wanted Marv to take over the day-to-day operations of the label and Eddie to handle promotions since that was his expertise. Dad would handle the creative side, as always. Eddie didn't like it one bit. He stared Marv dead in the eye and said, "I want you to buy me out of the company."

It would take roughly a year before my father cut ties with Eddie, but everyone knew Marv had won the battle. Marv had an advantage over Eddie beyond his white skin—he knew girls who liked to party. "I heard they liked threesomes," my mother says. "And you know, they were getting high. Marv along with Curtis. They both smoked pot and snorted cocaine. So, who knows what they did? I don't really; I was never there. [Curtis] was too trusting of people. If they said, 'We got you covered,' come bring some girls in, they have a party, he forgot about the business."

In such a way, my father went deeper into trusting the wrong people—accountants, employees, "friends." He knew someone was doing something wrong when the IRS began hounding him again. This time, they wanted more than his Webcor tape recorder. He owned a building with Marv in Berwyn, Illinois, which he had to sell to pay off the government.

"He didn't want to listen to me about a lot of things," my mother says. "I knew someone that was stealing from him, and I told him, and he said unless I told him who told me he was just going to let him steal. Someone would call me and say, 'You need to tell Curtis to watch out for so-and-so because he knows how to steal the money from him,' and Curtis, you know, he could have a whole lot of money and leave it there, go leave the building, and he doesn't know, it might be $5,000 in there, and then when he came back, it might be $4,200. And I would tell him, but he didn't listen to me." Again, for all his business acumen and obsession with owning himself, my father often acted directly against his own interests.

———————

Even though they had separated, my parents stayed in each other's lives, sometimes with disastrous consequences. Once, when Dad went over to visit, a man called the house for my mother. Tracy answered the phone, but when Dad found out it was another man, he snatched the phone and hung up. Then, he stormed into the bathroom, where my mother had just finished bathing Sharon, and started screaming. He pulled my sister out of the tub, knocked my mother down between the wall and the toilet, and kicked her. "I had a huge bruise on my thigh," my mother says.

It wasn't the only time he used physical violence. My mother recalls, "Another time when I wanted to do something, he wouldn't, and I think Kenny was there that time, and he punched me in my stomach. I started to call the police, you know, have him arrested, and Kenny asked me not to."

It's hard to know what was going on in my father's mind during those times. He was not a violent man by nature, but he was under incredible pressure and experimenting with mood-altering drugs—a dangerous proposition for a man who could shift into a foul disposition at a moment's notice, even when sober. There was no excusing his actions, and he didn't try. It wasn't the last time he'd use violence to control a woman, either.

Within the previous two years, my father had entered uncharted territory in every aspect of his life. He moved far from his relationships with Fred, Sam, Eddie, and my mother, and grew close to people who didn't have his best interests at heart. But at the same time, he had never been more successful. And he now lived and worked on his own terms. As the year ended, Eddie saw where things were headed. He made plans to sell his share of Curtom while Marv lured my father into moving the studio to the North Side of Chicago.

———

Dad had quit the Impressions in large part to spend more time at home working at Curtom, but with the wild success of his first three solo efforts, he found himself touring as much as ever. After one of his last shows of the year—a gig at Lincoln Center in New York City—writer Phil Fenty and producer Sig Shore slipped backstage with a script in hand and a proposition. "We hope that you might be interested in scoring this movie," they said as they handed him the script. My father almost fell out of his chair. He'd wanted this break for years, and it had finally come.

The result would define him for the rest of his life.

10

Super Fly

"Hard to understand, what a hell of a man,
This cat of the slum had a mind, wasn't dumb."
—"SUPERFLY"

Somewhere between New York and Chicago, late 1971—Sitting on an airplane, the *Super Fly* script in his lap, Dad couldn't stop the music from coming. "Wow, was I so excited," he said. "I'd written a song just flying back home from New York. It took me hardly no time to prepare the songs and that's how it began . . . I began writing immediately upon reading the script. I was making notes and coming up with the songs already. That was just a fantastic adventure for me."

Reading the terse script, he felt drawn to the main character, Young-blood Priest. By name alone, Priest was an obvious archetype, a broadly drawn amalgamation of every drug dealer and pimp who stalked the ghettos. The main difference—Priest wanted out. Curtis said, "I didn't put Priest down. He was just trying to get out. His deeds weren't noble ones, but he was making money and he had intelligence. And he did survive. I mean all this was reality."

Even closer to reality, my father felt, was Priest's fall guy, Freddie. "Reading the script, I started feeling very deeply bad for Freddie," he said. "Between his friends, his partners, and his woman, he was catching a hard time. 'Freddie's Dead' came to me immediately. While you might not know a lot of pimps and drug dealers, we do meet quite a few Freddies."

Dad crafted "Freddie's Dead" on the Fender Rhodes piano he kept in his basement bedroom of the three-flat house—he said it only took him five minutes to write. He liked to work late into the night, long after we'd fallen asleep. In the morning, sometimes we'd see the aftermath of a songwriting session. As Tracy recalls, "I remember all this legal paper balled up everywhere on the floor. And I remember picking one up to read it and it just said 'Freddie's Dead' on it. I was like, 'Who's Freddie? Who's dead?'"

Dad had another song already written—"Ghetto Child"—which he tried to cut during the *Roots* sessions. It fit the *Super Fly* script perfectly. He renamed it "Little Child Runnin' Wild," and as he explained, "I started writing ['Little Child Runnin' Wild'] three years ago. It never seemed to come out right, though. And then, all at once, while I was scoring the movie, everything fell into place."

To score the rest of the film, Dad received rushes of the scenes and watched them on a Sony VO-1600, a huge, heavy, professional piece of equipment that was a precursor to the VCR. The rushes came on three-quarter-inch videocassettes, each one the size of a book, featuring a timeline running across the bottom of the screen so he could sync the music exactly where he wanted in each scene. He had the machine set up in a room he used as a home studio, and sometimes he'd let us watch the tape while he worked. Other times, my brothers and I would sneak in and watch the famous bathtub love scene while he was napping.

Though we were still young, we'd grown accustomed to watching Dad work in such an intimate setting. He made a point of including us in his professional life whenever possible, often letting us sit in the Curtom studio as he recorded. We learned quickly, however, that watching someone write a song isn't nearly as exciting as listening to the finished product.

Dad was more than excited, though. On top of giving him a chance to score his first movie, the *Super Fly* script called for a cameo performance featuring "The Curtis Mayfield Experience," which would mark his first time on the silver screen. Because of scheduling conflicts, the band had to shoot the scene for the movie before recording the album, so late in December 1971, Dad called Craig, Lucky, Henry, and Tyrone and said in typical last-minute fashion, "Hey, we're going to go do this movie. We got to go to New York."

Dad had written a song called "Pusherman" for the scene, but he hadn't had a chance to work it out in the studio. Filmmaker Gordon Parks Jr. needed a finished song for the shot, though, so the band booked a session at Bell Sound Studios in New York to cut it. Craig recalls, "I think we went in at night, because we had to go do the movie thing the next day." The band hadn't heard any of the other songs my father had written, but if "Pusherman" was any indication, they were in for something special.

When they arrived on set, as Craig recalls, "That's when we found out what movie making is all about. We're just standing there, and they're adjusting the lights. They're trying to get all the entrances right and things." The band mimed the song while the actors attempted to nail the scene, take after take. The next day, they did it again. As my father learned on the first Impressions' tour, what once seems glamorous often becomes mundane when viewed up close. Movies were no different.

Shooting the scene was a bit tedious, but it only lasted two days, after which the band embarked on another European tour. They had a shaky opening at the Rainbow in London on Sunday, January 23, 1972. The support band, Bloodstone, went on more than an hour late and performed to an indifferent audience. During Curtis's set, the PA crapped out, and the sound engineer didn't know he had to make up for Curtis's soft voice and left the microphones too low. On top of that, Craig's guitar was beset with technical problems. Frustrated, my father ended the show early.

Despite these difficulties, a concert review in *NME* that appeared a week later provided a glimpse into the growing appreciation white audiences in England showed my father. Reviewer Roger St. Pierre wrote, "As for those who did turn out, apart from a fair leavening of blacks, they were the kind of audience you'd expect at any rock show . . . Perhaps the long-hairs have suddenly, belatedly but pleasingly, turned on to soul music; perhaps they've always secretly dug it anyway; perhaps they were there just because it's the latest trendy thing. But, maybe it's because—at long last—the barriers between musical forms are really coming down and good music per se is the new fad."

Whether or not those barriers were coming down in Europe, they still loomed large in America. This dichotomy became more confusing as Dad's popularity in Europe continued growing. He made several TV appearances there, including *The Old Grey Whistle Test* in England and *Beat Club* in Germany. In an interview with the German hosts, he explained his message music for a European crowd that didn't live the day-to-day struggles of life in America, saying:

> My comments I guess are more for the States, because black people in the States have gone through many of the things that I talk about—more so, I would imagine than in most countries, even though we do have the prejudices and the hang-ups of not only black people but most minority groups everywhere. I feel that it's very important to me to make people at least take in what I stand for, how do I feel, what do I represent. I think the masses overall today, when they come to see an artist, if they spent their money, they are more interested in the overall picture. Not just make me laugh, or make me feel good, but make me understand what you mean. What do you stand for? Love, appreciation, and anything else starts out first with respect. If I can establish some identity as to making you respect me as a human, and then accept me as an entertainer, then let's do that.

In his mind, that sort of respect wasn't just a personal need; it represented a way to cure the social ills he sang about. As he'd say years later, "Segregation will only end when people get to know the people they think they hate. To start to know somebody is to respect them."

One host asked him, "So your function is sort of, well, it is similar to that of a preacher?" My father replied, "I would suppose so. My grandmother was a preacher, and I came up in the church, not that I really try and relate my works with that, but I suppose in one way or another it did have a great effect to me as to my lyrics." The host then asked about his performance style: "You have this cool and very special way of performing, which is not the cliché of black music being performed. It's very cool, it's very in a way sophisticated, convincing. It's not ecstatic in the sense we apply the word 'ecstasy' to black music." "Well, I agree with that wholeheartedly," my father said. "I'm glad that at least in my presentation, I can bring about more status as to white people understanding that we are not as entertainers just people that turn flips, and holler 'Shake your shaggy shaggy,' and 'Do your thing,' but we also are people that think and want to progress and have culture and identity as well. Why not sell that in my music?" That was as full a summary of his musical philosophy as he'd ever given, and it helped create a European fan base that would sustain him in later years.

Apart from television shows, he mostly played military bases in France, England, and Germany, where all the soldiers said the same thing—"I'll be glad when I get back to the world." "Back to the world" was their slang for returning home. The phrase rang in my father's head, much like "It's all right" almost a decade before. He logged it in his memory for later use.

———

Dad returned home in February to finish *Super Fly*, but other obligations demanded his attention first. On February 22, he appeared on the *Dick Cavett Show* and felt snubbed when Cavett didn't invite him to sit for an interview as he did with so many other artists. Cavett's producer said, "What does he have to talk to him about?" My father recognized that comment as a dig. It was a negation of the massive success he'd achieved and the toil it took to achieve it.

Next, Dad returned to his old group. The Impressions hadn't recorded since *Check Out Your Mind* in 1970, so they hit the studio to cut the songs they'd been rehearsing at Fred's house. The resulting album, *Times Have Changed*, introduced Leroy Hutson as lead singer. Dad wrote seven of the eight songs on the album, including his most powerful antiwar song ever, "Stop the War," featuring a haunting, passionate vocal performance from Sam.

My father produced the album and played on it with Craig, Lucky, Tyrone, and Master Henry. *Times Have Changed* failed to chart, but it contained several powerful songs, including the beautiful title track, as well as a song my father would use later for himself called "Love Me." The Impressions' first effort without him might not have created a stir, but it was a strong album unfairly overlooked.

After wrapping *Times Have Changed*, Dad received more rushes of the *Super Fly* film and didn't like what he saw. He said, "Reading the script didn't tell you 'and then he took another hit of cocaine' and then about a minute later 'he took another hit.' So when I saw it visually, I thought, 'This is a cocaine infomercial.'" He was no prude, nor from what I heard was he a stranger to cocaine—I was told he'd begun experimenting with it by the time of *Super Fly*, and soon he would enter a period of heavier use. He had also lived the truth of the movie's seedy scenes during his childhood in the White Eagle. "I didn't have to leave my neighborhood to be surrounded by the things that *Superfly* is about," he said. "It was easier than most scripts because it was about an environment that I knew. It's not that the ghetto is thriving with pimps and pushermen, it's just they are a very visible part of the ghetto. If you stand on the corner, you're gonna notice the pimp, because he's so bright. If he goes by twice, you're gonna remember him and get to know him, while you might not remember somebody else who goes by five times. And you have to understand that half of every big city is the ghetto."

Still, he wanted no part of a movie that glorified these things. Instead of backing down, he doubled down. He crafted his songs into character studies, each one becoming its own movie in miniature. In a way, he became the film's conscience. "I did the music and lyrics to be a commentary, as though someone was speaking as the movie was going," he said. "It was important for me to counter the visuals—to go in and explain it in a way that the kids would not read it as an infomercial for drugs."

With the message in place, he needed the music to match, so he returned to the man who had done more for his music than anyone— Johnny Pate. Johnny still lived in New York, working as an A&R man, producer, and arranger for MGM Records. He got a call, and the soft, high voice on the other end said, "I can't do it without you." Johnny dropped his work and flew to Chicago.

As usual, Curtis brought in cassettes with snippets of guitar licks and vocal ideas. For the first time though, when Johnny heard the songs, he felt little inspiration to write arrangements. "Most of [the songs had] very few chord changes, very few melodic lines," he said. "'Pusherman,' 'Superfly,' 'Freddie's Dead,' if you listen to these closely enough, Curtis was almost rapping through these things." Johnny did get excited about "Eddie You Should Know Better"—"You've got chord structure, you've got beautiful chord changes, plus a great melody," he said—but for the rest of the material, scoring two-chord songs didn't leave a lot of room for a jazz cat with a full orchestra at his fingertips.

That simplification—the emphasis on rhythmic rather than chordal movement—had already pushed my father's music into new realms. It did the same for Johnny's arrangements. Despite the difficulties, or perhaps because of them, Johnny created unforgettable backdrops to the songs, jaw-dropping in brilliance and complexity. Harps, oboes, strings, horns, bells, and flutes do as much to paint a picture as the lyrics themselves.

The arrangements helped create an intricate tapestry of sound unlike anything Dad and Johnny had yet made together. Part of that intricacy came from the method of recording. "We had the chance to cut with a live orchestra," Craig says. "The advantage of it is, if you have full orchestra, when you place your licks, you don't have to worry about your licks bumping. You can hear everything that's going to go down."

Another part was how close my father, Craig, Henry, and Lucky had become from touring together. "As a guitar player, I wanted to make sure I had my stuff right," Craig says.

I played on every song. Curtis would drop out sometimes and just sing. He knew I could do that. I was the only guitar player on 'Freddie's Dead.' Curtis was in the control booth and Phil Upchurch couldn't be there, so I was the only one out there. So, I knew exactly where to put all the nuances, the little licks. The way we worked was that Curtis would play something and he relied on me and Lucky and Master Henry to put our parts onto his thing. He might have an idea, but in the end we was like a team, man. You don't even have to say nothin'. We just do it. I already knew what he was getting ready to do, and I can counter with something else.

Engineer Roger Anfinsen recalled working in a crammed studio with as many as forty musicians on some songs. Dad and the band were crowded in by harps, horns, strings, flutes, and other players, and background singers had to sing from the control booth. "This was the only time I worked in this fashion with Curtis," Anfinsen said. "It seemed about capturing a certain electricity, a live energy." They cut the songs in a mere three days, after which my father perfected his vocals. Then, everyone stepped back to admire the finished product.

The first seconds of "Little Child Runnin' Wild" grab the listener by the throat. Master Henry's percussive force mixes with undulating organ chords and the anguished wails of Craig's guitar, creating an eerie tension. Five quick raps on the snare drum break the tension, and the song kicks in.

The groove rides on a surreptitious riff, full of upbeats and hits on the third and fourth count of the second measure. It makes the standard 4/4 time signature feel off-kilter, enhancing the sense of anxiety. Lucky's bass propels the song—a role he filled for most of the album—while against a backdrop of morose horns and pizzicato strings, my father lays down some of his heaviest lyrics:

> Little child runnin' wild, watch awhile, you see he never smiles
> Broken home, father gone, mama tired, so he's all alone
> Kinda sad, kinda mad, ghetto child, thinking he's been had
> In the back of his mind he's sayin', "I didn't have to be here,

You didn't have to love for me, while I was just a nothing child
Why couldn't they just let me be?"

Never did his voice betray such sadness, such depth, such nuance of emotion.

Next comes the up-tempo magic of "Pusherman." The song is flashy, funky, streetwise. Upon impact, it hooks the listener with the sweet science of a pusher on the corner, spitting game. Master Henry's percussion dances around Lucky's dazzling bass line, while in a vocal style becoming familiar to him, my father almost raps the lyrics:

I'm your mama, I'm your daddy,
I'm that nigga in the alley,
I'm your doctor when in need,
Want some coke? Have some weed.
You know me, I'm your friend,
Your main boy, thick and thin,
I'm your pusherman.

He'd taken the rhythm of the street hustler and put it to music. As he explained, "It's the way a hustler really would come in with a superfly motive, superfly ego, and telling what his thing is really supposed to be . . . I think this one gets down."

The message shifts back to a minor key on "Freddie's Dead," where Curtis deals with the character that spoke to him most. His phrasing is again proto-rap as he lets loose a flurry of words, "Let the man rap a plan, said he'd send him home / But his hope was a rope, and he should have known." He deals with life in the space age, placing it in brutal contrast with the realities of ghetto life: "We're all built up with progress / But sometimes I must confess / We can deal with rockets and dreams / But reality, what does it mean?" Once again, Lucky's unforgettable bass riff drives the song.

"Give Me Your Love"—written for the bathtub love scene—sees my father taking his music down sensual alleys again, this time exceeding the raw sexuality of "Get Down." It begins with one of those signature

Curtis Mayfield guitar licks, all gorgeous hammer-ons and pull-offs, which Johnny smartly echoes on strings and harp. The song left room for Johnny to slip in a few accents, as well. "I was able to put a few other jazz licks in there that I couldn't always do with Curtis," he said. "But, there were holes enough in there for me to use them. I could use some percussive brass licks. I was able to do this on a few other cuts on *Super Fly*. Whenever I found a hole where I could shine, where I didn't cover up anything Curtis was doing, I took advantage of that as an arranger."

Johnny's favorite song, "Eddie You Should Know Better," clocks in at two minutes and twenty-one seconds—far shorter than the average for my father's post-Impressions work—but in that short span, he tells a vividly detailed story about Priest's right-hand man, one of the movie's most morally ambiguous characters.

The album ends with the title track, "Superfly"—a perfect character study of Priest and an encapsulation of the entire movie into three-and-a-half minutes. As far as infectious songs go, it is perhaps my father's best. Johnny's horns are somewhere between big-band swing and James Brown funk, the drums pound with the insistence of a hustler trying to score, the bass rumbles like a superfly hog, and the percussion adds a Latin flare with guiro and congas. When Curtis coos the chorus, the word "Superfly" rolls off his tongue, his inflection somewhere between delighted surprise and supreme cool.

Perhaps counterintuitively, writing to a script and telling other characters' stories allowed Dad to craft his most autobiographical lyrics ever. He wasn't just writing about Priest and Freddie; he wasn't just writing about junkies and pushers; he was writing about himself and his childhood. He was writing about the things he'd seen growing up in the White Eagle, the things he'd experienced living in one of the most segregated cities in the North and traveling through the South during the darkest hours of Jim Crow. His autobiography shines through in lines like "Hard to understand / What a hell of a man / This cat of the slum had a mind / Wasn't dumb," and "His mind was his own / But the man lived alone," and "Can't be like the rest / Is the most he'll confess."

He also recognized his adult life in the film rushes. In one scene, a street gang approaches Priest and tries to extort money in exchange for protection. My father had just lived through that exact trouble. One day, he walked into Curtom and found the Blackstone Rangers, one of Chicago's most notorious gangs, lurking in his office. They demanded money. Just like when the promoter in Atlantic City waved a gun in his face, my father remained cool. He had steel of his own in his desk drawer—a silver revolver with a white handle. He often kept it close in case a situation got out of hand. At home, he tucked it under his mattress or stashed it in the drawer next to his bed. Sometimes he'd even bring it on family outings for safety. One day, he showed it to me—"You see that?" he said. "Don't touch it."

Still, he wanted no part of the Blackstone Rangers. He cut a deal. "I'm not giving you any money," I recall him saying, "but I'll play a concert in Chicago and you can take the money and help the neighborhood." They never bothered him again.

That didn't mean he was safe, though. A black man making the money he made remained a conspicuous target, especially in a city with such strong Mafia ties. After fending off the Blackstone Rangers, Dad found himself in the shady clutches of Queen Booking again—the same company he bought into with Jerry a decade before and ultimately left because of the way the Mob took advantage of black artists. Now, Queen offered him a deal he couldn't refuse—a six-month contract to book a tour of white-college dates. The deal was short-lived, though, since Queen never followed through. Dad soon switched to William Morris, one of the biggest bookers around, and they scheduled more than eighty white-college shows. He hadn't given up on getting over to white crowds in America the way he did in Europe.

———

Though he navigated that treacherous world of gangsters and mobsters without losing control of himself or his money, he couldn't always navigate personal relationships with such finesse. While preparing *Super Fly* for release, Dad and Johnny got into an argument over the album's two instrumental tracks, causing an irreparable rift in their relationship.

The first of those tracks, "Junkie Chase," is a classic piece of blaxploitation music—all orchestral hits, rumbling bass, and wah-wah guitar. The second, "Think," features a guitar part that would surely have made Hendrix take notice. Both songs owe quite a bit to their orchestral arrangements, and Johnny wanted cowriting credit on them. My father refused to give it to him. Curtis the friend might have appreciated Johnny's contributions; Curtis the businessman didn't share credit—not with Carl Davis, not with Fred and Sam, and not with Johnny. When the final product hit stores, the album sleeve read, "Successfully arranged and orchestrated from the original dictations of Curtis Mayfield by Johnny Pate."

Johnny refused to back down. "I orchestrated and arranged the score to *Super Fly*, but Curtis Mayfield got all the credit," he told a reporter a month after the album's release. "Everybody is ego tripping and taking credit for things they didn't do." By December, Dad filed a lawsuit in New York's US District Court to declare himself the sole author and publisher of "Junkie Chase" and "Think." He also went after one million dollars' worth of damages for alleged defamation of character. His lawyer, Lew Harris, told *Jet* magazine, "We aren't denying that Johnny Pate performed a very useful service in the arranging of the songs, but he was an author for hire; he was paid for his service." In the same article, Johnny said, "I am entitled to half of the composing rights for those two tunes, because I wrote the melodic line for both."

In Craig's eyes, Johnny had a point. "Curtis couldn't write music down," he says. "So, he wasn't going to orally translate those harmonies or those hits. You can listen to it and tell this is some big-band arranger putting this down. So, really, after all the things those two had done like brothers in the past, it shouldn't have been a problem. That was just a poor way of doing something, as far as I'm concerned."

That was how my father had always done business, though, and that was how he'd keep doing it. Even near the end of his life, in an interview for the album's twenty-fifth anniversary, he framed the debate on his terms. "Most arrangers that I have used in the past will come in with their own contributions, but I was always careful to make changes and be assured that the music was still mine and there was no conflict in the music that was arranged against the basic rhythm pattern in the song itself," he said. "There's a Curtis Mayfield song that really has no singing or lyrics, which is called 'Think' from the *Super Fly* album that I especially appreciate when I listen to it. My art and my creativities were totally something that was of my own heart and mind. I could never let anybody dictate to me what I should write and how I would write it." Sharing writing credit would have meant sharing revenues, and Curtis had toiled his whole career to avoid that. As a result, he and Johnny would never work together again.

————

After Johnny left, Dad suffered another major split when Eddie sold his share of Curtom. Eddie had wanted out since Marv began angling for control in the late '60s. Now, the label Eddie worked so hard to help start was out of his hands for good. The record stickers still read Curtom, but for all intents and purposes, it had become CurtMarv. Marv lived on the North Side, and he'd already convinced my father to move the Curtom offices to a building at 5915 N. Lincoln Avenue—a more convenient location for him. Eddie planned to stay on the South Side. Thus, the split took on physical and emotional dimensions.

Eddie remembers those times with customary grace and good nature, saying, "I knew Curtis needed to stand on his own. I had to stand on my own too . . . You have to roll your sleeves up and say, 'Hey, Eddie Thomas, let's get busy. Let's start doing things.' That's what I did. I said, let me get busy and do my thing. I can do something. I'm not just relying upon anybody else's talent. We all got something to offer. You don't hold grudges."

The split took a toll on them both, though, and their relationship wouldn't mend for years. My mother is more candid about what went on behind the scenes. "I saw some changes when [Curtis] went from Eddie Thomas as the business partner to Marv Stuart," she says.

They brought [Eddie's wife] Audrey and I in it. When Eddie and Curtis fell out, they didn't want us to speak. We had to sneak to

speak and make phone calls. "Oh, he's coming in! Hang up!" Like
that. Everything was behind the scenes because they weren't friends
anymore. They had severed their business ties. I was upset about
that. I mean, this is your friend, how could you do that? And now
you want me to ignore and not speak, because you and Eddie are
not speaking anymore? I didn't like that.

There again emerged the cold side Tracy spoke of. It was a business
decision, and Dad knew how to separate his heart from his business.
Even though few understood why he trusted Marv, it felt like the right
choice to him. My mother tried to explain his reasoning, saying, "Marv
Hyman, that was a Jewish name, so of course he had more connections.
I did say something to [Curtis] and he said, 'Well Eddie can't, you know,
he's black! He's still trying to get a little crack in the door, but Marv can
open the door. And he can get better deals.'"

In my father's defense, like Priest and Freddie, he was forced into a
rigged situation that left him few choices. Radio had opened up some
since the Impressions' early days, and segregation was dead at least where
the law was concerned, but America remained a racist, segregated country in almost every station of life. My father grew tired of beating his
head against that wall. With the massive success of his first few Curtom
projects, he had reason to believe he'd made the right decision.

———————

The *Super Fly* soundtrack continued that massive success. It dropped
a month before the movie and shot to the top of the R&B chart. It
was an odd way to orchestrate a release, but a canny move in this case.
Making a blaxploitation film came with tremendous obstacles, and the
massive pre-publicity from the soundtrack helped overcome them. Fenty
and Shore had that in mind when they handed my father the script in
New York. They knew working with one of the hottest artists in the
world would help them secure backing, and as Dad wrote and cut the
soundtrack, Fenty got that backing. He went to Nate Adams, who owned
an employment business in Harlem. Adams said, "I had a good picture

of what was happening on the streets, as well as what was happening in the business world." He signed on.

Fenty also had producer Sig Shore on his side. He said, "Sig was ideal for this. He knew the market. He knew how to get things done. He knew how to hustle, how to put together an independent project with no money." Shore received money from two black dentists that lived in his neighborhood. Gordon Parks Sr. also pitched in roughly $5,000. "It was really a struggle from the very beginning," Shore said.

One struggle was overcome easily—casting the lead role. Fenty went to his friend Ron O'Neal, who was trained as a Shakespearean stage actor. It went without saying that *Super Fly* was not Shakespeare, but O'Neal felt a connection to Priest. He had grown up in a one-bedroom apartment on the West Side of New York and recognized himself in the script the same way my father did. "He really understood what that part was all about," Shore said.

They overcame another struggle with help from an unexpected place. In need of a superfly hog—the sweet street-hustler car they felt a character like Priest would drive—Adams serendipitously ran into a real-life pimp with just such a ride. "I can remember sitting in the shoe-shine parlor in the Theresa Towers, and a gentleman pulled up with this black Cadillac El Dorado with these big headlights," Adams recalled. "This gentleman walked in, and he was slick as he wanted to be. A guy by the name of KC. He sat down next to me on the rack, I'm getting my shoes shined, you know, so I go, 'Hey, man, that's a bad ride. We thinkin' about doing a movie, and I'd like to maybe let them look at your car to use in the movie.' So, he gave me his number. It took me three weeks to get in touch with him. Consequently, when we finally talked, he said, 'Man, ain't no niggas makin' no movies. You jeffin' me?'"

After Adams convinced him, KC let them use his car, which features heavily in the film. Fenty decided he wanted more than just the car, though. "We said, 'Let's put KC in the picture,' because KC was wonderful," Fenty said. "When we ran out of money, KC would just, [*snaps fingers*], 'Buy 'em some food.' He would buy food, he had his own wardrobe, and he knew what to say."

Even so, production difficulties haunted the actors and crew. "When you shoot a picture like this, you're very flexible," Fenty said. "If you can't get in someplace, or if you get thrown off of a corner, you can't just fold it and wait for tomorrow. You got to find something else you can get." Adams recalled, "We didn't have anything but raw bones and guts. We didn't have the luxury of saying, 'We can shoot this scene over.'" They didn't have the luxury of a professional wardrobe, either, so most of what the actors wore onscreen came from their own closets, or from Adams's bevy of fly vines.

After Warner Brothers agreed to back the film, they held a sneak preview in Westwood, a predominately white California neighborhood. Reviews came back tepid at best, and Warner Brothers threatened to back out. They were, after all, taking a chance on backing such a movie. Shore wheedled, saying, "What the hell did you expect in that theatre? This is a white-bread town." As he recalled, "The next picture they screened it with was with *Shaft* at the Fox Theatre in Philadelphia. Of everybody that came out, they were all raves."

Spurred on by my father's music, the movie caused a fracas when it opened in New York in August 1972. "We decided we would go down and watch the lines for the movie," Fenty recalled. "They ran out of tickets, and there was still a lot of line left. Somebody went around the side of the building, and they broke the door open. You saw this mass of people with police trying to stop them breaking into the theatre trying to see this movie. That was a very, very high moment for Gordon and myself. That was our little picture, and people were actually breaking into the movies to see it."

Super Fly briefly knocked off *The Godfather* as the highest-grossing movie in the country, and it was the third-highest grossing film of 1972. Dad took Tracy, Sharon, and me to the movie's premiere in Chicago. Even though I was only six years old, I still remember the excitement and electricity in the air. I had seen many of the scenes on video while he was in the process of making the soundtrack, but seeing it on the big screen with the score made it seem bigger than life. Obviously, *Super Fly* wasn't meant for a young audience, but I believe Dad was so proud of his accomplishment that he wanted to share it with us.

While the movie follows a pusher trying to escape street life, beneath the surface, it is about the same things my father had been singing about since "The Other Side of Town" and "Underground": the dynamics of power—who has it, who needs it, who is denied it.

The movie has a strong moral center. At the end, Priest wins through intelligence and cunning, not violence—although he did give the cops a good beat down before driving off with his life, woman, and money intact. As my father noted, "In all the films at that time black people were portrayed as pimps and whores, who usually got ripped off at the end. *Superfly* had enough mind to get out of all that, and let the authorities know that he saw through their games." In other words, unlike every other movie, this time the black man won.

Crowds loved it. Critics did not. They'd fallen hard for *Super Fly* the album, but a furor erupted over *Super Fly* the movie. The *Times* of London said, "You could find more black power in a coffee bean." Vernon Jarrett, a black reporter for the *Chicago Tribune*, called it a "sickening and dangerous screen venture," going on to say,

> In real life, white biggie Warner Brothers and white producer Sig Shore and black writer Phillip Fenty and black director Gordon Parks, Jr. got themselves together and are selling to the black community a cinema brand of cocaine designed to appeal to the same people that are the targets of the hard-drug traffic. The truth is— ain't nobody stuck anything to the man.

Tony Brown, dean of Howard University's School of Communication, said in a *Newsweek* cover story, "The blaxploitation films are a phenomenon of self-hate. Look at the image of *Superfly*. Going to see yourself as a drug dealer when you're oppressed is sick. Not only are blacks identifying with him, they're paying for the identification. It's sort of like a Jew paying to get into Auschwitz."

Critics couldn't stop the movie from influencing the culture, though. Soon, black men everywhere wore Priest's hairstyle, "the Lord Jesus," with long, flowing locks curled and pressed. Cadillacs, decked out à la Priest's

224

superfly hog, crept down ghetto streets across America, moving just slowly enough to give the whole neighborhood an eyeful. The clothing of the street hustler became mainstream fare, too—suits with wide lapels and intricate stitching, mink coats, and platform shoes with three-inch heels. That last sartorial trend couldn't have come soon enough for my father, who at five-foot-seven loved to wear platform leather and suede boots. In those boots, he stood two or three inches taller. Of course, he wasn't the first or last artist to surreptitiously enhance his height. Everyone from Bob Dylan to Prince took advantage of heels in the same way.

Critics also couldn't stop a generation of kids who lived through the realities on the screen from absorbing every nuance. A decade later, they'd dig through their parents' records and chop up beats they found from Curtis, James Brown, the Isley Brothers, and others, to create a new art form—hip-hop.

While James Brown was arguably the most influential of the group, an especially strong link exists between *Super Fly* and hip-hop. The movie's gritty depiction of street life, the way Ron O'Neal swaggers through every scene as if he owns the entire world, the gratuitous martial arts scenes, and Curtis's slick, streetwise songs—these elements are imprinted on KRS-One's *Criminal Minded*, Public Enemy's *It Takes a Nation of Millions to Hold Us Back*, Nas's *Illmatic*, the Wu-Tang Clan's *Enter the Wu-Tang (36 Chambers)*, Notorious B.I.G.'s *Ready to Die*, and Snoop Doggy Dogg's *Doggystyle*, among dozens of others.

As Public Enemy's Chuck D said, "When hip-hop became the thing, of course you're going to reach back to what influenced you, what touched you in the past. The words from Curtis Mayfield and the Impressions just meant everything. The rhythms and the pacing we might not have incorporated as much as maybe something more percussive and aggressive like a James Brown, but there was something in Curtis Mayfield's stance that we used."

The film inspired more than just a young generation of musicians. Armond White, film critic for the *NY Press*, said, "I remember in the theater in St. Louis, Missouri, in 1972—the climax was when [Priest] told the cop off. He says, 'If I so much as choke on a chicken bone' what would happen, and the entire theatre, including myself, we leaped to our feet, and we stood, and screamed, and applauded, and clapped our hands, and stomped our feet. It connected psychically with people at a perfect place and time to provide that kind of catharsis."

Michael Gonzales, noted R&B and hip-hop journalist, had similar memories. "The first time I saw *Superfly* was at the Lowe's Victoria on 125th Street," he wrote. "Next door to the Apollo, the theater was a hundred feet away from the pigeon-eyed view of the movie's opening shot. Filled with young folks who couldn't wait to enter into that playa playa netherworld of hustlers, scramblers, dames, and gamblers, folks were psyched. As the reel started rolling, music spilled from the speakers and the audience hummed along, mouthed the words, or sang aloud to the soundtrack." Gonzales also credited the "neo-psychedelic red logo" on the "Freddie's Dead" single with inspiring "a million graffiti artists."

Despite the success of both soundtrack and movie, though, the critical excoriation stung. My father, who never wasted time arguing with critics, fought back, saying:

The way you clean up the film is by cleaning up the streets. I can see where those guys are coming from, and how they look upon *Superfly* as a dope movie. But it's just as easy to see it as an anti-drug movie, which is what I think the critics don't give the people enough credit for seeing. I mean even an anti-dope commercial can be looked at as a dope commercial. You can't do nothing about drugs by pretending they don't exist. You just have to be able to give people credit for knowing what's good and what's bad. That's why I wanted "Freddie's Dead" put out as the single. Because the average dude realizes that he's more like a Freddie than a Priest. And Freddie's just the average guy who might have been able to be saved except that he fell in with the wrong crowd. More people are gonna realize that they're like Freddie and if they don't watch what they're messing with they'll end up dead. There's one other thing that the critics of *Superfly* seem to miss. For the budget of less than $300,000, there isn't that much you can do. The film had to be

about things that go on in the street because this is the only place
they could afford to shoot it.

In another interview, he continued his argument. "Forget the critics," he said. "Ask somebody who has had a true taste of street life. They
know this was the only way we could make an honest film about the
drug culture. Nobody called James Bond, Tarzan, or Frankenstein 'white
exploitation' movies. If there is a dollar to be made in adventure films,
why can't black people make it?"

Craig echoes that last thought. "This was another opportunity for a
black artist to do another movie score in that vein of what they call black
exploitation," he says.

It's exploitation, but at the same time, it seems like if you got that
many people workin', I don't know who you exploiting. It seems
like a black *employment* situation to me. All they were filming was
what was normal anyway. The type of cars and stuff that was in
Super Fly, hey, I seen that stuff back in '63, '64. The pimps around
here had those same kind of cars, and they were immaculately
dressed and all that . . . This is nothing new.

Even late in his life, Dad defended the movie. In a 1996 interview,
he said, "These films were positive for us. Prior to blaxploitation, we
didn't dare show any intellect in films. The black characters were always
getting killed. But with *Shaft* and *Superfly*, things were different."

For his part, O'Neal provided some of the most full-throated defense
of the movie. In an interview shortly after the release, he said, "*Super Fly*
is about people who don't believe in the American Dream at all—have
no reason to . . . What *Super Fly* does, I think it provides a measure of
hope in some lives that, believe me, do not get any spiritual enlighten-
ment from the Doris Day show. Black people that I've come in contact
with, they take a personal pride in my role in the film. There seems to be
a general feeling that they have advanced somehow. My success is indeed
a success for my people."

With *Sweetback,* *Shaft,* and *Super Fly,* the blaxploitation genre exploded. A pattern formed in which a world-class artist created an album that helped sell the movie and often overshadowed it. It happened with Bobby Womack's *Across 110th Street,* Roy Ayers's *Coffy* (written for the movie that introduced Pam Grier to the world), Marvin Gaye's *Trouble Man,* and James Brown's *Black Caesar*—all excellent albums that resulted in some of the best work by each artist.

Even Johnny Pate got back in the mix, scoring *Brother on the Run* and *Shaft in Africa.* Dozens of other examples exist, but of all these soundtracks, *Super Fly* remains in a class by itself. It transcends the genre and time period in a way no other blaxploitation soundtrack does. Perhaps that's due to its unprecedented and unrepeated success on the charts. Perhaps it's because my father spoke about real life issues that remain relevant some forty years later, and will likely be relevant in another forty years. Whatever the reason, critical opinion and cultural impact have set *Super Fly* apart from the competition—and it was damn stiff competition, too.

———

After the movie became a smash, it propelled the soundtrack to even further heights. Dad was no stranger to the top of the R&B chart, but *Super Fly* did something else—something Dad had never done before and would never do again. When the *Billboard* pop chart came out for the week of October 21, 1972, at number one with a bullet, it read: "Curtis Mayfield, *Superfly.*" After fourteen years in professional music, including countless albums and singles for dozens of other artists, he reigned supreme on the pop chart for the first and only time.

No other black artist had hit the top of the pop chart with an album like *Super Fly.* It was the grittiest, hardest album Curtis ever made. He painted his most unflinching picture of ghetto reality as black people experienced it—drugs, pimps, pushers, depression, despair, destruction. More than ever before, he spoke directly to the concerns of his people. He wrote no songs of conciliation, no messages of peace and understanding between races. In return for that, the public—both black and white—gave him the highest status in popular music.

It seemed contrary to everything black performers had experienced throughout history. For half a century or more, conventional wisdom held that white people wouldn't buy "race records," although white people had always discreetly listened to black radio stations. Such reasoning formed the underpinning of segregated radio. The only way black artists could break through those chains was to walk that tightrope between worlds, between voices. With *Super Fly*, Dad not only cut that rope, he replaced it with a new model of artistry.

One can debate forever the reasons why that happened. Certainly, the movement and the music of the 1960s helped make it possible. Perhaps the recent years of hard drugs, brutal assassinations, and bloody war also readied the record-buying public for *Super Fly*'s unflinching honesty. Regardless of why, however, *it happened*—and it would happen for black artists with increasing frequency in coming decades. It's hard to imagine the fearless honesty of hip-hop catching on with white suburbia—and influencing the music, culture, fashion, and language of the entire world in the '80s and '90s—if not for the success of an album like *Super Fly*.

———

At the moment of his greatest success, however, my father also had a moment of great weakness. His history of occasional abuse—the darkest realization of his insecurities—continued with Toni. On vacation in Nassau in October, right around *Super Fly*'s ascendance to the top of the pops, he and Toni got into a late-night argument as Tracy, Sharon, and I slept in another room. When the commotion startled me awake, I walked out to find policemen hulking in the doorway and Toni with a black eye. Dad never did these things in front of us, but we'd see the aftermath.

Toni lived with Dad in the three-flat house, and they had vicious fights there, too. "Everything was done behind closed doors," Tracy recalls. "She's cooking and next thing you know, it's like doors slamming and they'd fight. You heard the commotion; you heard the voice; you heard the screaming. [One time] me, Sharon, and Todd were out in the hallway. We were scared. I remember thinking, I'm the oldest; I've got to protect my brother and sister. I don't know what to do, though."

We already knew our father had two voices—the soft, whispering coo he used in songs, interviews, and normal interactions, and the stern, fatherly tone he used when we did something wrong. As he and Toni went at it, we learned he had a third voice—a trembling, frenzied scream that only came out in fights with women. "That was a whole other voice," Tracy says. "That went into a whole other realm. It was very shaky. It wasn't high-pitched—it was very manly, but shaky. And scary."

When the fighting stopped and things cooled down, Dad would return to his normal self—the affectionate, doting man who bought gifts and wrote love songs. That side of him attracted women; the other side made it hard for them to stay. He was an uncompromising partner in love, just as in business. He expected others to bend to his will, and they usually did. He never directed his violent side at Sharon, Tracy, or me—or any of his children—but physical abuse toward his significant others remained an occasional and inexplicable occurrence of weakness for some time.

Still, Dad and Toni stayed together. He still hadn't divorced Helen, so he invented a new term, calling Toni his "spiritual wife." Apparently it was good enough for her. At least for a while.

In November, Dad and his spiritual wife flew to New York to tape the first episode of a new ABC show called *In Concert*. The show featured concert performances from Curtis, Bo Diddley, Seals & Croft, Jethro Tull, and Alice Cooper, all taped at Hofstra University in Long Island.

Hanging out before the taping at Buddah's offices in New York, a publicist told Curtis that *Super Fly* had held the top position for another week. "We lost our bullet, but it was crowding up the page anyway," she joked. *Super Fly* would hold the top slot for four weeks in total.

My father then left for his taping. As he stepped in the elevator, Buddah copresident Neil Bogart yelled to him, "Curtis, wait! We're gold, Curtis! 'Freddie' was just declared gold!'" Bogart brought a bottle of wine and a glass. "Well, this is the first time we've ever partied in an elevator," my father said. Toni responded, "This is the first time for a lot of things, Curt."

Toni was right. All told, the singles "Freddie's Dead" and "Super-fly" both sold a million copies, and the album went double platinum, grossing $20 million. Just two decades before, young Curtis had listened to his mother cry herself to sleep because she'd given Kenny her last quarter as a birthday present. Now, on the strength of nine songs, he'd generated eighty million quarters. Such fortune boggled the mind of a ghetto child.

At the Hofstra concert, my father looked like the epitome of early-'70s cool—floppy cap hung rakishly over his ear, wire-rimmed granny glasses perched on the tip of his nose, superfly suit with wide lapels cut perfectly to fit his thin frame, patterned shirt open to the chest, lightning-white Fender Strat slung across his body. Surviving footage shows him leading a band that had become tight as hell—Craig's wah-wah guitar intertwines seamlessly, Master Henry hunches over his congas like a mad scientist, and Lucky's wiry frame humps the funk out of his bass. At one point, the camera pans to the audience, where a few black faces dot a sea of white college students, all of them going nuts, dancing whether they want to or not, the rhythm section leaving them no choice. As my father raps about the meaning of "Freddie's Dead," it's clear he's doing more than performing, he's delivering his message, perhaps to the people who needed to hear it most. Indeed, the white college students in the audience had most likely never seen a black man proudly singing the word "nigga," or heard about the real-life Freddies who died every day in the ghetto.

———

Dad's message was as important as it had ever been, as prospects for blacks had become more dismal in Nixon's America. Almost two decades after *Brown*, major challenges to desegregation still existed. A busing pro-gram, started as an attempt to give black students access to white schools, was met with refusal and violence. Even when the US Supreme Court ordered forty-one southern schools to desegregate, only six complied.

Meanwhile, 33 percent of blacks struggled below the poverty line, in comparison to 9 percent of whites, and the gains of the movement continued to erode. Nixon won reelection four months after *Super Fly*'s release, and it seemed the crusade against Jim Crow had officially ended. Nixon spoke of allowing any remaining segregation to go untouched. Statements like that made sure he won only 18 percent of the black vote.

Though conditions remained dire for the majority of blacks, the gains of the movement also flowered in important ways. Black politicians won elections that would have been impossible even a decade before, including mayoral races in Cleveland, Newark, and Gary. A few months before the *Super Fly* soundtrack's release, the first National Black Political Convention met in Gary, bringing together diverse members of the community like Jesse Jackson, Louis Farrakhan, and Shaft himself, Richard Roundtree. Shirley Chisholm, the first black female member of the US House of Representatives, became the first black woman to run for president in 1972, strengthening the burgeoning feminist movement. In addition, black enrollment in college had nearly tripled since the mid-'60s.

Despite those triumphs, the movement of the '50s and '60s had run out of momentum. The dozing conscience of the nation, which King and company startled awake, fell back into deep slumber. Leaders like Chisholm and Jackson tried to keep pushing in the nonviolent mold of King, while the Panthers tried to expand their influence without losing their edge—but as hard as the new crop of leaders worked, they failed to gain widespread traction. Artists stepped into this leadership void. It seemed they were the only ones left who could unite people around the old movement banner. And of all artists, people expected it and accepted it most from Curtis.

Even Marvin Gaye couldn't continue making message music—when he tried to duplicate the success of *What's Going On*, releasing a message song called "You're the Man (Part 1)," it failed to cross over. Gaye worried that he couldn't count on message songs to sustain his career, and with the exception of "Trouble Man," from his 1972 blaxploitation soundtrack of the same name, he went back to making pop music.

Unlike Gaye, Curtis had been a messenger for so long and done it so well, he'd earned special license to keep doing it. As SCLC's Andrew Young said, "You have to think of Curtis Mayfield as a prophetic visionary teacher of our people and of our time . . . Martin Luther King was trying to do it legally and morally, but there's a sense that the music has been more successful than the courts and the church. Even as I say that, I think of Curtis Mayfield as the church."

————————

After *Super Fly*, all of our lives changed forever. Dad became busier than ever before. He was in demand everywhere—in concert, on television, in the Curtom offices, and in the studio to cut with other bands on his roster. As his fame hit its peak, we became more conspicuous as well. Despite the added pressures of fame and his incredible schedule, however, Dad did what he could to include us in his professional life as well as his personal one. Whenever possible, he'd have us backstage at his concerts, where we'd often play chess before or between shows. He'd take us to television appearances and let us hang out in the control room during recording sessions. Watching Dad work, I began to envision myself working with him some day.

With *Super Fly*'s success, Dad also dramatically increased his earnings on tour. He began demanding a hefty sum of $12,500 per show plus percentages. Depending on the size of the crowd, he could walk away from a performance with as much as $25,000, and he usually performed three to four times a week. He also appeared on *Soul Train*—where we often accompanied him—lip-synching a bit awkwardly to "Superfly," "Pusherman," and "Freddie's Dead."

The first time Dad took us to a *Soul Train* taping was when the show was still produced in Chicago. It was great to meet Don Cornelius, and I was fascinated to see how a television show was produced. Dad always had a special relationship with Don. He was one of the first guests to appear on *Soul Train*, which helped boost early ratings and give the show legitimacy. Later, after the show moved to Los Angeles, we would fly out and view the production in its more famous, glitzy incarnation. On one of Dad's later appearances, Don asked Tracy, Sharon, and me if we wanted to go on the floor to be on the show with the other dancers. We were all too intimidated and declined the offer. We'd watched enough on TV to know those *Soul Train* dancers didn't mess around.

During an interview segment after the *Super Fly* performances, an amply Afroed Don offered Dad "personal congratulations on that great score you did," saying, "After hearing Isaac Hayes' *Shaft* score last year, I never thought I'd hear anything as good. And, needless to say, we did hear that in *Super Fly* this year." A young man in the audience named Anthony Cole then asked him, "Since *Super Fly* was a very controversial movie, what type of movie would you like to score next, if you had the opportunity?" "It's really hard to say," my father responded. "I didn't really pick *Super Fly*. It came to me. I prefer happenings." He wouldn't have to wait long for it to happen again.

———————

As 1972 came to a close, construction began on a sixteen-track studio at the new Curtom location, and Dad began writing a new album. Because of *Super Fly*'s massive clout, record stores around the world pre-ordered five hundred thousand copies of his new album, sight unseen and sound unheard. In other words, he had a gold album before he made it. He couldn't fail. That put him in a new and exciting position.

Of course, success is not always what it seems. My father had already learned that lesson. He had everything he'd always wanted—money, fame, family, a movie score, the most popular album in the country, his own label, complete control over his career, all the material comforts and conveniences possible, and as always, a generous share of women. He was only thirty years old. Yet, Eddie's warning that he was going to burn himself out was coming true. "I'm working 24 hours a day," he said. "This business involves mind and imagination. You can't sit back and enjoy 'normal' activity—it always involves work."

He had an unbelievable amount of creativity left within him, a deep well of songs that replenished at the same astonishing rate it always had. That well was in no danger of running dry, but he didn't know how long fans would keep coming back to it. In two years, he'd recorded six albums between himself and the Impressions. The four he made for himself—*Curtis, Curtis/Live, Roots,* and *Super Fly*—surpassed anything he'd done with the Impressions in terms of commercial success. If this wasn't the peak, how much higher could he climb? As he sang in "Superfly," "How long can a good thing last?" These thoughts crept into his mind.

"You never want to reach the peak," he said, "because after all, when you've gone all the way up, the only way to go is down."

11

Back to the World

"With such heavy burdens,
It's hard for one to think sometimes."
—"Sweet Exorcist"

Curtom Studio, North Side Chicago, 1973—After running errands with me on a Saturday afternoon, Dad stopped by his new office. Sitting at his desk, he pulled out his stash and rolled a joint. "Did you know your father smokes marijuana?" he asked nonchalantly, firing up the joint. "Yes," I said, although that wasn't entirely true. I knew he did something, because I'd smell the smoke and notice the goofy look on his face, but I didn't know what to call it until then. He occasionally smoked clove cigarettes, too, but he didn't drink much, and he didn't have many hobbies outside of music, so weed became a release valve for the ever-building pressure.

His office at the new North Side Curtom headquarters was the same size as the hovel that once housed his entire family at the White Eagle, but the room he now occupied served a far different function. He sat at the central hub of a humming business with managers, arrangers, artists, engineers, accountants, lawyers, secretaries, publicists, and distributors. The building also boasted a sixteen-track studio (soon upgraded to twenty-four tracks), "two of the juiciest psychedelic lounge areas around," according to *Jet* magazine, and several other offices.

The more Curtom grew, the more the label's day-to-day operations consumed Dad's time. Unfortunately, he never excelled at day-to-day operations. With the benefit of hindsight, he'd later admit, "That was probably no good for me, or the company, and for the customer that had so much expectation for me. The whole name of the game was to make money. The investors want to hear one thing—'I want to make money.' Probably what people should have done, and I probably should have done myself, was just laid back and kind of watched things for a while."

Laying back was never his thing. He was laid-back, sure, but he didn't *lay back*. His work ethic, always tremendous, now became superhuman as he entered the busiest phase of his career. "The name of the game is longevity," he told *Jet*. "Stars are made to burn out, and I don't intend to see that happen. And that's one reason why I try to do as many things and own as much of myself as possible. . . . Once you've become successful, you've got to work twice as hard to keep being successful. In other words, if I make a million dollars this year, I've got to make two million next year to support ongoing functions that I own." He didn't just want money, though. He wanted respect. "This is what makes me want to go higher on the ladder of success," he said. "I would like all types of people to listen to my music and get something out of my songs."

My father set out to gain that respect in unfamiliar territory. Curtom's new home on the urbane North Side was light years removed from the gritty South Side where he'd lived and worked most of his life. With the change of scenery came a change of personnel. Johnny was gone forever, along with Eddie. Craig joined Aretha Franklin's band, and only Lucky and Master Henry survived from the original group. Marv beefed up the in-house staff, bringing in a new crop of industry professionals to help with the minutiae of running a business. Leroy Hutson left the Impressions to start a solo career. On top of that, a new form of music began crowding the charts—disco. Despite these shakeups, Curtom stood on the cusp of a big year with album releases from the Impressions and Leroy, as well as my father's new album and a live recording/public-television broadcast featuring a retrospective of his entire career.

Continuing a frustrating trend, however, my father couldn't quite get out of his own way. *Super Fly* had earned four Grammy nominations, and Dad received an invitation to perform at the ceremony in early March 1973. Perhaps it was the added pressure of success, or perhaps it was the increased consumption of weed, but whatever the reason, that night his insecurities mushroomed into full-blown paranoia. When the time came for his performance, Dad waited in the wings while his band kicked into "Freddie's Dead." A fog machine spread smoky ambiance across the stage as he walked out. When he started singing, it didn't stop blowing. For the entire performance, billows of fog blocked him from the audience's view. He felt like a fool in front of his peers, not to mention the people tuning in on TV.

Then, *Super Fly* lost in every category, often to songs or albums that didn't approach its commercial or artistic impact. My father sulked back to his hotel room, crestfallen. Toni got in his ear and convinced him the whole thing was a white conspiracy—Whitey wouldn't let a guy who sang "Superfly" win. Seething, the smoke machine's fog still burning in his nostrils, he called Marv and demanded he cancel the college tour William Morris had booked for him.

Marv warned him, "You're going to be so caught up in lawsuits, it's not worth it," but for a man who changed his mind with such ease, my father could also be immovable as a boulder. Marv enlisted the help of Neil Bogart, and they went to my father's room to try to dissuade him, but he wouldn't budge. They cancelled the tour, he got sued and lost a good deal of money, and William Morris refused to work with him again.

He ran into similar trouble a few weeks after the Grammys at the Academy Awards. "Freddie's Dead" was nominated for Best Original Song but later deemed ineligible because the movie only features an instrumental version. Dad tried to play off the insult, saying, "I'm glad I was in a position to let everybody see what the Academy Awards are—a personalized social club with exclusive members. I'm from R&B music, so I'd rather lose an Oscar than to lose in the streets." But his words belied the damage to his ego.

Perhaps my father can be forgiven for his hasty reaction at the Gram-mys. After all, racism didn't end because *Super Fly* hit the top of the pop chart. Dad still struggled in a world with limited opportunities for black people, even famous ones. His records sold to white audiences as well as black ones, but he couldn't bridge the gap at concerts. He tried crossing over at the Aragon, a white rock club in Chicago, but received a cool reception. Promoter Jerry Mickelson took an unfortunate lesson from that show. "You learn the market," he said. "Take Curtis Mayfield. He was hotter than a pistol, and he died in the Aragon. So we learned that you can't do a black act up there." The success of black artists like Jimi Hendrix and Sly Stone with white rock crowds proved the lie in Mickelson's statement. Further proving it, Stone played the Aragon in 1974 and killed.

Even so, the fact remained that after escaping the chitlin' circuit, forces beyond Curtis's control still restricted his career. About crossing over, Marv said simply, "It didn't work. We wanted it, but it didn't work. His audience at concerts remained mostly black even through the '70s, but it didn't bother him. He was a realist and accepted it for what it was."

———————

He turned, as he always did, to music. Dad worked on the follow-up to *Super Fly* first. Like never before, he had the world by the ear. As always, he tried to fill that ear with a meaningful message. On his previous three studio albums, he'd dealt in-depth with many aspects of black life in America, but he hadn't yet touched the Vietnam War. He'd written peace anthems like "Stop the War" and "We Got to Have Peace," but these didn't examine the black experience in Vietnam, and he felt compelled as always to tell the whole story.

His transition from the movement to the war mirrored the world around him. White liberals had long since shifted their energy from civil rights to war protests, but by 1973, Vietnam consumed the black com-munity, too. The *Black Panther* newsletter printed a stark message aimed at black soldiers returning home, and it summed up the issues my father would put to music. "I know you dream about home," it read. "But when you come home, come home and realize that you have a fight here. . . . When you get back home, you're going to see that same oppression. They're going to promise you a job; but you're going to be out of a job."

Amid the din of war, Dad couldn't get one phrase out of his head, the one he'd heard the year before while touring army bases—"back to the world." It gave him an angle to tell his story, and he used it as the title for both the album and its leadoff track.

With *Back to the World*, he showed that he still had his finger on the pulse of the ghetto, even though he'd become a rich and famous man, now living in a swanky new condo near the top floor of 4170 North Marine Drive. From his perch atop the city, he wrote about a soldier just returned from war and the malice he faced on his return, much in the mold of Marvin Gaye's *What's Going On*, and much like the real-life experience of Uncle Kenny.

With Johnny gone, Dad brought in Rich Tufo to provide harmonic backdrops. Tufo served as a sort of utility man at Curtom, sometimes producing or arranging a session, sometimes handling paperwork or publicity. His work ethic rivaled my father's. "My day runs anywhere from fourteen to fifteen hours a day," he said. "It's divided up depending on whether I'm working on any particular project at the time. If I'm not, I may be dealing with publishing, copyright clearances, A&R."

My father worked with Tufo in much the same way he worked with Johnny. "Usually, when Curtis is ready to begin a project, he's already put down in demo form his ideas, songs, whatever," Tufo said. "Then, I take it from there—put down the rhythm charts. He may come in with a particular selection and we'll juggle around. Then we go in, do the rhythm tracks, the vocals, then add the sweetening. We usually lock ourselves in for a week. That's before we actually get into the studio—and we'll get together either here or at his home." Tufo's style was a departure from Johnny's, but his work helped usher in a new period of success for Dad's music, both as a solo artist and a writer/producer on multiple film soundtracks.

Back to the World was my father's second consecutive album to hit number one R&B, but it was a slight fall in fortunes from *Super Fly*.

The first single, "Future Shock," hit number eleven R&B but peaked at number thirty-nine pop. Dad's lyrics are as on point as ever, with lines like "Our worldly figures playing on niggers / Oh see them dancin', see how they dancin' to the 'Superfly.'" That line could have been a simple shout-out to his previous work or a searing comment to his listeners about missing the message behind the lyrics of his most famous album as they ate up the dance beats. Still, many critics panned the single for borrowing too heavily on sounds he'd already explored.

The album also contains one of my personal favorites, "Right On for the Darkness." The song wasn't released as a single, but it became one of my father's most influential cuts, reverberating through the hip-hop age. Many artists in the '90s sampled the song's opening guitar lines, most notably Chicago native R. Kelly on his 1999 smash hit "Did You Ever Think."

Back to the World was a solid effort, but on the heels of the monumental critical and commercial success of *Super Fly*, it was viewed as a slight disappointment. Critical failure can spell disaster for any artist, and *Back to the World* hinted at shifts in my father's music that would cause many critics to desert him as the '70s wore on. Perhaps the biggest shift was his increased use of falsetto. It was, as a *Rolling Stone* reviewer noted, "an intensely masculine falsetto," and he'd used it since the earliest days of the Impressions. But now he began using it almost exclusively, seldom dipping down into his natural register. His voice became higher and thinner than ever, which critics had complained about since *Curtis/Live*.

Also, the new studio changed the sound of his records. The drums are thinner. The bottom end—bass guitar and bass drum—punches rather than rumbles. The snare skews toward high frequencies, sounding more like a piccolo snare than the deep wooden *thwap* common in R&B music. Master Henry's polyrhythmic force fills less sonic space.

As Curtis's sound changed, disco moved the sound of the time in a different direction. Disco revolved around booming drums, slapping bass, slick production, catchy melodies, and glitzy string lines. Dad didn't pay much attention to that, though. He still shied away from listening to other people's music, and the few times he did, he seemed more interested in studying it than taking pleasure from it. While making *Back to the World*, for instance, Tracy recalls him putting on Marvin Gaye's "Let's Get It On" to get a sense of the tempo and dissect what had made the song such a huge hit. Disco didn't mean anything to him yet, but soon the forces of commercialism would bend him to its insistent beat.

For the time being, his fans stuck with him. They made *Back to the World* a commercial smash, although advance orders for the album had already guaranteed that. The success kept him in the public eye, including more appearances on *Soul Train*, and it also created a surge of interest in *Curtis*, which went gold that same month based on renewed sales.

———

After *Back to the World*, the Impressions began work on their next album, this time without Leroy Hutson at the helm. Instead of finding a new singer they cut the album, *Preacher Man*, as a duo. No Impressions album before or after features only two singers. The album was unique for another reason—for the first time ever, Curtis didn't write any of the songs. Instead, Tufo produced, arranged, and wrote most of *Preacher Man*. He provided strong material, but the album sunk like a stone, struggling to hit number thirty-one R&B and missing the pop chart. Modern critics have since burnished *Preacher Man*'s reputation, but that didn't help at the time.

A similar thing happened with Leroy's first solo album, *Love Oh Love*, which Curtom released next. It didn't place well on the charts, but like *Preacher Man*, Hutson's album is now considered a classic, if overlooked, piece of Chicago soul. Both albums proved how elusive and impossible it was to predict a hit.

For the final Curtom project of the year, my father gathered Fred, Sam, Jerry, Leroy, and Gene Chandler together for an era-spanning, lineup-shifting night of music. Channel 11 in Chicago broadcast the performance, and Dad recorded it as a celebration, a retrospective, and a reunion.

It was a good moment to look back. Over the previous three years, he had left the Impressions and hoisted himself and Curtom to the pinnacle of the music world. He'd changed the face of R&B and soul music, sold more records than ever, made more money than he could count, and crafted a legacy apart from his work with the Impressions. At the same time, he was always a man of few friends. As Curtom grew and my father grew closer to Marv, that became truer than ever. He'd lost (or severed) his close relationships with Eddie and Johnny. His relationships with Fred and Sam changed again now that he no longer wrote for them, and new faces at Curtom surrounded him. Perhaps a night with old friends would recharge his creative battery.

    With the amount of work he was about to undertake, he'd need it.

———————

Curtis in Chicago didn't approach the impact of his first live album, *Curtis/Live*, but it was an impressive showcase highlighting the best parts of Dad's career. The performances crackle with energy, beginning with a spirited rendition of "Superfly." Then, my father says, "Ladies and gentlemen, if we may, we would just like to take you back a ways. Before us we have a few gentlemen, and I count myself as part of us, a group known as the Impressions—still the Impressions." He introduces Jerry, Fred, and Sam, and says, "I'm going to let Sam speak on the song we want to present to you while I play on it." My father begins plucking the inimitable chords as Sam says, "This is a tune that takes us back to 1958—a tune entitled 'For Your Precious Love.'" Then, the Impressions drop into the gorgeous backing harmonies as if they'd never stopped singing them. With Jerry at the helm for the first time in almost fifteen years, they provide a jaw-dropping rendition of the song that started it all. For the people who had only just come to know Curtis through *Super Fly*, it provided a powerful lesson on the length and breadth of his career.

    Curtis in Chicago also features a sweet version of "If I Were Only a Child Again," featuring my brother, sister, and me. On the day of the taping, we were playing outside in the street, running around, getting dirty. Without consulting my mother, Dad called and in his typical spontaneous fashion said, "There's a car coming to get you guys." He didn't tell us why. A few minutes later a limousine pulled up and took us to Channel 11, where we found him in the midst of an intricate production. We watched most of the show from the crowd, but when he got to "If I Were Only a Child Again," he called us onstage.

When my mother saw the broadcast, she became furious—her children's first appearance on television showed us looking dirty, wearing raggedy play clothes. That was life with my father, though. The small details never occurred to him. He got the idea to have us appear on the show, and he did it. Making sure we put on clean clothes and looked presentable didn't cross his mind.

Before playing the song, Dad asked us what we wanted to be when we grew up. I said baseball player and Sharon said nurse. Then, he turned to Tracy. "Hey Tracy, what do you want to be when you grow up?" he asked in his soft voice. Tracy responded, "A musician." Tracy would make his dream come true.

As a child, Tracy picked up the guitar and soon moved to bass, but he never felt supported in his musical endeavors. There again came Dad's split personality as a Gemini—on one hand, Tracy says, "He mentored me, I looked up to him. He's the one that cared whether I ate. He put the clothes on my back. He was in my life as far as guiding me." On the other, when it came to music, he says, "I thought I was being more or less discouraged from playing. I would get derogatory comments every now and then. . . . I remember him getting mad at me because I couldn't tune my guitar when I was a little boy. I remember picking the guitar, and he's like, 'That's not in tune!' I'm thinking to myself, it sounds good to me. He picked the guitar up, tuned it, and gave it back to me, 'That's nice and tuned.'"

Perhaps Dad's complexities wouldn't allow him to recognize his son's burgeoning talent. The rejection made Tracy work harder to impress him, but it also showed the intricate inner workings that made it hard for Dad to deal with competition. It was almost a subconscious reflex—the same one that had left him the sole creative force at Curtom—and it continued throughout his life. In a few years, Tracy started a group called Sapphire that won two citywide talent shows in Chicago. Dad couldn't quite support that endeavor either. "He invited us to the studio," Tracy recalls.

> We recorded a session, and after the session, you know, you want to hear something good. All I remember him saying is, "OK, cat, this is what y'all should sound like." And he put on [his song] "Do Do Wap Is Strong in Here." And that was it. We just listened to it and said, "Well, I guess you don't like us." He just kind of laughed, and talked a little bit, and then left. It was subtle, I guess. He just didn't acknowledge if he heard me play. I remember him coming in the studio, and he was like, "Oh, cat, who's playing keyboard?" I said, "That's me, Dad." And he didn't say nothing. He just looked at me.

For a man not threatened by James Brown, Marvin Gaye, or Smokey Robinson, it is hard to understand why Dad felt threatened by his own son. Perhaps it was because he never had a father to look up to, and he struggled to understand Tracy looking up to him. Or maybe it was because he remained haunted by his past. In a short time, he'd gone from kids calling him Smut to people revering him all around the world. He pushed himself to become one of the first black men to own his own label, and he made himself a millionaire in a business designed to take advantage of him. Such dizzying changes of fortune didn't come with a guidebook. His subconscious insecurities could still complicate his life, even when his conscious mind didn't want them to. He had evolved beyond most of those hang-ups, and as he got older they bothered him less, but some scars remained on his psyche.

———

Curtis in Chicago features one other Impressions song of great significance beyond their brilliant performance that day. After "For Your Precious Love," Curtis, Fred, and Sam sing "I'm So Proud," the song that once inspired a young Bob Marley and the Wailers. The Wailers never tried to hide my father's influence on their music, and they'd already covered several of his songs, including "Long Long Winter," "I Made a Mistake,"

"Keep On Moving," and "Another Dance." When not covering Impressions songs, the Wailers often used them as inspiration for their originals, like "Diamond Baby," based on "Talking About My Baby." The influence went beyond Marley, too—as Wailers biographer John Masouri noted, Curtis's songs were the most covered, or "versioned," in Jamaican music.

Even though Marley and company had released four albums since the mid-'60s, they remained a regional act. In 1973, that changed. As Curtis cut *Back to the World*, the Wailers released their first album on Island Records, *Catch a Fire*, which rocketed them onto the world stage. Songs like "Slave Driver," "Concrete Jungle," and "400 Years" painted searing pictures of racism and its consequences that gave even Curtis a run for his money. At the same time, cuts like "Stir It Up" and "Kinky Reggae" showed how influential the Impressions' harmonic style remained on the burgeoning reggae stars.

When the Wailers performed on *The Old Grey Whistle Test*, the world began taking notice. Marley had just begun growing his dreadlocks, bringing Rastafarianism—an Ethopian-Hebrew spiritual belief system that became a political Black Power movement in Jamaica—to the mainstream. For the rest of the '70s, Marley would match Curtis album for album, carrying the torch of unflinching social commentary and setting it to new rhythmic structures like ska, rocksteady, and roots reggae.

Marley would pay his most enduring homage to Curtis and the Impressions with "One Love/People Get Ready," which became a defining anthem for the island of Jamaica. On the song, which the Wailers had first recorded in 1965 before Marley reworked it for his 1977 *Exodus* album, Marley quotes a large portion of "People Get Ready," making his strongest connection to Curtis and the group that had inspired the Wailers to form. For copyright reasons, Dad was even listed as cowriter of the song.

———

As 1973 ended, my father rode a wave of momentum that started with *Curtis*, hit an unprecedented peak with *Super Fly*, and rolled on with the success of *Back to the World*. He also entered his thirties, and a casual observer might have expected him to take a break and let others take over the business while he watched his royalty money roll in. Instead, he started a new label with Marv called Gemigo, cut two solo albums, and agreed to score two movies. He was never further from taking it easy. He stood in the middle of the most productive, creative, and successful run of his entire career. As Marv put it with a heaping of understatement, "Curt's pretty busy right now."

No matter how busy he was, he maintained a strong presence in his children's lives. When he was in Chicago, we'd never go more than a few days without seeing him. We often stayed at his house on the weekends, and when he went on tour, he made sure to send postcards and call whenever he could. We understood he didn't have a normal job, or keep normal hours, or live a normal life—in fact, many people in our lives never let us forget it. He'd take us to the studio often, where we watched him in the hustle and bustle, commanding his world. Because of his efforts, we knew him in a way he never knew his own father.

In 1974, Dad's world entered a state of flux. Curtom's distribution deal with Buddah was set to expire, and though Dad didn't know what would happen after that deadline, he poured himself into new work. Early in the year, the cast and crew of the movie *Three the Hard Way* shot scenes at Curtom as the Impressions recorded the soundtrack. Gordon Parks Jr. directed the movie, his second since *Super Fly*. The cast featured three of the biggest black action stars of the era—Jim Brown (*The Dirty Dozen, Slaughter*), Fred Williamson (*Black Caesar, Bucktown*), and Jim Kelly (*Enter the Dragon, Black Samurai*), as well as *Super Fly*'s Sheila Frazier. The Impressions also had their first acting gig in the movie.

Writing duties for the soundtrack fell on Lowrell Simon, who had scored minor hits under Carl Davis with his group the Lost Generation. Not long after, Simon would also write for another Curtom group called Mystique, featuring two former members of the Lost Generation.

After wrapping *Three the Hard Way*, Dad began work on another soundtrack, this one for the film *Claudine*. Since the film featured a female protagonist, he wanted a female vocalist. As luck would have it, Gladys Knight and the Pips had just left Motown and signed with Buddah in 1973, releasing "Midnight Train to Georgia," which hit number one pop and R&B and won a Grammy Award. They were hotter than ever, and they agreed to sing for *Claudine*.

As he had with *Super Fly*, my father related to the story of *Claudine* right away. The movie follows a single mother on welfare and the ravages it wages on her children, her romantic relationships, and her life. "I had experienced all of that growing up," he said. "Welfare, living in a home without a father; I knew welfare pretty good, because my mother was on it." Just like with *Super Fly*, he could get inside the characters and write about their lives with depth and empathy. In a way, *Claudine* also allowed him to pay tribute to his mother's struggles. On cuts like "Mr. Welfare Man," he seems to write in Marion's voice:

> *They just keep on saying I'm a lazy woman,*
> *Don't love my children and I'm mentally unfit*
> *I must divorce him, cut all my ties with him*
> *'Cause his ways they make me sick*
> *It's a hard sacrifice not having me a loving man*
> *Society gave us no choice, tried to silence my voice*
> *Pushing me on the welfare.*

Gladys Knight gives a superior vocal performance, capturing the anguish of so many women stuck in a similar situation. I watched many of Gladys's vocal sessions from the control booth and developed a huge crush on her. I'm sure I wasn't the only eight-year-old boy in love with her, but I got to watch her perform in a way few others have. I'll never forget the way she made time to talk to me during breaks in recording.

The next cut, "To Be Invisible," features some of my father's most heartbreaking poetry. Inspired by a scene in the film, he wrote about how poverty can steal one's individuality and control, with lines like "To be invisible will be my claim to fame / A girl with no name / That way I won't have to feel the pain." Again, Gladys's performance touches the soul, and Dad liked the arrangement so much he hardly changed a note when he recorded his own version for his next album.

Claudine also features the supreme funk of "On and On," which hit number two R&B and number five pop as a single, as well as another hit single in "Make Yours a Happy Home," and Gladys provides a beautiful rendition of "The Makings of You," originally from the *Curtis* album. The soundtrack shot to number one on the R&B chart, and the movie did just as well, grossing $6 million and earning a bevy of award nominations, including an Oscar nod for Diahann Carroll, Golden Globe nominations for Carroll and James Earl Jones, and a Golden Globe nomination for "On and On."

The only downside for my father was that the album came out on Buddah, not Curtom. Still, he climbed back on top doing something he loved. As he said years later, one of his favorite things was "hearing someone else record one of your songs, something that you had prepared, produced, and worked out for another artist—to find that it was a hit, to know that you could not only do for yourself, but you could do for others."

Dad also had plans to do for himself, and he began cutting his next album, *Sweet Exorcist*. Perhaps because of the demands on his time, he relied mostly on songs he'd given to others, including "Ain't Got Time" (the Impressions), "To Be Invisible" (Gladys Knight and the Pips), "Suffer" (Holly Maxwell), and "Make Me Believe in You" (Patti Jo). Still, he said, "The album allowed me to say some things I'd wanted to say for quite a while, things that were in my mind which I wanted to get out."

The retreads often followed the original versions closely, but there were important differences, especially on "Ain't Got Time." The song is funkier than the Impressions' version, and my father's phrasing is looser. He also augmented his voice with multitracked backing harmonies, a trick he'd use with great effect on his future work. He changed the song's structure, wrote a new chorus, and added new lyrics, including the lines "Make a mess of me / Which wasn't supposed to be / We were supposed to change / It couldn't be arranged."

He'd written the first version of the song—one of his last singles with the Impressions, recorded during the *Check Out Your Mind* sessions and released in early 1971—as his relationship with my mother crumbled. He cut the version on *Sweet Exorcist* with the new lyrics just as his relationship with Toni, his "spiritual wife," ended.

Dad never explained his breakup with Toni, but just before she disappeared he had a peculiar mishap, severing the tendon on his left middle finger. The injury was so serious he faced the prospect of never playing guitar again. He tried to play it off, saying he was holding a glass pot and it broke in his hand. Even as a child, I didn't buy that explanation.

Doctors reattached the tendon, but he couldn't straighten his finger, so he had to attend physical therapy. I sat with him in his rehab sessions, mulling over the accident in my mind. The best I could guess was that Toni stabbed him. I had no evidence, just a feeling. Their relationship was always volatile, and a stabbing certainly wasn't outside the realm of possibility.

Whatever happened with Toni, it didn't take my father long to find someone new. He met Altheida Sims through Craig and quickly fell in love again. They'd stay together until the end of his life. The new romance spurred one of his greatest love songs, the title track, "Sweet Exorcist," on which his falsetto sounds lighter, thinner, and more sexual than ever. As he coos and croons, guitars and organ weave around each other like lovers entwined. "Sweet Exorcist" is a mature love song, too, full of the contradictions of life. He sings about depression and hard times but also about the persevering power of love. He even mixes in message music, singing, "The love she gives, it makes me feel so black and proud." And he shouts out Annie Bell, singing, "I know I believe in the spirit, Traveling Soul was alone, a part of me."

Next is his version of "To Be Invisible," at which point his fans might have noticed that for the first time since he left the Impressions, he hadn't presented a single message song on his new album. He made a conscious decision to ease back on jeremiads after the success of *Super Fly*, proving himself a canny evaluator of his audience. "We've shouted the message from the roof-tops and if people haven't cottoned on to it by now then they never will," he said. "It's like a paper that carries nothing but headlines: in the end they lose all effect. To carry on writing in that vein would be just like beating people's heads against a brick wall and in the end they resent it." He also spoke about the direction he intended to go, saying, "It's now time to carry the message in a more personalized vein, that way people relate easier. General statements are all very well but fit the statement into a personal context which the listener can place himself into and you then have something with much more impact. That's the way I'm writing songs now."

With that in mind, the only message-like song on *Sweet Exorcist*—"Power to the People," an infectious anthem in the mold of "Keep On Pushing"—makes more sense. Unlike his previous solo work, it doesn't bite or sear. It encourages, lifts, prods. Critics lambasted the song's title and what they saw as its trite message, and by 1974, the phrase was indeed tired—the Panthers had used it as a motto, saying, "Power to the people; off the pigs," and John Lennon had a popular single of the same name in 1971. Still, the song is heartfelt and lyrically complex. Perhaps part of the song's joy comes from the fact that Nixon stood on the verge of resigning the presidency. He'd recently been caught up in the Watergate scandal, and the public hearings played out on national television. Dad had good reason to sing, "God bless great America!" Nixon was going down.

———

Despite a number-three R&B hit with the single "Kung Fu," however, *Sweet Exorcist* faced even more disapproval than *Back to the World*. A review in *Rolling Stone* was emblematic:

> Like many an overextended or depleted artist, Mayfield has dug into his past for material for this album, which sounds hastily conceived and then competently executed to meet some contractual deadline. Four of the seven tunes were written prior to 1971. . . . The very titles of the two new numbers, "Kung Fu" and "Sweet Exorcist," signal the lack of invention. . . . The music is competently routine. Almost all of it is in the *Superfly* boogie-down mold, but without the extras that made the best *Superfly* cuts stand out. . . . All

that's left is Mayfield's basic competence in using the studio. At this point, the *Superfly*-derived material the Motown writers have been coming up with for Eddie Kendricks is far superior to what May-field can come up with.

Robert Christgau, music editor of the *Village Voice* famous for his "Consumer Guide" record reviews, gave *Sweet Exorcist* a grade of C, call-ing "To Be Invisible" the only interesting song on the record. Of course, out of all reviewers of my father's post–*Super Fly* work, Christgau was usually most off point.

Dad rarely wasted his time paying attention to critics, but perhaps these reviews contained valid points. It was an undeniable fact that only two songs on *Sweet Exorcist* were new. My father had stretched himself way past thin and didn't have the time to create to his highest stan-dards. "I can't come in [to Curtom] and write, which I didn't know at the beginning," he said. "I thought I'd be able to do that, but when things start happening, there's decisions to be made, you have your other artists to deal with. So usually I find myself as a client in my own place—I have to call in and book my time like everyone else."

Sweet Exorcist also contained many halfhearted nods to current trends without fully engaging any of them. Most obviously, there was the title itself. Now a legendary horror film, *The Exorcist* came out at the end of 1973 and remained a cinematic phenomenon well into the next year when Dad released his album. While my father claimed the film had nothing to do with his album title, the comparison wasn't hard to make. At the same time, martial arts and Eastern mysticism became hot, due in large part to Bruce Lee's recent death and David Carradine's hit TV show, *Kung Fu*. It is worth noting that the top-selling single of 1974 was a disco song called "Kung Fu Fighting."

While Eastern mysticism had enthralled many black Americans for decades—Sun Ra, for example, had pushed it in Chicago since Curtis was a child—it now hit another renaissance in black culture. Still, *Sweet Exorcist's* far-out cover—"a skeletal Hokusai sea with reefs of doomed and skeletal men, which met with little critical favor," as one writer described it—drew questions from fans and critics alike as to what exactly my father was getting at. In an era when artists like Parliament, Earth, Wind & Fire, and Sly Stone took mysticism in R&B to new heights, *Sweet Exorcist* lacked the conviction to stand out in the crowd.

Despite these problems, the album sold. It went gold, hitting number two on the R&B chart. Continuing the downward trend since *Super Fly*, though, it only reached thirty-nine on the pop chart. The album also marked another shift in Curtis's music. From that point on, he returned to his Impressions-era ratio of one or two message songs per album, surrounded by love songs.

In a way, he had no choice. The Watergate scandal was everywhere, inescapable, thrust into the face of a generation still reeling from the Pentagon Papers' proof that the government had sent sixty thousand boys to die in Vietnam based on lies and deception. The public needed an escape from politics. Disco gave it to them.

My father seemed to need an escape, too. As his relationship with Altheida deepened, he became more of a recluse than ever. "His behavior patterns changed, and not for the good," Sharon says. "He was more withdrawn. They would just be in the room for hours and hours on end, and we would be left to our own devices." In the apartment on Marine Drive, Dad fell further into abnormal behavior. Some people whispered rumors attributing it to cocaine use. Tracy recalls seeing strange people hanging around, people we didn't know. "They would be feeding him information," Tracy says. "It felt strange, whatever it was."

We could only guess what was going on at the time. He never did anything in front of us. Instead, he stayed locked in his room while we entertained ourselves. He wasn't always getting high in his room—like his mother and Annie Bell before him, he did many normal, everyday things from that sanctuary, and because he kept such late hours, many times he'd just be in there sleeping. Still, as we got older we noticed the pattern getting worse, and we assumed why.

One day, as Sharon recalls,

they were in the room for so long, and we had nothing to do. We hadn't had anything to eat, there was nothing to do in that condo, and so they had all these boxes of tissues. We went on the balcony and started tossing tissues out into the open air and watching them float. Maybe an hour later, my dad comes out of the room, we all go out to get something to eat, and there are tissues everywhere down below. He made a comment about it like, "What in the world? I wonder what happened." I felt like that was definitely the beginning of him withdrawing and being irresponsible when it came to caring for his children when they were in his presence. That made me very angry. It made me not want to go and visit.

As he withdrew, the day-to-day issues of life—never his strong point—became even harder to handle. Stacks of unopened mail sat neglected on his table for months. Bank statements, bills, and letters piled up in forgotten corners of the apartment. Sometimes we couldn't get in touch with him because he'd forgotten to pay the phone bill and the phone company cut off his service.

Like always, he had the grand vision but needed others to execute it. For a man so concerned with control, this left him at the mercy of people who did know how to execute—people who couldn't write a song but could keep two sets of books, or lift a few thousand dollars here and there without him noticing. I noticed these things, though, and I became more interested in the business. I saw a way to protect my father by learning to do the things he couldn't. Later in life, I'd get my chance to try.

While life with my father became difficult during this period, the Gemini in him made sure that we also saw another, better side. As often as he withdrew, and as much as he broke promises—little things, like saying he'd show up somewhere and then forgetting to do it—he also proved his love for us constantly. Always a practical joker, he went out of his way to fill our lives with excitement. "I think he got a kick out of scaring us, like Halloween-type stuff," Tracy says. "He would set up these elaborate things because he was a very funny person. He liked magic. He would do magic tricks for us."

He showed us the world, taking us on vacations to California, Hawaii, the Bahamas, and other places, often on a moment's notice. He gave us advice, telling us over and over again the importance of owning ourselves. "He was always like the old wise man," Tracy says. "He would get astute—philosophical, really deep answers." He lectured on the dangers of borrowing money, especially from shady characters. "That's when they own you," he always said. He spent time with us, bringing us to Six Flags, playing chess, taking us shopping. He'd often pick us up after school, drive to a store, and say, "Pick out what you want."

He even doted on us. "He was always concerned with, 'You want something to eat, cat?'" Tracy recalls. "He always wanted to feed you. 'You want me to fix you some fish, cat?'" Sharon also remembered his efforts to maintain a presence in our lives, saying, "It felt like we were always in connection with him. I didn't feel like he was an absentee father. I felt like my mom did a good job and kind of insisting that he did interact with us, and I think that he made a pretty good effort to have us around him when he was in the studio."

He also protected us with a ferocity that let us know we could trust him when in need. At his house in Atlanta, which we visited often, we made friends with some white kids who lived nearby. One day as we swam in the pool, they came over and hurled rocks and racial slurs at us. When Dad found out, he shot out of the house in a fury with no shoes or socks on, chased the kids through the woods, caught one of them, and dragged him back to the house. As the boy wriggled and cried, his parents came to get him. My father laid into them and made them apologize. "He did what any father would've done to protect his children," Sharon says. "And he acted immediately. He didn't hesitate. He didn't even wait to put shoes on or anything; he wanted to know who was inflicting harm on his children. So I remember feeling like my dad is going to protect us."

Dad didn't face disrespect like that often. Most people stood in awe of him. Watching the way people reacted to him, we learned about the power of stardom. Each of us dealt with it in our own way, but we all learned what he already knew—fame and money cloud everything. They make everyone's motives suspicious. They make it hard to recognize one's real friends or know whom to trust. In my eyes, being Curtis Mayfield's son was the proverbial double-edged sword. It set me apart, but not always in a good way. I felt everyone wanted something. People always asked, "How's your dad doing?" No one ever asked about my mother.

That's not to say having a famous dad didn't come with many advantages. But sometimes such a thing precedes you. I often got upset when people introduced me as Curtis Mayfield's son, as if that's all I was. Sharon felt the same way. She says, "I didn't want to be identified as Curtis Mayfield's daughter. I just wanted to be like everyone. I've never in my whole life told anyone that Curtis Mayfield was my father. Anyone who knew, knew either before they met me, or they heard it from someone. And I remember times growing up that I denied it. I didn't want the attention. I didn't want the questions." The same held true for Tracy. "You don't want to tell people who your father is because there's a lot of jealousy out there," he says. "When some people found out or some kids found out, it wasn't a happy thing; it was more of a jealousy kind of thing."

While we understood his importance, the life we lived was all we knew. Others might have counted him as a hero; to us he was just Dad. "I have an early memory of being aware of other people's reactions to him in public," Sharon recalls. "I would think, 'Why are they so excited about him? He's just my dad.' I knew that he was a singer. I just thought, 'Well, he's not Michael Jackson.' At the time when I was growing up, the Jackson 5, they were just *it*."

We also learned how to deal with these things graciously. He made sure we appreciated what we had. We never had to worry about money, but he couldn't forget going to bed hungry while his mother wept, so he expected us to remain humble in the face of good fortune. He still lived modestly for a man of his means. His main extravagances were cars— with his *Super Fly* money he bought a 1974 convertible Rolls Royce Corniche, baby blue with cream interior. In summertime, he'd roll out with the top down, come around the house, drive it over to the office. Still, he never went for huge houses or flashy possessions, and even when it came to cars, he preferred bouncing around in his brown soft-top Jeep Wrangler.

While we learned to remain humble, he learned that we didn't always feel comfortable with shows of wealth. At the time, Sharon and I attended a Catholic school in a rough neighborhood. One day after school, my sister walked outside and, as she recalls, "Here comes Curtis Mayfield driving up in a Rolls Royce. The excitement that that would cause, and then me getting into that car, and everyone watching—that made me a little bit uncomfortable, and I remember asking, 'Dad, the next time you pick us up, can you park a little ways down?' He was tickled by it. The next time he parked half a block down from the school."

———————

After *Sweet Exorcist*, the Impressions released the *Three the Hard Way* soundtrack, which only hit twenty-six on the R&B chart and missed the pop chart. At the same time, they worked on another album called *Finally Got Myself Together*. Yet again, my father passed off writing duties, this time to a team of writers including Ed Townsend, the man the Impressions replaced in concert more than a decade before, the first time they played for Georgie Woods in Philadelphia. Townsend wrote the title track, which went to number one R&B—the only Impressions number-one hit my father didn't write. They would never reach the top of the charts again. Though the album did well, Fred and Sam could see they were no longer a top priority at Curtom. They began looking for a way out.

Finishing off a busy year, Curtom released four more albums in 1974—Leroy Hutson's *The Man!*, the Natural Four's self-titled album, Bobby Whiteside's *Bittersweet Stories*, and Curtis's third album of the year, *Got to Find a Way*. The last begins with a reworking of the song "Love Me," which he'd given to the Impressions on *Times Have Changed*. This time, it's called "Love Me (Right in the Pocket)," and is an undeniable piece of rhythmic, sexual soul. Again, my father sings near the top of his range, almost whispering the lyrics, and providing his own backing vocals—soulful "doo doos" and "mmhmms." The song also contains his clearest nod to Hendrix, as a wailing wah-wah guitar noodles over the entire thing, giving the listener a tantalizing taste of what a possible Mayfield/Hendrix collaboration might have sounded like.

The next song, "So You Don't Love Me," is another heartbreaking ballad of lost love. Again, he provides his own gorgeous backing vocals, and in the chorus he hits what might be the highest note of his career when he sings the line "I guess I got to find me a better place." Just like on "Sweet Exorcist," my father showed great maturity, singing again of the pain and struggle inherent in life. He'd written breakup songs before, but never had he approached the subject with such nuance and maturity.

Side A ends with another slow soul shuffle called "A Prayer," in which he dipped back into the gospel of his youth. Like in the previous song, his lyrics contain a mixture of world-weariness and hope, the kind only a true artist can convey. In a way, these were message songs—not about the movement, but about life in general, full of the accumulated wisdom of a man who had been on the top and the bottom and everywhere in between, who had seen great success and painful failure, who knew about love and hate, wealth and poverty, equality and discrimination, fame and obscurity.

The only real message song on the album, "Cannot Find a Way," is a dark answer to the album's title. The combination forms a poignant comment on what had happened to the movement—it began with a mass of people demanding a way forward and ended with the disillusionment of realizing that, in fact, they could not find a way. The lyrics serve as a sort of coda to the movement:

> People across the country, they all protest the same old news
> The white and black, rich and poor
> Find we're all standing in the same old shoes.
> We just cannot find a way
> Preacher man, trying to do the best he can
> But the text he preaches seems obsolete

> *And we suffer still over the land*
> *We just cannot find a way.*

In total, other than the sexy, upbeat opening track, *Got to Find a Way* plays like a man battling serious depression over losing love in his life and hope in the world. The album's strength is even more impressive considering that he'd already written two other albums that year. It remains one of my favorites, but at the time it removed my father further than ever from the disco craze. It also marked the worst chart showing yet for his solo career.

Critics once again lamented his music as being unfocused and drawing too heavily on *Super Fly*–type jams without the inspiration that made his previous work so strong. The slide in ratings still didn't concern him, though. He said, "I suppose I was somewhat arrogant about many songs. But, if I liked it and I felt it deep in my heart, it didn't matter if it sold or not. I was with it."

Modern critics have taken a kinder view, citing the album as a classic of '70s soul. AllMusic.com led the charge, saying that "Curtis Mayfield hit a stride during the '70s that was unparalleled among R&B/soul performers from an album standpoint" and that he "continued his run of excellent albums in the '70s with *Got to Find a Way*. This album had more love songs than some of his earlier material, although he didn't tone down his searing attacks on American injustice and hypocrisy. His vocals continued to be alternately poignant, urgent, and accusatory, while his lyrics, production, and arrangements were once again magnificent."

Dad paid the critics no mind, anyway. He had too much else to focus on, as always. Curtom prepared to switch its distribution to Warner Brothers Records in 1975, and while he wrote his next album, *There's No Place Like America Today*, two new movie offers came his way.

He wrote *There's No Place Like America Today* in Atlanta during two weeks of depression. "I just had to work this depth out of my system," he said. "Often it's hard to accept how bad things are, you want to think about how things should be, but sometimes it's good to take inventory, to face what's happening. If you know what the foundation is, then even when you're flying high, you know where you're going to land. It was a long way from *Superfly* . . . I don't think of it as depressing, more of a drama album."

In many ways, it was his last great message piece, ending a decade of making the most consistent and powerful message music of any artist of his era. As he described it, "*America Today* takes a hard look at some of the things that sour our life experience. . . . There is much to celebrate in America today that's good, even great. But for too many people, too often, there is still something sour waiting around the corner."

He spoke candidly about the album cover—a take on Margaret Bourke-White's classic black-and-white photograph, "There's No Way Like the American Way," but this time featuring a full-color image of a happy white family driving a comfortable sedan superimposed over a black-and-white photo of people waiting on a soup line. He'd begun thinking in terms of class, not just race, as he pondered his generation's place in American history, saying:

> It's not meant as a racial connotation but merely a difference in class situation. While the situation isn't as bad today as it was then, there is a general air of feeling that we may be headed in that direction . . . Of course, I'm aware that I couldn't be where I am today if I had lived forty years earlier and I'm pleased that things have improved so much during that time—but my arrival isn't of much help to the people who are suffering today because to them it's as real as it was for the people of the Thirties . . . In the Thirties, the doors simply were not open, it was as easy as that. I would have been too early and it wouldn't have mattered one little bit whether I had had the ability or not then.

America Today simmers with understatement. Unlike his previous solo albums, which were full to the brim with orchestration and percussion, he left the new songs full of space. They creep and crawl from the speakers as his falsetto draws the listener in close, producing an effect as devastating as anything he'd done.

The song "When Seasons Change" is one of the slowest Dad ever wrote. It unfolds with no urgency, secure in its power and message. He felt so strongly about it that in later years, he'd often use it to close concerts. His lyrics deal with themes he'd been exploring a lot on his last few albums, themes he learned as a child from his mother—despair, depression, and spiritual strength in the face of life's impossible vagaries. "Time make you suffer," he sings. "Praying to Jesus: 'Make me a little stronger' / So I might live the life a little bit longer . . . Look all around, and see yourself so weak and so vulnerable / So you try to be strong, but your money ain't too long, and it's so terrible."

He had good reason for those feelings at the time. Not only had the movement ended, it seemed the country was heading straight back into the nightmare that caused it to start. National unemployment rates for black people remained nearly double that of whites, racial violence broke out in Boston and Pensacola, Florida, and the *New York Times* reported that conditions in the Watts ghetto in Los Angeles were worse than before the 1965 riot. School busing remained a dangerous endeavor, with children often put in the middle of terrible violence as protestors hurled rocks or worse at the buses, and it would take another year for the Supreme Court to rule that private schools couldn't discriminate based on race, which meant that many white schools still refused to follow a twenty-three-year-old law.

My father didn't just witness these things on the news, either. He lived them. Police sometimes stopped him in Atlanta for the infamous crime of driving while black. One time it happened with Sharon in the passenger seat. He got out of the car to speak with the officers, who began asking questions that all had the same end in mind—how did a black man get such a nice car? As Sharon recalls, "When he got back in the car, I could sense that he was furious. He was livid. Steam was coming out of his ears. I said, 'What's wrong, Dad? What happened?' He said, 'Nothing, baby'—he always called me baby—and he mumbled something. I realized in that moment that they were just two white police officers who were harassing him for no reason."

As it happened to him, it also happened to his brother. Uncle Kenny moved to Atlanta, but he couldn't find work. He recalls:

I had two honorable discharges, twenty-three letters of appreciation, but all that still wouldn't get me a job. One time I went looking for a job out there. I was presentable, I felt, and I walked in this
place. It advertised that they were hiring, and I walked in and asked
the lady, "Ma'am, are you hiring?" She said, "No, not at the time."
I said, "OK, thank you, ma'am," because Mama always taught me
to be polite. I come out of there, and I was looking at the paper in
case there was something in that area, and a white guy come up to
me, and he said, "Are they hiring?" I said no. He said, "Well, I'm
going to go in there and check anyway." So he went in, and when
he came out he had a job.

Once again, the control Curtis earned with his music allowed him to
help his family in times of need. He gave Uncle Kenny a job with Curtom doing record promotion, covering radio stations in the Southeast
(he'd also hire Aunt Judy as a receptionist for a short time). "I basically
dealt with the secondary radio stations," Uncle Kenny says.

When they branched me out and started moving me north, then I
did Ohio, Illinois, Pennsylvania, and all that. The ma-and-pa stations, after they got to know you, there wasn't none of this payola
like there was with the big companies. They were good people. I
could walk in there with any of Curtis's product or anything off
the Curtom label, they would get on it and they would report it to
the trades. Everybody thinks that these big radio stations are the
ones that push the music. They was not back in them days. It was
always the ma-and-pa, the little small radio stations that pushed
your record up. Most of the time, all those guys wanted you to do,
you'd buy them a sandwich, take them to lunch. One guy out of
Birmingham, Alabama, Shelly Pope, he always wanted you to get
his laundry out.

Though his audience had declined, my father could still vent his feelings through music. On *America Today*, he drew on the spiritual strength
of Annie Bell to make sense of his country's state. Speaking about the

spiritual messages prevalent in the album, he said, "I'd like to think that you could sing most of my songs in a church or in a tavern or in the streets. I believe that every man not only has his God, but is, within himself, his God. Through having come up with my grandmother, and her being a preacher, I guess what I've taken from her is the ability to communicate these inspiring messages for those who want to take it." He also said that the song "Jesus" was "the closest I've come to real gospel since the 'Keep On Pushing' days."

Some critics saw *America Today* as a return to form. Others saw it as a further descent into unfocused jams. Christgau gave it a D+, saying, "It appears [Curtis] was seeking new standards of incoherence." Yet again, the trend continued—critical and commercial decline at the time but eventual vindication as future generations recognized it as a classic album. Still, it marked his third straight solo release that failed to meet his expectations of success and was an inauspicious start to Curtom's deal with Warner Brothers.

In fact, the Warner Brothers deal had gone sour almost before it started. Neil Bogart was the reason Curtom made the switch to Warner—he'd just left Buddah and started a label and promotional company under Warner Brothers' umbrella. Dad followed him with the understanding that Bogart would promote Curtom's product the same way he'd done with wild success at Buddah. As soon as the ink dried on Curtom's deal, though, Bogart split. Curtom hired its own promotion team, but it didn't have the pull of a major label behind it. This led to a further decline in Curtom's fortunes.

Luckily, while his solo albums failed to hit, he was able to keep his hard-earned spot at the top of the music world with the help of movies. For the rest of Curtom's stay at Warner Brothers, soundtracks kept them in business. Earlier that year, Warner Brothers had approached my father and asked him to score their new comedy, *Let's Do It Again*. According to some sources, they also asked him to star in the movie alongside up-and-coming soul man Al Green. Dad pulled out of the project because he didn't have the time and didn't like the script, but Warner Brothers went ahead with the film, hiring Bill Cosby, Sidney Poitier, and

Jimmie Walker (famous for portraying J.J. on the sitcom *Good Times*, set in Cabrini-Green).

After some convincing from Warner Brothers, Dad rejoined the project to write the soundtrack. The opportunity appealed to him because it "brought about a different type of thing because it was a comedy," he said. "And I wondered to myself what kind of songs I could write if I wanted to be funny."

As he wrote, he knew exactly whom he wanted to sing the songs— his old friends the Staple Singers, whom he'd known since his days on the gospel circuit with the Northern Jubilee Singers. "I could hear what was going to happen where," he said. "The songs were written specifically for the group. A lot of times, they can't hear what you can hear. Those are the tools of a creative person. You can actually see the whole picture— you see how it will turn out."

Like his last several albums, *Let's Do It Again* was remarkably strong and consistent. Somehow, he still hadn't run out of ideas. The material was also far more sexual than the Staples were used to. Mavis Staples recalled, "When we went into the studio and Pops heard his part—'I like you lady, so fine with your pretty hair'—he said, 'Man, I ain't singing that, Curtis,' and Curtis said, 'Pops, come on. It's a movie score. It's not changing your religion. Do it for me, please?' And Daddy just got tickled. He couldn't say no to Curtis. He was that inspiring."

The album went gold, and the title-track single hit the top of the R&B and pop charts. The movie also hit big with audiences, including a young kid in Brooklyn named Christopher Wallace. Late in the next decade, Wallace began rapping on street corners to entertain his friends, eventually making a demo tape under the name Biggie Smalls—the name of the outsized pimp in *Let's Do It Again*. A few years later, Wallace rose to the top of the music world as the Notorious B.I.G. with his debut album, *Ready to Die*.

By the end of the year, my father sputtered with exhaustion and still piled more work on himself. In 1975, he'd written a new solo album, two soundtracks, and Curtom had released albums from Leroy Hutson and the Impressions. They all toured the United Kingdom to support their albums, and when they came back, Warner Brothers relaunched the Gemigo label.

On top of that, Dad started another publishing company, Mayfield Music, which meant that Curtom now handled six of his publishing companies at once. He also joined Don Cornelius in an attempt to license a vacant AM radio station, which they hoped to make into a Top 40–styled black station. "I'm not really a radio man," Dad said, "but my music is on the radio a lot, and Chicago is my place of business, and I feel that my own ethics and community involvement would be a big asset to a radio operation." The plan never came together, but perhaps it was just as well. It's hard to imagine how he would have found the time to make it work.

In 1976, the Impressions released *Loving Power*, which didn't do much. Then they quit Curtom. Curtis had never been further from his old group, but he was too busy to dwell on it. After the Impressions left, he worked on finishing the second movie project he'd taken on the year before—*Sparkle*. He'd already written and recorded the entire album with his voice as a placeholder. "I was writing the songs not knowing really who was going to do them," he said. "I didn't know really until two or three weeks before we released the album who was going to sing it."

What he didn't say was that someone had already sung it—the film's cast, including the future costar of *Miami Vice*, Philip Michael Thomas. Understandably, the cast members reacted with dismay when they heard their version of the soundtrack was scrapped because Curtis didn't like it. Lonette McKee, one of the female leads, said, "The next thing I knew, Curtis Mayfield was giving an interview saying he couldn't understand how they could cast unknowns . . . He made it hard, deliberately setting the keys of the songs in uncomfortable registers for all of us."

Whether or not that accusation was true, it's hard to blame my father for making the switch. At the end of 1975, Atlantic Records' in-house legend, Ahmet Ertegun, approached Dad about working with Aretha Franklin. Like Curtis, the Queen of Soul had recently released a string of unsuccessful albums. She listened to the music he'd written for *Sparkle* and jumped on board. "I'd never gotten into Aretha until this," Dad said. "I was very pleased with my music and the contents even before I knew she was going to do it. And her singing just brought everything together."

Recording only took five days because, as Franklin recalled, "[Curtis] likes to work fast." Also, they worked well together. "He pretty much let me have a free hand," she said. "Our only real disagreement was over one note—he wanted me to sing one way, but I had another way in mind. So we recorded both versions, and what you hear on the album is his concept. He was the producer, so I let him produce." Even when producing a woman who many believe to be the greatest singer of all time, my father wouldn't relinquish control.

The *Sparkle* soundtrack hit number one R&B, as did the single "Something He Can Feel." The album went gold that year, proving Dad's music could still captivate the music world. Tracy recalls him saying he liked *Sparkle* best out of all the albums he'd made, but it continued a frustrating trend—even though his music remained strong, it seemed he could only succeed when someone else sang his songs.

With his next solo album, *Give, Get, Take and Have*, he sought to break that trend. He wrote a batch of songs aimed at the pop charts, even giving a brief nod to the disco craze on "Party Night." That song in particular was a microcosm of the forces directing his songwriting. It showed a man torn between his heart and commercialism, between the music he loved and the music that was currently popular. As a result, the album doesn't quite cohere despite excellent songs like "In Your Arms Again," "This Love Is Sweet," and "P.S. I Love You." The only bright spot commercially was that the single, "Only You Babe," hit number eight R&B.

Give, Get, Take and Have was his worst-selling solo album yet, and another critical failure. With the pressure of running Curtom taking up more mental space than ever, and with his family life deteriorating from increasing solitude and probable drug use, he simply didn't have time to construct an album as seamless and powerful as *Curtis* or *Super Fly*.

Creating a work of art takes absolute focus, ample time, and unrelenting determination. My father only had the latter. He'd always said he wanted his music to be about more than "shaking your shaggy shaggy." He wanted to give people something to think about while they danced. But several of the songs on *Give, Get, Take and Have* feature some permutation of the phrase "shake it," with nothing more serious as a counterbalance. It seemed he was giving in.

Perhaps he had to. On top of dicso's prominence, other factors played into Curtis's continued decline, and Marv spoke candidly about them in a 1976 interview with *Blues & Soul* magazine. One was the racism still prevalent in radio programming. "They tell you, go across town and get me a hit black record and we'll listen," Marv said.

> Then you get them a hit black record and they'll tell you it's too black. I've heard that expression, "too black," for years. I would love for a pop station to actually explain to me what that means. . . . Maybe if I printed our lacquers white—they'd play them. It affects your dollars, it affects your growth. Maybe if we had artists crossing over to the mass white market, we'd be signing rock acts as well. It limits us, truthfully. I think it's a disgusting situation. I'll give you an example: we just had the number one R&B record in the country with "Something He Can Feel." It never crossed over to the white market. It sold 800,000 singles and the album's nearly platinum.

Also, because he was either busy in the studio or locked in his room at home, he hadn't toured much since *Super Fly*. "Curtis hasn't been out for three years and I think his sales have suffered as a result," Marv said. "He felt that after touring for years, he wanted to see his children grow up. . . . I know in '77 he's going to tour. It hurts any artists not to tour. It's a commitment that the artists have to their fans." My father blamed it on his workload, saying, "I'm usually working on one situation or another—and that's why I haven't been on the road as an artist, more or less."

Though he'd grown tired of touring, the road was always a source of inspiration. From "He Will Break Your Heart" to "It's All Right," Dad wrote some of his greatest songs sitting in a car on tour, guitar resting in his lap. That source of inspiration had vanished in recent years.

Still, he felt optimistic. "I'd like to think that this company can become another Motown, as famous as all the things that Berry Gordy did for his company," he said. Marv echoed that statement, saying, "He's thirty-four and has spent seventeen years on the charts. His contribution to black music is beyond comprehension. His contribution to music throughout the world is the same. So I don't look at Curtom as 'What are we doing today'—I look at it as what are we doing today *and tomorrow*."

Dad had multiple plans for tomorrow, including two new film soundtrack projects and a new solo album. By this point, he had pushed himself dangerously close to burnout, yet he didn't rest for a moment. The first of the two films he scored, *Short Eyes*, was based on a popular Broadway play of the same name, and it dealt with one of the few issues of black life my father still hadn't touched—prison. The term "short eyes" was prison slang for a pedophile, and the movie followed a man accused of pedophilia as he made his way through the complex social structure of prison life.

Short Eyes was my father's fifth soundtrack, but unlike his other soundtrack work, this time he invested a good deal of money in the film. He also landed his first dramatic role as Pappy, a wizened old prisoner who doles out advice and sings "Do Do Wap Is Strong in Here" from the soundtrack. With so much of Curtom's money on the line, my father needed the movie to succeed as much as he needed the soundtrack to succeed. Neither did.

Perhaps the subject matter was too heavy for the times. "We got great recognition and real good write-ups," Dad said. "However, it was probably too real. When we did it, it was during the times of escapism and *Star Wars*." The *New York Times* gave the movie a breathless review, saying it was "eloquently adapted" from the play. The review even praised

Dad's turn on the big screen—"Curtis Mayfield, the singer and composer, makes a brief, very effective appearance as an older prisoner who
wears 'granny' glasses and believes there should be some decency even
among people fighting to hang on to the bottom rung of the ladder."

Still, the movie flopped. Though the soundtrack was full of Curtis's
most incisive social commentary since *Super Fly*, it was also a disaster,
only reaching number fifty-nine on the R&B chart. Again, the failure
didn't make much sense for either project. It showed how critical appro-
bation and artistic quality don't guarantee commercial success.

My father felt proud of the album, especially the cut "Do Do Wap Is
Strong in Here." Many critics count it as among his best songs—impossi-
bly funky and lyrically dazzling. Personally, I didn't like it as a kid; it didn't
seem radio friendly to me. His response when I told him that: "Don't
listen to it, then." The album also features "Back Against the Wall," a
heartbreaking look at prison life that pulls from a deep gospel well, while
cuts like "Need Someone to Love" and "A Heavy Dude" lived up to his
usual standard of quality. But, *Short Eyes* broke the spell he'd cast on his
fans over the course of two decades. With the failure of the movie and
soundtrack, my father's reign in the music world suffered a mortal blow.

———————

Short Eyes almost bankrupted Curtom, putting extra pressure on Dad to
come up with a hit. His second movie soundtrack that year, *A Piece of
the Action*, didn't provide it. The album served as an interesting comparison to *Let's Do It Again*, as Mavis Staples sang the songs (this time by
herself) and the movie starred Sidney Poitier and Bill Cosby once again.
"I remember when Curtis called me to work on *A Piece of the Action*,"
Mavis said. "He'd run into some kind of trouble, and he was on a tight
deadline. So he called and said, 'Mavis, I'm in a bind,' and I said, 'Okay,
Curtis, I'm on the way.' All of the musicians ended up spending the
night in the studio, sleeping over two nights to get the album done."

The trouble Mavis referred to involved Roberta Flack, whom my
father first hired to sing the songs. She came into the Curtom studio to
record but couldn't produce the sound he wanted. Tracy, who watched

the scene unfold from the control booth, recalls, "I remember Dad giving her instructions, and he wasn't really feeling her. She asked for the lights to be turned out and she's singing, and you couldn't see anything, you could just hear her voice. She wanted it totally pitch black out there, I guess to maybe get into the mood, but he still wasn't satisfied. She's more of a mellow, precise intonation type of singer. He wanted that soul and that grit. Sometimes he could be very hard to please, very hard to please."

Dad had always been that way, and he remained that way, as Tracy would learn when he went on tour with him years later. "He would get upset, like, 'You better deliver right away. You ain't got two, three minutes. I want to hear it right now,'" Tracy says.

> You had to be doing something for him. Because he would let you know. He would say, "Hey, cat. That ain't happening. This is what you need to be doing." Just like that. He didn't pull no punches. He had a very clear idea of what he wanted at all times, and he heard very well what was going on. And he would stop you or stop the music. He would put his hand out. He wasn't a very mean person, very pleasant even when being decisive of what he wanted. But he would be very direct, and say, "Hey, that ain't happening."

Despite getting exactly what he wanted out of Mavis, *A Piece of the Action* failed. Yet again, my father churned out excellent soul music in a disco-dominated world. Two months later, *Saturday Night Fever* hit theaters, and with it came the Bee Gees' mammoth soundtrack, which reigned atop the *Billboard* album chart for twenty-four straight weeks and sold more than fifteen million copies. At that point, Marv's exhortations to make a disco record became more powerful, but my father wasn't ready to relent. Instead, he recorded *Never Say You Can't Survive*, a collection of soulful love songs that sounded pleasant enough but went nowhere on the charts. Now, he had another problem—moneymen at Warner Brothers began turning the screws, tired of investing in product that didn't sell.

———

The failure of *Never Say You Can't Survive* ended 1977 on a bitter note. Dad knew something had to change, but at the same time, he'd almost burned out his creative spark. In the seven years since he'd gone solo, he'd written fifteen studio albums—ten for himself, one for the Impressions, and four for other artists—and released two live albums. This surge of creativity came after he'd already toiled nearly twenty years in the business, writing hundreds of songs for the Impressions and others. It is hard to think of a musician of any era who kept up that level of output for so long, let alone one who did it with such consistency and commercial success. James Brown might have been the hardest-working man in show business from a performance perspective, but my father could have claimed the title of hardest-working man in the record business.

Dad's decline in popularity had less to do with the quality of his work than it did with the tastes of his audience. Like anyone in charge of running a business, he had to respond to the market. As he watched artists like the Bee Gees, Gloria Gaynor, KC and the Sunshine Band, and Donna Summer tear up the charts with feel-good disco songs, the pressure mounted.

His response to that pressure marked the lowest point of his career.

12

When Seasons Change

"I'll play the part I feel they want of me
And I'll pull the shades so I won't see them seein' me
Havin' hard times"
—"HARD TIMES"

*W*ally *Heider Studios, Los Angeles, mid-1978*—Backed into a creative corner, Curtis cut a disco album. For the first time in his career, he relinquished lead writing duties on half the songs and most of the recording took place outside Chicago. Curtom arranger Gil Askey penned much of the A-side for *Do It All Night*, producing three meandering disco tunes that limp from the speakers. Dad gave the worst vocal performances of his career on these songs, sounding bored, unconvinced, and barely present. The song "Party, Party" is emblematic, full of bad lyrics delivered with little conviction. The man who once sang, "There'll be no more Uncle Tom, at last that blessed day has come," now sang, "Dance, dance, dance, here's your chance, party, party."

The market forced his hand. In 1978, Curtom teetered on the brink of collapse, and he'd been stubborn long enough in the face of changing tastes. In an ironic twist, the control he'd established over himself and his career forced him into that corner—too many people relied on him, too many people had invested in him, and since he could no longer provide hits to keep them all in business, he had to do whatever it took to steady the ship.

Unfortunately, *Do It All Night* did little except obscure his true identity. "It didn't have much to do with me, it was Marv's thing," Dad said.

> He wanted us to have a disco hit. Linda Clifford was having some success on the dance scene, and he thought that's the way we should go. I had spread myself a little thin what with the *Short Eyes* movie score at that time, which cost Curtom a lot, as well as many other recording and tour commitments . . . I think that maybe I should have taken a break at that time and reflected on just what was going on, and not have listened so much to other people, but there were lots of pressures on all of us to turn things around.

Part of that pressure came from Linda's success. She was the only Curtom artist to make a meaningful mark on the disco scene, especially with her album *If My Friends Could See Me Now* and its eponymous single, which hit the top of the new *Billboard* dance chart in 1978. Dad coproduced that album and wrote several songs on it, including "You Are, You Are," which he also sang on *Do It All Night*. It shone a lone bright spot in a year of artistic darkness.

Before *Do It All Night*, he had collaborated again with Aretha Franklin, hoping to repeat the success of *Sparkle*. Franklin had no idea what to do with disco either, and the resulting album, *Almighty Fire*—which my father wrote, produced, and recorded at Curtom—failed by Franklin's standards. It broke her streak with Atlantic Records of fourteen straight top ten R&B albums, including ten that went to either number one or two.

That was Atlantic's problem, though. *Do It All Night* was Curtom's. The album set a new low for my father's solo career, selling worse than anything that preceded it. *Rolling Stone* called it his "flimsiest solo album yet, an indifferent collection of flaccid disco songs," and went on to say a few more hurtful things, even taking a potshot at *Sweet Exorcist*.

The album also finished Curtom's distribution deal with Warner Brothers, hanging the albatross of failure around Curtis's neck as he

searched for new distribution. In the last two and a half years, no Curtom album had even touched the *Billboard* Top 100. Except for the brief
period after Jerry left the Impressions, my father's commercial viability
had never been more in doubt. Unlike those early days, though, he didn't
seem to have an answer.

For his next album, he doubled down on disco, giving up even more
control of his music. This time, he surrendered production duties to
Norman Harris, Bunny Sigler, and Ronald Tyson of the Philadelphia
International label. They wrote much of the album, with Gil Askey con-
tributing on two songs. For a man who always pursued total control
of himself and his music with fanaticism, Dad had taken another huge
departure. He felt it was necessary, though, especially since the pressure
of running a business had only grown after *Do It All Night* failed. "To
show your own value, you must make hit records," my father said. "It just
can't be me, me, me. That always fails. Every once in a while even the best
of the best have to say, okay maybe I better let somebody who's proven
themselves with a new track record do something to keep me going."

He felt a kinship with the folks at Philly International. The label
started as the brainchild of Kenny Gamble, Leon Huff, and Thom Bell,
and released huge hits from the O'Jays, Harold Melvin and the Blue
Notes (featuring future star Teddy Pendergrass), and Chicago native
Lou Rawls, among many others. If my father had to give up control, he
found the right people to give it to.

The resulting album, *Heartbeat*, marked his most complete capitula-
tion to disco. Though low on artistic vision, it hit number nineteen on
the R&B chart and gave him his highest placement on the pop chart in
five years. The single—a duet with Linda Clifford called "Between You
Baby and Me"—was one of the only songs on the album Dad wrote
alone, and it fared best on the charts, which made him happy. The album
also featured "You're So Good to Me," a lively steppers cut that was sampled often in the next decade, most notably as the musical backdrop to
Mary J. Blige's "Be Happy," from her triple-platinum *My Life* album
in 1994. Of course, that success didn't help *Heartbeat* at the time of its
release.

My father felt ambivalent. "It wasn't so bad," he said. "I liked the music. It was strange how *Heartbeat* worked out. Other people's styles could never express me the way I expressed myself. All my life the music I made only sold when I was being me, when I was just being Curtis. When I tried to be other than what I was, you could forget it. I had to be me to be a singer at all."

He'd tried to be a disco artist for the past three years with disappointing results. And he was an astute evaluator of his own voice—it effused a world-weary wisdom, a deep sadness, and a deeper strength in the face of that sadness. These things fit gospel and soul music to a tee but had no place on the dance floor. As a result, when he tried to do middle-of-the-road dance tunes, the lyrics clashed with the tenor of the voice singing them. He came closest with *Heartbeat*—its limited success attracted RSO Records, which purchased Curtom's distribution rights, but the move wouldn't mean much. Curtom hobbled on its last legs, and my father didn't have the energy or ideas to revive it. Disco, along with a string of poor albums and dismal sales, beat the fight out of him. He was exhausted and overworked. For the first time, he contemplated slowing down.

"Those were some strange times for me," he said. "I had done so well for myself for such a long time. As far as my doing songs with messages, disco interrupted it very much. The name of the game these past few years has been escape. People have been going off and doing their thing since time began. But it's important that they remember themselves and who they are." He even revealed bitterness over the disco craze. "So many of the lyrics were just, 'Dance, dance, dance, let's get the hell outta here, cause it's rough on the bottom,'" he said. "At times escape means you're closing your eyes and ears to what's going on. Then when you open them up, it's even more screwed up than before you closed them. You wish you had just gone on and lived through it."

Even as he said that, my father continued to live in his own state of escape. More and more, he lived like a shut-in, staying locked behind his bedroom door. He even ate many meals in his room. His solitude would get worse in coming years.

As the '70s waned, disco crumbled and a new generation of artists emerged in the ghettos and projects of New York. Two neighborhoods in particular—Queensbridge and the Bronx—experienced a renaissance with new styles of fashion, dance, and music that borrowed heavily from R&B and funk music, my father's included. He remained far from all that, though. More than ever, he looked inward, contemplating his past while considering what to do with his future.

His next album, *Something to Believe In*, nodded to the post-disco sounds that would come to dominate R&B music in the early 1980s, but for the most part, it was a return to the deep soul and gospel roots that run through his best work. On the album, he decided to remake "It's All Right," with backing vocals from Sharon and me.

The version of "It's All Right" we cut provides an interesting counterpoint to the original. As soul-music historian Craig Werner wrote, it "underscores the changes in Mayfield's energy since the high point of the Movement. The Impressions' version of the song radiates an energy of connection, especially when the three voices come together at the ends of lines. The 1980 recording accentuates the distance between the lead singer and the backup singers, who sound like they're located in a different room. You can feel the call and response falling apart." Of course, Sharon and I were not the Impressions, and it wasn't 1963 anymore. Regardless, my father felt happy enough with the results to put it on the album.

Werner's assessment of the rest of the album was also on point. "If 'It's All Right' suggested that Mayfield had lost control," he wrote,

> the best songs on the album—"People Never Give Up," "Never Stop Loving Me," and the searching "Something to Believe In"— demonstrated his profound understanding of the gospel vision. Even as he stood alone on the dance floor, contemplating the inevitable collapse of the disco community, Mayfield testified to the power of love. But whatever the lyrics might claim, the sound warned forebodingly of the coming world in which nothing was going to be all right.

After the triumphs and heartbreaks of the '60s and '70s, no one knew what to expect from the new decade. In the '80s, black people continued the symbolic act of renaming, adopting the term African American to pay homage to their historical roots. Despite this progress, it seemed the beautiful moment to change America had passed.

From the beginning, Dad looked at the '80s askance. Less than ten years prior, he said in an interview, "I think people in general will finally find that violence . . . is really not the way," and he'd spoken of "living in harmony, which might sort of force the establishment, who say their way is the only way, to finally feel there is another way to make things work out." With Ronald Reagan spearheading a conservative backlash, Dad couldn't muster the same hope in the '80s. Now he said, "Everything's changed and nothing's changed. . . . If it has always been that way, what makes you think it's going to change? It's like a bowl of fat, whichever way you tip it, the rich stuff's going to be on top and the lean stuff's gonna be underneath."

As usual, he hadn't completely given up hope. *Something to Believe In* showed him still trying to motivate his audience, only he didn't have the same audience anymore. Few listened. The album didn't sell, and Dad entered a new part of his career where he accepted his declining popularity with wisdom and resignation. "Stars are made to burn," he said. "Does it matter whether there is a time when you're not number one? It only gave me time to put some of my main thoughts toward other important things, like being a father. It's the media that always asks, 'Why aren't you still as big as you were?' Well, why aren't I still twenty-two?" In a way, it took the pressure off him and allowed him to return to making the music of his heart.

Where poor decision-making had marred his career for the past five years, bad luck now played just as large a part. When he came off a tour with Linda Clifford, RSO collapsed, and Dad had to shut down Curtom, firing fifty-five employees, including many who had worked for him since the beginning. It seemed his dream of owning his own label, which he'd toiled at for a quarter century, had finally died. "I had the ambition to want to be rich like Motown and Berry Gordy," he said.

I was striving for that like you can't *believe*. Everything I was doing was pulling myself up by my boot-straps, both with OKeh and with the Impressions, who were working three-hundred-sixty-five days a year. With every little bit that was done I could see myself closer to the dream. But it took a little bit more than I could handle myself to make another Motown. It just wasn't in the cards for one man to run a publishing company, be a recording artist, and be a producer.

He added a bit of searing self-evaluation, as he often proved capable of, saying, "You'd be surprised how many businessmen ain't businessmen when it comes to trying to collect for everything they do."

Mourning the loss of Curtom, he also cut ties with his hometown and moved to Atlanta full time. "That Chicago weather," he said, trying to paint a bright picture on his departure. "Man, that Hawk'll get you." There were other reasons for the move, though. Chicago's race problems persisted—a 1980 census named it the most segregated city in the country—and my father found himself in the ironic position of feeling more comfortable as an African American in the South. "I've always felt that the mass of black people in Atlanta were trying to achieve things, run businesses, own their own homes," he said. "Maybe that was because of what they were up against, it's segregation that politicizes black people, makes them hold together. Atlanta was Martin Luther King's home, and the lifestyle is very positive."

Chicago was not the same city my father grew up in, either. Record Row was defunct—the labels had gone out of business or moved their operations to other cities. The place that once held some of the most groundbreaking, world-beating music on the planet quickly deteriorated into an empty echo chamber. "The music scene was kind of drying up in Chicago," my father said. "All the musicians moved to either L.A., New York or Philly. Of course, you know Chicago is my home. I love it, but my needs and my desires were quite different. I guess after coming up in the city all your life, you can appreciate a little bit of ground around you. Atlanta had trees, space, some of those things you want to have. It was a good place for the children."

That last part was especially important. Music had enthralled him
for more than two decades. It dictated his life, defined him, made him a
millionaire, gave him the pride and security he had never had as a ghetto
child. It took him around the world several times over, introduced him
to the highest echelons of business and art, made him an icon to his generation. At the same time, it commandeered his time and commanded
his focus. As the 1980s began and he looked ahead to his thirty-eighth
birthday, my father shifted his focus for the first time since high school.
"Life isn't just music," he said. "Go to your family. Raise your kids. Find
out what you're all about other than music."

———————

Of course, he was still mostly about music. Though he'd just witnessed
the death of his greatest dream with the loss of Curtom, he set about
planning the construction of a new studio next to the house in Atlanta
so he could be both a father and musician in the same place. "I saw the
situation as an ideal opportunity to unite all my business and family life
in one place," he said. "One day I hope to reactivate Curtom records.
I still own the name and all the masters, and there is some great, as yet
unissued music there that should be released."

In late 1981, he got in touch with Neil Bogart, his old friend who
once represented Curtom at Buddah. Bogart had just started a new label,
Boardwalk, and accumulated a diverse roster including Ringo Starr, Joan
Jett, the Ohio Players, and Harry Chapin. Just like old times, Bogart
came through. My father had a new label.

Recording in Atlanta, he made *Love Is the Place*. "At that time, I
wasn't so hot so we were all looking for the right recipe to bring me
back," he said. Against all odds, they found it—sort of. Curtis, working
again with cowriters, created a strong and consistent album. He wrote
songs in a feel-good mode that also had substance, strong hooks, and
soul. The first single, a calypso-tinged love song called "She Don't Let
Nobody (But Me)," hit number fifteen on the R&B chart, his highest
showing since 1976. The second single, "Toot an' Toot an' Toot," also did

well compared to his recent releases, reaching number twenty-two R&B. It marked his last significant showing on the charts.

Love Is the Place left him unsatisfied, though. Once again, other people wrote for or with him on many of the songs, and after years of declining popularity, he faced the exasperating reality of not calling the shots. "I wanted it to be a lot funkier, but then I suppose that's what Boardwalk were trying to get away from," Dad said. "They didn't want to do an album that was a hundred percent Mayfield." Still, feeling momentum building, he worked on his next album, *Honesty*, and reconnected with another old friend who would help revive his career overseas.

———

By that time, John Abbey, Dad's old friend from England, also lived in Atlanta. One night, John walked into Morrison's Restaurant and saw my father sitting across the room. "Curtis was there with his posse as usual, all the deadbeats who followed him around," John says. "I went over, came behind him like how you do with kids, you put your hand on their eyes and say, 'Guess who this is.' And he just sat there and said, 'Hey, John Abbey.' And that was it. It was like I'd just seen him the day before."

As they resumed their friendship, my father discussed where his career stood and the frustration he felt at losing control over its direction. "I think he was kind of disillusioned with the industry," John says.

> I think there was a battle going on in his mind over exactly what he wanted to do. There were times when he said, "I'm just going to retire." There were other times when he wanted to reinvent himself. Part of the thing that was holding him back was that he saw his music a certain way. And I know he wasn't willing to meet anybody halfway. His music was his music, and that was one of the artistic problems that he had with record companies later on when he wasn't the superstar in terms of selling records, because in the record industry you're only as good as your last record. There was a resentment that he felt that people were trying to tell him how to

reinvent himself. His thing was, "If I'm going to reinvent myself, I'm going to do it myself."

In fact, Dad did feel those things. When he spoke about them, anger burned through his usually cool demeanor. "I've been in this business for thirty years, so I can see through all the bullshit," he told an interviewer. "A record deal is like a marriage, you have to be totally satisfied with your partner, and I don't want someone who . . . does a half-assed job. I want to give everything and be given everything."

Since he had little traction in the United States, he asked John about touring overseas, like they did in the early '70s. John worked with a Japanese company at the time and within a few months he had put together a Japanese tour. It went so well, my father instructed him to "just keep doing it." The next summer, Dad had European and South African tours booked. He also went on a "Silver Anniversary" American tour with Jerry and the Impressions—a victory lap, as they celebrated twenty-five years in the business.

Needing a bass player for the tour, Dad turned to Tracy, finally honoring his son's passion to play music. At that time, Tracy was pursuing a music degree at Eastern Illinois University, but when he got the call, he couldn't wait to join the band. Unfortunately, the other band members weren't as excited. "The musicians gave me hell," he recalls. "I was miserable. I guess they thought I wasn't good enough. These were the best players from Chicago, and here I am playing with them—a little punk kid, they thought."

A month passed on the road before the band backed off and showed him respect. "I had to prove myself nightly," he says. "Everybody got solos, so if the audience liked your solo, we'd say you 'got a good house.' The audience let them know I was OK. They couldn't go around that, because I got the audience approval. So I didn't need theirs anymore."

On tour, Tracy met Curtis Mayfield the businessman, not the dad. He'd caught glimpses of that man hanging around the studio as a child, but now he worked for him. He learned Curtis Mayfield always got his money up front. "He didn't go on stage one time in San Diego on the

Silver Anniversary tour," Tracy says. "They didn't have all of our money, and they were trying to get him to go on stage. I remember him talking to the promoter, and he was very stern. He said, 'I'm not getting on that stage without my money.' And they kept trying to get him on stage, and he said, 'You all need to clear the bar.' The audience had to keep drinking because they had to get enough money from the bar to pay us before we got on stage. They waited a long time. I'm talking about at least forty minutes to an hour, we did not go on that stage."

He also learned Curtis Mayfield knew a few tricks when it came to playing music. "I didn't tune to F-sharp, of course," Tracy says. "I used standard tuning. I remember him wanting to show me what he wanted me to do for 'Superfly,' the buildup at the end. He said, 'Give me your bass.' I'm thinking to myself, 'What is he going to do with that? What is he going to show me?' So he picked up my bass and he played exactly what he wanted me to play. That blew me away. I didn't know he could even play regular bass. That's like, 'I'm going to play in this language, and I'm playing this language too.' Not many people can do that. And I saw him do it regularly."

While Tracy knew about his dad the Gemini, he learned Curtis Mayfield was just as impulsive and unpredictable on stage as he was at home. One night, the band sweated it out at a nice theater in front of three thousand people when Curtis Mayfield turned to Tracy and said, "Hey, cat—'We People Who Are Darker Than Blue.'" Tracy looked down at his feet. "Dad," he said, "The band doesn't know that song." Curtis Mayfield shot him a look and retorted, "Don't worry about it. Follow me." He kicked into a song his band had never rehearsed. "You could hear a pin drop," Tracy says. "I looked up at the keyboard player, and he looked at me like a deer in headlights, and I'm like, 'I can't do nothing about it, man. We in it now.' We were all sucking air right there—why are you going to do that to us? But that's the kind of performer he was. He felt it. He wanted to do it at that point, and it was done. And we didn't mess up, either."

The tour had many high points, including a concert in Chicago where the mayor pronounced it "Curtis Mayfield Day." Press reviews ranged

from enthusiastic to laudatory, including a rather colorful description in
NME of a show in Los Angeles:

> There were no strings attached, just brass and reeds, Curtis's son
> Tracy on bass, and six black gents in white tuxedos with satin
> lapels: Nate Evans' quarterback shoulders, Vandy Hampton's Pro-
> fessor Cornelius perm, the smile Sam Gooden's been wearing for
> forty-nine years, the grizzled grey pate and granpappy specs of Cur-
> tis Mayfield, Fred Cash's tongue rolling over his lower lip like an
> uncooked chipolata, and, one unto himself, Jerry Butler, with his
> eyelids at half-mast like those of a blind man.

Just as my father gained some momentum, though, bad luck came calling
again, this time wrapped in tragedy. After coming off the road with the
Impressions, he learned Neil Bogart had died of cancer, sending Boardwalk into a freefall. Within days, he embarked on another European
tour. The audience Dad had attracted on his trips there in the early '70s
with Craig, Master Henry, Lucky, and Tyrone, created a surge in popularity that had only grown despite his declining fortunes in America. As
one reviewer noted, "Curtis delivers sixty magical minutes, backed by a
group, including his son Tracy on bass, that steams through the set—top
musicians each one, they have come straight off an American tour on
which Curtis and Jerry Butler together celebrated the twenty-fifth anniversary of the Impressions. Mayfield is visibly amused when mention of
them draws a puzzled silence from the young crowd."

When he returned to America, Boardwalk stood on the verge of
collapse. With the help of Epic Records, they eked out the release of
Honesty, which didn't sell well, and then Curtis found himself without a
label again. It was a trio of hard blows—an old friend dead, a record deal
defunct, and an album failed.

He dealt with it by retreating further into the confines of his room.
"After touring, Dad shut down," Tracy recalls. "You wouldn't hear from

him for months. And it'd be many times we'd go over his house, and you would have to talk to him through the door. He would not come out the room. He wouldn't take phone calls. He wouldn't return phone calls."

Dad had a nice setup in the basement with a big screen TV, and we'd often play chess or shoot pool down there, but he seemed to prefer the solitude of his room. I never knew exactly what he did in there, but many people around us believed Dad was sinking further into drugs, possibly cocaine. I never saw him do it, but it seems plausible. Regardless of what he was doing, when I'd knock on his bedroom door and say, "Dad, I'm hungry, come make me something to eat," and he'd talk through the door instead of opening it, I knew something was amiss.

During that period he became more unpredictable, lending credence to the possibility of a growing drug habit. We never knew which promises he'd keep. Sharon says, "I felt like I couldn't rely on him to do things. I remember [when I visited him in Atlanta] he often wouldn't pick me up from the airport. I'd call him and say, 'Dad? I'm here.' He'd say, 'Oh yeah, I'll be right there,' or, 'Oh, Robert, he will send someone out.' And I didn't like that. I didn't like someone else picking me up. I wanted him to pick me up."

Tracy experienced similar feelings. "We've all been disappointed a lot by his personality," he says. "I mean, just promising us something, just spending time with us and he wouldn't show up. [He was] always making promises. I was trying to get a record contract at one point for myself, he'd just have me record all these tracks and make promises that he wouldn't deliver. Then, you know, I'd bust out more tracks, and he'd make more promises, and he wouldn't deliver on those."

He also continued his spotted history of physical abuse toward women, now with Altheida. I remember seeing her with a black eye and asking what happened. She made an excuse for it, but we knew what was going on. In his personal life as well as his creative one, my father had sunk to a low point.

His Gemini duality made him strive to be a family man despite his shortcomings as a partner, and in quick succession, he and Altheida had six children, leaving him with ten children spread across three separate families. He wanted us all to get along and made an effort to include everyone in trips and activities. We also spent a good amount of time with Curtis III and Helen. "Helen was extremely nice to us," Tracy recalls. "Never once did I feel any negativity from her." Sharon, however, noticed tension between Dad and Helen when he'd drop us off.

Perhaps naturally, tensions also simmered among ten children vying for one man's time and attention, and three women wanting to make sure he allocated that time and attention fairly. As usual, Dad could see the big picture—having a lot of children and remaining close to each of them—but he struggled with the day-to-day reality of making it happen. "You have to create the conditions for that to happen," Sharon says. "You have to nurture that type of environment, because it does not just happen. One of my first memories, I remember my dad introducing me to Curtis III and saying, 'This is your brother.' I was confused about who are these people I don't know?"

Dad kept his mother and grandmother close. I remember my great-grandma Sadie vividly—she'd smoke cigarettes all day, perched by the window in the third-floor apartment where my grandmother lived. Even in her eighties, she was feisty and funny. For her part, my grandmother still followed her son's career closer than any fan. She proudly kept a box of newspaper and magazine clippings, adding to it every time a new story appeared. We'd even see Mannish every now and again—my father never fostered a relationship with his father, but he still welcomed the old man into his house for Thanksgiving or Christmas dinner.

———————

Despite the hardships of the past few years, *Honesty* proved my father could write a great song when he stayed true to himself. Songs like "If You Need Me" and "What You Gawn Do?" lived up to his best standards. The latter featured another Caribbean arrangement and lyrics about the islands, perhaps as a tribute to his recently departed protégé Bob Marley, who had died of cancer at age thirty-six in 1981. Dad hadn't lost his social or political edge in the Reagan era, either, as he showed in the song "Dirty Laundry." He sings, "Dirty laundry in the country /

Can't trust Uncle Sam / Broken link / Future sinking / And no one gives a damn." But he was not the man to comment on the Reagan years. That job fell to a new era of musicians who had learned from his work. Several months before *Honesty* came out, Grandmaster Flash and the Furious Five released their seminal single, "The Message." The song set the tone for artists like N.W.A, KRS-One, Public Enemy, and others who would define hip-hop in the next few years. In many ways, "The Message" was *Super Fly* set to a new form of music. It's hard to miss my father's imprint on the song's lyrics and point of view.

In fact, Dad's music played a huge role in the development of hip-hop, even as he faded from the public eye. While artists like James Brown and Stevie Wonder remained cultural icons—and Bob Marley's fame reached the stratosphere with the posthumous best-of compilation, *Legend*—Dad seemed resigned to his status. "I don't feel that I'm a great success," he said.

It takes a lot of ego and playing a role that I'm not. I like the idea of having money. I'm very happy that I'm in an area that people turn their heads and listen, that I've got respect and naturally, I feel proud of myself. And then, every couple of years, when you get the money in, you wonder if you're winning or losing. I cherish the time I can get away from it all.

At the same time, he remained hopeful. "These are not easy times, yet they are not hopeless times," he said. He just needed a break.

———

Ernest Hemingway once wrote:

In going where you have to go, and doing what you have to do, and seeing what you have to see, you dull and blunt the instrument you write with. But I would rather have it bent and dull and know I had to put it on the grindstone again and hammer it into shape and put a whetstone to it, and know that I had something to write about,

than to have it bright and shining and nothing to say, or smooth
and well-oiled in the closet, but unused.

Those words could sum up my father's career. In a span of twenty years,
he put his instrument on the grindstone again, and again, and again,
more than almost any artist of his generation. He crafted an immortal
legacy from it. He dulled and blunted it and still demanded more of it.
Now, for the first time, he rested it.

He spent much of the mid-'80s away from music, learning to be
a father first and world-famous musician second. Gray crept into his
beard. He put on weight. Life changed, as it must. He spent some time
in the Curtom Atlanta studio tinkering with new sounds, but he didn't
have a clear direction or a record deal. He filled most of his time with
ordinary things—cooking, going to the store, tooling around town in
his brown Jeep. In 1983, I began college at Morehouse in Atlanta, and
I'd visit the house on weekends, where the Rolls Royce sat in the garage
dusty, unused, battery dead, tires low. I'd clean it up, charge it, and take
it out for an occasional spin. Sometimes I'd even ask to drive his new
Corvette. He was always good about it—he'd just give me the keys and
I'd take off.

Aunt Carolyn and Uncle Kenny visited him in Atlanta often, and
they found that as much as life had changed, Curtis remained in many
ways the same frustrating man. "He enjoyed people, he enjoyed family,"
Aunt Carolyn recalls. "But he would enjoy you for a while, and the next
thing you know, he would disappear in his room. You went home. Or,
you just enjoyed the rest of your day and knew that was him; that was
part of his personality. I think everybody you talk to can tell you another
side of him. That's a Gemini. Everybody you talk to, they know a different side."

Uncle Kenny developed his own way to deal with my father's capricious nature. He says, "I wouldn't go out there all the time, but I could
always tell when my brother wanted to be bothered, because he'd send
somebody looking for me, so that meant Curtis want to be bothered.
Curtis was a Gemini, you know. Wishy-washy. I remember one time I

was out there, and Curtis told Altheida, 'Get all the kids together, we're going to go to the other house and swim.' So, she's up there getting all these rug rats together, and she comes down and says, 'We're ready.' Curtis was laying up on the couch asleep, and he gets up and says, 'Ready for what?'"

A few years prior, he'd finally divorced Helen, but he didn't marry Altheida, causing trouble with Aunt Carolyn. "Me and Theida, we got in the biggest thing," Aunt Carolyn says. "I said, 'You got all these babies and you ain't married? Every man I ever had, he married me.' She obviously would go up and tell Curtis about it, and he'd tell her—he wouldn't tell me—he'd tell her, and I know he told her because the next day, the conversation would come back around, and she would tell me what he said. One time he told her that she was his 'spiritual wife.' I said, 'Ain't no such thing!'"

Still, my father loved being with his family, and he always tried to include all his children in his life. Years ago, he'd become a photography fanatic, and now he enjoyed taking hundreds of pictures, developing them in his own darkroom and documenting his life during the first significant break he'd taken since 1958.

At the same time, Dad also spent more time in his bedroom hidden from the outside world. His life continued taking on the detritus of addiction, which only fed the rumors of cocaine use. His career floundered. The house in Atlanta sat unkempt and dirty. His relationships deteriorated. "No one was taking care of the house," Sharon remembers.

> No one was taking care of the children. It was dirty. I didn't want my feet to touch the floor. The cabinet's hanging off by a single screw. I withdrew from him, and I stopped wanting to come and visit. We had some bumps in the road during that time when I was in high school. I remember he called me one day. My mother said he was drunk. I couldn't tell. But he called me one day, and he was angry with me because I was acting like I didn't want to see him. I wasn't returning his phone calls. He was using profanity towards me, and I got really upset. I was crying. My mother took the phone

and started telling him that he's not going to call up here and upset
me and talk to me in that way.

While he lost control of his career to changing musical tastes, he lost
control of his personal life to drugs. Family relationships became strained.
Tracy stopped touring with him in the mid '80s and began running the
studio. "It was very frustrating because at that point I was managing the
studio, and I needed him a lot sometimes for some decision-making
things," Tracy recalls. "And that was tough that he wouldn't even return
my calls. I couldn't get in touch with him."

After a misunderstanding between Altheida and Tracy, Dad shut
down the studio completely. "I was managing the studio, and all of a
sudden, the next day, the doors were locked," Tracy says. "I had to find
another job. Supposedly they were remodeling in there but there wasn't
nothing going on. It was ridiculous." Curtis III also caught the brunt of
Dad's wrath. Curt played saxophone and was asked to go on his first tour
with his father but got kicked off at the last minute after a screaming spat
that almost came to blows.

As all this happened, my father talked about reviving Curtom. He
still hadn't given up, but he needed a distributor, so along with William
Bell and a few other artists, he brought a proposal to John Abbey. "They
didn't have a record deal," John says. "They had kind of been mistreated
and cheated by some of the other companies. They were disenchanted.
They said, 'Why don't you start a distribution company so that we can
put out product through you?'"

John started Ichiban Records. "It was something that Curtis pushed
me into," John says, "And when he did, I pushed back and said now
you need to do your part. And he did." Because RSO wouldn't release
the name Curtom without payment, my father signed a deal with John
under the moniker CRC—Curtom Record Company, later called Curtom Records of Atlanta, Inc.—and began recording a new album called
We Come in Peace with a Message of Love.

The album is uneven, and it failed to chart. As John says,

Some of the tracks were very good, but there were tracks that he would put on albums that people thought, "Curtis, why are you putting that on there?" It was the way he saw it. We had discussions that I won't say got heated, because that never happened, but certainly there was definitely disagreement there, because looking at it as a record company, you want it to sell the best you could. And you knew that once it got out there in the marketplace, people aren't going to be kind like we are. Some of the reviews on the *We Come in Peace* album were not really that great, and I think that hurt him.

After *We Come in Peace*, perhaps realizing that he could no longer dominate commercially, my father stepped even further from the spotlight, taking the longest recording break of his career. Five years would pass before he recorded again. In that time, he fell further into obscurity in America, but his popularity continued overseas. He formed a new road band called Ice-9 featuring Lee Goodness on drums, Buzz Amato on keyboards, and Lucky's brother LeBron Scott on bass. They toured Europe and Japan in 1986 and '87, including places my father had never been, like Austria, Spain, Scotland, France, Germany, Holland, Belgium, Switzerland, Denmark, and Sweden. Even in semiretirement, he still didn't know how to take it easy.

By that point, I had graduated from college and decided to go on the road with him for the first time, acting as a glorified roadie. I spent almost three months in Europe, riding around drinking all the European beer I could hold. My father was never a big drinker—when he did drink, he preferred cheap wine or a three-dollar bottle of champagne. One of my jobs on tour was bringing girls backstage that the band picked from the audience. I'd introduce them to my father, but he had mellowed quite a bit from his younger days of chasing women. Now, he just felt anxious to get back home and see Altheida.

The tour gave us precious time together, and we talked through the days and nights on long bus, plane, and train rides. We also discussed working together in a more formal sense, giving me a chance to put my college degree to work and fulfilling my childhood hope of protecting him by handling the finer points of business he often missed.

Dad particularly enjoyed performing in England because the people there loved him. He also liked Germany, where he played several military bases. Being a reformed sports car fanatic, he loved watching the German roadsters zoom by on the Autobahn. He'd stare at them between games of chess on the bus. In fact, that trip marked the first time I ever beat him at chess. Even though he'd taught me to play as a child, he never let me win—that just wasn't his nature—so my victory felt even sweeter.

In the summer of 1987, the band cut *Live in Europe* at the Montreux Jazz Festival and released it on CRC/Ichiban. "I think all of us were very lucky that that was so well-received," John says. "I think that gave him a lot of confidence back." Dad certainly seemed to grow in confidence as the European crowds flocked to see him. He sold out venues in every country and performed at a few summer festivals, where he absorbed the energy of fifty thousand screaming fans. He said, "You have to remember that when I was having all my hits in the States, my records really weren't being exposed properly in Europe. So maybe this is like a catch-up situation. People seem more loyal in Europe. I see some of the same faces at my concerts each time I come over, and that's a comfortable feeling."

He also got another shot recording a movie soundtrack for Keenen Ivory Wayans's blaxploitation parody film *I'm Gonna Git You Sucka*. Wayans asked him to score the whole movie, and Dad tinkered around in the CRC studio for a while, but the result sounded thin and low on inspiration. Wayans scrapped it and only included one song of my father's, "He's a Flyguy." It appeared next to songs by artists who counted Curtis as a hero. One of them was KRS-One, whose group, Boogie Down Productions, had just released their 1987 album, *Criminal Minded*, which many credit with starting gangsta rap. Years later, KRS paid my father homage, saying, "Curtis Mayfield was hip-hop."

As the 1980s came to a close, my father found a new niche. He didn't have to record unless he felt the urge, and he could count on his loyal fan base overseas to sustain him between records. He felt pride as he watched his influence spread through the younger generation of musicians. More and more artists sampled his music, including Eric B. & Rakim, LL Cool J, Big Daddy Kane, N.W.A, and Biz Markie. Listening to what they did with his songs, my father gained an affinity for hip-hop. "I don't see any great differences between what people are expressing now and what we used to do," he said at a time when the new art form was under serious critical and cultural attack. "There's observations on contemporary goings-on, personal freedoms, civil rights, and discriminations of minorities. Then of course, there's always love, the ins and outs and movements and the happenings of love."

Responding to critics' complaints against sampling—one of the most controversial aspects of the new music—he said, "It's not that they can't create; they've made a new way of creating by sampling. These are new ways of putting music together, which is fantastic. It's as if you put together a collage of pictures into a pattern, so you look at it from afar and say, 'Wow look at that,' and then you come up close, and these are pictures that you are familiar with put together in a different manner."

He understood the role his music played in the new art form, but he knew his boundaries. His attempt at making disco had taught him a valuable lesson—he had to stay true to himself regardless of changing tastes. "We're talking about character here," he said.

> You can't expect everyone to like you, but they're sure as hell not going to like you if you jump around trying to accommodate, and can't find yourself. I like a lot of today's fire-up party sounds, but if I borrowed those sounds, who could trust me? Who could feel they know my character? If I'm to retain any credibility, I have to be myself. There's a time for every mood, and even the kids into techno-rap may want to step into the cultural museum and pull out some Mayfield. Hopefully I'll be one of those treasures that will always be there.

In 1989, he toured with the Impressions again through Chicago, Detroit, and Philadelphia, mirroring the first tour they did after the success of "For Your Precious Love" thirty years before. The next year, he had two projects on his mind—a new album and movie soundtrack. It was almost like old times.

Shortly after *I'm Gonna Git You Sucka*, my father and I became more serious about working together. In July 1990, I left my job in Chicago and moved to Atlanta, where Ichiban gave me a desk in their office. Dad dumped a stack of boxes on me, and I began sorting through them—old contracts, the Warner Brothers deal from 1975, concert agreements. I had joined the family business.

One of my first assignments was helping coordinate Dad's involvement with the *The Return of Superfly* soundtrack. It was the second *Super Fly* sequel—he'd wisely rejected an offer to score the forgettable *Super Fly T.N.T.* in 1973. On the three songs he contributed, he explored a new R&B subgenre called new jack swing, and he cut a hit single alongside rapper Ice-T with "Superfly 1990." I felt I was making a smooth entry into the music business, until it came time to shoot a music video with Ice-T.

Dad and I bought tickets together to fly from Atlanta to New York City for the video. We were scheduled to arrive the day before shooting began. When it came time to leave, I knocked on his bedroom door. Speaking through the door as usual, he said, "Go ahead. I'll come tomorrow morning." I tried to convince him to come with me, but he refused and assured me he would be there for the shoot. The next morning, he didn't show up. He wasn't even in New York City. I sweated it out, assuring the record executives from Capitol he would be there, not entirely sure myself if it was true. They began shooting other scenes to avoid blowing the budget, and several hours later, in walks Curtis Mayfield as if nothing had happened. Somehow he could get away with these things, and everyone loved him and his performance. For my part, I was just happy he didn't leave me hanging. Even so, I decided to approach him about his drug use. I had recently witnessed a deal take place in his driveway, and I asked if he was OK. He told me not to worry about it. We never spoke of it again.

Soon after, New York state senator Marty Markowitz invited my father to play an outdoor concert series he staged every year in Flatbush, Brooklyn, at Wingate Field. "Curtis Mayfield was making a comeback, and he was certainly an icon of the black community," Markowitz says. "There was certainly a lot of respect, and devotion and love, and that's why I hired him." Ice-9 was scheduled to tour Europe again the next week, and Dad figured it would be a good chance to get the band geared up while making some money.

He flew to New York, leaving the band to drive the equipment from Atlanta in a van. I considered driving with them, but I didn't feel like sitting in a van for twelve hours, so I stayed home. I spoke to him by phone before the concert, and he sounded in high spirits. Promoters expected a big turnout at the show. Weathermen predicted a bad storm, but Dad didn't pay it much attention. If they had to cancel because of rain, the band still got paid.

Before we hung up, I said, "How's the weather?" Hazy, overcast, hot, he said. "You think it's going to rain?" No, he said. "You know if it does rain you still get your money?" I know, he said. My father had performed in concert thousands of times—he wasn't scared of a little bad weather.

Besides, he always felt safest on stage.

13

Never Say You Can't Survive

"A terrible blow, but that's how it go."
—"Freddie's Dead"

Wingate Field, Brooklyn, August 13, 1990—A heavy storm slithered across the Empire State, menacing Senator Markowitz. He didn't want to cancel the show—ten thousand people had already shuffled into the park and taken seats or splayed on blankets in the grass. They came to see Curtis Mayfield, and Markowitz felt it his duty to ensure that happened. He hounded his weather contacts, hungry for updates. As showtime approached, he got word that grim weather rumbled an hour away. He decided to put my father on early, thinking even if they had to cancel, Curtis might at least get off *one* song.

Hanging out in his trailer, Dad heard about the early start time from his road manager Vince and agreed to it. Markowitz remained antsy. He approached the opening act, Harold Melvin and the Blue Notes, with the storm in mind. "Listen, you get on stage to get everyone ready to go," he said, "and then I'm going to bring Curtis Mayfield up, because most people are here for him." Markowitz cut the Blue Notes' set in half, down to twenty minutes, which they performed dutifully. No rain yet. So far, so good. Ice-9 hustled on stage and exploded into the opening strains of "Superfly," drums thump-thump-thumping, bass pulse-pulse-pulsing.

Markowitz ascended the stairs on back of the stage, pausing to give a quick greeting to Curtis, who hung out waiting for his cue. It was the first and last time they would ever speak. Markowitz stepped to the microphone, front and center. "Ladies and gentlemen, we've decided that we're going to bring up Curtis Mayfield," he said. "I'm thrilled . . ." and as soon as he hit the word "thrilled," something wrenched the first two rows of spectators from their seats and dumped them on the ground like several hundred discarded dolls.

Markowitz stood confused. Then he felt it—a hurricane-force blast of wind. Stacks of speakers on the front of the stage—big mothers, heavy and stout—fell off like they were committing suicide. Trees thrashed above the panicking crowd. Markowitz didn't know what to do. He was in the middle of an introduction. The band was playing. Composing himself, he said, "Ladies and gentlemen, Curtis Mayfield," and turned to hand over the microphone. My father strode toward Markowitz, axe slung across his body. Halfway there, Hell paid him a visit.

It happened in a matter of seconds, starting with the wind that had thrown the first two rows from their seats and razed the speakers. The gust also toppled the cymbals on the drum riser. Lee Goodness leaned back and caught them with his left arm, keeping the beat with his right. As Markowitz turned with the microphone, another gust heaved the front lighting truss off the ground and sent it tumbling, knocking the back truss off the stage as it fell. Markowitz collapsed in fear, lying on his stomach. The front truss plunged down, down, down, like a freight train dropped from the sky. As it plummeted, stage lights fell from it like raindrops.

One of those falling raindrop lights cracked Curtis on the back of the neck and crumpled him to the ground. Then the falling truss pulverized the tom drums with a mighty crash. If Lee hadn't leaned back to catch the cymbals, it would have severed his arms, maybe worse. His bass drum stopped the truss before it could squash my father like a bug.

Dad blacked out, came to, and discovered neither his hands nor arms were where he thought they were. He lay splattered on the stage, helpless as an infant. People screamed and cried and hollered, everyone in frantic motion, running for their lives.

Then it rained. Big drops. Torrents poured from the sky; thunder exploded like shrapnel. Lee rushed over to his bandleader. "Are you all right?" he yelled into the rain. "I think so, but I can't move," my father groaned, sodden in the squall, powerless to take cover. He kept his eyes open, afraid that if he closed them he'd die. Someone covered him with a plastic sheet, and everyone waited without breath until an ambulance arrived. "I knew what had happened right away," my father told an interviewer later. "The first thing I told myself was just to stay alive."

Nothing was assured beneath the plastic sheet. The ambulance rushed him to Kings County Hospital. In the only stroke of luck that day, the hospital stood right next to the field. Paramedics saved his life, but not his body. After stabilizing him in traction, doctors told him the brutal truth—the stage light had crushed several vertebrae. Paralyzed from the neck down, he would never walk, let alone play guitar, again.

He was forty-eight years old.

The road manager, Vince, called me. It felt surreal—Dad and I had just discussed the weather on the phone. I reminded him he'd get paid even if he didn't perform. Worse still, I was supposed to drive up with the band. Had I been there, who knows what might have happened differently. I felt unimaginable guilt. More than that, I feared for his life.

Altheida made arrangements to fly to New York the next day. I stayed with the kids, who were too young to go and too young to stay home alone. Uncle Kenny and his wife came to relieve me, and I left the next day. Already media requests for interviews came pouring in. Tragedy had us all scrambling.

When I arrived, my father's body was wracked with pneumonia. His system couldn't fight the sickness after enduring such trauma. Seeing him hooked to a ventilator, in traction, I almost broke down and had to step out of the room. Gathering myself, I walked back in and stood over his bed. Tears welled in his eyes. I'd never seen him cry before. He couldn't speak, but he mouthed the words, "Take care of the finances."

In the hardest of circumstances, we show our true selves. Even at death's door, my father's first thought ran to finances. It was never money he cared about. It was always what money represented—the ability to take care of his family and ensure his children would never suffer the way he had. Without a working body, he couldn't guarantee that anymore.

On some level, he knew he'd lost more than just control of his body. He'd lost his guitar, his other self, the love of his life. With it, he lost the magic that gave him control of his life—music. Music broke him out of the ghetto; music bought his mother new furniture and a refrigerator full of food; music granted him the power to raise his friends from poverty; music eased his insecurities; music made him a messenger and a hero; music inspired the movement; music brought money, fame, and an incredible lifestyle; music gave his brother and sister and sons jobs when they needed work. Because he could control music, he could control his world. With cruel irony, fate snatched that control from him in the exact place where he had earned it—the stage.

———

Soon after I arrived at the hospital, Tracy, Sharon, and Curtis III did too. Sharon recalls, "When I got there, he had that halo on. He was lying on his back. I was so devastated to hear what happened and to see him in this way. I asked for people to leave because I wanted to pray. I laid my hands on him, and I prayed over his body. He had tears coming out of his eyes. I remember that, because I rarely saw my father be emotional in a way that he had tears. It was really, really, really tough. There were lots of times when I just couldn't see him that way."

Tracy recalls sitting at Dad's bedside, reading messages that came in, not knowing how else to help. "I remember reading a telegram from Eric Clapton," he says. "Some other famous people sent him a telegram, so he had people caring about him all over the country, sending him all these flowers and telegrams. It was not a lot of interaction at that point. We were just there day and night just to be around him."

The show of love from peers in the music world boosted my father's spirits, but there wasn't much any of us could do to make his situation better. I'd often try to get his mind off it, maybe get some laughs going, but no one could ignore the heartbreaking truth. The man who once controlled everything now couldn't even go to the bathroom without help.

Politics set in immediately, making everything more difficult. My father served as the linchpin of a complex social structure—three often-separate families, three mothers of ten children ("I wouldn't do that to one woman," he used to joke), and a bevy of business connections. Then, of course, there was Marv—ever the opportunist, he reinserted himself into the mix after a long absence. No one but Curtis could keep all those factions together.

When the press came calling, I handled their inquiries. I didn't look for that role; it fell on me, with my father's approval, because I had just taken charge of Curtom. Curtis III felt slighted, saying it was his duty as oldest son. That created a wedge, but we quickly settled the issue. Still, as my responsibilities grew after the accident, it seemed everyone wanted to shove wedges between my father and me.

It took years for these wedges to become major problems, though. In the hospital, the only thing we all cared about was the man trapped in traction. After a week or so, the pneumonia subsided and the doctors deemed him safe for transport to Atlanta. He flew on a Medevac plane with Altheida to Atlanta's world-class Shepherd Center, where he received extensive therapy. He still had bone fragments in his spinal cord, and they surgically extracted them. They also fused his spine together and supported it with metal plates and screws so he could hold his head up.

Dad began rehab, training with various pieces of equipment including a giant motorized wheel chair he could operate by mouth. He never learned to use it. His attitude was, "Fuck it, just push me." For the rest of his life, that lumbering, heavy contraption sat unused in his room while we pushed him around in a regular wheelchair.

He also received counseling at the hospital. He learned, barring a miracle of modern science, he'd never move his limbs again. As the reality of his situation dawned on him, he tried to make sense of what had happened, saying:

We arrived [at the venue] at about eight-thirty or nine. It was bigger than I thought. We pulled up behind the stage. I met a few people, shook a few hands, got my money—my balance in advance.
All the normal things. I'm in the safest place in my life, doing my
work. I was to close the show, but it was running a little late, and I
was asked to go on stage a little early so people who were there to
see me wouldn't be disappointed. No problem. I was happy to do
that. I tuned my guitar and jumped into my stage clothes . . . I had
my guitar on and I'm walking up these sort of ladder steps, a little
bit steep but not so steep you couldn't walk up them. I get to the
top of the back of the stage, I take two or three steps, and . . . I don't
remember anything. I don't even remember falling. Next thing I
know, I was on the floor with no guitar, no shoes on my feet, no
glasses on, and I was totally paralyzed. One moment I was smiling,
going toward the stage, and the next moment my eyes were looking
straight up to the sky. The only thing I could move was my neck. I
looked about me, and I was completely sprawled like a rag doll all
over the floor.

Even as he told the story, he couldn't quite believe it. It was the type of
freak accident that makes no sense no matter how many times one goes
over it. The best he could say was, "It happened, and it happened fast.
I never even saw it coming." His recollection that the show ran late is
interesting—perhaps no one told him the real reason Markowitz asked
him to go on early. Maybe, had he known about the weather, he would
have refused. Maybe, had I been there, I could have played bad cop and
refused for him. As with any tragedy, there were a million maybes.

———————

After more than two months at Shepherd, Dad grew tired of life in a
hospital bed. There was only so much rehab he could do, and even that
wouldn't bring his body back. He began lobbying for release, and when
his doctors finally assented, he called me to pick him up immediately. I
said I'd have to arrange for a van to help transport him, but he shot back,

"No, come get me now." I raced over in my two-door Mazda, and the staff helped me use a lift to get him into the front seat. They gave me a huge strap, which I wrapped across his chest, under his arms, and around the back of the car seat to secure him. Slowly, cautiously, I drove him home. It was close to Thanksgiving.

Returning home from the hospital, he faced the greatest challenge of his life—learning to live without a body. It forced him to give up all control. He thought he wouldn't experience much physical pain as a result of the paralysis. He was wrong. "Aches come and go," he said. "I have a lot of complications, the effect of low blood pressure, chronic pain, things no one really could see or would even know unless you were around people with spinal cord injuries. I'm trying to maintain the status quo, but the hardships are many as are the complications. Sometimes you don't have answers."

He couldn't regulate his body temperature, and the Hawk he left behind in Chicago now seemed to live inside him. We piled blankets on him, struggling to keep him warm, but other symptoms we could do nothing about. He suffered from phantom hands—an agonizing sensation he compared to thrusting his arms in a bucket of writhing snakes. Atrophy set upon his muscles, and his feet began to curve downward from lack of use. Diabetes became a serious problem too, and the fingers that once effused elegant guitar licks now served solely as pincushions, caked in dried blood and wrapped in bandages from constant blood-sugar tests. On top of that, he suffered perennial urinary-tract infections as a result of his ever-present catheter.

His life crashed to a halt. No more performing, no more traveling, no more writing. At home, he stayed stuck in bed all day and night with the TV on. The first-floor library became his bedroom, and he sat there passively observing life go on around him. Interview requests flooded in, which gave him something to think about, and he did have days when the darkness lifted a bit, but just as often, his mood turned despondent. Always a man of capricious mood swings, he struggled to maintain a sense of hope and happiness while adjusting to a living nightmare.

Dad never succumbed to self-pity, though. As Marv recalls, "He never said, 'Why me?' He'd say, 'Why not me? It could happen to anyone.'" Still, he suffered mightily. Every night, he lay trapped as the snakes slithered around his arms and a simple itch could drive him to insanity. He'd call out in the darkness, begging for someone to come ease his pain. Sharon recalls, "When I would go to visit, I would hear him in the middle of the night calling out for Altheida. And I just felt such hopelessness. He would just call for her, and call for her, and call for her incessantly through the night."

Home healthcare workers came to ease Altheida's burden, but she still worked herself to the bone. One night, exhausted, she put a candle near the wall and forgot it. The wallpaper ignited. Soon, flames engulfed the second floor of the house. They had to evacuate fast, wheeling Dad beneath billows of black smoke and deadly fire. He watched his home burn, knowing if no one had been there to save him, he would've burned with it.

More bad news followed. Dad kept his old master tapes in the basement, and when the fire-hoses extinguished the blaze, they also doused some of the most famous recordings in soul music history. I went back and salvaged everything I could. Some tapes survived, and I began the process of digitally remastering them, culminating in more than fifteen reissues from the Curtom catalog on compact disc. Many tapes, however, we lost forever.

___

For Dad, life had become apocalyptic. In a matter of weeks, he lost the use of his body and much of his life's work, and he had to evacuate his home. We kept trying to take his mind off of his trouble. I'd go over and watch basketball games with him, and Sharon resumed one of her favorite father-daughter activities. "When I was a little girl in the old house on Austin Road, sometimes he would be in bed, and he would lay on his stomach and watch nature shows," she says.

He always loved nature shows. I would sit on his back and get a comb and a brush. He had a little bald spot. I would just play in his hair, and rub the oil on his bald spot. I would take the comb and run it through his beard, and I would touch his face. And I would kiss his face. He would just smile. He would eat it up. So I remember after the accident, sometimes if I were in the room with him, I would scratch his beard and kiss him and touch his head. Just things like that. And he would smile. He liked it.

Tracy delved into researching spinal cord injuries, looking for a miracle. Soon, the Miami Project to Cure Paralysis contacted us. Ray Chambers—former owner of the New Jersey Nets, founder of the philanthropic Amelior Foundation, and board member of the Miami Project—sent his own private jet to pick us up and fly us to South Florida. We stayed two days in Miami, where Dad received some more hard news—the longest living quadriplegic on record survived ten years. In the end, Dad would live just over nine.

In a bizarre way, some issues improved after the accident. Because he couldn't move, he couldn't retreat from the world anymore. He couldn't stay in his room, lost in a haze of drugs. He became Dad again. Tracy says,

At this point, there was no more locking yourself up in a room for months. There was no more didn't answer phones. All that changed. Now he answered the phone, he did talk to you. He couldn't hide in the room and lock up. So, the relationship as far as just sitting there and talking with him got better, because you were actually able to sit down, and he couldn't move. I spent a lot of time talking with him. He would always talk when he was feeling pain. That's one of the things that he would voluntarily always talk about: "I just wish this pain would go away." And he would describe what it was. He said it felt like worms was eating his flesh.

Some things about Dad didn't change at all. "He got mad from that bed, too," Tracy says. "He didn't play around, even though he was bound in that bed, can't move. You'd hear that voice that you've heard since you were a little kid. So, it commands you, it draws you in. The same person is still there."

Though he struggled to maintain his spirit, my father's life became an endless combination of medications and physical hardships. At one point he had some fifteen prescriptions for various ailments. "I think overall I'm dealing with it pretty good," he said to an inquiring interviewer, "but you can't help but wake up every once in a while with a tear in your eye." To another, he expressed cautious hope:

> Some good doctor somewhere may have come up with that magical
> way of bringing back to life what is paralyzed. Until that happens,
> I fear I will probably be this way until my death. The character,
> they say, is in the head. It's not what's below my neck, it's what's
> above. So I hope to stay in good care and carry on. I have no pity on
> myself, nor do I look for it. You can understand sometimes when
> I wake with tears; sometimes you just feel like you're bound in a
> mummy wrapping, and you just can't get out.

The next few years were a battle against atrophy—both of his spirit and body. Sometimes his sense of humor shined through. "I'm a fifty-four-year-old quadriplegic, and there's not too much demand for that these days," he said wryly. But no amount of humor could mask the intense physical and spiritual pain he confronted all day, every day.

———

The outside world gave him few reasons for hope. Race relations in America seemed worse than at any point since King's death. Reagan's successor, George H. W. Bush, presided over a deeply conservative country and a new generation that had little sympathy for civil rights. A study concluded nearly half of African American children lived in poverty, and a national poll showed only 15 percent of white men (and 16 percent of white women) felt the government was obligated to do anything about it. In 1991, Los Angeles police beat Rodney King, an African American man, within inches of his life. Even though there was gruesome video evidence of the crime, the following year the jury acquitted all officers involved.

The resulting L.A. riots painted a heartbreaking, frustrating picture of how little had changed since a similar police incident had set off the Watts riots almost thirty years before. This time, after six days of looting, shooting, smashing, and burning, the damage totaled more than one billion dollars, with more than fifty deaths, two thousand injuries, and seventeen thousand arrests.

Meanwhile, in early 1993, three white men in Valrico, Florida, doused an African American man with gasoline and set him on fire. Around the same time, another African American man moved to Vidor, Texas, after a federal court ordered the town desegregated, which meant almost four decades after the movement began, pockets of complete segregation still existed within America.

Dad was keenly aware of these events. He couldn't avoid them as he sat stuck in front of the TV all day and night. He didn't want to avoid them, either—one of his favorite programs was the nightly national news. It frustrated him that he couldn't counter these issues with music anymore, but that didn't mean his music career was over. In 1991, the Rock and Roll Hall of Fame inducted the Impressions, and late the next year an all-star cast of musicians recorded a tribute album featuring selections from Dad's entire body of work. Around the same time, the City of Chicago renamed Hudson Avenue "Honorary Curtis Mayfield Avenue," and even today, the street sign stands outside the Cabrini row house where he once lived. These events flattered and revitalized him. Then, he learned the Grammys would honor him with a Legend Award. It felt good after the *Super Fly* snub twenty years before. At the Grammy ceremony, Jerry, Fred, and Sam wheeled him onstage where he gave a short speech. They ended with a chorus of "Amen." It was the last time my father sang in front of an audience.

————

As he struggled to face each day, I stayed busy working on remasters and licensing the Curtom back catalog. The added attention after the accident pushed my father's music to a peak it hadn't seen in almost two decades. This led to a legion of samples in hip-hop and R&B songs, as well as TV and film licenses.

It also had unintended consequences for our relationship. I saw his insecurities surface again—sometimes it seemed he felt jealous of me because I did all the things he no longer could. After I bought the house on Austin Road in Atlanta from him, I formed my own independent label—Conquest—of which Dad owned a share. At the same time, outsiders intent on regaining control of my father's affairs began undermining our relationship, saying that I focused on too many other things and not solely on his business. My father and I discussed being wary of anyone who would try to undermine the relationship between a father and son, and for the time being he continued to support me. As outsiders took their shots, there also appeared to be a growing perception with some in the family that I was somehow Dad's favorite, the one getting special considerations others didn't get. The truth was, nobody else in the family was prepared to run Curtom, and most of the money I made came from the producers and artists I managed at Conquest, not from my father or Curtom.

Regardless, the misperception persisted. Then, for reasons obvious to me, Marv began driving a wedge. Because Dad couldn't hold a phone, he conducted all his calls on speakerphone, which meant I overheard many one-sided conversations where Marv tried to make me look inept and self-interested. If I scored a deal to place one of Dad's songs in a film, Marv felt he could've wheedled more money out of it. If I licensed a song to a commercial, Marv thought I didn't drive a hard enough bargain.

I tried to explain that my quotes were the same as Warner Brothers', who still had a stake in the publishing. For instance, if a company wanted to license a song for an ad campaign, they'd approach both Warner Brothers and Curtom to see how much it would cost. If Warner quoted $30,000 for the track on the publishing side, I would charge the same on the master side. This was an industry custom. I also used most-favored-nation clauses to ensure market rates, and I relied on many leading industry professionals who allowed me to use them as a resource, knowing the gravity of what I was up against.

Regardless, after several years of hearing what I was doing wrong—or wasn't doing right—my father began to believe the talk. I had several heated conversations with Marv, but by early 1995, I felt everyone aligning against me and grew tired of the constant stress. While working on an employment contract, my father promised me a piece of Curtom. After some last-minute changes, the contract became so stacked against me, I refused to sign it. I decided to focus on my label and told Dad I wanted to resign. "No, don't do it," he said. "I still need you." Despite my reservations, I stayed on. For the first time in years, he had plans.

———

After years of adjusting to life as a quadriplegic, Dad set his mind on making a new album. "I always said I would not be singing till my sixties or seventies, not unless I really wanted to," he told the press. "Now I feel like I want to." As he began figuring out how to record without the use of his body, I continued licensing his music.

Nike had a series of barbershop commercials featuring legendary athletes like George Gervin, and they wanted legendary music to accompany it. When the press picked up the story about my father's new album-in-the-making, Nike asked him to do an original track for the commercial, rather than licensing an old one. I felt excited because I put the deal together—$60,000 for one commercial that would run for a couple of weeks. I brought it to my father, who agreed to cut a new song for Nike.

He still didn't feel comfortable singing, and his first few dry runs didn't go well. He had little control over his diaphragm, and when he tried to sing, his body tensed up. Instead of the famous, smooth falsetto, strange sounds came out of his mouth. Disappointed, he decided to read the lyrics instead of singing them. I explained that the ad agency wanted him to sing, but he refused. We got into a nasty fight about it, and in the end, he won. He read his lyrics over the music, and Nike rejected it. I tried to salvage the situation, wanting to protect my father even though I didn't agree with what he had done. In the end, Nike used the track and hired a sound-alike to sing it.

We still got paid, but after that, our relationship quickly deteriorated. As Dad worked on his new album, I spent more time on my own
projects. The chatter grew louder—I wasn't paying enough attention to
him; I just used him to further my own career; other people could do a
better job. In early 1996, I got a letter from Marv telling me I was fired.
My father hadn't said a word to me about it, and the wedge I felt others trying to force between us since his accident finally drove us apart.
We exchanged heated words. I told him off and cut all communication.
Throughout my entire life, no matter what Dad did or who was mad at
him for it, I knew I wanted to keep a relationship with him. Now, for the
first time, I wanted no part of him.

I got a job on Wall Street and moved to New York as he finished making
New World Order. To make the album, he worked with other musicians
and producers who sent tracks and sat at his bedside discussing what he
wanted to add to their ideas. The first song he worked on this way was
"Back to Living Again," written with gospel singer Rosemary Woods.
"It's not about dying," Dad said. "It's about living again . . . I always need
a good challenge to push me or dare me."

Here was something more than a good challenge, though. For one
thing, he couldn't use a tape recorder to save his ideas, making the creative
process exasperating. "I have ideas," he said, "but if you can't jot them
down or get them to music they fade like dreams." He also missed his
guitar dearly. "For expression and harmony, my guitar was like another
brother to me," he said. "I mourn my guitar to this day. I used to sleep
with my guitar. I'd write five songs a night—a day. When I couldn't find
answers, I would write songs. When I was heartbroken, I would write
songs. It was my own way of teaching myself."

His problems were just beginning, though. He had difficulty speaking loudly as a result of the paralysis, and singing was nearly impossible.
He found a way around this too, singing while lying down at a slant
or sometimes flat on his back, using gravity to help his diaphragm and
lungs work. He could only sing a few lines at a time, which the producers
spliced together to form a complete take.

Dad didn't write any of the songs on the album by himself—a first in his entire career. Rather, he relied on producers. He contributed lyrics, verses, hooks, and other snippets, but he needed them to form the ideas into songs.

A production team called Organized Noize came to assist. The trio of Sleepy Brown, Rico Wade, and Ray Murray was famous for working with Atlanta hip-hop superstars OutKast and had just produced "Waterfalls," a number-one hit for TLC. They helped produce some of the best music my father had made in more than a decade. For a time, they also leased the Curtom Atlanta studio in the house on Austin Road before building their own facility. "Curtis worked so long and hard on that project," Brown said. "Sometimes he was in obvious pain, but he just worked through it. He was always asking us to criticize the work, so we could make it better."

Roger Troutman of the 1980s funk band Zapp also helped. Troutman brought a recording console and hard drive to the house, ran some speakers into my father's room, and put a microphone in front of him. Dad cut two tracks from bed, including a remake of his classic, "We People Who Are Darker Than Blue."

The loss of both voice and guitar—the two things that *defined* Curtis Mayfield—left him frustrated and depressed. "[I can't sing] in the manner as you once knew me," he said. "I'm strongest lying down. I don't have a diaphragm anymore, so when I sit up I lose my voice. I have no strength, no volume, no falsetto range, and I tire very fast. I'm sorry to say that my style of playing is probably gone forever—the tuning—I can't play it and there's no one to teach it." But he felt proud of the album. "It took all of my know how," he said, "and we got it done."

Then, Lucky died. Dad had known Lucky since he toddled around in diapers. After the Impressions lost their road band in 1968, Lucky became a fixture in Dad's life—as a musical director, bass player, creative companion, and friend. He died of a blood clot to his lungs, a sudden and unexpected end.

Despite that hard blow, when *New World Order* came out on October 1, 1996, it strengthened my father. He proved to himself that he could still create and take care of his family—which by this point officially included Altheida, whom he finally married after his accident. "My particular thing is how, within my limits, to still find ways to earn a decent living, just prove to myself that I'm doing the best that I can do," he said.

> How many fifty-four-year-old quadriplegics are putting albums out? You just have to deal with what you got and try to sustain yourself as best you can and look to the things that you can do, so that's how I'm looking at things. I'm devoting what time I have to my children. I'm trying to get the rest of them out of here to college. I've got a very strong woman. You never know who's going to take that stand and say, "Hey, I'll do it." Nobody wants to do it, but she's been around all these years.

Like most albums during the last twenty years of his career, *New World Order* is uneven—and like most of the work during that period, it contains flashes of brilliance. The title track and superb cuts like "Ms. Martha" and "Back to Living Again" show just how sharp my father's creative mind was, even if his body no longer cooperated in the songwriting process. He also remade one of the most underrated songs from the Impressions' catalog, "The Girl I Find," and he cut a first-rate ballad with "No One Knows About a Good Thing (You Don't Have to Cry)." The album's crowning moment is "Here but I'm Gone," a haunting, hypnotic song that is as good musically, lyrically, and melodically as anything he'd ever done.

New World Order put him in the context of mid-'90s R&B and hip-hop, which suited him better than any style since pre-disco days. Dad said,

> Fusing elements of hip-hop on this CD was not so much a concession to the times, as much as it was a connection to the times. We all have to grow. You have to stay true to yourself while recognizing and acknowledging what's going on now. Fortunately we had a lot of the young people who always admired my work so they could put music together that was of the Nineties and all I needed to do was just lay my signature down. They're all great producers and

have great ideas but they were all very kind and always left the parts for Curtis.

The album went to number twenty-four R&B, his best showing in nearly twenty years. It brought a rare moment of happiness to a man who hadn't experienced many in recent memory, and the renewed focus made him feel vital again. Interview requests came pouring in, as did two Grammy nominations. The Soul Train Music Awards honored him with the Heritage Award. He was back in the game.

———

A few months before the Soul Train awards, I flew to Atlanta for a weekend visit. I hadn't spoken with Dad since our falling out six months prior, but I had run into someone who knew him and heard he wanted to see me. I went to his house, we both apologized, and our relationship resumed. Perhaps he knew he didn't have long to live.

For the first time, he spoke to the press of total retirement. "I've been doing this since I was seven, professionally since I was fifteen," he said. "I turned sixteen in the Apollo Theater. I'm a fighter, but it's best at this point to go on and retire and be appreciated for whatever you have done."

He spent his last years in swift decline. In February 1998, doctors amputated his right leg below the knee due to a complication of diabetes. By many accounts, a diabetic amputee has a worse five-year prognosis than anyone, except those with the most severe forms of cancer. They die piece by piece, suffering. After the amputation, he sank into misery, avoiding interviews.

Early in 1999, the Rock and Roll Hall of Fame came calling again, this time to induct Curtis as a solo artist. His spirits lifted one last time, and he began making plans to attend the ceremony. Before he could leave, diabetes struck again. He went to the hospital, where doctors discussed taking his other leg. He refused.

Marv went with Altheida to accept the award. He gave a moving speech, despite the squabbles of previous years—and perhaps as a last olive branch before the nasty fights that erupted after my father's death.

"The honor that you bestowed upon [Curtis] tonight moved him a great deal," Marv said.

> He wanted me to say the following things. First of all, he wants
> to thank the recording industry . . . and his fans, who have made
> it all possible. The artists, through the years, who have recorded
> his music, that have kept his music alive the last nine years, with
> the evolution of hip-hop and rap, all of you that have sampled his
> music, from Coolio to Dr. Dre, Tupac, Puff Daddy, Lauryn Hill,
> who just mixed and did a duet with Mr. Mayfield—all of you have
> made his life worthwhile. I said to Curtis, "There's nothing I can
> say with the circumstances [that] befell you." He says, "Don't feel
> sorry for me; it could've happened to anybody. I was just there."
> . . . All I can say to all of you in the Rock and Roll Hall of Fame:
> thank you—thank you for honoring my friend while his eyes are
> still open.

After the ceremony, Dad faded quickly, one foot on Earth, one in the hereafter. Just before Christmas, he called Sharon and said, "I need you to come to Atlanta right away." She sensed something in his voice, something urgent and grave.

Sharon says:

> I don't know anything about death, but I sensed that he knew he
> was leaving. He asked me to come, and that always meant a lot to
> me. He was in bad shape when I saw him. He wasn't well. I remem-
> ber talking to him the day before we left, and it was gibberish.
> I guess when his blood sugar got really low, his communication
> was unintelligible. It was just sounds, and whenever that happened,
> it would frighten me so much. It would make me cry because I
> wouldn't know what to do or what to say. His eyes would be pierc-
> ing me, and he would just be talking and making these sounds and
> noises, and I don't know if he was aware of it. When we left, on the
> drive back to Chicago, I said, "I think that's going to be it."

Three days before Christmas, Dad slipped into a coma. An ambulance took him to North Fulton Regional Hospital in Roswell, Georgia, where he hung on for a few days. The day after Christmas, as dawn crept over the dew, his spirit finally gave out. I had recently relocated back to Chicago and was alone at my mother's house that day. It was cold and overcast, the Hawk threatening outside. The radio murmured quietly in the background, and I heard my father's name cut through. I began listening closely as a somber DJ on V103 announced that Curtis Mayfield, iconic Chicago musician, had just died. That's how I found out. No one in the family had called me yet; I heard it on the radio.

At that moment, I didn't know what to think or how to feel. I knew he had been deteriorating rapidly. The last time I saw him he looked like he was tired of fighting and ready to leave. A part of me felt relief that he was gone and didn't have to suffer any longer. Another part of me felt alone, with no father to be there for me if I really needed something. As the news settled on me, I began thinking of my dad and what he was for me, good and bad, throughout life. I was thankful for all he had done for me and for what he represented in my life. It was truly sad to see him cut down when he was still relatively young with so much more life to live. I felt sad that he would never see his future grandchildren and continue to shape and share life experiences with his own kids as we continued to grow as adults.

I mourned privately, quietly, knowing that his transition necessitated a transition of my own. I also knew controversy and family fights would soon take center stage over the sizable estate Dad left, and unfortunately, that's exactly what happened. Dad was the rock, the glue that kept us all more or less together. Now he was gone.

My dad once said, "As I sum it up, I just want folks to say he didn't do bad with his life in inspiring others." Of course, he did so much more. In fifty-seven short years, he changed the course of music history while influencing one of the greatest movements for human freedom ever mounted. He triumphed over a system created to keep people with his skin color

in subservience and constant poverty. He catapulted himself to the top
of his profession with a mixture of brilliance and dogged determination.
He became one of the first African American men in America to own his
own record label, and one of the first in music history to retain almost all
his publishing rights. He invented his own style of guitar—often copied
but never duplicated—and his songs defined the Chicago Sound. Above
all, he never strayed far from his commitment to sing for his people,
speak truth to power, and give voice to those who had none.

He was similarly prolific in his personal life. He loved his children
and his family deeply, and despite his imperfections, he never stopped
working to create a better life for us all. He tried to live up to the best
sentiments contained in his music, and when he failed, he tried again.
He protected and provided for his mother, his sisters, his brother, his
wives, his girlfriends, his children, and his friends. Even in the darkest
moments, we always knew where he was, and who he was, and how
much he loved us. His father never gave him that gift. He made sure he
gave it to us.

———————

At the funeral, Jerry, Sam, and Fred carried Dad's casket. They sent him
off with a somber performance of "Amen." The song connected Curtis to his beginning. It spoke of the spirit—the same spirit he met as
a child in Annie Bell's church . . . *Amen, amen, amen, amen, amen . . .*
the same spirit that suffused songs like "Keep On Pushing" and "People Get Ready" . . . *See the little baby wrapped in a manger on Christmas
morning . . .* the same spirit that infused the movement with hope and
courage . . . *Singing in a temple, talking with the elders, tomorrow there's
wisdom . . .* the same spirit that compelled him to warn about Hell below
and the Pusherman . . . *Down at the Jordan, John was baptizing and sav-
ing all sinners . . .* the same spirit that gave him strength to endure tragedy and calamity at the end of his life . . . *See him at the seaside, talking
with the fishermen, and made them disciples . . .* the same spirit that new
generations still find in his music . . . *Amen, amen, amen, amen, amen.*

The same spirit that makes him impossible to forget.

Lasting Impressions

"I still feel as if I'm here, but I'm gone."
—"Here but I'm Gone"

***H**is music still lives.* Like the movement that inspired him—and that he inspired—it is woven into the fabric of today even if it seems the stuff of yesterday. Hip-hop and R&B stars still sample him, eager to connect to his branch on music's evolutionary tree. That branch gets stronger with time, putting forth countless flowers—from Erykah Badu to Kanye West, Jay Z, Eminem, Ludacris, Rick Ross, Drake, and dozens more.

Yet, just like the movement, his social mission remains incomplete. The problems he sang about persist. Late in 1992, PBS reconvened the roundtable discussion they'd televised nearly thirty years before featuring James Farmer, Wyatt Tee Walker, Malcolm X, and Alan Morrison. Of the four, only Farmer and Walker still survived. Their views on the movement had lost the rush of optimism shown in 1963. "There's the illusion that progress has been made," Walker said in 1992, "but the reality is that what progress has been made has been more cosmetic than it has been consequential." Farmer concurred: "Racism is here, and now we've got to exert the same kind of energy and diligence in fighting against racism as we did in fighting against Jim Crow."

Since then, as my father once said, everything has changed and nothing has changed. If he were alive today, he would surely be knocked out by the direction music has taken. Hip-hop dominates the world, and many black artists have continued in his footsteps of owning their own labels. He would have rejoiced at achieving the once-impossible dream of electing an African American president. Indeed, though he was never a political man, he once hosted a fundraiser at Curtom in Atlanta for Jesse Jackson's 1988 presidential bid, hoping to see that dream come true in his lifetime.

He would also find much to feel despondent about. Poverty rates for most minorities in America remain more than double that of whites, the US Supreme Court has continued dismantling the legislative gains of the movement, and racial violence remains an ever-present danger for those who are darker than blue. From the killing of an unarmed Florida teenager in 2012 to an instance of police brutality that ignited riots in Ferguson, Missouri, in 2014, to the slayings of Eric Garner, Tamir Rice, and too many others, America's problem with race continues to rear its ugly head. A new generation must now deal with the same old issues, ask the same old questions, and fight to find new answers.

Though he isn't here, my father is still part of that fight. His music speaks as powerfully to the times we live in as it did to his own. His songs remain vital, uncompromising, and true. His message endures—a message he refused to abandon even in the darkest of times. If he were alive today, he'd urge us to keep on pushing, to never give up, to get ready for something better. He wouldn't be able to help himself.

After all, as the man himself once sang:

> *Pardon me, brother,*
> *I know we've come a long, long way*
> *But let us not be so self satisfied*
> *For tomorrow can be an even brighter day.*

Acknowledgments

I'd like to extend my most sincere thanks to my mother, Diane Mayfield, my grandmother Marion Jackson, Uncle Kenny, Aunt Judith, Aunt Carolyn, Eddie Thomas, and Jerry Butler, without whom this book would not be possible.

Big thanks to Travis Atria, for his dogged determination, thorough research, and creativity, all essential to this book.

Special thanks to Sharon Mayfield Lavigne, Tracy Mayfield, Herb Kent, John Abbey, Craig McMullen, Lee Goodness, Martin Markowitz, Lebron Scott, Marv Heiman, Michael Putland, Jim McHugh, Steven Ray, David Ritz, Thomas Flannery, David Vigliano, Adam Burns, Tyler Francischine, Ashley Belanger, Annie Niemand, the staff of Alfred Music/Warner/Chappell Music, and Yuval Taylor and the Chicago Review Press staff for their time and contributions.

Finally, I'd also like to say thank you to all my friends, my wife, and my family, who have supported and encouraged me in this endeavor.

Travis Atria would like to thank: *Kathy Atria for teaching me to write. Drew Atria for introducing me to the music of Curtis Mayfield. Kyle Donnelly, Eric Atria, and Collin Whitlock for love and support. Ashley Belanger for skills and advice. Everyone in the Mayfield family who made me feel welcome in this momentous endeavor.*

Song Credits

AMEN
Words and Music by CURTIS MAYFIELD and JOHNNY PATE

CANNOT FIND A WAY
Words and Music by CURTIS MAYFIELD

CHOICE OF COLORS
Words and Music by CURTIS MAYFIELD

DIRTY LAUNDRY
Words and Music by CURTIS MAYFIELD

FREDDIE'S DEAD (Theme from *Super Fly*)
Words and Music by CURTIS MAYFIELD

GHETTO CHILD (LITTLE CHILD RUNNIN' WILD)
Words and Music by CURTIS MAYFIELD
© 1971 (Renewed) WARNER-TAMERLANE PUBLISHING CORP.
All Rights Reserved
Used by Permission of ALFRED MUSIC

HARD TIMES
Words and Music by CURTIS MAYFIELD
© 1975 WARNER-TAMERLANE PUBLISHING CORP.
All Rights Reserved
Used by Permission of ALFRED MUSIC

HERE BUT I'M GONE
BY CURTIS MAYFIELD, IVAN MATIAS, ANDREA MARTIN
MARQUEZE ETHRIDGE, RICO WADE, PATRICK BROWN, AND
RAYMON MURRAY
© 1996 WARNER-TAMERLANE PUBLISHING CORP., MAYFIELD MUSIC
and WARNER/CHAPPELL MUSIC LTD. (PRS)
All Rights on Behalf of Itself and MAYFIELD MUSIC
Administered by WARNER-TAMERLANE PUBLISHING CORP.
All Rights on Behalf of WARNER/CHAPPELL MUSIC LTD.
Administered by WB MUSIC CORP.
All Rights Reserved
Used by Permission of ALFRED MUSIC

I PLAN TO STAY A BELIEVER
Words and Music by CURTIS MAYFIELD
© 1971 (RENEWED) WARNER-TAMERLANE PUBLISHING CORP.
All Rights Reserved
Used by Permission of ALFRED MUSIC

(DON'T WORRY) IF THERE'S A HELL BELOW, WE'RE ALL GOING TO GO
Words and Music by CURTIS MAYFIELD
© 1970 WARNER-TAMERLANE PUBLISHING CORP.
All Rights Reserved
Used by Permission of ALFRED MUSIC

MR. WELFARE MAN
Words and Music by CURTIS MAYFIELD
© 1974 (RENEWED) WARNER-TAMERLANE PUBLISHING CORP. and
TODD MAYFIELD PUBLISHING (NS)
All Rights Administered by WARNER-TAMERLANE PUBLISHING CORP.
All Rights Reserved
Used by Permission of ALFRED MUSIC

THE OTHER SIDE OF TOWN
Words and Music by CURTIS MAYFIELD
© 1970 (RENEWED) WARNER-TAMERLANE PUBLISHING CORP.
All Rights Reserved
Used by Permission of ALFRED MUSIC

PEOPLE GET READY
Words and Music by CURTIS MAYFIELD
© 1964 (Renewed) WARNER-TAMERLANE PUBLISHING CORP. (BMI)
and MIJAC MUSIC (BMI)
All Rights Reserved
Used by Permission of ALFRED MUSIC

PUSHERMAN
Words and Music by CURTIS MAYFIELD
© 1972 WARNER-TAMERLANE PUBLISHING CORP. and
TODD MAYFIELD PUBLISHING
All Rights on Behalf of Itself and TODD MAYFIELD PUBLISHING
Administered by WARNER-TAMERLANE PUBLISHING CORP.
All Rights Reserved
Used by Permission of ALFRED MUSIC

SO YOU DON'T LOVE ME
Words and Music by CURTIS MAYFIELD
© 1974 (RENEWED) WARNER-TAMERLANE PUBLISHING CORP.
All Rights Reserved
Used by Permission of ALFRED MUSIC

SUPERFLY
Words and Music by CURTIS MAYFIELD
© 1972 (Renewed) TODD MAYFIELD PUBLISHING and
WARNER-TAMERLANE PUBLISHING CORP.
All Rights Administered by WARNER-TAMERLANE PUBLISHING CORP.
All Rights Reserved
Used by Permission of ALFRED MUSIC

SWEET EXORCIST
Words and Music by CURTIS MAYFIELD
© 1974 (RENEWED) WARNER-TAMERLANE PUBLISHING CORP.
and TODD MAYFIELD PUBLISHING
All Rights Administered by WARNER-TAMERLANE PUBLISHING CORP.
All Rights Reserved
Used by Permission of ALFRED MUSIC

THIS IS MY COUNTRY
Words and Music by CURTIS MAYFIELD
© 1968 (Renewed) WARNER-TAMERLANE PUBLISHING CORP.
All Rights Reserved
Used by Permission of ALFRED MUSIC

TO BE INVISIBLE
Words and Music by CURTIS MAYFIELD and RICHARD TUFANO
© 1974 (RENEWED) WARNER-TAMERLANE PUBLISHING CORP. and
TODD MAYFIELD PUBLISHING
All Rights Administered by WARNER-TAMERLANE PUBLISHING CORP.
All Rights Reserved
Used by Permission of ALFRED MUSIC

WE PEOPLE WHO ARE DARKER THAN BLUE
Words and Music by CURTIS MAYFIELD
© 1970 (RENEWED) WARNER-TAMERLANE PUBLISHING CORP.
All Rights Reserved
Used by Permission of ALFRED MUSIC

Notes

1. The Reverend A. B. Mayfield

were worth almost $800: Hall, "Mean Price by Gender."

Louisiana citizens lynched: "Lynching by State," Charles Chesnutt Digital Archive.

"Up and down Indiana and Wabash and Prairie": Wilkerson, *Warmth of Other Suns*, 268–269.

"There was nothing to block or buffer": Rawls, "Dead End Street."

2. My Mama Borned Me in a Ghetto

"Until the 1943 uprising in Detroit": Wilkerson, *Warmth of Other Suns*, 131.

"Mom had this great big pot": Carolyn Mayfield, interview by Atria and Mayfield.

"Mama was kind of on the timid side": Ibid.

"She was always around": Ibid.

"I guess pimps are a luxury": Page, "Does Curtis Mayfield Sincerely Want to Be Rich?"

"Many Christmases, we didn't have anything": Carolyn Mayfield, interview by Atria and Mayfield.

"If anything went on, we looked to him": Ibid.

"De times is mighty stirrin'": Dunbar, "How Lucy Backslid."

"It is a peculiar sensation": DuBois, *Souls of Black Folk*, 3–4.

"When other children came by to play": Monroe Anderson, "From Superfly to Super Star."

"He used to stand on the tree stump": "Darker Than Blue," *Omnibus*.

"She was a reasonable mother": Ibid.

"I never will forget": Carolyn Mayfield, interview by Atria and Mayfield.

"Aside from the gospel music": Valentine, "Curtis Mayfield in the Talk-In."

"a whiskey-drinking Democratic precinct captain": Werner, *Higher Ground*, 36.

3. Traveling Souls

"It wasn't a pleasant home": Carolyn Mayfield, interview by Atria and Mayfield.

"My father had a doctor": Butler, interview by Atria and Mayfield.

"We sang traditional gospel songs": Ibid.

"I never really had to acquire an interest": Werner, *Higher Ground*, 35.

"*[Eddie Patterson] brought a guitar with him*": Light, "Lasting Impression."
"*The church had plenty of little affairs*": Werner, "Curtis Mayfield."
"*A group of white boys*": Butler with Smith, *Only the Strong Survive*, 22.
"*They seemed to know only one phrase*": Ibid.
"*It was a twelve-string*": "Soul of an R&B Genius," *Guitar Player*.
"*When I first started playing guitar*": Valentine, "Curtis Mayfield in the Talk-In."
"*It was my other self*": Gonzales, "Curtis Mayfield."
"*My education didn't give me any background*": Alexander, "The Impressions."
"*When we were little she told us*": Carolyn Mayfield, interview by Atria and Mayfield.
"*Brown v. Board was what the grown-ups talked about*": Butler, interview by Atria and Mayfield.
"*We felt we were up in Pill Hill*": Carolyn Mayfield, interview by Atria and Mayfield, 2013.
"*It was really high-class living*": Page, "Does Curtis Mayfield Sincerely Want to Be Rich?"
"*We used to harmonize and sing Frankie Lymon*": Aletti, "Jerry Butler."
"*We were all trying to sing*": Werner, *Higher Ground*, 68.
crowds of eager young kids lined up: Ibid., 69.
"*We thought that this would all be over*": Garrow, *Bearing the Cross*, 26.
"*We'd tell him to get away from us*": Werner, *Higher Ground*, 68.
"*Once they'd gone to bed, I'd slip out*": Bowman, booklet for *Movin' On Up*.
"*Arthur was stockily built*": Butler with Smith, *Only the Strong Survive*, 38.
"*If you join us, man, with the way you play*": Ibid.
"*We woodshedded for a good year*": Werner, *Higher Ground*, 69.
"*The Medallionaires thought they were hot stuff*": Thomas, interview by Atria and Mayfield.
"*Their harmony was mind blowing*": Ibid.
"*We couldn't get through a song*": Ibid.
"*I can't see it on a marquee*": Ibid.
"*What's the new name then?*": Goins, "Soulful Conversation."

4. The Original Impressions
"*I had never heard of [Eddie Howard]*": Butler with Smith, *Only the Strong Survive*, 40.
"*She talked very fast*": Ibid.
"*Vee-Jay had an employee lounge*": Davis, *Man Behind the Music*, 44.
"*We thought they were ridiculous*": Butler with Smith, *Only the Strong Survive*, 40.
"*Gee, I really want to record you guys*": Ibid., 42.

"*That's it! That's it!*": Werner, *Higher Ground*, 74.

"*Here comes the rip off*": Butler with Smith, *Only the Strong Survive*, 43.

"*We were very happy and very grateful*": Ibid.

"*I ain't gonna lie*": Ibid., 44.

"*a huge room with the control room way up in the air*": Callahan, "Vee Jay Album Discography."

"*Four or five takes later*": Butler with Smith, *Only the Strong Survive*, 44.

"*When we heard that song coming across*": Butler, interview by Atria and Mayfield.

"*I knew that Curtis, Sam, Arthur and Richard didn't like it*": Butler with Smith, *Only the Strong Survive*, 50.

"*By the time he got through talking*": Ibid.

"*The rift over the phrase*": Ibid.

"*You can understand all these fellows*": Werner, *Higher Ground*, 76.

the market featured "*cigar-chomping hawkers*": Butler with Smith, *Only the Strong Survive*, 53.

"*We were treated like a bunch of kids*": Ibid., 52.

"*Don't worry*": Ibid.

"*dressed like some fairytale prince*": Ibid., 53.

Larry started his rap: "*Ladies and gentlemen*": Ibid.

"*I got the same feeling that night*": Ibid., 54.

"*didn't even buy us a hamburger*": Ibid.

"*Curtis was so broke in those days*": Gonzales, "Gangster Boogie."

"*Mrs. Washington was a very hip old lady*": Butler with Smith, *Only the Strong Survive*, 66.

"*She sure did bless the hell out of us*": Ibid.

"*Wait a minute!*": Ibid., 56.

"*We used to play tricks on one another*": Ibid., 174.

"*I felt like a stranger*": Ibid., 66.

"*Jocko was number one*": Ibid., 58.

"*Since we were going to New York*": Butler, interview by Atria and Mayfield.

"*Y'all take that white shit someplace*": Butler with Smith, *Only the Strong Survive*, 59.

"*I'll tell you what to do*": Ibid.

"*Plenty of junkies and rats*": Ibid.

"*Every junkie and booster in Harlem*": Ibid., 61.

"*We had sold only so many records*": Ibid., 63.

"*Turn on American Bandstand*": Ibid., 110.

"*Nixon has a genius for convincing one*": Garrow, *Bearing the Cross*, 119.

"*This is the creative moment*": Ibid., 124.

"*We were making more money*": Butler with Smith, *Only the Strong Survive*, 68.

"We never had decent-looking furniture": Carolyn Mayfield, interview by Atria and Mayfield.

"All of a sudden, the smells we used to ignore": Butler with Smith, *Only the Strong Survive*, 68.

"Helen used to come over the house": Carolyn Mayfield, interview by Atria and Mayfield.

"We let Richard go ahead": Thomas, interview by Atria and Mayfield.

"Young girls, seeing the spectacle": Butler with Smith, *Only the Strong Survive*, 67.

"They all interviewed us": Ibid., 68.

"Okay, baby," Abner said: Ibid., 70

"Arthur pitched a bitch": Ibid., 71.

"[Mom] bought this great big freezer": Carolyn Mayfield, interview by Atria and Mayfield.

"I found out later": Thomas, interview by Atria and Mayfield.

"Hey, this a great record": Lewis, "The Impressions."

"We scuffled some": Werner, *Higher Ground*, 79.

For a few months, they scraped by: Ibid.

"There were so many fights": Gonzales, "Gangster Boogie."

"He was always coming round and looking through my bag": Williams, "Everything Was a Song."

"We were still living in Cabrini-Green": Kenny Mayfield, interview by Atria and Mayfield.

"I beat her up, and the next thing I heard": Carolyn Mayfield, interview by Atria and Mayfield.

"I don't think that relationship": Thomas, interview by Atria and Mayfield.

"Man, I don't know anybody's songs": Butler, interview by Atria and Mayfield.

"When Jerry called, I had nothing": Werner, *Higher Ground*, 81.

"I was his chauffer—or flunky": Thomas, interview by Atria and Mayfield.

"We were living together": Ibid.

"I was making history": Ibid.

"I can assure you that we did it very poorly": Butler, interview by Atria and Mayfield.

"He always had an instrument": Ibid.

He introduced it to Eddie: Thomas, interview by Atria and Mayfield.

"I was there with my tin cup": Ibid.

"I used to take him out to dinner": Ibid.

"This is me, man": Ibid.

"Eddie was such a hustler": Werner, *Higher Ground*, 83.

Harris said, "No, I can't see this group": Thomas, interview by Atria and Mayfield.

"He was black, and I'm black": Ibid.

"Being with Jerry Butler, I know a lot of DJs": Werner, *Higher Ground*, 83.

"Man, we're going to have to roll our sleeves up": Thomas, interview by Atria and Mayfield.

"I could see it coming, but I didn't know": Butler with Smith, *Only the Strong Survive*, 92.

"Everybody who was part of the Impressions": Ibid.

5. Keep On Pushing

"Brill was a building where songwriters would go up": Dwyer, "In a World of Songwriting."

"If a songwriter was doing a demo session": Ibid.

"I believed very early in life": Light, "Lasting Impression."

"Publishers were hitting the lottery": Gonzales, "Gangster Boogie."

"My friends were being intimidated": Butler with Smith, *Only the Strong Survive*, 108.

"Once they saw that, they released it": Thomas, interview by Atria and Mayfield.

"I was scared to death": Lewis, "The Impressions."

"Girls were there by the fortress": The History Makers.

"Man, you think the people are gonna like me?": Farberman, "Q&A: The Impressions' Fred Cash."

"The country was our neighborhood": Werner, *Higher Ground*, 85.

"We went downtown to pay the ticket": Ibid.

"Oh Lord, it was rough": Atria, "The Message."

"A lot of auditoriums that we played": Ibid.

"You had your room": Ibid.

"When the fellows would go out to have fun": Werner, *Higher Ground*, 86.

"During those times of my life": Werner, "Curtis Mayfield."

"Our style was so different": Pruter, *Chicago Soul*, 139.

"They were wanting to do stuff like Little Richard": Lewis, "The Impressions."

"Sam, Curtis, and I had become really tight": Bowman, booklet for *Movin' On Up*.

"I wanted Curtis more for his guitar": Page, "Does Curtis Mayfield Sincerely Want to Be Rich?"

"Because I play with my fingers": "Soul of an R&B Genius," *Guitar Player*.

"My voicings are different": Ibid.

"I chose to use Johnny in particular": Pruter, *Chicago Soul*, 74.

"I used to go out to Curtis' house": Ibid., 73.

In the furtive early days of their relationship: Diane Mayfield, interview by Atria and Mayfield, 2013.

"They were taking me out of my range": Peck, Galloway, and Gulotta, *Movin' On Up*.

"We were trying to establish something": Bowman, booklet for *Movin' On Up*.

"In gospel, you knew how to sing lead": Werner, *Higher Ground*, 120–122.

Dad "got to talking and running off at the mouth": Werner, "Curtis Mayfield."

"I drove most of the time": Atria, "The Message."

"He knew that I liked coffee": Davis, *Man Behind the Music*, 55.

"Which one do you like?": Ibid., 56.

"A lot of [Curtis's] entertainment friends": Kenny Mayfield, interview by Atria and Mayfield.

"That was my first introduction to arranging": Werner, *Higher Ground*, 120.

"My group's the Impressions": Peck, Galloway, and Gulotta, *Movin' On Up*.

"He started putting brass": Ibid.

"I never tried to cover what Curtis was doing": Ibid.

"We didn't record anything else": Carmichael, "Curtis Mayfield."

"When we recorded that song, I discovered": Peck, Galloway, and Gulotta, *Movin' On Up*.

"That song bought Sam's home": Atria, "The Message."

"The hatred was strong, strong": Thomas, interview by Atria and Mayfield.

"The Negro is shedding himself of his fear": Garrow, *Bearing the Cross*, 273.

"I started out reading the speech": Ibid., 283.

"You know, this dream of King's": Marable, *Malcolm X*, 257.

"We aren't going to stop": "Race Relations in Crisis," *The Open Mind*.

"If the NAACP can tell me": Malcolm X, interview at UC Berkeley.

"[Curtis] would never share": Davis, *Man Behind the Music*, 58.

"If you made a dollar": Gonzales, "Gangster Boogie."

"The record company called and said": Carmichael, "Curtis Mayfield."

"We were fascinated by": Steffens, "Soul Survivor."

"Hey man, come and listen to this": Lewis, "The Impressions."

"I wrote something that maybe can help": Bowman, booklet for *Movin' On Up*.

"I'm living": Courter, "R&B Trio, with Two Chattanooga Members."

"All I needed to do was change": Werner, *Higher Ground*, 118–119.

"It wasn't like they were starstruck": Tracy Mayfield, interview by Atria and Mayfield, 2014.

"Man, you look like Curtis Mayfield": Kenny Mayfield, interview by Atria and Mayfield.

"On the end of 'I've Been Trying'": Peck, Galloway, and Gulotta, *Movin' On Up*.

"Dear Mother": Author's collection.

"On his part, I didn't feel any iota": Tracy Mayfield, interview by Atria and Mayfield, 2014.

"He had poor table manners": Diane Mayfield, interview by Atria and Mayfield, 2014.

"The building basically was white people": Ibid.

"They called us names": Ibid.

6. People Get Ready

"The fragile unity that had made possible": Marable, *Malcolm X*, 297.

In what he called "a deep mood": Werner, *Higher Ground*, 125.

"Curtis would usually bring me the material": Peck, Galloway, and Gulotta, *Movin' On Up.*

"The Temptations went out and did": Carmichael, "Curtis Mayfield."

My father said, "Well, we got 'People Get Ready'": Bowman, booklet for *Movin' On Up.*

"The song touched me quite a bit": Peck, Galloway, and Gulotta, *Movin' On Up.*

"Lyrically you could tell": Bowman, booklet for *Movin' On Up.*

"There's no room for the hopeless sinner": Williams, "Everything Was a Song."

"I was observing things": Werner, "Curtis Mayfield."

"'People Get Ready' was one that we used": Peck, Galloway, and Gulotta, *Movin' On Up.*

Some churches changed the final couplet: Bowman, booklet for *Movin' On Up.*

"It was so different": Ibid.

"I'm not totally about being just": Salewicz, "Keep On Pushing."

"When we came out, it was like": Bowman, booklet for *Movin' On Up.*

"We did a lot of shows with James Brown": Peck, Galloway, and Gulotta, *Movin' On Up.*

"We were doing a show with him at the Regal": Ibid.

"It is wrong—deadly wrong": Garrow, *Bearing the Cross*, 408.

Forman wasn't alone in advocating: Ibid., 410.

"I never will forget, I was looking": Atria, "The Message."

"They thought they had the cream": Thomas, interview by Atria and Mayfield.

"We would go to friends' houses": Diane Mayfield, interview by Atria and Mayfield, 2013.

"He seemed like butter": Ibid.

"He picked my friends": Ibid.

"He was a better father": Ibid.

"Because of who he was": Ibid.

She yelled, "I want to work!": Ibid.

"He was always up late writing": Ibid.

"King had this naive faith": Garrow, *Bearing the Cross*, 455.

"I have never seen": Ibid., 544.

"You ain't never seen": Werner, *Higher Ground*, 124.

"[Curtis] just kind of lost his way there": Atria, "The Message."

"This fella, you could just talk to him": Werner, "Curtis Mayfield."

"This is the twenty-seventh time": Churcher, "Stokely Carmichael."

"The only way to end": Bauerlein et al., *Civil Rights Chronicle*.

"I have seen many demonstrations": James, "Martin Luther King Jr. in Chicago."

"I don't know what the answer to that is": Garrow, *Bearing the Cross*, 497.

"We raised the hopes tremendously": Ibid., 540.

"For years I labored with": Ibid., 562.

One journalist pointedly predicted: Ibid., 568.

"I asked Hendrix who": Shadwick, *Jimi Hendrix: Musician*, 78.

"I really like Curtis Mayfield": Ibid., 84.

"There were dark days before": Garrow, *Bearing the Cross*, 569.

"They don't plan to just burn": Ibid., 570.

"I have found out that all that I have been doing": Ibid., 580.

"That song came to me in a dream": Gonzales, "Gangster Boogie."

it was *"a message to all"*: Burns, *People Never Give Up*, 44.

"I was listening to all my preachers": Werner, *Higher Ground*, 140.

"Curtis had written some real tough lyrics": Peck, Galloway, and Gulotta, *Movin' On Up*.

"They thought that we had become militant": Ibid.

"I've run into frustrating obstacles": Ibid.

"I wasn't a quitter": Werner, *Higher Ground*, 143.

"Mom would take us": Tracy Mayfield, interview by Atria and Mayfield, 2013.

7. Curtom

Abernathy rushed over to him: Garrow, *Bearing the Cross*, 624.

"That's one place that anybody could find you": Thomas, interview by Atria and Mayfield.

"How are young people supposed to feel": Witter, "Now More Than Ever."

"Now that they've taken Dr. King off": Kurlansky, *1968*, 117.

"A truck came through here": Whitaker, *Cabrini Green*, 25.

"Black people had torn it up": Ibid., 26.

"Donny could do everything": Goins, "Soulful Conversation."

"One thing you knew": Thomas, interview by Atria and Mayfield.

"With my own label": Berry, "Curtis Mayfield's 'Super Fly.'"

"On to Chicago": Swanson, *Chicago Days*, 212.

"I only look upon my writings": Werbin, "Curtis Mayfield's Biggest Score."

"The style, the clothes, the wide pants": Werner, *Higher Ground*, 142.

"It's hard work running between the studio": Burns, *People Never Give Up*, 49.

"When you get your record on the radio": Thomas, interview by Atria and Mayfield.

"Half a million start selling": Ibid.

"We've been pushed into corners": Foner, *The Black Panthers Speak*, 28.

"a movement that will smash": "Stokely Carmichael," Biography.com.

"They aren't a national organization": Alexander, "The Impressions."

"They had a thing going on back then": Kenny Mayfield, interview by Atria and Mayfield.

"A lot of Curtis's music reached way over there": Ibid.

"Here I am over [in Vietnam]": Ibid.

"I'll never forget it, I got off the boat": Ibid.

"Uncle Sam wants YOU": Bauerlein et al., *Civil Rights Chronicle*.

"U.S. Negro armymen!": Ibid.

"My conscience won't let me": "Ali: A Living Legend," *Like It Is*.

"My face during those years": Williams, "Everything Was a Song."

"There was one guy in charge": Stuart, interview by Atria.

"As green as he was": Werner, *Higher Ground*, 160.

"The road wears a man down": Alexander, "The Impressions."

"They were coming down a big double highway": Alexander, "The Impressions."

"They was messed up": Ibid.

"He had the guy at the body shop to fix it": Diane Mayfield, interview by Atria and Mayfield, 2013.

"I think they just didn't think that Sam and I": Atria, "The Message."

"Now that I have money I spend": Alexander, "The Impressions."

"That was a heavy blow": Werner, "Curtis Mayfield."

"That was one of the hardest": Atria, "The Message."

"He didn't read music": "The Impressions: Part 2," *Beldon's Blues Point*.

"When we came out in 1958, Lucky and his brother": Werner, "Curtis Mayfield."

8. Now You're Gone

"Baby, I'm not going to give you any money": Alexander, "The Impressions."

"The girls would all line up backstage": Thomas, interview by Atria and Mayfield.

"Street clothes, no suits or ties": Alexander, "The Impressions."

"We don't have a choice of colors": Ibid.

"'Choice of Colors' isn't for Whitey": Ibid.

"People didn't like it too much": Bowman, booklet for *Movin' On Up*.

At eleven o'clock the following morning: Alexander, "The Impressions."

"I can't get into anything": Ibid.

"You try to present yourselves": Ibid.

"You wouldn't be-lieve that smoke": Ibid.

"I wasn't dropping acid": Gonzales, "Gangster Boogie."

"Man, we can't stand this drummer": Fischer, interview by Atria.

"If you see me with a younger woman": Ibid.

While the Impressions rehearsed: Peck, Galloway, and Gulotta, *Movin' On Up*.

"*Sometimes we'd drive*": Fischer, interview by Atria.

"*Your services were welcome*": Ibid.

"*I shouldn't even be traveling*": Alexander, "The Impressions."

"*We'd get up at eight or nine*": Ibid.

"*I still play semi-pro baseball*": Ibid.

"*I used to write all the time*": Ibid.

"*which means responsibilities, securities*": Ibid.

"*Being an entertainer, even though it's beautiful*": Ibid.

"*When Curtis Mayfield would sing*": Peck, Galloway, and Gulotta, *Movin' On Up*.

That last one was a favorite: Fischer, interview by Atria.

"*Curtis was not hard to work for*": Ibid.

"*Everyone makin' it [is] a singer-songwriter*": Werner, *Higher Ground*, 155.

"*I suggested to him that he just focus*": Goins, "Soulful Conversation Thomas."

"*[Curtis] is writing the songs*": Alexander, "The Impressions."

9. Move On Up

"*Over there you could get the purest stuff*": Kenny Mayfield, interview by Atria and
     Mayfield.

A Time magazine poll in 1970: Foner, *The Black Panthers Speak*, xxiv.

"*Every one who gets in office promises*": Ibid., 64.

"*That was a tune that I didn't*": Carmichael, "Curtis Mayfield."

"*Of course, the Impressions were just the perfect bunch*": Peck, Galloway, and Gulotta,
     Movin' On Up.

"*Not being with the Impressions*": Galloway, liner notes for *Roots*.

"*I've been on the road for twelve*": Abbey, "Curtis Mayfield: No Longer an
     Impression."

"*Fred, I'm going to try to go*": Peck, Galloway, and Gulotta, *Movin' On Up*.

"*Leaving the Impressions was a lot like*": Burns, *People Never Give Up*, 62.

"*I felt bad for a simple reason*": Atria, "The Message."

"*You saw a good and evil*": Tracy Mayfield, interview by Atria and Mayfield, 2014.

"*The Impressions are still the Impressions*": "Impressions Lose Curtis Mayfield,"
     Rolling Stone.

Eddie recalled dozing off: The History Makers.

"*There were movements sometimes*": Werner, *Higher Ground*, 159.

"*He used to sit down with Lucky*": "The Impressions: Part 2," *Beldon's Blues Point*.

As Andrew Young said, "It's 'jigger'": Peck, Galloway, and Gulotta, *Movin' On Up*.

"*Songs like 'We People Who Are Darker Than Blue'*": Galloway, liner notes for *Roots*.

"*It was the '70s*": Gonzales, "Curtis Mayfield."

"I took it as a person that was very, very angry": Peck, Galloway, and Gulotta, *Movin' On Up.*

"The latter part of the '60s": Galloway, liner notes for *Roots.*

"It just wasn't my plan": Valentine, "Curtis Mayfield in the Talk-In."

"My thoughts were that if we were to": Abbey, "Curtis Mayfield: No Longer an Impression."

"What we did in the UK": Abbey, interview by Atria and Mayfield.

"Him being there, in my opinion": Ibid.

"It was misleading sometimes": Ibid.

"He was a very genuinely kind man": Ibid.

"[Curtis] wanted me to move into an apartment": Diane Mayfield, interview by Atria and Mayfield, 2014.

"They were calling them the 'Jamaican Impressions'": "The Impressions: Part 3," *Beldon's Blues Point.*

"Me and [Marv] were driving into Chicago": Galloway, Liner notes for *Super Fly.*

"Man, I don't even know the names": McMullen, interview by Atria, 2012.

"We were fortunate enough to find a studio": Valentine, "Curtis Mayfield in the Talk-In."

"Lately my lyrics have been more conscious": Van Matre, "Mayfield's Message."

"[Melvin] went out and made a movie": DVD special features for Parks, *Super Fly.*

"As I suffered through Sambo": Bauerlein et al., *Civil Rights Chronicle.*

"When I first heard What's Going On": Burns, *People Never Give Up*, 75.

"A year ago, I'd have been pleading": Williams, "Putting Something on Our Minds."

"The all-too-brief, spur-of-the-moment": Nathan, "Curtis Mayfield."

"Probably the most significant factor": Ibid.

"If you've ever walked into a large hall": Mayfield, *Curtis Mayfield "Rapping."*

"I don't think we should stop demanding it": Symes, "Curtis Mayfield."

"If ever you could gather up a bunch of kids": Galloway, liner notes for *Roots.*

"Everyone knows we have a pollution problem": Symes, "Curtis Mayfield."

"I was never crazy about my ability": Galloway, liner notes for *Roots.*

"I was in love with this particular lady": Ibid.

"I believe my vocal is stronger": Burns, *People Never Give Up*, 70.

"I think my music is aimed at a general audience": Ibid., 72.

"Those concerns are not just black problems": Ibid., 72.

"With me running cross country we figured": Symes, "Curtis Mayfield."

"It's sort of funny": Ibid.

"We're working on several new things": Ibid.

"I told Curtis, 'If we want Marv Stuart'": The History Makers.

"I want you to buy me out": Thomas, interview by Atria and Mayfield.

"I heard they liked threesomes": Diane Mayfield, interview by Atria and Mayfield, 2014.

"He didn't want to listen to me": Ibid.

"I had a huge bruise": Ibid.

"Another time when I wanted to do something": Ibid.

"We hope that you might be interested": Peck, Galloway, and Gulotta, *Movin' On Up*.

10. Super Fly

"Wow, was I so excited": Werner, *Higher Ground*, 161.

"I didn't put Priest down": Ibid.

"Reading the script, I started feeling": Gonzales, "Gangster Boogie."

"I remember all this legal paper": Tracy Mayfield, interview by Atria and Mayfield, 2014.

"I started writing ['Little Child Runnin' Wild']": Berry, "Curtis Mayfield's 'Super Fly.'"

"Hey, we're going to go do this movie": McMullen, interview by Atria, 2012.

"I think we went in at night": Ibid.

"That's when we found out what movie making": Ibid.

"As for those who did turn out": St. Pierre, review of Mayfield at the Rainbow.

"My comments I guess are more for the States": Witter, "Now More Than Ever."

"Segregation will only end when people": Ibid.

"My grandmother was a preacher": Peck, Galloway, and Gulotta, *Movin' On Up*.

"What does he have to talk": Werbin, "Curtis Mayfield's Biggest Score."

"Reading the script didn't tell you": Ibid.

"I did the music and lyrics": Light, "Lasting Impression."

He got a call: Peck, Galloway, and Gulotta, *Movin' On Up*.

"Most of [the songs had] very few chord changes": Ibid.

"We had the chance to cut": McMullen, interview by Atria, 2012.

"As a guitar player, I wanted to make sure": Ibid.

"This was the only time": Gonzales, "Gangster Boogie."

"It's the way a hustler really would": Mayfield, *Curtis Mayfield "Rapping."*

"I was able to put a few other jazz licks": Peck, Galloway, and Gulotta, *Movin' On Up*.

"I orchestrated and arranged the score": Gonzales, "Gangster Boogie."

"We aren't denying that Johnny Pate performed": Ibid.

"Curtis couldn't write music down": McMullen, interview by Atria, 2012.

"Most arrangers that I have used in the past": DVD special features for Parks, *Super Fly*.

"I knew Curtis needed to stand": Thomas, interview by Atria and Mayfield.

"I saw some changes": Diane Mayfield, interview by Atria and Mayfield, 2013.

"Marv Hyman, that was a Jewish name": Ibid.

"I had a good picture": DVD special features for Parks, *Super Fly.*

"Sig was ideal for this": Ibid.

"I can remember sitting in the shoe-shine parlor": Ibid.

"We said, 'Let's put KC in the picture'": Ibid.

"When you shoot a picture like this": Ibid.

"We didn't have anything but raw bones and guts": Ibid.

"What the hell did you expect": Ibid.

"We decided we would go down": Ibid.

"In all the films at that time": Witter, "Now More Than Ever."

"You could find more black power": Strick, "Congress Dances."

"sickening and dangerous screen venture": Jarrett, "Cocaine Cinema Exploits Blacks."

"The blaxploitation films are a phenomenon": Werbin, "Curtis Mayfield's Biggest Score."

"When hip-hop became the thing": Peck, Galloway, and Gulotta, *Movin' On Up.*

"I remember in the theater in St. Louis, Missouri": DVD special features for Parks, *Super Fly.*

"The first time I saw Superfly": Gonzales, "Gangster Boogie."

Gonzales also credited the "neo-psychedelic": Ibid.

"The way you clean up the film": Werbin, "Curtis Mayfield's Biggest Score."

"Forget the critics": Page, "Does Curtis Mayfield Sincerely Want to Be Rich?"

"This was another opportunity": McMullen, interview by Atria, 2010.

"These films were positive for us": Gonzales, "Curtis Mayfield."

"Super Fly is about people who don't believe": DVD special features for Parks, *Super Fly.*

"Everything was done behind closed doors": Tracy Mayfield, interview by Atria and Mayfield, 2014.

"That was a whole other voice": Ibid.

"We lost our bullet": Werbin, "Curtis Mayfield's Biggest Score."

"Curtis, wait! We're gold, Curtis!": Ibid.

"You have to think of Curtis Mayfield as a prophetic visionary": Peck, Galloway, and Gulotta, *Movin' On Up.*

"personal congratulations on that great score": "Curtis Mayfield / The Main Ingredient / Hank Ballard," *Soul Train.*

"I'm working 24 hours a day": Berry, "Curtis Mayfield's 'Super Fly.'"

"You never want to reach the peak": Nathan, "The Curtom Story."

11. Back to the World

"two of the juiciest psychedelic": Burgess, "Curtis Mayfield Keeps On Pushin'."

"That was probably no good for me": Werner, *Higher Ground*, 205.

"The name of the game is longevity": Burgess, "Curtis Mayfield Keeps On Pushin'."

"This is what makes me want to go higher": Ibid.

"You're going to be so caught up": Stuart, interview by Atria.

"I'm glad I was in a position": Berry, "Curtis Mayfield's 'Super Fly.'"

"You learn the market": Werner, "Curtis Mayfield."

"It didn't work": Stuart, interview by Atria.

"I know you dream about home": Foner, *The Black Panthers Speak*, 89.

"My day runs anywhere from fourteen to fifteen hours": Nathan, "The Curtom Story."

"Usually, when Curtis is ready to begin": Ibid.

"an intensely masculine falsetto": Davis, review of *Back to the World*.

"He mentored me": Tracy Mayfield, interview by Atria and Mayfield, 2014.

"He invited us to the studio": Ibid.

"Curt's pretty busy right now": Burns, *People Never Give Up*, 78.

"I had experienced all of that": Gonzales, "Gangster Boogie."

one of his favorite things was "hearing someone else record": Peck, Galloway, and Gulotta, *Movin' On Up*.

"The album allowed me to say some things": Werner, *Higher Ground*, 207.

"We've shouted the message from the roof-tops": St. Pierre, "Curtis Mayfield."

"Like many an overextended or depleted": Gersten, review of *Sweet Exorcist*.

"I can't come in [to Curtom] and write": Nathan, "The Curtom Story."

"a skeletal Hokusai sea": Clive Anderson, liner notes for *Sweet Exorcist & Got to Find a Way*.

"His behavior patterns changed": Sharon Mayfield, interview by Atria and Mayfield.

"They would be feeding him information": Tracy Mayfield, interview by Atria and Mayfield, 2014.

"they were in the room for so long": Sharon Mayfield, interview by Atria and Mayfield.

"I think he got a kick out of scaring us": Tracy Mayfield, interview by Atria and Mayfield, 2014.

"He was always like the old wise man": Ibid.

He even doted on us: Sharon and Tracy Mayfield, interviews by Atria and Mayfield, 2014.

"He did what any father would've done": Sharon Mayfield, interview by Atria and Mayfield.

"I didn't want to be identified": Sharon and Tracy Mayfield, interviews by Atria and Mayfield, 2014.

"I have an early memory of being aware": Sharon Mayfield, interview by Atria and Mayfield.

"Here comes Curtis Mayfield": Ibid.

"I suppose I was somewhat arrogant": DVD special features for Parks, *Super Fly*.

"Curtis Mayfield hit a stride during the '70s": Wynn, review of *Sweet Exorcist*.

he *"continued his run of excellent albums"*: Wynn, review of *Got to Find a Way*.

"I just had to work this depth out": Witter, "Now More Than Ever."

"America Today takes a hard look": Burns, *People Never Give Up*, 103.

"It's not meant as a racial connotation": Abbey, "Curtis Mayfield: Love to the People."

"When he got back in the car": Sharon Mayfield, interview by Atria and Mayfield.

"I had two honorable discharges, twenty-three letters": Kenny Mayfield, interview by Atria and Mayfield.

"I basically dealt with the secondary radio stations": Ibid.

"I'd like to think that you could sing": "Soul of an R&B Genius," *Guitar Player*.

the song *"Jesus"* was *"the closest I've come"*: Abbey, "Curtis Mayfield: Love to the People."

"It appears [Curtis] was seeking": Christgau, review of *America Today*.

The opportunity appealed to him: Nathan, "The Curtom Story."

"I could hear what was going to happen": Ibid.

"When we went into the studio": Vanhorn, "Best of '99."

"I'm not really a radio man": Burgess, "Curtis Mayfield Keeps On Pushin'."

"I was writing the songs not knowing": Nathan, "The Curtom Story."

"The next thing I knew, Curtis": Werner, *Higher Ground*, 211.

"I'd never gotten into Aretha until this": Nathan, "The Curtom Story."

"[Curtis] likes to work fast": Werner, *Higher Ground*, 212.

"They tell you, go across town": Nathan, "The Curtom Story."

"Curtis hasn't been out for three years": Ibid.

"I'm usually working on one situation": Ibid.

"He's thirty-four and has spent seventeen years": Ibid.

"We got great recognition": Werner, *Higher Ground*, 209.

"Curtis Mayfield, the singer and composer": Canby, review of *Short Eyes*.

"I remember when Curtis called me": Werner, *Higher Ground*, 209.

"I remember Dad giving her instructions": Tracy Mayfield, interview by Atria and Mayfield, 2014.

"He would get upset": Ibid.

12. When Seasons Change

"It didn't have much to do with me": Burns, *People Never Give Up*, 135–136.

Rolling Stone called it his "flimsiest": Tucker, review of *Do It All Night*.

"To show your own value": Werner, *Higher Ground*, 220.

"It wasn't so bad": Ibid., 221.

"Those were some strange times": Ibid., 219.

Craig Werner wrote, it "underscores": Ibid., 223.

Werner's assessment of the rest: Ibid.

"I think people in general": Valentine, "Curtis Mayfield in the Talk-In."

"Everything's changed and nothing's": Witter, "Now More Than Ever."

"Stars are made to burn": Werner, *Higher Ground*, 268.

"I had the ambition to want to be rich": Salewicz, "Keep On Pushing."

"That Chicago weather": Werner, *Higher Ground*, 232.

"I've always felt that the mass": Witter, "Now More Than Ever."

"The music scene was kind of drying up": Werner, *Higher Ground*, 232.

"Life isn't just music": Peck, Galloway, and Gulotta, *Movin' On Up*.

"I saw the situation as an ideal opportunity": Burns, *People Never Give Up*, 177–178.

"At that time, I wasn't so hot": Werner, *Higher Ground*, 268.

"I wanted it to be a lot funkier": Burns, *People Never Give Up*, 179.

"Curtis was there with his posse": Abbey, interview by Atria and Mayfield.

"I think he was kind of disillusioned": Ibid.

"I've been in this business": Witter, "Now More Than Ever."

"The musicians gave me hell": Tracy Mayfield, interview by Atria and Mayfield, 2014.

"I had to prove myself nightly": Ibid.

"He didn't go on stage one time": Ibid.

"I didn't tune to F-sharp": Ibid.

"Hey, cat—'We People'": Ibid.

"There were no strings attached": Hoskyns, review of Mayfield, Butler, and the Impressions at the Greek Theatre.

"Curtis delivers sixty magical minutes": Salewicz, "Keep On Pushing."

"After touring, Dad shut down": Tracy Mayfield, interview by Atria and Mayfield, 2014.

"I felt like I couldn't rely on him": Sharon Mayfield, interview by Atria and Mayfield.

"We've all been disappointed a lot": Tracy Mayfield, interview by Atria and Mayfield, 2014.

"Helen was extremely nice": Ibid.

"You have to create the conditions": Sharon Mayfield, interview by Atria and Mayfield.

"I don't feel that I'm a great success": Nathan, "The Curtom Story."

"These are not easy times": Werner, *Higher Ground*, 237.

"In going where you have to go": Bouchard, *Hemingway*, 119.
"He enjoyed people": Carolyn Mayfield, interview by Atria and Mayfield.
"I wouldn't go out there": Kenny Mayfield, interview by Atria and Mayfield.
"Me and Theida, we got in": Carolyn Mayfield, interview by Atria and Mayfield, 2013.
"No one was taking care": Sharon Mayfield, interview by Atria and Mayfield.
"It was very frustrating": Tracy Mayfield, interview by Atria and Mayfield, 2014.
"I was managing the studio": Ibid.
"They didn't have a record deal": Abbey, interview by Atria and Mayfield.
"It was something that Curtis": Ibid.
"Some of the tracks were very good": Ibid.
"I think all of us were very lucky": Ibid.
"You have to remember": Werner, *Higher Ground*, 269.
"Curtis Mayfield was hip-hop": KRS-One, interview by Atria
"I don't see any great differences": Werner, *Higher Ground*, 279.
"It's not that they can't create": Light, "Lasting Impression."
"We're talking about character here": Witter, "Now More Than Ever."
"Curtis Mayfield was making a comeback": Markowitz, interview by Atria.

13. Never Say You Can't Survive
"Listen, you get on stage": Markowitz, interview by Atria.
Markowitz ascended the stairs: Ibid.
"I think so, but I can't move": Goodness, interview by Atria.
"I knew what had happened": Werner, *Higher Ground*, 267.
"When I got there, he had": Sharon Mayfield, interview by Atria and Mayfield.
"I remember reading a telegram": Tracy Mayfield, interview by Atria and Mayfield, 2014.
"We arrived [at the venue]": Light, "Lasting Impression."
"It happened, and it happened fast": Williams, "Everything Was a Song."
"Aches come and go": Werner, *Higher Ground*, 267.
"He never said, 'Why me?'": Stuart, interview by Atria.
"When I would go to visit": Sharon Mayfield, interview by Atria and Mayfield, 2014.
"When I was a little girl": Ibid.
"At this point, there was no more": Tracy Mayfield, interview by Atria and Mayfield, 2014.
"He got mad from that bed": Ibid.
"I think overall I'm dealing": Light, "Lasting Impression."
"Some good doctor somewhere may": Ibid.
"I'm a fifty-four-year-old quadriplegic": Burns, *People Never Give Up*, 238.

a national poll showed only 15 percent: Bauerlein et al., *Civil Rights Chronicle*.

"I always said I would not be singing": Gonzales, "Curtis Mayfield."

"It's not about dying": Peck, Galloway, and Gulotta, *Movin' On Up*.

"I have ideas": Burns, *People Never Give Up*, 223.

"Curtis worked so long": Van Nguyen, "Back to Living."

"[I can't sing] in the manner": Burns, *People Never Give Up*, 214–215.

"It took all of my know how": Ibid., 230.

"My particular thing is how": Werner, *Higher Ground*, 270.

"Fusing elements of hip-hop on this CD": Ibid., 286.

"I've been doing this since I was seven": Ibid., 287.

"The honor that you bestowed upon [Curtis]": "Marv Stuart Hyman on Curtis Mayfield at the Induction Ceremony," Rock and Roll Hall of Fame official website.

"I don't know anything about death": Sharon Mayfield, interview by Atria and Mayfield.

"As I sum it up": Werner, *Higher Ground*, 287.

Lasting Impressions

"There's the illusion that progress": "Race Relations in Crisis," *The Open Mind*.

Bibliography

Abbey, John. "Curtis Mayfield." *Blues & Soul*, February 1972.

———. "Curtis Mayfield: Love to the People." *Blues & Soul*, June 1975.

———. "Curtis Mayfield: No Longer an Impression." *Blues & Soul*, September 1970.

Aletti, Vince. "Jerry Butler." *Rolling Stone*, April 30, 1970.

Alexander, Michael. "The Impressions." *Rolling Stone*, December 27, 1969.

Anderson, Clive. Liner notes for *Sweet Exorcist & Got to Find a Way*. Charly Records, 2001.

Anderson, Monroe. "From Superfly to Super Star." *Ebony*, July 1973.

Atria, Travis. "The Message." *Wax Poetics* 61 (March 2015).

Bauerlein, Mark, et al. *Civil Rights Chronicle: The African-American Struggle for Freedom*. Lincolnwood, IL: Legacy, 2003.

Beldon's Blues Point. "The Impressions: Part 1 of Our Interview with Original Member Sam Gooden" April 20, 2013. http://beldonsbluespoint.blogspot .com/2013/04/the-impressions-part-1-of-our-interview.html.

———. "The Impressions: Part 2 of Our Interview with Original Member Sam Gooden" April 22, 2013. http://beldonsbluespoint.blogspot.com/2013/04 /in-part-2-of-our-interview-with-sam.html.

———. "The Impressions: Part 3 of Our Interview with Original Member Sam Gooden" April 24, 2013. http://beldonsbluespoint.blogspot.com/2013/04 /in-part-iii-of-our-interview-sam-gooden.html.

Berry, William E. "Curtis Mayfield's 'Super Fly' Music Makes $20 Million." *Jet*, May 31, 1973.

Biography.com. "Stokely Carmichael." Accessed June 6, 2016. www.biography .com/people/stokely-carmichael-9238629.

Bouchard, Donald F. *Hemingway: So Far from Simple*. Amherst, NY: Prometheus, 2010.

Bowman, Rob. Booklet for *Movin' On Up: The Music and Message of Curtis Mayfield and the Impressions*. Universal Music Group, 2008. DVD.

Burgess, A. Ace. "Curtis Mayfield Keeps On Pushin' Message Music." *Jet*, February 12, 1976.

Burns, Peter. *People Never Give Up*. London: Sanctuary, 2003.

Butler, Jerry, with Earl Smith. *Only the Strong Survive*. Bloomington: Indiana University Press, 2000.

Callahan, Mike. "Vee Jay Album Discography Part 12: Correspondence, Corrections, Updates," Both Sides Now Publications, December 21, 2006. www.bsnpubs.com/veejay/veejaymail.html.

Canby, Vincent. Review of *Short Eyes*. *New York Times*, September 28, 1977. www.nytimes.com/movie/review?_r=3&res =9504E7D91638E334BC4051DFBF66838C669EDE.

Carmichael, Rodney. "Curtis Mayfield, Still Making His Impression Felt." *Creative Loafing Atlanta*, July 15, 2010. http://clatl.com/atlanta /curtis-mayfield-still-making-his-impression-felt/Content?oid=1720299.

Charles Chesnutt Digital Archive. "Lynching by State." Accessed May 6, 2016. www.chesnuttarchive.org/classroom/lynchings_table_state.html.

Chicago Defender. "It's Curtis, 1975." June 3, 1975.

Christgau, Robert. Review of *America Today*. Consumer Guide, *Village Voice*, ca. 1975. Reprinted on author's official website. www.robertchristgau.com /get_artist.php?name=Curtis+Mayfield.

Churcher, Kalen M. A. "Stokely Carmichael, 'Black Power' (29 October 1966)." Voices of Democracy, July 24, 2009. http://archive.vod.umd.edu/civil /carmichael1966int.htm#_ednref.

Courter, Barry. "R&B Trio, with Two Chattanooga Members, Still in the Public Eye after 50 Years." *Times Free Press*, December 2, 2012. www.timesfreepress .com/news/2012/dec/02/rb-trio-with-two-chattanooga-members-still/.

Davis, Carl. *The Man Behind the Music*. Mattson, IL: Life to Legacy, 2009.

Davis, Stephen. Review of *Back to the World* by Curtis Mayfield. *Rolling Stone*, July 19, 1973. www.rollingstone.com/music/albumreviews/back-to-the-world -19730719.

DeCurtis, Anthony. "The Soul of Soul." *Rolling Stone*, February 3, 2000.

DuBois, W. E. B. *The Souls of Black Folk*. Chicago: A. C. McClurg, 1904.

Dunbar, Paul Laurence. "How Lucy Backslid." In *The Complete Poems of Paul Laurence Dunbar*. New York: Dodd, Mead, 1913.

Dwyer, Jim. "In a World of Songwriting, at the Top of the Pack." *New York Times*, August 28, 2009. www.nytimes.com/2009/08/30/nyregion/30about.html.

Farberman, Brad. "Q&A: The Impressions' Fred Cash on Curtis Mayfield, Politics in the '60s, and the Venues His Band Played Back in the Day." *Village Voice*, July 19, 2012. http://blogs.villagevoice.com/music/2012/07/the_impressions _fred_cash_interview.php.

Foner, Philip S. *The Black Panthers Speak*. New York: Da Capo Press, 1995.

Galloway, A. Scott. Liner notes for *Roots* by Curtis Mayfield. Rhino Records/ Curtom, 1999.

————. Liner notes for *Super Fly* by Curtis Mayfield, 25th anniversary ed. Rhino Records, 1997.

Garrow, David J. *Bearing the Cross: Martin Luther King, Jr. and the Southern Christian Leadership Conference.* New York: Quill, 1986.

Gersten, Russell. Review of *Sweet Exorcist* by Curtis Mayfield. *Rolling Stone*, August 1, 1974.

Goins, Kevin. "A Soulful Conversation with Eddie Thomas." Examiner.com, May 18, 2009. www.examiner.com/article/a-soulful-conversation-with-eddie-thomas. Page discontinued.

Gonzales, Michael A. "Curtis Mayfield: Mighty Mighty." *Vibe*, April 1996.

————. "Gangster Boogie." *Wax Poetics*, 2009.

Gore, Joe. "Curtis Mayfield: 1942–1999." *Guitar Player*, April 2000.

Gray, Tracy. "Mayfield Scores with 'Superfly'." *Chicago Tribune*, September 10, 1972.

Guitar Player. "The Soul of an R&B Genius." August 1991.

Hall, Gwendolyn. "Mean Price by Gender." Afro-Louisiana History and Genealogy, accessed September 2, 2014. www.ibiblio.org/laslave/calculations .php.

History Makers, The. www.thehistorymakers.com.

Hoskyns, Barney. Review of Curtis Mayfield, Jerry Butler, and the Impressions, at the Greek Theatre, Los Angeles. *NME*, July 16, 1983.

James, Frank. "Martin Luther King Jr. in Chicago." *Chicago Tribune*, January 3, 2008.

Jarrett, Vernon. "Cocaine Cinema Exploits Blacks." *Chicago Tribune*, September 13, 1972.

Junior, Chris M. "'Precious Love' for the Impressions: Socially Conscious '50s and '60s Vocal Group Keeps On Pushing After 50 Years." *Goldmine*, August 15, 2008.

Kot, Greg. "The Impressions Keep On Pushing." *Chicago Tribune*, June 28, 2012. http://articles.chicagotribune.com/2012-06-28/entertainment/chi -impressions-interview-fred-cash-interviewed-20120628_1_brooks-brothers -sam-gooden-fred-cash.

Kurlansky, Mark. *1968: The Year That Rocked the World.* New York: Random House, 2004.

Lewis, Pete. "The Impressions: Everlasting Impressions." *Blues & Soul*, May 18, 2011. www.bluesandsoul.com/feature/678/the_impressions_everlasting _impressions/.

Light, Alan. "A Lasting Impression." *Rolling Stone*, October 28, 1993.

Like It Is. "Ali: A Living Legend." WABC-TV, first aired June 26, 1980.

Malcolm X. Interview at UC Berkeley, October 11, 1963. www.youtube.com /watch?v=iTOn8JtN4c0.

Marable, Manning. *Malcolm X: A Life of Reinvention*. New York: Penguin Books, 2011.

Mayfield, Curtis. *Curtis Mayfield "Rapping."* Curtom, 1972. LP.

Mitchell, Gail. "Mayfield Remembered as R&B Pioneer." *Billboard*, January 8, 2000.

Mundy, Chris. "Curtis Mayfield Paralyzed." *Rolling Stone*, October 4, 1990.

Nathan, David. "Curtis Mayfield: The Speakeasy, London." *Blues & Soul*, July 9, 1971.

———. "The Curtom Story." *Blues & Soul*, December 14, 1976.

National Archives. "Teaching With Documents: The Civil Rights Act of 1964 and the Equal Employment Opportunity Commission." Accessed October 4, 2014. www.archives.gov/education/lessons/civil-rights-act/.

Obrecht, Jas. "Curtis Mayfield: The Messenger Returns." *Guitar Player*, December 1996.

———. "Keep on Pushing: A Curtis Mayfield Tribute." *Guitar Player*, June 1994.

Omnibus. "Darker Than Blue: Curtis Mayfield." BBC, first aired March 21, 1995.

Open Mind, The. "Race Relations in Crisis." PBS, first aired June 12, 1963; rebroadcast and updated November 13, 1992.

Page, Clarence. "Does Curtis Mayfield Sincerely Want to Be Rich?" *Chicago Tribune*, February 10, 1974.

Parks, Gordon, Jr., dir. *Super Fly*. Orig. rel. 1972; Warner Home Video, 2004. DVD.

Peck, David, Phillip Galloway, and Tom Gulotta, dirs. *Movin' On Up: The Music and Message of Curtis Mayfield and the Impressions*. Universal Music Group, 2008. DVD.

Pruter, Robert. *Chicago Soul*. Urbana: University of Illinois Press, 1991.

Rawls, Lou. "Dead End Street." On *Too Much!* Capital Records, 1967.

Ritz, David. *Divided Soul: The Life of Marvin Gaye*. New York: Da Capo Press, 1985.

Rock & Rap Confidential. Obituary for Curtis Mayfield. December 1999.

Rock and Roll Hall of Fame official website. "Marv Stuart Hyman on Curtis Mayfield at the Induction Ceremony." *Rock and Roll Hall of Fame*. Accessed August 4, 2014. http://rockhall.com/inductees/curtis-mayfield/transcript/marv-stuart-hyman-on-curtis-ma/.

Rolling Stone. "Curtis Mayfield." August 12, 1985.

———. "Impressions Lose Curtis Mayfield." October 1, 1970.

Salewicz, Chris. "Keep On Pushing: Curtis Mayfield." *Face*, 1985.

Shadwick, Keith. *Jimi Hendrix: Musician*. San Francisco: Backbeat Books, 2003.

Smith, R. J. *The One: The Life and Music of James Brown*. New York: Gotham Books, 2012.

Soul Train. "Curtis Mayfield / The Main Ingredient / Hank Ballard." Syndicast Services, first aired January 6, 1973.

St. Pierre, Roger. "Curtis Mayfield: Where He's Been and Where He's Going." *Let It Rock*, October 1972.

———. Review of Curtis Mayfield at the Rainbow, London. *NME*, January 29, 1972.

Steffens, Roger. "Soul Survivor." *Beat* 12 (1993): 44–46.

Strick, Philip. "Congress Dances and Sings." *London Times*, March 2, 1973.

Swanson, Stevenson. *Chicago Days: 150 Defining Moments in the Life of a Great City*. New York: McGraw-Hill, 1997.

Symes, Phil. "Curtis Mayfield: Soul Music's Elusive Dynamo." *Disc and Music Echo*, December 4, 1971.

Tucker, Ken. Review of *Do It All Night* by Curtis Mayfield. *Rolling Stone*, October 5, 1978. www.rollingstone.com/music/albumreviews/do-it-all-night -19781005.

Valentine, Penny. "Curtis Mayfield in the Talk-In." *Sounds*, February 5, 1972.

Van Matre, Lynn. "Mayfield's Message Checked Out." *Chicago Tribune*, October 10, 1971.

Van Nguyen, Dean. "Back to Living: Curtis Mayfield and the Making of 'New World Order.'" *PopMatters*, April 7, 2010. www.popmatters.com /feature/120209-back-to-living-curtis-mayfield-and-the-making-of-new -world-order/.

Vanhorn, Teri. "Best of '99: Friends, Family Recall Curtis Mayfield's Influence, Persistence." MTV.com, December 27, 1999. www.mtv.com/news/620073 /best-of-99-friends-family-recall-curtis-mayfields-influence-persistence/.

Watson, Beatrice. "From Bea to You." *Chicago Defender*, January 2, 1965.

Werbin, Stu. "Curtis Mayfield's Biggest Score." *Rolling Stone*, November 23, 1973.

Werner, Craig. "Curtis Mayfield." *Goldmine*, July 1997.

———. *Higher Ground*. New York: Crown, 2004.

Whitaker, David T. *Cabrini Green in Words and Pictures*. Chicago: W3 Chicago, 2000.

Wilkerson, Isabel. *The Warmth of Other Suns: The Epic Story of America's Great Migration*. New York: Vintage Books, 2010.

Williams, Richard. "Everything Was a Song." *Independent*, February 27, 1994. www.independent.co.uk/arts-entertainment/arts--everything-was-a-song -curtis-mayfields-voice-used-to-be-one-of-the-sweetest-sounds-in-soul -music-three-and-a-half-years-ago-it-fell-silent-when-mayfield-was-paralysed -now-as-the-stars-pay-tribute-on-an-album-of-his-songs-he-gives-a-rare-and -candid-interview-1396804.html. Page discontinued.

———. Obituary for Major Lance. *Indepdendent*, September 12, 1994. www .independent.co.uk/news/people/obituary-major-lance-1448552.html.

———. "Putting Something on Our Minds." *London Times*, July 31, 1971.

Witter, Simon. "Now More Than Ever: Curtis Mayfield." *i-D*, September 1987.

Wynn, Ron. Review of *Got to Find a Way* by Curtis Mayfield. AllMusic.com, accessed May 5, 2016. www.allmusic.com/album/got-to-find-a-way-mw0000186170.

———. Review of *Sweet Exorcist* by Curtis Mayfield. AllMusic.com, accessed May 5, 2016. www.allmusic.com/album/got-to-find-a-way-mw0000186170.

Interviews

Abbey, John. Interview by Travis Atria and Todd Mayfield, 2014.

Butler, Jerry. Interview by Travis Atria and Todd Mayfield, 2013.

Fischer, André. Interview by Travis Atria, 2012.

Goodness, Lee. Interview by Travis Atria, 2011.

KRS-One, interview by Travis Atria, 2010.

Markowitz, Martin. Interview by Travis Atria, 2011.

Mayfield, Carolyn. Interview by Travis Atria and Todd Mayfield, 2013.

Mayfield, Diane. Interview by Travis Atria and Todd Mayfield, 2013.

———. Interview by Travis Atria and Todd Mayfield, 2014.

Mayfield, Kenny. Interview by Travis Atria and Todd Mayfield, 2013.

Mayfield, Sharon. Interview by Travis Atria and Todd Mayfield, 2014.

Mayfield, Tracy. Interview by Travis Atria and Todd Mayfield, 2013.

———. Interview by Travis Atria and Todd Mayfield, 2014.

McMullen, Craig. Interview by Travis Atria, 2010.

———. Interview by Travis Atria, 2012.

Stuart, Marv. Interview by Travis Atria, 2014.

Thomas, Eddie. Interview by Travis Atria and Todd Mayfield, 2013.

Index

Abbey, John, 187, 190, 279, 288
ABC/Paramount Records, 75–76, 116, 123–124, 140, 162, 165, 171
and the Impressions, 79–80, 90, 93, 98, 130–134
Abernathy, Ralph, 37, 109, 135
Abner, Ewart, 45–46, 48–50, 52–53, 56, 61, 65–66, 68, 78
Ace, Johnny, 98
Across 110th Street (film), 227
Adams, Dr. Jo Jo, 22
Adams, Nate, 220–222
African Americans
    changing terminology regarding, ix
    in Chicago, 5–9, 12–14
    duality within, 17, 18
    electoral successes of, 231
    in Florida, 29
    and jazz, 18
    revolutionary sentiments of, 177
    in Vietnam War, 149
    See also civil rights movement; racism
"Ain't Got Time" (Impressions), 248
Alexander, Michael, 157
Ali, Muhammad, 149, 150
"All You Need Is Love" (Beatles), 129
Almighty Fire (Franklin), 272
Alphatones, the, 36, 37, 40
Amato, Buzz, 289
Amelior Foundation, 303
"Amen" (Impressions), 104, 314
American Bandstand (TV show), 50, 54, 61, 81, 156, 161
Amos, John, 194, 195
Andrews, Lee, 55, 57
Anfinsen, Roger, 214
Apollo Theater (Harlem), 50, 56–62, 80–81, 87–88, 133, 200, 225
Aragon club (Chicago), 238
Armstrong, Louis, 20, 51
"As Long as You Love Me" (Impressions), 79
Askey, Gil, 271, 273
"At the County Fair" (Impressions), 48, 67
Atco Records, 139

Atlanta, Georgia, 64–65, 260, 277, 299
    Curtis's home in, 190, 254, 277–278, 286–287, 306
    riots in, 125, 129
Atlantic City, New Jersey, vii–viii, 72, 217
Atlantic Records, 139, 264, 272
Austin, Sil, 66
Avant, Clarence, 76
Ayers, Roy, 227

Baby Huey. *See* Ramey, James
Baby Huey and the Babysitters, 150
Bacharach, Burt, 77
Back to the World (Mayfield), 239–241, 245, 250
Badu, Erykah, 315
Baker, Josephine, 56
Band of Gypsys, 170
Bandera label, 44, 46
Bandstand Matinee (TV show), 50, 52, 53
Banks, Ernie, 189
Barnevilles, 91
Bass, Ralph, 43
Beach Boys, the, 103, 122
Beatles, the, 95, 99, 103, 122, 128, 129, 145, 168
    disbanding of, 175
    outfits of, 88
Bee Gees, the, 269–270
Bell, Thom, 273
Bell, William, 288
Bells of Joy, the, 22
Benson, Al, 21
Berry, Chuck, 22
Big Beat, The (TV show), 60
Big Time Buck White (play), 163
Billboard magazine, 116, 140
    charts, 85, 227, 269, 272–273
Birmingham, Alabama, 95–96, 109, 115, 126, 129
Bishop, Joey, 161, 164
Bitter End club (New York), x, 190, 191
Biz Markie, 291
Black Belt (Chicago), 6, 7

Black Caesar (film), 227
Black Liberation Army, 175
Black Panther (newsletter), 147, 238
Black Panther Party, 125, 127, 131,
    147–149, 170, 177, 250
Black Power movement, 125–126, 131, 143,
    147–148, 158–159, 163, 245
Blackstone Rangers (gang), 217
blaxploitation films, 194–195, 218,
    220–227, 231, 290
Blige, Mary J., 273
"Blowin' in the Wind" (Dylan), 98
Blue Notes, the, 273, 294
Blues & Soul magazine, 187, 196, 266
Boardwalk label, 278–279, 282
Bogart, Neil, 190, 229, 237, 262, 278
    death of, 282
Bonnevilles, 91
Booker T. and the M.G.'s, 95
Bourke-White, Margaret, 259
Boyce, Al, 36
Bradley, Jan, 90, 123
Brooks, Arthur, 38, 46, 48, 65–67
Brooks, Gwendolyn, 22
Brooks, Richard and Arthur, 38–40, 51, 54,
    59, 63–66, 73, 83–84, 91, 98, 104
Brother on the Run (film), 227
Brown, James, x, 133, 146, 161, 169, 224,
    227, 270, 285
    and funk, 122, 128, 216
Brown, Jim, 246
Brown, Oscar, Jr., 202–203
Brown, Sleepy, 309
Brown, Tony, 223
Brown v. Board of Education of Topeka, 32,
    33, 197, 230
Brownlee, Archie, 22
Bryant, Roy, 33
Bryson, Peabo, 203
Buddah Records, 133, 138, 140, 190, 200,
    229, 262
    and *Claudine* album, 248
    and Curtom Records, 141, 246
Bush, George H. W., 303
Butler, Billy, 36, 99, 113, 116
Butler, Jerry, 26–27, 39–67, 70–76,
    116–117, 171, 282, 241–242, 282, 314

Cabrini-Green housing projects (Chicago),
    34–36, 41, 66, 68, 69, 107, 108, 137
    and Curtis Mayfield Avenue, 305
    Curtis's desire to leave, 62–63
    riots in, 137
    as setting of *Good Times*, 263
Calla Records, 124
calypso music, 278

Camad label, 124
Cameo Parkway label, 123
"Can't Satisfy" (Impressions), 122
Capone, Al, 6
Capris, the, 36
Carmichael, Stokely, 115–116, 125, 131,
    136–137, 147
Carradine, David, 251
Carroll, Diahann, 248
Carter, Calvin, 44–47, 58–59, 66–68, 78
Carter, Vivian, 47
Casablanca Records, 140
Cash, Fred, 38–39, 67, 88, 184–185,
    241–242, 244, 256, 305
    and Curtis's departure from the
        Impressions, 178–179
    at Curtis's funeral, 314
    draft scare, 80
    in the Impressions, 67, 80–85, 88, 90–95,
        100–103, 116, 153–158, 161–168
    marries, 69
    tensions with Curtis, 134, 140, 151, 155,
        172, 177
Cashbox magazine, 140
Catch a Fire (Wailers album), 244
censorship, 132, 164, 171
Chambers, Ray, 303
Chandler, Gene, 84–85, 87, 94, 99, 116,
    180, 241
"Change Is Gonna Come, A" (Cooke), 98
Charles, Ray, 36–37, 40, 58, 75, 80, 146
Chattanooga, Tennessee, 38–39, 41, 67, 83
Check Out Your Mind (Impressions), 174,
    177, 178, 185, 211, 248
Chedwick, Porky, 74
Chess Records, 45, 123, 90
Chicago, Illinois
    African American community in, 5–9,
        12–14
    Black Belt in, 6, 7
    and civil rights movement, 115, 116,
        120–122, 126, 127
    club scene in, 22, 35, 51
    criminals in, 6, 79, 217
    Democratic National Convention of 1968
        in, 142, 144, 170
    the Hawk (wind), 7, 29, 43, 190, 301, 313
    jazz in, 22
    the Loop, 68, 130, 137
    racial mixing and segregation in, 6–7,
        31–32, 35, 101, 121
    radio stations in, 21, 22
    Record Row in, 43, 75, 277
    Red Summer of 1919 in, 6
    rioting in, 6, 125, 126, 137, 138
    See also specific locations in Chicago

Chicago Black Renaissance, 22
Chicago Cubs, 167
Chicago Defender (newspaper), 33
Chicago Housing Authority, 35, 63
Chicago Sound, 85–86, 146, 176
  Curtis's influence on, 85, 314
Chiffons, the, 75
Chisholm, Shirley, 231
Chi-Sound label, 124
chitlin' circuit, 70, 79, 82, 91, 136, 238
"Choice of Colors" (Impressions), 148,
    152–153, 158–159, 164, 166, 178, 183
Christgau, Robert, 251, 262
Chuck D, 224
Civil Rights Act of 1964, 95, 101, 114, 121,
    129, 177
civil rights movement, 3, 21, 69, 101, 192
  Curtis and, ix, 113
  Martin Luther King Jr.'s death and, 135,
    136
  sit-ins, 69
  violence against, 95, 114, 115
  See also King, Martin Luther, Jr.
Clark, Dee, 49
Clark, Dick, 54, 61, 81, 113, 156
Clark, Samuel, 76, 80
Claudine (film), 246–248
Claudine (soundtrack album), 248
Cleaver, Eldridge, 147
Clifford, Linda, 272, 273, 276
Clowns, the, 55, 57
Club DeLisa (Chicago), 22
Coasters, the, 63–64
Cobbins, Robert, 158, 169
cocaine, 176, 204, 212, 223, 252, 283, 287
Coffy (film), 227
Cole, Nat King, 18, 86, 120
Coltrane, John, 56
Columbia Records, 85
Congress of Racial Equality (CORE), 21, 97,
    115, 148–149
Conquest, June, 138
Conquest label, 306
Cooke, Sam, 58, 98, 103
  as Curtis's hero, 20, 22, 27, 36, 78
  murder of, 108
  and SAR label, 78, 146
Coolio, 312
Cooper, Alice, 229
Cooper, Willie (grandfather), 4
CORE. *See* Congress of Racial Equality
Cornelius, Don, 232, 264
Cosby, Bill, 262, 268
country music, 18, 44, 80
  and the Roosters, 41
Cox, Billy, 180

CRC/Ichiban Records, 288, 290
Curtis (Mayfield), 179, 185–187, 190, 193,
    195, 199, 241, 249
Curtis in Chicago (Mayfield), 242, 244–245
Curtis/Live! (Mayfield), 192–194, 240
Curtis Mayfield Avenue, Chicago, 305
Curtom Records, 163, 166, 239, 256, 261, 264
  attempted gang shakedown of, 217
  and Buddah Records, 141, 246
  decline of, 262, 268, 271–274
  demands on Curtis, 140, 141, 143, 154,
    161–162, 187, 236, 251
  Eddie Thomas and, 79, 138, 140, 141,
    145, 171, 204, 206, 219–220
  founding of, 79, 133–134, 138–145
  growth of, 150–156, 166, 171, 202–204,
    235–236
  investment in *Short Eyes*, 267–268
  Marv Stuart and, 150–151, 154–155, 171,
    204, 219–220, 267, 306–307, 308
  offices/studios of, 138, 219, 233, 235–236,
    286, 309
  revival of, 288
  shutdown of, 276–278
  Todd Mayfield and, x, 299, 302, 305–307,
    308
  and Warner Brothers Records, 258, 262,
    272–273, 306
Curtom Records of Atlanta, Inc., 288

Daley, Mayor Richard J., 101, 120
Davis, Carl, 44, 84–87, 89, 92–93, 99–100,
    189, 218, 246
Davis, Miles, 18, 51, 56, 90
Daylie, Holmes "Daddy-O," 21
Del-Phis, the, 123. *See also* Martha and the
    Vandellas
Della (TV show), 151
Dells, the, 36, 51
Democratic National Convention of 1968,
    142, 144, 170
Detroit, 12, 29, 31, 39, 50–53
Dick Cavett Show, 211
Diddley, Bo, 229
Dillard, Moses, 203
Dion and the Belmonts, 75
"Dirty Laundry" (Mayfield), 284–285
disco music, 240, 241, 251–252, 269–272
  Curtis and, 258, 265, 271–274, 291
  origins of, 236
  waning of, 275
Dixon, Dallas, 36
Dixon, Larry, 52, 53
DNC. *See* Democratic National Convention
"Do Do Wap Is Strong in Here" (Mayfield),
    244, 267–268

Do It All Night (Mayfield), 271–273
Domino, Fats, 75
"(Don't Worry) If There's a Hell Below, We're All Going to Go" (Mayfield), 175, 180–185
doo-wop, 19, 21, 36, 40, 46–47, 55, 68, 73–74, 98, 138
    competing groups, 38
    the Impressions and, 83–84, 98, 103
Dr. Dre, 312
Drake, 315
Drifters, the, 49, 99
Du Quoin, Illinois, 18, 27
DuBois, W. E. B., 3, 17
"Duke of Earl" (Davis), 84–85
Dunbar, Paul Laurence, 9, 16–17, 18
    influence on Curtis, 58, 131, 143
Dylan, Bob, 98, 103, 122, 197, 224

Earth, Wind & Fire, 195–196, 252
Eastern mysticism, 251–252
Ebony magazine, 97
Ed Sullivan Show, The, 52, 99, 197
Eisenhower, Dwight D., 61
Ellington, Duke, 51
Eminem, 313
End Records, 84
Epic Records, 282
Ertegun, Ahmet, 264

Fabulous Impressions, The (Impressions), 127, 128
Famous Flames, the, 49
Farmer, James, 97, 115, 313
Farrakhan, Louis, 231
Fascinations, the, 123–125, 127
Fenty, Phil, 206, 220–223
Ferguson, Missouri, 316
"Find Another Girl" (Butler), 83
Fischer, André, 163, 166
Fisher, Bob, 91
Five Blind Boys of Mississippi, the, 22
Five Chances, the, 38
Five Royales, the, 83
Five Stairsteps, the, 123, 127, 138, 139, 141
Flack, Roberta, 139, 268
Flamingoes, the, 51
"For Your Precious Love" (Impressions), 40, 43, 45, 48–52, 55, 60–62
Forman, James, 115
Four Tops, 82, 122, 162, 171
Frankie Lymon and the Teenagers, 49
Franklin, Aretha, 79, 128, 146, 236, 264–265, 272
Frazier, Sheila, 246
Freed, Alan, 60, 61

"Freddie's Dead" (Mayfield), 208, 213, 215, 225, 230, 237, 294
funk music, 74, 83, 248
    Curtis and, 176, 177, 184, 192, 268, 279
    James Brown and, 122, 128, 216
"Future Shock" (Mayfield), 240

Gamble, Kenny, 273
Garvey, Marcus, 3, 31
Gaye, Marvin, x, 84, 144, 195, 227, 231–232, 241, 244
Gaynor, Gloria, 270
Gemigo label, 246, 264
"Get Down" (Mayfield), 197, 199, 215
Gibson, "Master" Henry, 180, 184, 212–215, 230, 236, 240
Gillard, Sadie Ann (grandmother). *See* Washington, Sadie Ann
Give, Get, Take and Have (Mayfield), 265–266
Godfather, The (film), 222
Gonzales, Michael, 225
Good Times (TV show), 263
Gooden, Samuel, 38–42, 181, 184–185, 190, 211–212, 241–242, 244, 256, 305
    and Curtis's departure from the Impressions, 178–179
    at Curtis's funeral, 314
    in the Impressions, 48, 59, 63–67, 73, 84–88, 90–95, 110, 132, 156, 158–161, 165, 167
    tensions with Curtis, 134, 140, 151, 155, 172, 177
Goodness, Lee, 289, 296–297
Gordy, Berry, 52, 73, 146, 267, 276
Gospel Clefs, the, 40
gospel music, 38, 91
    the blues and, 30
    Curtis and, 22, 28–30, 98, 111–112, 131, 262, 275
    the Impressions and, 74, 91, 99
    Marion Washington Mayfield and, 19
    Sam Cooke and, 27
Got to Find a Way (Mayfield), 256–258
Great Migration, 3, 4, 9, 12, 111
Green, Al, 262
Greenwich Village, 191
Gregory, Dick, 101
"Grow Closer Together" (Impressions), 83
"Gypsy Woman" (Impressions), 73–76, 79–80, 89, 186

Haley, Alex, 200
Hamilton, Roy, 50
Hampton, Riley, 176, 181–183
Hancock, Herbie, 22

Harlem, New York, 58–60. *See also* Apollo
    Theater
Harold Melvin and the Blue Notes, 273, 295
Harris, Lew, 218
Harris, Norman, 273
Hathaway, Donny, 124, 138–139, 144, 150
Hathaway, Eulaulah, 139
Hawk, the (Chicago wind), 7, 29, 43, 190,
    301, 313
Hawkins, Charles, Jr. (uncle), 9, 24–26,
    29–30, 72
Hawkins, Coleman, 51
Hayden, Horace, 9
Hayes, Isaac, 195, 233
"He Will Break Your Heart" (Butler), 72–73,
    267
Heartbeat (Mayfield), 273–274
Hearts, the, 55, 57
Heiman, Marv. *See* Stuart, Marv
"Hell Below" (Mayfield), 175, 180–185
Hemingway, Ernest, 285
Henderson, Jocko, 57, 60
Hendrix, Jimi, 92, 128–129, 145, 170, 191,
    238
    and the Bonnevilles, 91
    Curtis's influence on, 91–92, 128–129,
        257
    death of, 180
    guitar virtuosity, 218
High Chaparral club (Chicago), 180
Hill, Lauryn, 312
hip-hop music, 38, 139, 185, 228
    creation of, 223
    Curtis's influence on, 181, 240, 285,
        290–291, 306, 310, 312, 315
    and *Super Fly*, 224
Hofstra University, 229–230
Holland, Brian, 144
Holland, Eddie, 52, 84, 144
Holliday, Billie, 56
Honesty (Mayfield), 279, 282–285
Hooker, John Lee, 18, 20, 21
Horne, Lena, 18
Howard, Eddie, 44
Howlin' Wolf, 18, 21, 50
Hudson, Pookie, 46
Huff, Leon, 273
Hutson, Leroy, 124, 178, 211, 236, 241,
    256, 264
Hyde Park, Chicago, 137
Hyland, Brian, 186

"I Made a Mistake" (Impressions), 104, 244
"I'm A Telling You" (Butler), 83
I'm Gonna Git You Sucka (film), 290, 292
"I'm So Proud" (Impressions), 100

Ice-9 (road band), 289, 293–294
Ice-T, 292
Ichiban Records, 288, 290, 292
Impressions, the, vii, viii, 42–48, 79–82,
    87–94, 309, 310
    on Alan Freed TV show, 60, 61
    Apollo Theater debut, 56–62
    aversion to dancing, 92–93, 114
    changing vocal style and interplay, 91, 104
    and doo-wop, 83, 84, 98
    first film appearance, 246
    first professional recording date, 46–47
    first promotional tour, 50–52
    and funk, 177
    and Gospel music, 91
    influence on the Wailers, 100–101
    loss of backing band, 153–154
    and Marv Stuart, 151
    Rock and Roll Hall of Fame induction,
        305
    singing battle with the Temptations, 110
    and soul music, 45
    uniforms of, 50–51, 88, 143, 158
    and Vee-Jay Records, 43–46, 67–68
    See also specific songs and albums
In Concert (TV show), 229
Internal Revenue Service (IRS), 70–71, 204
Island Records, 245
Isley Brothers, 91, 122, 146, 224
"It's All Right" (Impressions), 92, 94, 96, 98,
    267, 275

Jackson, Albert (stepfather), 35, 106
Jackson, Jesse, 127, 231, 316
Jackson, Michael, 255
Jackson, Walter, 86
Jackson 5, 138, 139, 255
Jamaica, 100–101, 190, 245
James, Etta, 176
Jarrett, Vernon, 223
Jay Z, 139, 315
jazz
    African American musicians and, 18
    in Chicago, 22
    and the Chicago Sound, 85
    radio programs, 21
    Ray Charles and, 37
    Soupy Sales and, 51
Jet magazine, 33, 140, 193, 218, 235
Jeter, Claude, 19
Jethro Tull, 229
Johnson, Lyndon B., 96, 104, 115, 141
Jones, James Earl, 248
Jones, Melvin, 163, 166, 169, 171, 172
Jones, Ruby, 202, 203
Joplin, Janis, 180

Kahn, Tom, 120
Kane, Big Daddy, 292
KC and the Sunshine Band, 271
"Keep On Keeping On" (Mayfield), 198
"Keep On Pushing" (Impressions), ix, 77,
    101–104, 111–113
Keep On Pushing (Impressions), 103–106,
    146
Kelly, R., 240
Kennedy, John F., 69, 80, 95–96
Kennedy, Robert F., 141–142, 168
Kent, Herb, 21, 38, 40, 54, 67, 99
Khan, Chaka, 163
King, B. B., 75, 80, 81, 85, 194
King, Carole, 77
King, Coretta Scott, 130
King, Martin Luther, Jr., 37, 38, 168, 232,
    277
  assassination of, 135
  in Chicago, 115, 116, 120–122, 126, 127
  and Dwight D. Eisenhower, 61
  home burned, 81
  "I Have a Dream" speech, 96, 102, 125
  influence on Curtis, 38, 61, 62, 96, 101,
    134, 146
  March on Washington, 95, 96
  march to Selma, 114
King, Rodney, 304
King Records, 43
Kings County Hospital, 297
Kinks, the, 103
Knight, Gladys, 79, 246–248
Kodaks, the, 57
Kool Gents, the, 49
Krakatoa, East of Java (film), 196
Kramer, Eddie, 191
KRS-One, 223, 285, 290
Ku Klux Klan (KKK), 81, 149
Kulick, Bob, 128
"Kung Fu" (Mayfield), 250–251
Kung Fu (TV show), 251

LaBelle, Patti, 55, 56, 82
Lance, Major, 68, 86, 87, 92, 93, 98, 99,
    116, 180, 187
Last Poets, the, 182, 194
Laurie Records, 75
Lee, Bruce, 251
Legend (Bob Marley album), 285
Lennon, John, 145, 250
Let's Do It Again (film), 262–263, 268
Let's Do It Again (soundtrack album), 263
Lewis, John, 109
Lewis, Ramsey, 22
Lilies of the Field (film), 104
Lincoln, Abraham, 96

Lincoln Center, 206
Little Anthony and the Imperials, 84
"Little Hell" neighborhood, Chicago, 34
Little Richard, 84, 91
Little Walter, 30
"Little Young Lover" (Impressions), 83
Live in Europe (Mayfield), 290
LL Cool J, 291
"Long Long Winter" (Impressions), 104,
    145, 244
Los Angeles, 113, 161, 232
  Watts riot in, 121, 260
Lost Generation, the, 246
Louis, Joe, 56
Lounsbury, Jim, 50, 68
Love Is the Place (Mayfield), 278–279
"Love Me (Right in the Pocket)" (Mayfield),
    vii, 256
"Love to Keep You in My Mind" (Mayfield),
    199
Loving Power (Impressions), 264
Lubinsky, Herman, 43
Ludacris, 313
Lymon, Frankie, 36, 49, 60
lynchings, 2, 33, 64, 81, 143

Malcolm X, 32, 96, 97, 101, 315
  assassination of, 109, 177
"Mama Didn't Lie" (Fascinations), 123
"Man's Temptation" (Chandler), 87
Marable, Manning, 109
March on Washington (1963), 95–96
Marina Towers (Chicago), 107
Markowitz, Marty, 293–295, 299
Marley, Bob, 100, 104, 190, 244, 245, 285
  death of, 284
Marquette Park (Chicago), 126
Marshall, Thurgood, 21, 32
Martha and the Vandellas, 95, 110, 123. *See
    also* Reeves, Martha
Marvelettes, the, 84, 110
Masouri, John, 245
Maxwell, Holly, 248
Maxwell Street Market (Chicago), 50, 158
Mayfield, Altheida Sims (wife), 248, 252,
    283, 287–289, 296, 298, 302, 311
  marries Curtis, 309–310
Mayfield, Annie Bell (grandmother), 1–13,
    15, 18–20, 31–33, 54, 62, 72, 101,
    107–108
  changes name to Mayfield, 8
  death of, 165
  influence on Curtis, 54, 89, 101, 112,
    261–262
  spiritualist beliefs, 3–4, 8, 20, 26, 29, 76
  temperament, 25–26

and Traveling Souls Spiritualist Church, 22–27, 40, 314

Mayfield, Carolyn Mercedes (sister), 13–16, 19–20, 24–26, 32–36, 62–63, 66, 69, 286–287

Mayfield, Curtis, career and work
acts in *Short Eyes*, 268
becomes the Impressions' lead singer, 66–67
and Chicago Sound, 85–86
cigar-selling job, 68–70
decision to go solo, 177–180
decline in popularity, 270
disdain for "party music," 94–95
early musical interest, 18, 27
European tours, 187, 200, 203, 209–210, 280, 289
first arranging work, 93
first film score, 206–212
forms Ice-9 road band, 289
forms the Alphatones, 36
founds Curtom Records, 79
founds Gemigo label, 246
gives up guitar, 296–297, 300–301, 308–309
Grammys Legend Award, 305
hit singles, 134
influence on Jimi Hendrix, 128–129, 145
joins the Roosters, 40
loses copyright infringement suit, 122
master tapes lost in fire, 302
OKeh Records work, 84–87, 89
publishing rights, 78, 314
and Queen Booking, 79
radio station bannings, 132
radio station license quest, 264
Rock and Roll Hall of Fame inductions, 305, 311–312
"Silver Anniversary" American tour, 280
socially conscious music, 98, 101–103, 111–112, 131–132, 143, 146
tape recorder use, 70, 87, 308
teaches self guitar, 28, 30–31
touring, 64, 80–81, 108, 153, 160–162, 165–167, 178, 266
unique guitar style, 30, 36, 59, 85–86, 314
United Kingdom tours, 187, 188, 196, 290
See also specific songs and albums

Mayfield, Curtis, life
adjusting to prosperity, 72
birth of, 10, 11
children, 89–90, 98, 130, 132, 167, 243–244, 246, 253–256, 266–267, 287–288, 298–299, 313–314
death of, 313–314
diabetes, 301, 311
early role models, 11
extravagances of, 255, 256
home fire, 302
income tax problems, 70, 71, 204
leg amputation, 311
nicknames, 15, 169, 188
paralysis of, 294–303
schooling, viii, 31, 32, 35, 40, 68
serious finger injury, 249
womanizing, viii, 64, 71, 72, 88, 118, 123, 133, 141, 165, 201

Mayfield, Curtis, personal traits
abusive behavior, 205, 228, 229, 283
business sense, 78, 89, 90, 99
controlling nature, ix, 67, 78, 89–90, 117–119, 139, 155, 297
drug use, 162, 204, 205, 212, 235, 252, 283, 292,
duality, ix, 90, 117, 154, 156, 191, 243, 281, 283, 286
ignoring other musicians, 122, 240, 241
impulse traveling, 254
insecurity, viii, ix, 35, 78, 103, 140, 228, 237
lack of friends, 154
late-night habits, 82, 120, 208, 252
lifestyle choices, 89, 256, 298
mood swings, 117, 205, 301
musical genius, 28, 70, 85, 90, 99–100, 188, 196
performing magic tricks, 254
physical characteristics, ix, 15, 86, 103, 140
practical joking, 59, 253
reclusiveness, viii, x, 117, 189, 252
reluctance to share, 99, 163, 219
reluctance to vote, 121
singing voice, 28, 36, 104, 153
smoking, 235
sports car enthusiasm, 154, 290
temperate drinking habits, 289
variant speaking voices, 229

Mayfield, Curtis "Curt Curt," III (son), 98, 105–106, 186, 284, 288, 297–298

Mayfield, Curtis Lee "Mannish" (father), 7, 8, 13, 105, 284
birth of, 4
changes name to Kenneth Washington, 13, 19
children, 13, 19
deserts family, 13
marries Marion Washington, 9, 10
name changed to Mayfield, 8
temper of, 12

Mayfield, Diane (partner), 87–89, 105–108, 120, 139, 189, 200–202, 205, 219–220, 243
changes name to Mayfield, 107

children, 117, 123, 130, 132
relationship difficulties, 117–119, 123,
    130, 133, 140–141, 205
separation from Curtis, 172, 185, 188–
    189, 199
Mayfield, Gary Kirby (brother), 13, 15, 25,
    35
    death of, 105, 165
    encephalitis, 13–14
Mayfield, Helen (wife), 63–64, 69–71, 80,
    87, 89, 284
    children, 89–90, 98
    separation and divorce from Curtis, 105,
        107, 229, 287
Mayfield, Judy (sister), 13, 25, 107, 140,
    189, 261
    birth of, 12
Mayfield, Kenneth (brother), 19, 31, 69,
    105, 205, 239, 286, 297
    birth of, 13
    on brother's music, 148
    and Curtom Records, 260–261
    Vietnam service, 130, 148–150, 176
Mayfield, Marion Washington (mother), 9,
    13–20, 25, 30, 32, 34–35, 189
    abusive boyfriend Eddie, 14–15
    artistic talents, 16
    children, 11–14, 31
    depression, 13, 19–20
    and Diane Mayfield, 108
    financial problems, 12–14, 19
    marries Albert Jackson, 35
    marries Curtis's father, 10
    musical interests, 18, 19
Mayfield, Mercedes (aunt), 4, 8, 9, 24, 25,
    112
Mayfield, Sharon (daughter), 185–186, 205,
    222, 228–229, 233, 243, 275
    birth of, 130, 132
    on Curtis, 252–256, 260, 283–284,
        287–288, 298, 302–303, 312
Mayfield, Todd (son), 228
    birth of, 117, 123
    and Curtom Records, x, 299, 302,
        305–307, 308
    enters Morehouse College, 286
    forms Conquest label, 306
    tours Europe with father, 289
Mayfield, Tracy (son), 88, 185–186, 222,
    233
    on Curtis's career and music, 103, 179,
        208, 241, 265, 268–269, 281–283
    on Curtis's paralysis, 298, 303
    on family life, 107, 122, 133, 179,
        228–229, 252, 253–255, 284
    manages family studio, 288

musical interest, 243–244, 280–285
name changed to Mayfield, 107
Mayfield, Walter "Wal" (stepfather), 7, 72
Mayfield Music, 264
Mayfield Records, 123, 124
Mayfield Singers, 124, 179
McCullen, Tyrone, 190, 209, 212, 282
McKee, Lonette, 264
McKissick, Floyd, 116, 125
McMullen, Craig, 163, 168, 190–191, 197,
    209, 212–214, 230, 236
McPhatter, Clyde, 49, 64
Medallionaires, the, 36, 41
Melvin, Harold, 273, 294
Memos club (Chicago), 39
Memphis, Tennessee, 135
Mercury Records, 41, 43, 68
Meredith, James, 95, 125
Metromedia Records, 139
Mickelson, Jerry, 238
Midnighters, the, 83
Milam, J. W., 33
Miles, Buddy, 180
Miller, Patty, 202
Miracles, the, 73, 84, 87, 93, 103, 110
Mitchell, Mitch, 128
monkey dance fad, 92–93
"Monkey Time, The" (Lance), 92–93,
    99
Montgomery, Alabama, 37, 115
Montgomery, Tammy. See Terrell, Tammi
Montreux Jazz Festival, 290
Moore, Gatemouth, 22
Morgan, Irene, 21, 37
Morrison, Alan, 97, 315
Morrison, Jim, 197
Moses, Bob, 116
Motown label, 52, 73, 84, 95, 100, 122–123,
    251
"Move On Up" (Mayfield), 185, 187, 196
Muhammad, Elijah, 31
Murray, Ray, 309
Muszynski, Vi, 44–46
Mystique, 246

NAACP, 3, 21, 32
Nashville, Tennessee, 39, 91–92
Nathan, David, 196, 197
Nation of Islam, 31–32
National Association for the Advancement of
    Colored People (NAACP), 3, 21, 32
National Black Political Convention, 231
National Colored Spiritualist Association of
    Churches, 26
Natural Four, the, 256
Negro spirituals, 26, 111

Never Say You Can't Survive (Mayfield), 269–270
new jack swing, 292
New Musical Express. See NME magazine
New World Order (Mayfield), 308–310
New York City, 77–79, 190–192, 206, 229, 292. *See also* Apollo Theater; Harlem
Newton, Huey, 125, 147, 177, 195
Nixon, Richard, 144, 147, 175, 197, 231, 250
    and civil rights, 61, 141
NME (*New Musical Express*) magazine, 209, 282
Northern Jubilee Singers, the, 28–30, 52, 263
Notorious B.I.G., 224, 262
N.W.A, 139, 285, 291

O'Jays, the, 79, 273
OKeh Records, 84–87, 89–90, 123–124, 143, 176, 180, 277
    and Curtis, 84–87, 89, 98, 100, 106, 116, 119, 144
"On and On" (Knight), 248
One by One (Impressions), 120, 121
O'Neal, Ron, 221, 224, 226
"O-o-h Child" (Five Stairsteps), 138
Opals, the, 116
Operation Breadbasket, 127
Organization of Afro-American Unity, 109
Organized Noize, 309
OutKast, 309
Overa, Madame Mary, 8

Panama Limited (train), 5, 8, 112
Parks, Gordon, Jr., 195, 209, 221, 246
Parks, Gordon, Sr., 223
Parks, Rosa, 37
Pat, Alley, 64
Pate, Johnny, 93–94, 102–104, 110–111, 123, 132, 193, 227
    arranging work, 85–86, 181, 216–219, 236
    moves to New York, 176, 213
Patterson, Eddie "Paddyfoot," 26, 28
Pentagon Papers, 197, 252
"People Get Ready" (Impressions), ix, 1, 110–114, 178, 245
People Get Ready (Impressions), 113, 116, 146
Philadelphia International label, 273
Philadelphia, Pennsylvania, 54–56, 65, 74
    radio stations, 74
    riots in, 55
Piece of the Action, A (film), 268–269
Pilgrim Travelers, the, 22

Pill Hill, Chicago, 34
Players, the, 36
"Please Please Me" (Beatles), 95
Poitier, Sidney, 104, 262, 268
Pope, Shelly, 261
"Power to the People" (Mayfield), 250
practical joking, 56, 59, 253
Presley, Elvis, 47, 57, 77
Price, Lloyd, 75
Prince, 224
psychedelic revolution, 122, 129, 176
Public Enemy, 224, 285
Puff Daddy, 312
Pullman porters, 8
"Pusherman" (Mayfield), 209, 213, 215

Queen Booking, 79, 217

R&B
    Billy Butler and, 113
    Curtis and, 80, 85, 94, 99–104, 112, 186, 188
    Elvis Presley and, 57
    the Impressions and, 91
    Jerry Butler and, 72, 73
    Marvin Gaye and, 95, 152
    radio programming and, 21, 129
    Ray Charles and, 36–37, 40
    the Wailers and, 190
Ra, Sun (Sonny Blount), 22, 251
race riots, 12, 13, 125
    in Chicago, 6, 31, 125–126
    in Detroit, 12
    in Los Angeles, 121
    in Philadephia, 55
racism, 32–34, 81, 220, 238
    in Chicago, 121
    in Jamaica, 101
    in the North, 127
    in radio, 118, 186, 266
    in the South, 81
    in television, 61, 164
    in Vietnam, 149
radio broadcasting, 21–22, 47–48, 64–65, 71, 75, 102, 129, 261
    black-owned stations, 64
    censorship, 132
    ethnic programming, 21
    racism in, 186, 228, 266
"Rainbow" (Chandler), 65, 87, 116
Ramey, James "Baby Huey," 150, 151, 187, 203
    death of, 180
Rastafarianism, 245
Rawls, Lou, 7, 273
RCA Records, 75, 78

Reagan, Ronald, 276, 285
Record Row (Chicago), 43, 75, 277
Red, Piano, 64
Redding, Otis, 95, 103, 114
    death of, 146
Reed, Jimmy, 21, 50
Reese, Della, 151
Reeves, Martha, 82, 123. *See also* Martha and
    the Vandellas
Regal Theatre (Chicago), 41, 80, 114, 123
reggae, 245
Return of Superfly, The (film), 292
Revolver (Beatles), 122
rhythm and blues. *See* R&B
Ridin' High (Impressions), 121, 122
"Right On for the Darkness" (Mayfield), 240
Robert and Johnny, 55, 57
Robinson, Smokey, 73, 82, 93, 110, 144,
    196, 244
Rock and Roll Hall of Fame, 305, 311, 312
rock 'n' roll music, 47, 128
rocksteady music, 245
Rolling Stone magazine, x, 138, 156, 157,
    173, 199, 240, 250, 272
Rolling Stones, the, 103
Ronettes, the, 123
Roosters, the, 38–42, 67
    change name to the Impressions, 41–42
Roots (Mayfield), 197–200, 203, 208
Ross, Diana, 88, 175. *See also* the Supremes
Ross, Rick, 315
Roundtree, Richard, 231
RSO Records, 274, 276, 288
Rustin, Bayard, 120

"Sad, Sad Girl and Boy" (Impressions), 90,
    91
Sales, Soupy, 51
Salt-N-Pepa, 139
Santana, Carlos, 158, 168
SAR label, 78, 146
Saturday Night Fever (film), 269
Savoy Records, 43
Scepter Records, 75
Schiffman, Bobby, 58
Schwartz, Red, 61
SCLC. *See* Southern Christian Leadership
    Conference
Scott, Annie Bell (grandmother). *See*
    Mayfield, Annie Bell
Scott, Elmore (great-grandfather), 1, 2
Scott, Joseph "Lucky," 156, 163–166,
    169–172, 180–181, 212–215, 236, 282
    death of, 309
Scott, LeBron, 289
Scott, Lula (great-grandmother), 1, 2, 4

Scott-Heron, Gil, 182
Seale, Bobby, 125, 147
Seals & Croft, 229
Sears, Zena, 64
Seward Park (Cabrini-Green), 36
Shaft (film), 195, 222, 226–227, 231, 233
Shaft in Africa (film), 227
Shakur, Tupac, 139, 312
Shepherd Center (Atlanta), 299
Shirelles, the, 75
Shore, Sig, 206, 220–223
Short Eyes (film), 267–268, 272
Short Eyes (soundtrack album), 267–268
Sigler, Bunny, 273
Simon, Lowrell, 246
Simon, Paul, 77
Sims, Altheida (wife). *See* Mayfield, Altheida
    Sims
Sims, Gerald, 87
Singer, Manny, 74
ska music, 245
Slabo, Gary, 176, 181
Smith, Huey, 55, 57
Smith, Reggie, 38
SNCC. *See* Student Nonviolent
    Coordinating Committee
Snoop Doggy Dogg, 224
sock hops, 38, 54
"Something He Can Feel" (Mayfield),
    265–266
Something to Believe In (Mayfield), 275–276
soul music, 258
    Aretha Franklin and, 128, 146, 264, 265
    Baby Huey and the Babysitters and, 150
    and the Chicago Sound, 85, 146
    Curtis and, 242, 269, 274, 302
    Leroy Hutson and, 241
    Nat King Cole and, 86
    Otis Redding and, 146
    in United Kingdom, 196, 209, 210
Soul Rebels (Wailers album), 190
Soul Stirrers, the, 28
Soul Train (TV show), 232–233, 241
Soul Train Music Awards, 311
Soulfully (Impressions), 121–122
Southern Christian Leadership Conference
    (SCLC), 38, 114–115, 120, 127, 131,
    135, 148
Spaniels, the, 36, 46, 51
Sparkle (film), 264, 265
Sparkle (soundtrack album), 264–265
Specialty Records, 19
Spector, Phil, 77
Spiritualism, viii, 3–4, 8, 26, 29
St. Pierre, Roger, 209
Stairsteps. *See* Five Stairsteps, the

Staple Singers, the, 22, 28, 263
Staples, Mavis, 263, 268–269
Staples, Pops, 263
Stoller, Mike, 77
Stone, Sly, 133, 150, 181, 238, 252
Story Sisters, the, 57
"Straight Outta Compton" (N.W.A), 139
Stratocaster guitars, 128
Stuart, Marv, 150–155, 160–162, 190,
    236–238, 246, 266–267, 310–312
  encourages Curtis to go solo, 171
  friction with Eddie Thomas, 171,
    204–206, 219–220
  friction with Todd Mayfield, 306–308
  insistence on street clothes on stage, 158
Stubbs, Levi, 162
Student Nonviolent Coordinating
    Committee (SNCC), 115–116, 125,
    127, 148–149
Suitor, Eddie, 88
Sullivan, Ed, 52, 99, 197
Summer, Donna, 270
Summers, Bill, 74
Super Fly (film), 207–234, 237–239
Super Fly (soundtrack album), 214–221, 223,
    227–230, 236–237
Super Fly T.N.T. (film), 292
"Superfly" (Mayfield), 43, 207, 216, 230, 237
Supreme Court. See US Supreme Court
Supremes, the, 84, 103, 116, 122, 175
Swan Silvertones, the, 19
"Sweet Exorcist" (Mayfield), 23, 235, 249
Sweet Exorcist (Mayfield), 248–252, 272
Sweet Sweetback's Baadasssss Song (film),
    194–196
"Sweet Was the Wine" (Mayfield), 47
"Swing Low, Sweet Chariot" (Negro
    spiritual), 104
Swope, Lillian, 137
Symphonics, the, 138

Tamla Records. See Motown label
Tampa, Florida, 29–30
Tams, the, 80
Teenagers, the, 49
television broadcasting, 60, 164
Temptations, the, 122, 190
  singing battle with the Impressions, 110
Terrell, Tammi, 75, 175
Tex-Town Display, 203
There's No Place Like America Today
    (Mayfield), 258–262
"This Is My Country" (Impressions), 142–
    143, 146, 159
This Is My Country (Impressions), 144, 145,
    158

Thomas, Catherine, 38
Thomas, Eddie, 41–50, 64, 66, 68, 70–76,
    80–81, 95, 116, 136, 157, 180
  and Curtom Records, 79, 138, 140, 141,
    145, 204, 206, 219–220
  friction with Marv Stuart, 171, 204–206,
    219–220
Thomas, Emanuel, 38
Thomas, Philip Michael, 264
Thomas, Rufus, 95
Three the Hard Way (film), 246
Three the Hard Way (soundtrack album), 256
Thumbs Up club (Chicago), 150
Till, Emmett, 33, 34–81
Time for Teens (TV show), 68
Times Have Changed (Impressions), 211,
    212, 256
"To Be Invisible" (Knight), 247–249, 251
Toni (partner), 200, 201, 228–230, 237,
    249
Tosh, Peter, 100
Townsend, Ed, 55, 256
Traveling Souls Spiritualist Church, 23–27,
    40, 314
Trouble Man (film), 227
Troutman, Roger, 309
Tufo, Rich, 239, 241
Turf restaurant, 77, 78
Turner, Big Joe, 22
Turner, Ike and Tina, 158
Tyler the Creator, 139
Tyson, Ronald, 273

"Um, Um, Um, Um, Um, Um (Curious
    Mind)" (Lance), 99–100
"Underground" (Mayfield), 198–199, 223
Union Hall (Chicago), 22
United Kingdom, 187–188, 196, 290
  soul music in, 209–210
  See also Blues & Soul magazine; NME
    magazine
Universal Negro Improvement Association, 3
University of Mississippi desegregation, 95
Upbeat (TV show), 183
Upchurch, Phil, 70, 213
Uptown Theater (Philadelphia), 55–56, 74,
    80, 110
US Supreme Court, 21, 37, 147, 316
  and school desegregation, 32, 33, 197,
    230, 260

Van Peebles, Melvin, 194
Vandellas, the, 95, 110, 123. See also Reeves,
    Martha
Vastola, Gaetano "Big Guy," 79
Vaughan, Sarah, 56

Vee-Jay Records, 44–50, 54, 61, 67, 78, 85,
    95, 124, 171, 176
  and the Impressions, 43–46, 67, 68, 116
Verve Records, 176
Vibrations, the, 99
Vietnam War, 80, 129, 130, 147–149, 176
  casualties of, 175, 252
  Curtis and, 238
  Kenneth Mayfield in, 130, 148–150,
    176
  protests against, 197
voodoo, 4
Voting Rights Act of 1965, 121, 129

Wade, Rico, 309
Wailer, Bunny, 100
Wailers, the, 100–101, 104, 190, 244. See
    also Marley, Bob
Walker, Jimmie, 263
Walker, Margaret, 22
Walker, Shirley, 123
Walker, T-Bone, 85
Walker, Wyatt Tee, 97, 315
Wallace, Christopher, 263
Warner Brothers films, 222–223
Warner Brothers Records, 258, 262–263,
    269, 272
Washington, Ann (half sister), 19, 108, 119
Washington, Dinah, 18
Washington, Edith (aunt), 16
Washington, Gracie (stepmother), 19
Washington, Kenneth (father). See Mayfield,
    Curtis Lee "Mannish"
Washington, Kenneth "Joe" (grandfather), 9
Washington, Marion (mother). See Mayfield,
    Marion Washington
Washington, Mrs. (healer), 54
Washington, Sadie Ann (grandmother), 9,
    13–16, 93, 108, 140, 284
Washington, Son (uncle), 16
Washington, Tanya (half sister), 19
Washington, Zora, 138
Watergate scandal, 250, 252
Waters, Muddy, 13, 18, 20–21, 30, 50, 103,
    199
Watts riot (1965), 121, 260
Wayans, Keenen Ivory, 290

We Come in Peace with a Message of Love
    (Mayfield), 288–289
"We People Who Are Darker Than Blue"
    (Mayfield), 183–184, 309
Weathermen, 170, 175
Webster, Don, 183
Weems, James, 36
Wells, Mary, 87
"We're a Winner" (Impressions), 131–133,
    148, 171, 193
We're a Winner (Impressions), 141, 146
Werner, Craig, 275
West, Kanye, 315
What's Going On (Gaye), 195, 199, 231, 239
"When Seasons Change" (Mayfield), 260
Where the Action Is (TV show), 113
Whisky a Go Go, 151
White, Armond, 224
White, Maurice, 22
White Eagle Hotel (Chicago), 15, 16, 19, 58,
    107, 117, 155, 212, 216
Wilkerson, Isabel, 7, 12
William Morris Agency, 217, 237
Williams, Eugene, 6
Williams, Hosea, 121
Williamson, Fred, 246
Wilson, Jackie, 52, 73, 82, 84, 114, 153
Windy C label, 123, 125, 130, 138
Winstons, the, 139
Womack, Bobby, 227
Wonder, Stevie, x, 84, 95, 144, 286
Woods, Georgie, 54, 55, 61, 74, 110, 256
Woods, Rosemary, 308
Woodstock concert (1969), 170, 172
Wright, Frank Lloyd, 6
Wright, Richard, 22
Wu-Tang Clan, 224

Yakub's History theory, 31
"You Always Hurt Me" (Impressions), 128
"You Must Believe Me" (Impressions), 104
"You Send Me" (Cooke), 36, 41
Young, Andrew, 113, 135
Young Mods' Forgotten Story, The
    (Impressions), 151–153

Zapp (band), 309